WE ALL WENT TO PARIS

So we beat on,
boats against the current,
borne back ceaselessly into the past.

F. Scott Fitzgerald

WE ALL WENT TO PARIS

AMERICANS IN THE CITY OF LIGHT: 1776-1971

Stephen Longstreet

The Macmillan Company, New York, New York

The Macmillan Company
866 Third Avenue, New York, N.Y. 10022
Collier-Macmillan Canada Ltd., Toronto, Ontario

Library of Congress Catalog Card Number 78-165572
FIRST PRINTING

Printed in the United States of America

to T. M.

*I was struck last evening with something that Jonathan
Sturges . . . mentioned to me. . . . We were talking of
W.D.H. [William Dean Howells] and of his having seen
him during a short and interrupted stay H. made 18
months ago in Paris—called away—back to America,
when he had just come—at the end of 10 days by the news
of the death—or illness—of his father. He had scarcely
been in Paris, ever, in former days, and he had come
there to see his domiciled and initiated son, who was at the
Beaux Arts. Virtually in the evening, as it were, of life, it
was all new to him; all, all, all. Sturges said he seemed sad—
rather brooding; and I asked him what gave him
(Sturges) that impression. "Oh—somewhere—I forget,
when I was with him—he laid his hand on my shoulder
and said à propos of some remark of mine: 'Oh, you are
young, you are young—be glad of it: be glad of it and* live.
*Live all you can: it's a mistake not to. It doesn't so much
matter what you do—but live. This place makes it all
come over me. I see it now. I haven't done so—and now
I'm old. It's too late. It has gone past me—I've lost it.
You have time. You are young. Live!'"*

HENRY JAMES' NOTEBOOKS

Contents

WE ALL WENT TO PARIS

Introduction

He carries his horizon with him and remains
rooted at home.
    GEORGE SANTAYANA

A STEADY, mounting migration, a return eastward to Mother Europe, began when the Americans were still colonists, and it has been going on ever since. At times it was a trickle, at times a flood toward Paris. It did not begin with Benjamin Franklin or James Whistler, nor end with Gertrude Stein or Jackie Onassis. It included geniuses, fools and drunkards, Wesleyans, cultists and jazz musicians.

Some stood at the Ritz bar. Some were presented at the court of Louis XIV. One came to sell Napoleon a submarine (Robert Fulton), another broke his wrist showing off before a lady (Thomas Jefferson), yet another bedded—in his mind—with Mata Hari (Ernest Hemingway). There were poets E. E. Cummings and T. S. Eliot; novelist F. Scott Fitzgerald; painters Winslow Homer, Mary Cassatt. But also came the hunters of women, the benefactors of the *grandes horizontales* like Cora Pearl and the original of *Camille*. The smooth snobbery of Henry James was balanced by Jim Europe's AEF Army Band with the braying sound of American Jazz.

For Gertrude Stein and her "Amazon henyard" Paris was the center of the universe. For other Americans, after power and talent had begun to seep away in the Great Depression, it was "Babylon Revisited." George Santayana, who viewed with mock disdain so many Americans abroad in the late nineteenth and early twentieth centuries, stood to one side politely and observed, "Henry [James] liked to see things as they are, and . . . afterwards to image how they might have been." As for others, "Those who become expatriates out of hatred for their home . . . are as bound to their past as those who hate their parents." The American exile community is "an international intelligentsia adrift amid unsuspected currents and wrecked, one by one, on the reefs of El Dorado."

Not quite all. A great many came to seek out the little Paris *pied-à-terre*, to escape the remarkable material culture at home; others came to share the drive of the *demi-monde* to Longchamps in fine equipages, to be lusty and sensual (often guilt ridden as was fitting for an American), to be part of the epoch of luxury, pleasure, gaiety—to be known as one of the *jeunesse dorée, bons vivants,* men about town.

There were Americans in silk knee breeches at the French court, some of whom stayed to see the king and queen lose their heads. Others, like John Adams and John Jay, wrote in letters and journals of this evil place. Some stood under the tinkling chandeliers of the Opéra, applauding the quadrille from *Orphée aux Enfers.* Americans remembered the grim days during the nineteenth-century siege of Paris when the saraband of the *pétroleuses* was danced in the ruins of Paris, and how the government's firing squads slaughtered thousands of the dancers. Sometimes it was just Tortinis on the Boulevard des Italiens to eat ices, or Bignon's restaurant to sample la Belle Aurore.

It was also the Paris where Henry Miller stole an overcoat, bargained with a six-franc whore, and discovered Céline's surreal prose. Where James Baldwin was arrested for stealing a bed sheet. And where Stephen Vincent Benét wrote not of the *Revue Bleue* or the American millionaire who gave one of *les femmes galantes* of the town a box of *marrons glacés,* each wrapped in a thousand-franc note. No, in Paris he wrote of the Union cavalry and the massacre of Indian women, children, and old men.

> I shall not rest quiet in Montparnasse . . .
> I shall not be there, I shall rise and pass,
> Bury my heart in Wounded Knee.

Munching brochettes (or hashish), touring the Louvre, or being seen with Sinclair Lewis drunk at Jimmy's or Harry's bar, many Americans have not been able to resist Paris. Were they drawn by the Balzacian *comédie humaine* or the chic chaff of *The Sun Also Rises?* For over two hundred years we all went to Paris, or dreamed of going.

From John Adams sniffing in Puritan disdain at Franklin's sexual appetite to the exiled figures of the Bostonians in the Jamesian carpet, one can follow a trail. Pork packers and wealthy merchants sought titles for daughters or social status as collectors. Intellectual lesbians and homosexuals moved to escape social scorn or live out some sublime fantasy.

This book was a long time growing. I first saw Paris at the age of five, with my mother in attendance. I remember some parks, a few Parisian gamins tossing balls, a shimmering dessert of marvelous pink. Also the gentlemen in top hats and long cigarettes—how was I to recognize the true *boulevardier?*—much music and the clicking of glasses, the rustle of what could only be indiscreet underwear. I recall faces and shapes that later I was told were of social importance or involved with the music and painting that men on a café *terrasse* said was avant-garde. It was only in the last part of the 1920s, when I was a teen-age painter, that the charm and genius and color and tone of Paris began to fill out with reality the too much reading in the pages of Balzac, Stendhal, *Trilby*, *La Bohème*, the first parts of Proust's *A la Recherche du temps perdu*, and such odd volumes as Restif de la Bretonne's *Les Nuits de Paris*.

Much later I felt the need to know how many other Americans had been to Paris. I began to collect memoirs, copies of letters and journals of Americans who had been to or gone to live in Paris. I began to list them, some famous, some not, some notorious with white velvet waistcoats and Fabergé cigarette cases. And so many in penury, ill, or neurotic, those who imagined themselves dedicated to the arts; so many who had little talent for making their dreams come about, but who settled for an emerald scarfpin, hung midway between art and society.

Some lived with the wounding phrase, the venomous epithet, and a lot were of marvelous resilience; they existed with hard-grained, unquenchable vitality or a benign madness, lost in some quixotic quest. They came: Sherwood Anderson, Isadora Duncan so sublimely self-assured, Buffalo Bill and his Wild West Show. And some sank to suicide, with no leaven of complacency having decided that you can't go home again. The man from the Embassy came to the Paris morgue to view the remains on a marble slab.

From the thousands of Americans who have been to Paris, lived in Paris, I have picked a representative assortment of men and women, most of them known, but some not, some neglected by fame, others—just one or two—whose identity is cloaked here at their own request.

The problem of gathering research has been that in some cases there is almost no source material, in others there is too much, most of it so mixed with myth and legend (as in the case of Gertrude Stein and Ernest Hemingway's world of the Twenties prophesying doom or fame) that almost all published memoirs must be suspect. There is so much in literary heroism that destroys modesty and fact.

I have, whenever possible, gone to letters, newspapers, journals of the time for flavor, have tried to probe into how Parisians lived at those special times when the Americans were there, and how they reacted to them, and how the Americans acted and reacted to Paris. It has not been an easy task, but from unpublished papers I have had some clues, and from survivors whom I have talked to in the last thirty years there may be a personal sense of the color and life of those who were there. The artists' studios, the *salles privées*, from the Quatre-Arts Ball to the gossip of *tout Paris*, all is here.

This is not formal history—political or economic—but a story for the intelligent reader, and I have used the history of kings, politicians, generals, and critics only where it was part of the lives of those of whom I write. If I have ventured into some discussion of the art of painting and writing, the world of the grand courtesans, it is to help picture and understand the persons involved. While I have published works as a social historian and as an art and literary critic for many years, this book makes no claim to delve deeply into other fields—political changes, the history of dynasties, revolutions, battles, and dates. Nor can anyone explain spontaneous daemonic genius.

From dining at Voisin's to donning a Pacquin frock, I seek the personal story. As to the condition of the casual American in Paris or the permanent exile, I agree with Henry James that Americans "have a superstitious valuation of Europe."

While rereading the final version of the manuscript of this book, I was struck by certain personalities whose attitudes I had not planned to give so much space to, commentators pushing themselves forward almost unannounced. As examples: Benjamin Franklin expands beyond his legend; Henry James seems to dominate the middle section, without any effort on the part of the author; Gertrude Stein looms larger than in the first notations—at least as a personality; the Richard Wright story is heartbreaking. Also in studying memoirs, journals, and letters, some unpublished or in out-of-print sources, the sensual details of certain lives could not be separated from their existence in Paris, their reasons for being there. Some of this has been retained, but this is not a book for the scandal hunter, the seeker of mere sensation.

Voices seem to rise from the past to try and explain why so many Americans came and stayed, why there was this division in the native mind that carried over in a choice between home and exile. Perhaps no one states it better than George Santayana: "The truth is that . . . one-half of the American mind has floated gently in the backwater, while, alongside, in invention and industry and social organization, the other half of the mind was leaping down a sort of Niagara Rapids. The one is all aggressive enterprise; the other is all genteel tradition."

In Paris the genteel tradition died with Edith Wharton. The leapers dominated the last decades. They, too, loudly repeated old sentiments. As Henry Miller put it: "In Paris, out of Paris, leaving Paris, or coming back to Paris, it's always Paris and Paris is France and France is China . . . afternoons sitting at La Fourche, I ask myself calmly: 'Where do we go from here?' "

What is the true flavor? The drawled accents of grand salon conversation?

("We were discussing adultery."

"So sorry. Tonight I've come prepared only on incest . . .")

Sometimes in the background of postilions in their red liveries, or of F. Scott Fitzgerald at the Ritz bar, if one has read too much and remembers one's own uncles returning from a crusade called the Great War, there comes the faint sound of grouped Brooklyn, Kansas, Texas voices singing, "How you gonna keep 'em down on the farm, after they've seen Paree . . . !"

MIRADERO ROAD, CALIFORNIA.
PARIS, FRANCE.

Book One
EARLY AMERICANS

CHAPTER 1

Franklin in Paris

*I find that I love company, chat, a laugh, a glass
and even a song, as well as ever.*

BENJAMIN FRANKLIN

I N THE FALL of 1776, the armed American vessel *Reprisal*, a privateer,
beat its way toward the French coast carrying a septuagenarian grandfather and his two young grandsons, boys sixteen and seven years of age.
It was a thirty-day voyage through storms and high pitching seas, with
British men-of-war on the alert for a rebel against the king. The old man
was Benjamin Franklin, appointed by the Continental Congress as Com-
missioner to the Court of France to work toward an alliance, in a mutual
war against the Hanoverian King George III. It was a page of transitory
history caught for a moment in the perils of the sea.

Three commissioners had been appointed to go to Paris. One, Thomas
Jefferson, withdrew because of his wife's illness, and he had been replaced by one of Franklin's enemies, Arthur Lee. Silas Deane, the third
member, was waiting for Dr. Franklin in Paris, where the overtures
were becoming epilogues. There is little doubt that the British would
have hung the old man if they had captured him. Safety became real as
the ship touched French soil, and Franklin came on shore at Auray, an
inlet in Quiberon Bay in Brittany. A showman always, Franklin was wearing a fur cap of marten skin and Quaker-colored brown clothes. The trip
had weakened the old man; the diet of salt meat had brought on an
attack of scurvy, so the fur cap helped to hide the scorbutic rash on the

big bald brow. He showed no signs of expectancy—rather a Voltairian calm.

The British secret service reported with that bland sense of grieved directness that its members feature: "The famous Doctor Franklin is arrived at Nantes with his two grandchildren. They came on an American privateer . . . I cannot but suspect that he comes charged with a secret commission from the Congress and as he is a subtle, artful man, void of all truth, he will in that case use every means to deceive . . . the French . . . to draw them into an open support of that cause . . ."

On December 21 Franklin entered Paris. There had been much talk and gossip about this American. The curious, cheering, admiring people of Paris followed Franklin to the Hôtel d'Hambourg in the Rue de l'Université where Silas Deane lived. The old man could hardly pass inside. The women of Paris treated him like a Messiah, trying to touch his coat as he passed, hunting his face for some clue, as if he carried a universal secret, some mystic assurance. It was clear Franklin would have to find a place to live away from the mob, where he could play the cat and mouse game of diplomacy, where, with hope, anticipation could turn into achievement.

The solution for a comfortable corner came from Donatien le Rey de Chaumont, who offered the American a place on his estate in Passy, just across the Seine from Paris, to the northwest. It was a setting for a *grand seigneur*, rising from the river with well-built assurance in its detail, free of the stink and noise and wood-fire smoke of the heart of the city. Here in an entire wing that became the Hôtel Valentinois (*hôtel* in French means a private mansion) the old man settled. Every morning when weather permitted he and his grandsons went down to the river for a swim. Although a roisterer at times, Franklin had a tenacity for activity that amounted to genius. He had always shielded his private life with a carefully prepared facade. "In order to secure my credit and character I took care not only to be in reality industrious and frugal but to avoid all appearances to the contrary. I dressed plainly; I was seen at no places of idle diversion. I never went out a-fishing or shooting."

All his life women fascinated him. "That hard-to-be-governed passion of youth hurried me frequently into intrigues with low women that fell in my way, which were attended with some expense and great inconvenience, besides a continual risk to my health by a distemper, which of all things I dreaded, though by great good luck I escaped it." From these intrigues came a son named William, born when Franklin was twenty-five. The identity of the mother was unknown, perhaps a servant girl, Barbara, afterward employed in the Franklin home.

Franklin was once briefly engaged to marry—this ended when he insisted on a dowry to pay his debts. He renewed acquaintance with a Deborah Read, who had been abandoned by her husband. Franklin took her as a wife in 1730, a common-law marriage because of the legal problems posed by the missing husband. Deborah accepted Franklin's bastard into the household.

Franklin was no stranger to Europe or its atrophied society. He had been there as a youth in 1724 as a printer's apprentice, and again in 1744 and 1759. He was a much traveled man for his time. In 1768 he had recorded his impressions of France in letters home, written from Paris.

I took the Resolution of making a Trip with Sir John Pringle into France. We set out the 28th past August, 1767. All the way to Dover we were furnished with Post Chaises, hung so as to lean forward, the Top coming down over one's Eyes, like a Hood, as if to prevent one's seeing the Country; which being one of my great Pleasures, I was engag'd in perpetual Disputes with the Innkeepers, Hostlers, and Postillions about getting the Straps taken up a Hole or two before, and let down as much behind, they insisting that the Chaise leaning forward was an Ease to the Horses, and that the contrary would kill them.

At Dover . . . we embark'd for Calais with a Number of Passengers who had never been before at sea. They would previously make a hearty Breakfast . . . But they had scarce been out half an hour before the Sea laid Claim to it, and they were oblig'd to deliver it up . . . If you ever go to Sea, take my Advice, and live sparingly a Day or two beforehand . . . We got to Calais that Evening. Various Impositions we suffer'd from Boatmen, Porters, etc. on both Sides of the Water. I know not which are the most rapacious, the English or French, but the latter have, with their Knavery, the most Politeness.

Franklin was a sensual man who delighted in women and observed them closely:

The women we saw at Calais, on the Road, at Bouloigne, and in the Inns and Villages, were generally of dark Complexions, but arriving at Abbeville we found a sudden Change, a Multitude of both Men and Women in the Place appearing remarkably fair . . .

As soon as we left Abbeville, the Swarthiness return'd. I speak generally, for here are some fair Women at Paris, who I think are not whiten'd by Art. As to Rouge, they don't pretend to imitate Nature in laying it on. There is no gradual Diminution of the Colour, from the full Bloom in the Middle of the Cheek to the faint tint near the Sides, nor does it show itself differently in different Faces. I have not had the Honour of being at any Lady's Toylette to see how it is laid on, but I fancy I can tell you how it is or may be done. Cut a Hole of 3 inches Diameter in a Piece of Paper; place it on the Side of your Face in such a Manner as that the Top of the Hole may be just under your Eye; then with a Brush dipt in the Colour, paint Face and Paper together; so when the paper is taken off there will remain a round Patch of Red exactly the Form of the Hole. This is the Mode, from the Actresses on the Stage upwards thro' all Ranks of Ladies to the Princesses of the Blood, but it stops there, the Queen not using it, having in the Serenity, Complaisance and Benignity that shine so eminently in, or rather through her Countenance, sufficient Beauty, tho' now an old Woman, to do extremely well without it.

As an American on tour he went to court and dined with Louis XV and his queen. "There was every kind of Elegance except that of Cleanliness, and what we call Tidyness. Why should they be allowed to out do us in any thing?"

Paris agreed with him:

In the fortnight since London, the Variety of Scenes we have gone through makes it seem equal to Six Months living in one Place. Perhaps I have suffered a greater Change, too, in my own Person, than I could have done in Six Years at Home. I had not been here Six Days, before my Taylor and Perruquier had transform'd me into a Frenchman. Only think what a Figure I make in a little Bag-Wig and naked Ears! They told me I was become twenty Years younger, and look'd very galante; So being in Paris where the Mode is to be sacredly follow'd I was once very near making Love to my Friend's Wife.

And there is some doubt that he didn't.

But now, on this special mission to Paris, he was not there for pleasure or to describe the ladies, but to attempt to save the failing American Revolution. Only French aid, soon and in quantity, would do it; and he was the major pleader, the best man available for it. Perhaps the *only* one with his knowledge of Europe and his skill in knowing the nature of man.

So he swam and planned. There was a public bathhouse on a barge opposite the Tuileries from which he often went swimming. In the off hours Franklin actually used this bathhouse barge as a meeting place, a rendezvous point for talking in secret with certain people. An Englishman, spying on the Americans, was told to seek out a Paris contact described to him as "a stout, elderly gentleman known to be a strong swimmer." The attendants had no trouble pointing out Dr. Franklin, the old duffer who looked so incapable of duplicity.

Times were desperate for the thirteen rebel colonies. Some said 70 percent of the people were loyalists and supported the king. Not enough men wanted to serve under Washington. Needed were arms, ships, can-

non, gunpowder, uniforms, and the permission for young French gentlemen of fortune, or lack of it, to accept commissions as officers under the
Virginian planter, George Washington. Human inconsistency racked the
Congress. The Philadelphia Quakers mostly sold only to the British for
gold.

France itself was leaning—some felt tottering—toward revolution, a
class war of intellectuals inciting the mob against the king, against a
Bourbon monarchy that was a facade of the royal and divine right of
kings. Already one mob, led by fishwives, had come barging out to the
gates of Versailles, faced off the Swiss Guard, and cried out their grievances, the clichés, the aberrations of the rabble rousers.

Louis XVI was not a bad man; he was a rather stupid, kindly man set
in royal complacency and traditional extravagance, with a silly wife,
Marie Antoinette, who tugged a cow's udder over a silver pail playing
milkmaid in her Petit Trianon. She gave champagne suppers while the
king, a skilled locksmith, followed his hobby with oily fingers. Transitory
pleasures, pride, tradition misruled.

Some ministers saw ruin, but that cry was of long standing, the petit
bourgeois always lamenting the heavy taxes. The middle class never understood it was there to be exploited from above and below. Soon would
come the activities of the *Tiers État*, the meeting of the States-General in
the Salle des Menus Plaisirs. Already Danton, Marat, Robespierre were
active—besides the pleaders of the rational agnosticism of Voltaire, the
irrational deism of Rousseau.

Franklin was a significant figure for all of France, the fur-hatted, wig-
less, simple American from a fresh new country. The intellectuals raised
on Jean-Jacques Rousseau's idea of the Noble Savage and the philosophers of the Rights of Man and Liberty cheered Franklin. The bourgeoisie saw him as one of themselves, a businessman, a practical inventor, a
family man with, well, was it a dozen or so illegitimate children? A man is
a man for all that, said the *Parisiennes*.

The poor, the mob, the rabble were always ready to idolize any figure
who rose above their own sad state and who, like Franklin, seemed such a
child of nature. So they cheered him as he passed. To Paris the American
was a hero in a fight for liberties they were told could be theirs. Some
knew his real worth—Voltaire and scientists like Lavoisier or the experimenter Laplace; these knew of his mind. They saw no simple old fellow
beaming on the mob, playing good neighbor Bonhomme Richard for the
king's grace.

Nor did Franklin's shrewdness escape the wary sleek statesmen, Turgot

and Vergennes, or Beaumarchais, who came to deal and intrigue with him. Actually a kind of stiff peace still prevailed between France and Hanoverian England's Lord Stormont, British ambassador to the Court of Louis XVI. Stormont did not underestimate the old lightning-snatcher; the old man could be trouble, he existed like some insistent nuisance of an elderly uncle.

The Comte de Vergennes, the king's foreign minister, was not sure the American rebels could ever tear themselves loose from England. Yet England was a menace to France. The old struggle for power, for the first position, had a long and bloody history kept open like a wound between the two nations. The French people in shops and streets were for liberty for the American colonies. The firebrands, agitators, fanatics felt that if the American Revolution succeeded, who knows, perhaps in France, too, there would come the day of cocking one's snout at a king. So the pressure for an alliance, for aid to America was strong and loud. The court could not shrug evasively.

The invented firm of Roderigue & Company—really the wily Beaumarchais—got two million francs in loans from the court of France (and England!) and arranged for shipments of war supplies to America. However Franklin and his two commissioners had not yet been invited to court. All dealings with Vergennes were secret cloak-and-dagger stuff. Franklin had accepted the fiction that officially for France no commitment had been made.

Yet on the daily side of life's little duties Franklin enjoyed himself. The street shops and barrows of Paris contained good feeding and he delighted in the *charcuteries* full of things to coax the appetite: truffled pigs' feet, turkey pâté (the native American bird exalted), goose livers, wild boar's-nose jelly, bronze-colored whole truffles. The street shops were loud with the sounds of Strasbourg geese, Muscovy ducks; available were blood sausages the size of a hangman's noose, deep sea oysters, armor-clad sea spiders to drown in spicy sauces, and hairy leeks for salads. Franklin's meals were Lucullan.

The young Americans in Paris knew the white Calabria wine of the town, the apprentice temptresses of the shops—aged thirteen to fifteen but ripe for passion. Paris hummed with expectations for the Americans as the colonies never did. They went to the Jardin des Tuileries for the news and gossip to bring back to Dr. Franklin, and they watched the grand funeral cortèges form at the Place de la Grève. They were patrons of the Palais Royal, which the Duke of Orléans rented out for cafés, for entertainments, brothels—where the agitators came, scandalmongers, drinkers of mocha brews. "In the cafés one is half suffocated by the press of people." The other side of life was La Pologne (Poland) Route, kingdom of the flea-infected ragpickers, the shoeless poor who would carry the pikes when the Bastille fell, stab a Swiss guard in the liver.

Franklin was aware that there were no newspapers that amounted to anything and he had ears every place. For us in an age of fast and shallow communication the isolation from the outer world of those days must seem suffocating.

It was an active Paris the Americans experienced in its plenty and its poverty, elbow to elbow. The workers existed in their hovels at Saint Paul, Croix Rouge, the Rue Saint Denis. The world of milliners, notion shops, dry goods, clothing offered itself on the Rue Saint Martin, rubbing against the wilder, more stylish world of the Théâtre Français, Bonne Nouvelle, the Palais Royal. How safe it all seemed to Franklin's staff—the rich bourgeoisie snug in the Faubourg Saint Germain, the Marais, the Temple. It was a Paris that was to change when Baron Haussmann cut it up like slices of Brie cheese and let in the light. There were still one-cart lanes around Saint-Germain-des-Prés, the Pantheon. Perhaps Franklin enjoyed the afternoon plays of the marionettes in the Place Louis XV; he was a man who delighted in what would later be called *genre*.

Franklin—not yet seen by the king—did not take umbrage at the situation; beggars don't criticize the flavor of the cake.

The image of Franklin in the American mind is as false as that of the schoolbook Washington or Lincoln. The plaster saints or folksy characters that maudlin historians and novelists have turned them into miss the living vital men of blood and passions, incertitude and curiosity. Franklin was never "Poor Richard," a flat, overly simple provincial character he invented to push the sale of his Almanacs. Franklin was *not* simple, folksy, frugal, or even by the Puritan standards of the day very moral, for all his worsted stockings. He loved ease and comfort, had a great desire, a natural drive for sexual intercourse beyond the dour embrace of his wife. He looked at many women with the pleasure of expectancy.

So Franklin was in Paris, and the true man was not that of the old, wise-quipping codger polishing apples. At Passy he settled in comfortably, his senses wide open; Passy was in fact a sort of American Embassy. He hired a good *maître d'hôtel*, a full staff of servants. He also put down a fine cellar of wine, the work of an expert and gourmet. To start with 260 bottles of red Bordeaux, 150 red Burgundy, 400 bottles of assorted white wines including the best champagne. For the servants this democrat added 200 bottles of *vin ordinaire*. And for low fellows who had no palate, forty-five flasks of rum.

His digestion did not slacken with age. He retained that fruitful aware-ness of the body's delights, visiting the oyster cellars and dining at his favorite cafés, the Turc and the Paphos. An average dinner at Franklin's Passy table was a good solid joint of beef, veal, or mutton, followed by chicken or duck or wild small game, two vegetables, two dishes of sweets, a pastry, two kinds of fruit in winter (four in summer), a platter of assorted mild and strong cheeses, biscuits, a plate of bonbons, ices all around once a week (two times a week in summer). He enjoyed the table and was not annoyed by laughter at meals.

As for the staff, besides his two fellow commissioners, there was his grandson Temple to help with the pile of paperwork, aided at times by John Adams' son, John Quincy Adams, acting as a clerk. The confidential secretary, Edward Bancroft, was too fully trusted by Franklin, the wise and shrewd. Bancroft, blatantly respectful, was actually a British agent, and many copies of Franklin's letters were sent on to the London Office of Information.

So for all his rational skepticism Franklin was taken in, and he took no warning when Juliana Ritchie, the wife of a Philadelphia merchant who lived in France, wrote in January, 1777, warning him that Paris crawled with spies. He answered her:

I have long observ'd one Rule which prevents any Inconvenience from such Practices. It is simply this, to be concern'd in no Affairs that I should blush to have made publick, and to do nothing but what Spies may see & welcome. When a Man's Actions are just and honourable, the more they are known, the more his Reputation is increas'd and establish'd. If I was rue therefore that my Valet de Place was a Spy, as probably he is, I think I should not discharge him for that, if in other Respects I lik'd him.

A Paris police report got into the paper, *Nouvelles de Divers Endroits,* August 20, 1777.

Certain sinister-looking persons, seen lurking around Dr. Franklin's lodging at Passy, and others no less suspected, who have even penetrated to his presence upon different pretexts, have led the government to give positive orders to the Lieutenant General of Police to watch over the safety of this respectable old man, and take all the precautions to this end that prudence could suggest.

The British ambassador, Lord Stormont, got information via a tree in the Tuileries gardens—the spy post office. Communications were in a bottle placed near the roots. "The bottle to be sealed and tyed by the

Neck with a common twyne, about half a Yard in length—the other end of which to be fastened to a peg of wood split at the top to receive a very small piece of Cord—the bottle to be thrust under the Tree, & the Peg into the Ground on the west side."

Communications were written in invisible ink, visible when the paper was warmed at a fire. Information about ships and cargoes destined for America was sent to Stormont from Franklin's office by Bancroft. One document had instructions as to the subjects that Lord Stormont wished to know; communication to be carried on by "Doctor Edwards," a disguise for Edward Bancroft.

The progress of the Treaty with France & of the Assistance expected, or Commerce carryed on in any of the ports of that Kingdom—The same with Spain, & of every other Court in Europe. The agents in ye foreign Islands in America, & the means of carrying on the Commerce with the Northern Colonys . . .

Franklin's & Dean's Correspondence with the Congress, their Agents; and the secret as well as the ostensible Letters from the Congress to them. Copys of any transactions committed to Paper, & an exact account of all intercourse & the subject matter treated of, between the Courts of Versailles & Madrid, and the Agents of Congress.

Lord Stormont also desired information on:

Names of the two Carolina Ships, Masters both English and French, descriptions of the Ships, & Cargoes: the time of sailing, & the port bound to—The same Circumstances respecting all equipments in any port in Europe; together with the names of the Agents imployed. The intelligence that may arrive from America, the Captures made by their privateers, & the instructions they receive from the deputys.

Franklin was concerned with the purchase of ships, the commissioning of captains with cargoes to pick up at ports of France, Spain, and Holland, where they were to carry them, how to avoid capture, and similar business. We know the contraband game was mostly successful.

So things went. A semisecret existence for the American.

CHAPTER 2

America and France

To none man seems ignoble, but to man. . . .
EDWARD YOUNG

O N SEPTEMBER, 1777, news came to Paris that the Americans had had a great military victory over the British at Saratoga. The Parisians went dancing in the streets, crying out jeers at Gentleman Johnny, General John Burgoyne, the beaten general. The French even made up a word, *burgoinisse,* meaning to be badly defeated in love, in gambling, in business. Franklin was the hero of the mob as it became clear the king would soon give them a war with England and an alliance with the rebel colonies. "Liberty!" cried the mobs, "this is a fight for liberty!" An ironic warning, or it should have been, to a French king.

The first Paris victim of the far-off battle was Beaumarchais. He driving hell-for-leather to tell Franklin the news of Saratoga. His horses bolted and wrecked the carriage, wrecked Beaumarchais; a task nearly completed by his surgeon. Battered, in pain, Beaumarchais wrote:

This propitious event is balm to my wounds. Some god has whispered in my ear that King Louis will not disappoint the hopes of the faithful friends whom America has acquired for herself in France. It is my voice which calls out on their behalf from beneath my blankets: "Out of the depths have I cried unto thee, Oh Lord! Lord, hear my prayer."

Even if the writer seemed to be in fever, the king was now in a mood to come into the open on the side of the Americans.

The British were frankly worried. They sent out a peace feeler of their own, ordering their spy Paul Wentworth to Paris to talk to Franklin.

With an air almost of self-parody Franklin set out to play a sly game. The old fox played off the English peace offer (it would meet nearly all American claims, but no independence from England) against the French delay (for actual, large scale, open help). The spy went back with the word that Dr. Franklin claimed he had to have instructions from Congress and the added twist to the British lion's tail that the English were being "savage" in the war. The French prepared a treaty and Franklin hoped to send it home to Congress. On February 6, 1778, history could record:

> The signatures were affixed to a Treaty of Commerce, and Treaty of Amity and Alliance, between France and the United States. The French Government . . . solemnly disclaimed all intention to reconquer Canada. No condition whatever was exacted from America, except a promise that she would never purchase peace with Great Britain by consenting to resume her subjection to the British crown.

Franklin, the showman, signed wearing a worn, faded costume. Following the signing there was finally the presentation at court. He wore no formal dress, no wig, no sword—a full shrug at protocol. For an eyewitness account of "republican simplicity" we go to Madame du Deffand:

> Mr. Franklin has been presented to the King. He was accompanied by some twenty insurgents, three or four of whom wore a uniform. Franklin wore a dress of reddish brown velvet, white hose, his hair hanging loose, his spectacles on his nose, and a white hat under his arm. I do not know what he said, but the reply of the king was very gracious, as well towards the United States as towards Franklin their deputy. He praised his conduct and that of all his compatriots . . .

The King said to the American, "Firmly assure Congress of my friendship." And with a sigh of his natural unsureness about everything, added, "I hope this will be for the good of the two nations."

Marie Antoinette was playing cards for high stakes, but she interrupted her play to make small talk with Franklin, then with the charm some recorded, she begged him to stand by her side while she continued to play; a sign of royal graciousness to this old savage from the wild world across the sea.

As for the pleased Congress, it wiped out the commission of three and named Benjamin Franklin as "sole plenipotentiary." The message was carried to France by the young Marquis de Lafayette, who had been serving as an aide to General Washington. So, *seconde enfance moins morose,* Franklin entered a livelier second childhood of the spirit.

John and Abigail Adams—with a certain queasiness toward Paris—didn't approve of the old man and his still active interest in women. Their frozen Puritan souls blanched at his small indecencies, his relish at the sight and feel of women's flesh.

Wrote Adams of Franklin: "He loves his ease, hates to offend, and seldom gives any opinion till obliged to do it . . . Although he has as determined a soul as any man, yet it is his constant policy never to say yes or no decidedly but when he cannot avoid it."

And of Franklin's friend, Madame Helvétius, prim Abigail could write of madame's frizzled hair!

"Over it she had a small straw hat, with a dirty gauze half handkerchief round it, and a bit of dirtier gauze than ever my maids wore was bowed on behind . . . I own I was highly disgusted, and never wish for an acquaintance with any ladies of this cast . . . She had a little lap-dog, who was, next to the Doctor, her favourite. This she kissed, and when he wet the floor, she wiped it up with her chemise . . . manners differ exceedingly in different countries."

It had to be admitted the old man saw even his country in a sexual content. As a letter shows:

I think that a young State like a young Virgin, should modestly stay at home, & wait the Application of Suitors for an Alliance with her; and not run about offering her Amity to all the World; and hazarding their Refusal. My colleagues have this day proposed to me to go to Holland on this Business; but tho I honour that nation, and esteeming the People, and wishing for a firm Union between the two Republics, I cannot think of undertaking such a Journey without some assurances of being properly received as a Minister of the United States of America. Our Virgin is a jolly one; and tho at present not very rich, will in time be a great Fortune, & where she has a favorable Predisposition, it seems to me to be well worth cultivating.

Frankly, Benjamin Franklin's life in Paris was a problem to the early American historians. Most of them were from Boston, and usually stained with Puritan prejudice about the good Dr. Franklin's public (and private) display of interest in the pleasures of the flesh. They saw the sexual drive as a lachrymose, unprincipled disaster.

Our times, being more tolerant, can expand on Franklin's delight in sexual freedom; and he could, at seventy-four, write to his niece, Elizabeth Partridge, of his enjoyment of Paris, of the *Parisiennes.*

This is the civilest nation upon Earth. As for the rumors about "the Kindness of the French Ladies to me" . . . Your first Acquaintances endeavour to find out what you like, and they tell others. If 'tis understood that you like Mutton, dine where you will find Mutton. Somebody, it seems, gave it out that I lov'd Ladies; and then every body presented me their Ladies (or the Ladies presented themselves) to be *embraced,* that is to have their Necks kiss'd. For as to kissing of Lips or Cheeks it is not the Mode here, the first, is reckon'd rude, & the other may rub off the Paint. The French Ladies have however 1000 other ways of rendering themselves agreeable; by their various Attentions . . .

The trouble was that the hedonist Franklin entered American folk history as the frugal Poor Richard, that fictional character; as a fuddy-duddy, a bald old man with a fringe of lank hair, peering at us over his bifocals, uttering wise old sayings. This is one of those distortions that makes true the remark that "history is lies agreed upon." Even his first editor and biographer, Albert Henry Smyth, had to admit Franklin smoothed his problems, his official worries "by social diversions. He was admired by philosophers and petted by society; and he found himself as much at home in the salon of Madame d'Houdetot or Madame Helvétius as in the laboratory of Lavoisier, the clinic of Vicq-D'Azyr, or the cabinet of Vergennes. Never lived a man more idolized. Curious crowds followed him with applause when he walked abroad; men carried their canes and their snuff-boxes *à la Franklin,* fair women crowned him with flowers, and wrote him roguish letters."

He does not relate that pretty ladies sat on the philosopher's lap and were petted, and there was what a later time would call necking.

The Hôtel Valentinois (the large private residence) was the pride of the Brillons, and there Madame Brillon was always delighted to receive the American, her husband being usually away from home dallying with his official mistress. He was a connoisseur of the carnal tendencies of Paris. If Madame's daughters were present there was music, games. But Franklin asked for private meetings and total surrender of madame's body; according to some historians he was rejected by the lady on the ground it would spoil their pleasant relationship. Yet the cuddling seems to have reached a very physical and exotic pitch. Wrote the lady in what can only be sexually intimate terms:

Do you know, my dear Papa, that people have the audacity to criticize my pleasant habit of sitting upon your knees . . . I despise slanderers and am at peace with myself, but that is not enough, one must submit to what is called *propriety,* to sit less often on your knees. I shall certainly love you none the less, nor will our hearts be more or less pure; but we shall close the mouths of the malicious and it is no slight thing even for the secure to silence them.

It is the letter of a teasing woman who has surrendered part way and still leaves hopes of further possibilities. But Franklin, as in the much later "September Song," was not a man for the waiting game. He had—to quote a vulgar frontier expression—more than one fish on his string. He would dine twice a week with Madame Brillon, and Saturdays with Madame Helvétius, widow of the philosopher, Claude Arien Helvétius. At sixty, Abigail Adams sneered, Madame Helvétius made a great show of fancy vulgarity. Franklin, while merely sexually interested in Madame Brillon, wanted marriage with Madame Helvétius. As a widower he was not too involved with memories of his own wife.

Franklin's marriage to his American wife, Deborah, had not been all cooing and loving. In 1774, while in England, he had been cross at her for not writing information often enough. "Why might I not have expected the same Comfort from you, who used to be so diligent and faithful a Correspondent . . . ?" Deborah didn't answer why, and she died in December of that year. She had never been accepted by those who honored Franklin as a great man. Wrote historian Paul Conners of her:

There was one taint, however, that no amount of skill could fully erase—the more conspicuously lower-middle-class qualities of his wife Deborah. A carpenter's daughter, she knew her way around a shop and was a helpmate to Benjamin in his work as printer-stationer-bookseller and postmaster . . . But she was plain, at times embarrassingly loud and, in short, not the sort that the wives of Franklin's more select acquaintances would welcome . . . Franklin's amorous adventures in the better circles abroad proclaimed a latent yearning for a wife more genteel and witty.

In his direct, opulent hedonism Franklin, from the depths of his experiences, never hid his susceptible sensibilities in any esthetic subtlety. Certainly Madame Helvétius met his standards; she was charming and perhaps witty. But she rejected his offer of marriage, and this threw him into a strange condition. According to a letter Franklin wrote her when rejected, he rushed home and threw himself in great despair onto his bed. The whole situation to us seems preposterous: the elderly philosopher, victor and loser of many amorous engagements, acting like a rebuffed adolescent, a callow Romeo. He then wrote to the lady that on his bed of despair he suddenly found himself in a vision of Paradise. There he asked to see Madame's dead husband, M. Helvétius himself. And when that worthy man stood before him, Franklin was received with much courtesy. The letter goes on . . .

. . . having known me by reputation, he said, for some time. He asked me many things about the war and about the present state of religion, liberty, and government in France. "You ask nothing then," I said to him, "about your dear friend, Madame Helvétius, and yet she still loves you to excess. I was with her less than an hour ago." "Ah!" he said, "you remind me of my former happiness. But we must forget if we are to be happy here. For several years at first I thought of nothing but her. At last I am consoled. I have taken another wife; the most like her I could find. She is not, it is true, altogether so beautiful, but she has as much good sense and plenty of wit, and she loves me infinitely. She studies continually to please me, and she has just now gone out to search for the best nectar and ambrosia to regale me with this evening. Stay with me and you will see her." "I perceive," I said, "that your former friend is more faithful than you; she has had several good offers and has refused them all. I confess to you that I have loved her, to madness; but she was cruel to me and rejected me for love of you . . ." Then the new Madame Helvétius came in with the nectar; immediately I recognized her as Madame Franklin, my former friend. I claimed her again, but she said coldly, "I was a good wife to you for forty-nine years and four months, almost half a century. Be content with that. I have formed a new connexion here which will last for eternity." Indignant at this refusal from my Euridice, I at once resolved to quit those ungrateful shades, return to this good world, and see again the sun and you. Here I am. Let us avenge ourselves. The faithless Mrs. Franklin married again, so let us avenge ourselves . . .

The letter is such a simple Freudian document that one can only pass it off as an old man driven by sexual pressures to fantasize his not so subconscious desires in this rather calculated fantasy of wish fulfillment. An offer to trade his dead wife for the philosopher's living one. No matter how one views the incident, one cannot, as some historians do, dismiss it all as the senile dream of an impotent old man. Did they, did they not avenge themselves?

Franklin was often at the salon of the Comtesse d'Houdetot. She had once been the great passion of Jean-Jacques Rousseau. In Franklin's honor she gave a *fête champêtre* and wrote some verse for him. During the recitation wine was drunk as each verse ended; there were over a dozen verses.

Her farewell verse of the evening began:

> Législateur d'un monde, et bienfaiteur des deux,
> L'homme dans tous les temps te devra ses hommages.

Franklin's letters to her later from America show he had not changed his idea that beautiful witty women are not above being physical love objects. Whatever his state at the time, he was no canting hypocrite. He made his desires clear.

Physically he suffered painfully from the gout, and wrote an essay: *Dialogue Between Franklin and the Gout*. Said Gout: "You ate and drank too freely and too much indulged those legs of yours in their indolence . . ." Franklin denies he is "a glutton and tippler" but he is told he overdoes the "quantity of meat and drink proper for a man who has given up exercise."

He stuck to one principle: "A man and a woman are like a pair of scissors. Neither one is any good without the other."

Paris existence, Paris food, and the gaiety of life all appeared available to him. Unlike the dour Adams couple, Franklin wanted to leave no facet of life untried. When the ladies said his gout came from his eating and drinking, he replied, No! when he was younger and the ladies were kinder with their favors he had no gout. Now, if they would surrender to him what he wanted, the gout would leave him. As he wrote to Madame Brillon: "I will mention the Opinion of a certain Father of the Church which I find myself willing to adopt though I am not sure it is orthodox. It is this, that the most effectual way to get rid of a certain Temptation is, as often as it returns, to comply with and satisfy it . . ." So beating by over a hundred years Oscar Wilde's remark, "The best way to resist temptation is to yield to it."

Certainly Franklin at his Passy estate, printing his *bagatelles* as he called his little essays, lived well, surrounded by ladies, not all of whom were as unyielding as the mesdames appeared to be before final surrender. Franklin, respected as sage and seer, handler of the needs of Congress and America in the long cruel war of the forests against the Hanoverian king, like an ancient Greek was making his own morality. As for the Parisian setting, he knew it was a way of life all silk and scent on top, yet a dark brooding yeast of the revolution-to-come already fermenting, about to explode almost as soon as he, the old man, went home, his task done and done well. Perhaps he lit the fuse or loaned the match for the French Revolution.

John Adams, who might as well have been in a New England village rather than in Paris with his sour wife, watched Poor Richard's creator cavorting with the daughter of Franklin's host, called—but not by the Adams—"Mademoiselle de Passy, the most beautiful girl in France." Adams, who placed admiration of beauty as among the Puritan sins, could record that at "the age of seventy-odd Franklin has lost neither his love of beauty nor his taste for it."

When the frisky miss, Mademoiselle de Passy, was announced as engaged to the Comte de Claermont Tonnerre, Franklin wrote the girl's mother that it gave him great pleasure, "Madame, my respected neighbor,

to learn that our lovely Child is soon to be married with your Approbation & that we are not however to be deprived of her Company. I assure you that I shall make no Use of my Paratonnerre to prevent this Match. I pray God to favor it with his choicest blessings, and that it may afford many Occasions of Felicity to all concerned . . ."

Paratonnerre is what the French called his invention of the lightning rod. In fact lightning rods were the mode all over Paris from the Faubourg St. Honoré to the prisons. Mr. Franklin's *paratonnerres* on rooftops were like the radio and TV aerials of later days, a social status symbol for a host as great as truffled *foie gras* or woodcock *flambée à la riche.*

Franklin continued to combine science with a little lusting after women. At the home of the academician Jean-Baptiste le Roy, Franklin's scientific talk was mixed with flirting with Madame le Roy, whom Franklin addressed as "my little pocket wife"; in French coming out as his *petite femme de la poche.* The husband seemed to shrug it off and added a drinking song which, aided by his three brothers, he warbled to his American guest:

> With glass in hand
> Let us sing to our Benjamin!

Madame le Roy, with or without vanities and flipperies, did she indulge in some intimate relationship with their guest? One can interpret their exchange of letters as one wishes. Of those that survive here are some samples beginning with a text by madame:

"Will you, my dear friend, dine with me Wednesday; I am most desirous of seeing and embracing you."

Franklin answered he would "most certainly not fail to be at your house next Wednesday. I take too much pleasure in seeing you, in hearing you talk and too much happiness when I have you in my arms to forget an invitation so precious."

Just before Franklin left Paris, she wrote him a good-bye. "My dear, good friend. I promise you that as long as I continue to breathe the breath of life your little pocket-wife will love you. She embraces you with all her heart."

It was more than a series of poses or baroque exuberances.

He was still a sensual, thinking, far-reaching, inexhaustible, complex man. His warmth and interest in all living matter and the future are expressed in a letter of 1780. It was written to Joseph Priestley, showing his mind was not always on the hips of Madame le Roy or one of his other lady friends. He wrote that the rapid progress of truth "occasions my regretting that I was born so soon. It is impossible to imagine the Height to which may be carried in a thousand years, the Power of Man over Matter. We may perhaps learn to deprive large Masses of their Gravity, and give them absolute Levity, for the sake of easy Transport. Agriculture may diminish its Labour and double its Produce; all diseases may by sure means be prevented or cured, not excepting even that of Old Age, and our Lives lengthened at pleasure even beyond the antediluvian Standard. O that moral Science were in as fair a way of Improvement, that Men would cease to be Wolves to one another, and that human Beings would at length learn what they now improperly call Humanity."

He seems to be seeing into the future, the age of the ticking Doomsday Bomb, immoral and revolting national actions in Vietnam. Perhaps this contorted doubt about humanity was caused by a severe attack of gout at Passy. He was not, as we've noted, an abstemious feeder or drinker. He developed into a wine collector, favoring burgundies, and tippled a great deal of Nuits St. Georges at table. There was always plenty of rum, beer, Madeira, and wine in his cellars. He practiced no bleak, Calvinistic restraint on his appetites.

Perhaps it was his age that made him continue a variegated hunt for experiences; his wonder at when death would come. Most likely he felt in good living he was balancing the horror of life on earth as he measured the planet's doses of war and famine, fanatics' ideas, the plunder and greed of the politician, those thieves in high places. He saw the rabble rousers at their work on the Paris streets, in cafés, preaching in salons. In his private letters the high-liver, the pincher of girls, the seducer eyeing a countess, is brooding and pessimistic. Writing to Priestley he says he would rejoice much,

if I could once more recover the Leisure to search with you into the Works of Nature; I mean the *inanimate,* not the *animate* or moral part of them. The more I discover'd of the former, the more I admir'd them; the more I knew of the latter, the more I am disgusted with them. Man I find to be a Sort of Being very badly constructed, as they are generally more easily provok'd than recon-cil'd, more disposed to do Mischief to each other than to make Reparation, much more easily deceiv'd than undeceiv'd, and having more Pride and even Pleasure in killing than in begetting one another; for without a Blush they assemble in great armies at NoonDay to destroy, and when they have kill'd as many as they can, they exaggerate the Number to augment the fancied Glory; but they creep into Corners, or cover themselves with the Darkness of night when they mean to beget, as being asham'd of a virtuous Action. A virtuous Action it would be, and a visous one the killing of them, if the Species were really worth producing or preserving; but of this I begin to doubt.

It is a sad message on human failings and human motivations. It is more than Hellenic and Stoic, and brings to mind the last words of the dying H. G. Wells, another womanizer and believer in science: "Damn you all, I warned you!"

There was no ostentation or decadence in Franklin's grim viewpoint— just the summing up of an old man who wanted to be relieved of duty and sail for home. He had had his fill of court rakes, patricians unaware the sky would soon fall, courtiers, dandies. Yet so great was his adapt-ability that for the citizens of Paris he retained that image of the simple seer, serenely radiant with no frivolous elegance, priggishness, or pompos-ity. He had none of the greasy smugness of a Tartuffe, of a modern Secretary of State. He could agree with Descartes: *Cogito ergo sum*—I think therefore I am.

So life must go on—for all the shared absurdity of man—with its small pleasures, excitements such as the September day, 1783, when Franklin was seventy-seven, and he wrote of a large balloon going up "to give man the Advantage of Flying."

In November he watched the balloon carrying into the sky the first men to leave the planet, Pilatre de Rozier and the Marquis d'Arlandes, who were carried across the Seine, all Paris below them cheering. The next month Jacques Alexandre Chartes, using hydrogen (made by pouring sulphuric acid over iron filings) instead of hot air, rose up two thousand feet over the Tuileries. Franklin and all the Americans on hand joined Paris in the cheers. Paris was the flying capital of the world. Kitty Hawk and the Wright brothers' motored flight were just a little more than a century away; Franklin would have been delighted with Orville and Wilbur.

Like the Wright brothers, who thought the perfection of human flight "would make war impossible," Franklin, too, felt invasion from the air would make war a foolish venture.

Convincing Sovereigns of the Folly of wars may perhaps be one Effect of it; since it will be impracticable for the most potent of them to guard his Dominions. Five thousand Balloons, capable of raising two Men each, could not cost more than Five Ships of the Line; and where is the Prince who can afford so to cover his Country with Troops for its Defence, as that Ten Thousand Men, descending from the Clouds might not in many places do an infinite deal of mischief, before a Force could be brought together to repel them?

His version of parachute troopers did not envision the bestial horrors of napalm, defoliating a nation's earth, coming from the air. This was the main fault of the men of the Age of Reason; they overlooked the possibility of the Age of the Common—too Common—Man in power.

The French court continued to relish its contact with Franklin, but was still cold to John Adams. Adams, it appeared, bristling with importance, rubbed Vergennes, the king's director of aid to the Americans, the wrong way. Adams could not understand the French aristocrats' stiff, formal respect for style and dignity, the mellowing prurience of their sophistication. This mutual disdain became so pronounced that the French asked Congress to withdraw Adams from Paris.

In 1782 Congress sent another raw diplomat to Paris, John Jay, to join Franklin and take part in the peace negotiations which were taking place there with the English after Cornwallis' defeat, with the aid of French arms and men, at Yorktown. Europe irked John Jay, and he wrote to Congress his experiences had been "one continued series of painful perplexities and embarrassments." When Jay joined Franklin and John Adams at Versailles, the intrigues and protocol further alienated him from the French and the French scene. Like Adams, it all suggested to him something like Trimalchio's banquet in Petronius' *Satyricon*.

Jay was foolish and naive enough to think France had helped America because of the kindness in human nature. He was shocked to discover it had all been a power play, as Franklin explained, a game involving the map of Europe, the balance of power among the nations, France, England, Spain, and others. Franklin tried to cool Jay and Adams down. But Jay kept crying out, as he discovered duplicity on duplicity, "The dignity of the Congress will be in the dust."

Franklin, aware of the need of dealing off the cuff, rolling with the punches, put it directly to Jay. "You are prepared to break our instructions?" The instructions were to make a peace—breaking them could renew the war.

Jay, smoking a long clay pipe ("The Indian's Revenge," the tobacco habit, held him victim), in rage threw the pipe into the fireplace. "If the instructions conflict with America's honor, I would break them like this."

The peace treaty in the end was signed, and all parties moved to Passy to celebrate with Dr. Franklin and some French guests. It was a good treaty for that day. "His Britannic Majesty acknowledged the United States to be free and sovereign . . . there shall be a firm and perpetual Peace between his Britannic Majesty and the said States."

Franklin's gout got a bit of punishment that glorious day. He wanted to go home; he was old, he was in pain. Philadelphia was the place he wanted to be his last sight of earth. But Congress asked him to stay on. A peace was as hard to process as a war. Adams and Jay lacked Franklin's skill and knowledge of getting along with the French. He felt his duty to accept an inescapable fate:

I may as well resolve to spend the remainder of my days here; for I shall be hardly able to bear the fatigues of the voyage in returning. During my long absence from America, my friends are continually diminishing by death, and my inducements to return in proportion.

The French Revolution was six years away. Franklin was a member of a radical secret society in Paris called the Nine Sisters. They called him the Venerable and crowned him with laurels. Did Franklin know the society was a fomenter of revolution? He had translated into French the book of state constitutions of the colonies that influenced the French revolutionaries' thinking in many ways. Franklin's line of thought was the mood of Voltaire, Diderot, Mably, Locke, Rousseau. The book he got past the keeper of seals was a testament of revolution. Those historians who feel Franklin was a dupe of the secret society, the Nine Sisters, hardly know the practical alertness of their man. He would not plot against the king, but he could seriously encourage ideas in politics as revolutionary as those he had in science. He was aware of dimensions beyond reason and experience—impulses that could not be checked.

He had also written an essay against the whole idea of hereditary titles.

I only wonder that, when the united Wisdom of our Nation had, in the Articles of Confederation, manifested their Dislike of establishing Ranks of Nobility . . . a Number of private Persons should think it proper to distinguish themselves and their Posterity, from their fellow citizens, and form an Order of hereditary Knights in direct opposition to the solemnly·declared Sense of their Country! I imagine it must be likewise contrary to the Good Sense of most of those drawn into it by the Persuasion of its projectors, who have been too much struck with the Ribbands and Crosses they have seen among them hanging to the Button-holes of Foreign Officers.

He was talked out of publishing this essay in Paris, but it circulated privately among the French intellectuals and the Paris citizens. Mirabeau used Franklin's text in his own directions to the revolutionary conspirators. Both the American Revolution and Franklin's presence and writings had a great deal to do with the mood and methods of the French storms ahead. He aided in clarifying numb aspiration for change, mapped the intolerable boils of society, encouraged the fortuitous play of change and chance.

In 1785, on the second of May, Franklin at last got from Congress permission to go home. He was to be replaced by Thomas Jefferson, Envoy Plenipotentiary of the United States.

It was late in the old man's life. Could Franklin make the trip home, take the fearful land journey in French coaches over muddy rutted holes called French roads, then the long difficult sailing-ship trip across the wide ocean? The first ship to leave from Le Havre was in August. He'd try and reach it alive.

He began to give away his things: an armchair to an abbess with a broad beam; his magic cane with its hidden compartments to another. Madame Veilered got a tea table; his landlord, who refused all rent, got another table. Louis XVI gave Franklin a miniature of himself set with over four hundred bits of diamonds. The queen sent Franklin her personal litter and its two large mules to carry him to the ship. Franklin's printing press and assorted items were packed in one hundred eighteen boxes for the trip to America. He was ready. Travel, he knew, was the ability to confront whatever can be imagined.

On the afternoon of July 12, Franklin left for home. There was a party of admirers and the curious in the courtyard, "a great concourse of people," a mournful silence, interrupted by a few sobs. Jefferson was there in this Paris suburb to see the old chief off. "When he left . . . it seemed as if the village had lost its patriarch." The litter was comfortable and in a carriage behind it rode his two grandsons.

As he leaves Paris, what was Franklin really like, what had he accomplished?

In the *Digest of International Law* it is written of the Congress of Vienna: "The imposing fabric constructed by Metternich, and Nesselrode, and Talleyrand, with such lofty disregard for national liberties and popular rights, has long ago perished, while Franklin's work endures to this hour."

The historian George Otto Trevelyan wrote that Franklin was an ambassador "which the world had never seen before, and will never see again until it contains another Benjamin Franklin. Tried by the searching test of practical performance, he takes high rank among the diplomatists of history. His claims to that position have been vindicated in a manner worthy of the subject."

Franklin shocked the early editor of his writing, Albert Henry Smyth:

We may track him through the thirty years of the *Gazette* by the smudgy trail he leaves behind him. His humour is coarse and his mood of mind Rabelaisian. His "salt imagination" delights in greasy jests and tales of bawdry. He came of a grimy race of hard-handed blacksmiths, and they had set their mark on him. With all his astonishing quickness and astuteness of intellect and his marvelous faculty of adaptation, he remained to the end of life the proletarian, taking an unclean pleasure in rude speech and coarse innuendo. He out-Smolletts Smollett in his letters to young women at home and experienced matrons abroad. Among the manuscripts in the Library of Congress . . . are productions of his pen, the printing of which would not be tolerated . . . It is no use blinking the fact that Franklin's animal instincts and passions were strong and rank, that they led him to the commission of many deplorable *errata* in his life.

His grandsons even tampered with his *Autobiography*: the line "Franklin wished to leave Boston because he had got a naughty girl with child" reads in their version, he "had had an intrigue with a girl of bad character."

Jefferson, who replaced Franklin in Paris, wrote: "The succession to Dr. Franklin at the court of France was an excellent school of humility. On being presented to any one as the minister of America, the commonplace question used in such cases was, '*Il est vous, Monsieur, qui remplacez le Docteur Franklin?* Is it you, Sir, who replace Dr. Franklin?' I generally answered, 'No one can replace him, Sir, I am only his successor.'"

On the twenty-fourth Franklin crossed the channel to England, the

only one among his party who was not seasick. We shall leave him at
Cowes—the rest of Benjamin Franklin's story is not part of this book—
leave him with this simple note from his diary after crossing the channel:
"I went at noon to bathe in St. Martin's salt-water hot bath and, floating
on my back, fell asleep and slept near an hour by my watch without
sinking or turning! A thing I never did before and should hardly have
thought possible. Water is the softest bed that can be . . ."

And add his own suggestion for his epitaph:

The Body
of
Benjamin Franklin
Printer
(Like the cover of an old book
Its contents torn out
And stript of its lettering and gilding)
Lies here, food for worms.
But the work shall not be lost
For it will (as he believed) appear once more
In a new and more elegant edition
Revised and Corrected
BY THE AUTHOR

CHAPTER 3

A One Leg American—
Gouverneur Morris

There are few sensible people, we find, except
those who share our opinions.

LA ROCHEFOUCAULD

E ARLY IN THE YEAR 1789 there arrived in Paris President George Washington's private agent, a man of thirty-seven, with a wooden leg and a seared arm. Gouverneur Morris was a most remarkable man with an insatiable appetite for experience, who, as an agent and then as ambassador to France, lived through the king's last days, the French Revolution. He kept a detailed personal journal, not only of world-shaking events but also of a passionate love affair of ecstatic delight and of certain agonies and delinquencies.

Of all the Americans of historic importance of those days, Morris alone seems a modern man, seen as if directly out of some stockholders' meeting or one of those corporation heroes featured in the pages of *Fortune* Magazine. While Washington, Jefferson, Franklin, the Adamses, Hamilton are still to most of us figures in clubbed hair and tricorn hats, Morris strikes us, perhaps because of his gusty, alert journal, as being one of us—a man with a direct masculine intimacy, harassed by daily events, always wondering of tomorrow's, directly engaged in the business of doing and being. No intangible facade of a faded past emerges from his self-portrait.

There is a story, which he does not tell himself, of bloodthirsty mobs during the Terror of the French Revolution stopping his carriage, ready to drag him out and hack him to bits, murder him as one of the hated upper class. Pushing out his wooden leg to give them a good look at the American oak shaft, he shouted, "Goddamn you—*me* an aristocrat! Who lost his leg in the cause of American liberty!" One version of the story is that as they prepared to hang him, and before he made his speech, he unfastened the wooden leg and waved it over his head as a weapon to point up his words. Whichever version may be true, the mob cheered and applauded and let him pass . . . If he must wear some image of the past, he could have been a Roman of the Aurelian period.

Morris had lost his leg not in war, nor—so wrote Lord Palmerston—as was gossiped, in escaping a betrayed husband. In 1781, driving a pair of wild horses in a phaeton, Morris was tossed onto the road, his left leg catching in a wheel, being so badly mangled it had to be amputated. The seared arm was the result of an accident with boiling water as a child. However, scarred and stumping on his wooden limb, he was the solid American agent in revolutionary France, though the truth was he himself was not much given to democratic principles, fearing the mass, the brainless mob—one historian called him, "More royalist than the king." He was distrustful of all extremes but his own.

From a portrait by an untalented Swiss artist, we have a fairly good picture of the man: attractive without being overly handsome, some extra length of nose, a powerful virile male. He was an overcharged, sensual man, always involved with women. The picture is in profile, showing a humorous but firm mouth with ironic corners. The lips of a passionate personality (if facial readings mean anything). It was the kind of face we are told women like for its virile qualities. However, all these assumptions may only be so after our reading the journal. He was, it was said, a man who would not mislay himself, no matter what he faced. When all the ambassadors in Paris fled the city, he alone did not pack up when the Terror was at its height and horrifying apprehensions filled everyone's mind behind locked doors.

Morris stood well over six feet tall, in an age when people were shorter and smaller than we are today. The body was that of an athletic outdoor man, and in his mid-fifties he shot the St. Lawrence in an Indian canoe. He was an early Hemingway man, hunter, fisherman, horsebreeder, woodsman, camper, great walker, and gentleman farmer.

In an age of the unwashed, Morris bathed daily and changed his linen, visited his primitive dentist regularly. He took no snuff, smoked no tobacco, but was a boozer and suffered many a hangover, often several times a week. He posed for the body of French sculptor Houdon's great statue of George Washington.

Morris himself was a hard worker, man of energy, and had a low opinion of mankind, didn't care for others' opinions. But on official business for his country he proved a person of trust, of splendid diplomatic ability. Duty was first with Morris, even when he was involved in a most passionate love affair and the lady was causing him the usual problems of intrigue and secret meetings, and her husband was proving difficult. Morris was a bachelor until fifty-seven, but, as he wrote, "engaged in the war of the Paphian Queen." Early historians called his sexual drive "Gallantries."

Morris liked the good life, was a social climber, and sighed over his faults. Unlike James Boswell, the great biographer of Samuel Johnson, who was promiscuous with street women and drabs, Morris preferred bedding down with ladies of rank and those with minds and wit and social connections. Sadly enough, at times his great love affair in Paris took place in hallways, coaches, even in doorways.

It is one of the ironic mysteries of history that this man, Gouverneur Morris, who did so remarkable job as private agent for Washington and as minister to France, is almost unknown to the average educated American, while lesser lights have monuments and often mythical places in our history.

Morris was born in 1752. His parents were in middle age when they conceived him, and he came late to a large family. He fought his way out of the dull, fairly well-off, indifferent family life to become one of the youngest members of the Continental Congress. During the revolution Morris managed a major part of the financing of the war. He was a vital force in the making of the Constitution, and when President Washington wanted someone to go to France as his agent to assist Thomas Jefferson, our minister there, he picked Morris. He was to work on the matter of the debts we owed France, to work out credits, to see to the involved talks on how to keep the French from demanding too much from a new country that had so little. And to report on the rising tide of revolution. He agreed with Dr. Johnson: "Every man has to utter what he thinks truth, and every other man has the right to knock him down for it."

It was in Paris in his hotel in the Rue de Richelieu, in the stationer's shop in the Rue Neuve-des-Petits Champs, that Morris bought the first green, vellum-bound blank book of what was to be in time the twelve volumes of his *Diaries*, from which we gather such a close-up picture of him and of the French court during the Revolution and the Terror that followed.

Among the first notes we find he mentions he saw the play *The Misanthrope* by Molière, acted "inimitably well." He dined with Jefferson and his daughters at the American legation in the Champs Elysées. The two men got on well. Jefferson was an intellectual, a student of the arts, a widower. In Paris, while trying to engage in a love affair with a married Englishwoman, to show her how virile he was, he leaped over a fence and badly smashed his wrist. But the talk between Jefferson and Morris was mostly of the problem of the rising discontent in France and the complex business of finances between the French and the Americans.

It is time to let the lady enter.

On March 21 of 1789, Morris was at the home of a French family when in walked Madame Adele Flahaut, and the agony and pleasures of a prolonged affair of two hearts and bodies began to move about the stage in that exquisite irritability and sensibility called love. She was twenty-eight, married, with mink-colored hair (once the fashionable heavy powder was removed), heavy-lidded, "mysterious brown eyes." She spoke English. Her husband was a worn-out rake of sixty-three. In his journals Morris merely wrote just then that she was "a pleasing woman," and added, as if he knew the gossip, not "a sworn enemy of intrigue." One bright Sunday the two ran into each other in the gardens of the Tuileries; there is a hint that some sort of meeting had happened not by accident.

The Flahauts, in this disintegrating society, lived in one of the king's palaces, the Louvre (not then a museum); and a filthy, dirty place it was—its halls and doorways were horrors of smells and messes to Morris, who bathed and owned changes of linen. Sanitary ideas and plumbing were not part of French palace life. Court people had the habit of relieving themselves on the stairs, in the halls; so one must walk with care and hold one's nose.

Morris did again meet Adele, at home, and the long flirting, moving toward an affair, began. The king's way of supporting the couple was to let them live in the palace and give them eleven thousand francs a year—there was also a pension of four thousand more. Adele's old husband had a post called "Director of the Gardens of the King." There is doubt if he did much, and his wife's debts ran high. Extra-marital intimacies, it may be added, were socially expected.

There was a child in the family, not old Flahaut's, but the result of an affair with a priest, Charles Maurice de Talleyrand-Périgord, better known to history as just Talleyrand, the most gifted and cunning diplomat and politician that France—or perhaps Europe—ever produced. He managed to serve the king, then the Revolution, and then Napoleon. That took survival of a high order. He had another son by another married woman who became the famous romantic painter Delacroix. Talleyrand's other children are too numerous and vague to bring up here. Exciting, irreverent about God, and mocking, he remained friendly with Adele.

Adele herself is spoken of as being kind and sweet, lips bee-blown, the figure full and well curved. An engraving of her suggests the beauty, bearing, temper, passion the artist is not talented enough to capture fully.

Invited to have dinner, Morris found Adele Flauhaut in bed, she having, it appeared, forgotten. She did not ask him to join her under the sheets. On later visits Morris met Talleyrand, who was still good friends with the mother of his son. If Morris had a wooden leg as a lover's handicap, Talleyrand, under his bishop's robe, had a club foot. Today one can see both the wooden leg and the brace of the club foot preserved in a museum.

Was Adele a flirt? Morris was new to her, but Talleyrand's friendship went back ten whole years. There was a court saying: One only could die for the first love; the others burn in the wound a short time.

Morris had affairs of state. Trouble was brewing in France, and he talked to Jefferson and Lafayette, giving good advice on the mounting crisis as to how the king could hold the country together. Soon there were bread riots and the part of the population that was the mob and the agitators began to sharpen pikes and talk of coming days of revenge on the *aristos*. Morris wrote Washington: "The great mass of the common people have no religion but their priests, no law but their superiors, no morals but their interests . . ." Morris witnessed the king and queen address the States General that was taking over control, it was hoped, for the welfare of the country. It all ended with *"Vive la Reine!"*

Still, there was time for the charming French woman. Morris played tric trac and backgammon with Adele, but not love; and later wrote sourly of a poor lunch of a "mackerel, pigeon, fresh eggs and asparagus." Like Franklin and Jefferson he was a gourmet. As a poet we have some verse he wrote on a pad for Adele—perhaps he had used it before:

> No lover I. Alas too old
> To raise in you a mutual Flame.
> Then take a Passion rather cold
> And call it by fair Friendship's Name.

The husband asked for a translation into French—got some satisfaction from the result. He had long ago learned to eat umbrage like cake. Morris visited Adele at her *toilette*, and she dressed before him *and* her husband with "perfect decency even to the shift." The husband left. The two came intimately together at last (but some of the journal here has been edited out by later editors). "We sit down with the best disposition imaginable but instead . . ."

They became lovers then and there. But he had other duties. Returning from a trip to London for Washington, Morris found Adele out of town— ninety miles away in the country—and with deflated concupiscence proceeded to get roaring drunk with two French friends and a Pole. The hangover was fearful. Adele, hearing of his return, rode fifteen hours in a wretched, rattling coach over ninety miles of rutted roads to be with him. They met and had a hasty sexual encounter in the Louvre. One historian calls their behavior "wanton and flagrant," but to us today, with our more public acceptance of sexual themes and images, we see merely two worldly people in love, in physical contact, the stuff of our films and raunchy novels.

Some have suggested that Adele was planted as a spy by the wily Talleyrand. But no such evidence has come to light. Adele was a young woman, married to an old man, and here was Morris, a still virile, strong American. From the journals, she seems to have been sexually insatiable at this time. As for Morris, he is delighted, but he does not talk of love to her. They jest, make happy, lewd remarks as lovers will. They fight a bit, there are tears, the whole armory of passion involved in a new affair is in use. When he misses her as she performs her special duties on visits to the court, Morris can write: "Come, lovely Woman, who so long delayed." It was the age of capital letters for Love and Passion.

Meanwhile Jefferson left France, having been appointed Secretary of State, leaving Mr. William Shore to carry on for America with Morris. Suddenly Adele was sure she was pregnant, and if so, being *triste*, it would be best to "talk of the future until the husband returns, and then . . . add one more to the number of human existences." In plainer words, give the husband the impression when he returned to his wife's bed that the child was his. But it was a false alarm.

Adele was a sensitive, nervous person, held to rigid court protocol, and sometimes she was too high strung to be with Morris. He noted in his journal of times he went to bed, alone, "vexed," another time she pleaded "too much fatigued for Love's Dispute," and gave him Voltaire's erotic story *La Pucelle* to read. *La petite mort* (French for orgasm) had to be caught on the run. Adele was not an easy mistress to please or under- stand. But there were moments, Morris recorded, when "we join in fer- vent adoration to the Cyprian Queen . . . I leave her reclined in the sweet tranquility of nature well satisfied. . . ." It is like a polite line from *Fanny*

Hill. Neither coarse nor vulgar, but amusingly indecent. As the English author Lawrence Sterne wrote: "They do these things better in France."

At this time Morris was also engaged on American diplomatic matters, meeting leaders, talking to bankers, drawing up figures on wheat and corn, on commercial ideas, and listening to the sounds in the street, becoming more and more involved with French friends he had made in their talk of change, *change.* Morris was not a great believer in Liberty with a big L, nor of the People with a big P. He was a student of human nature and he felt the American Revolution had been lucky in having few criminal or addled minds involved (Benedict Arnold excepted). He felt the French revolutionaries—he saw them as dregs and debris—were not to be trusted. This was both the snide attitude of a native American and the cynical appraisal of a man of the world who found European mankind deceitful and brutish. He never held ideals of perfection nor hoped for the common man to be anything but common and dangerous, and a fool when he gathered as a rabble.

Morris' great treat was to see Adele in her bath water tinted with milk. As it was a social custom among her class, he added, "Appearances are scrupulously observed between us." They usually met in a hurry in dark corners, in coaches, banging out the dust of borrowed couches. It is doubtful if during this period the lovers ever spent the night together with their clothes off or with candlelight. This may have been from a certain shyness on Morris' part to expose his badly seared arm and the stump of his missing leg. Romance as written of in that period is all flowers and pastoral meetings in gardens, all frivolity and levity. But we find in the journals the facts that Adele was often ill with bad colds, that she still suffered from the results of her son's birth, the *accoucheur* having damaged her at the delivery. Morris notes he was in pain, the stump of his amputated limb had turned mean. He was in agony at times and had to leave off his heavy wooden leg and rest. Once he fell down the filthy stairs at the Louvre and tore his knee breeches. We catch the drama, the color of the *mise-en-scène.* He was jealous of Talleyrand who acted as if he were still Adele's lover, and most likely may have been. Morris would leave Adele's side in a huff when Talleyrand became too charming toward her. She would follow Morris out onto the reeking dark staircase, begging him to be sensible. Once she even offered to have him sneak back and spend the entire night with her (the husband slept alone in a room below). But Morris was so angry he refused even that grand offer. It can be assumed he, as yet, feared to fully expose that seared arm and the stump to a perhaps boisterous mistress.

Revolution was near. Danton was crying, "Lafayette is the eunuch of the Revolution!" To which Lafayette responded by abolishing all titles and coats-of-arms. Mirabeau delivered a fine oration on news of the death of Franklin, of which the French had just heard. The whores of Paris, too, wanted certain titles abolished and petitioned the National Assembly for the "abolishing of the titles *garces, putains, toupies, maquerelles.*" Semantics in the flesh trade was part of the revolutionary problem.

Adele confessed to Morris she was sleeping with Talleyrand again, and Morris shouted he would possess her for "the last time." But, of course, the affair went on, both aware of the absurdity of society and the attending joys of copulation.

The Austrians were sending an army to aid the king, a king whom Morris pitied, a "sovereign, humbled to the level of a beggar's pity, without resources, without authority, without a friend." The nobles began to prepare for the worst. Talleyrand wrote his will, making Adele his sole beneficiary, and left it with her; he was in fear of assassination. (Later he took the will back.)

Morris watched the impotence of the court. The mob broke into the king's rooms at the Tuileries, courtiers defended him with knives, forks, and pistols until Lafayette came up panting with the National Guard. On a more personal level Adele asked Morris would he marry her, *if* she were widow? Answer *yes* or *no*. Morris gave neither. Love, both discovered, is the finest of all instruments of torture. Tom Paine was in Paris trying to publish his *Rights of Man*. Morris disliked Paine—a man of absolutes about liberty and justice—and told him he had urged Paine's dismissal from Congress.

There were small lovers' rewards. Morris had the treat of twice more seeing Adele taking her milk bath. But rioting at the Tuileries continued and Lafayette fainted at the head of his troops. Somehow history cast him as a sort of comic relief to the revolution. He emerges with a minimum of gratitude for his efforts. Morris reported he had eaten his first frogs' legs and John Paul Jones, the famous American sea captain—unemployed— came to see him.

On the twenty-first of June the royal family tried to escape from the Tuileries but bungled the flight to Varennes. It was hoped that the king, a good horseman, could reach Germany in about a day's ride. But that was not to be. The royal family was escorted back to the palace in disgrace. On July 4 Americans in Paris celebrated *their* revolution (already back home some preferred calling it the War of Independence). Soon after that Adele and Morris at a window of the Russian Embassy watched the ashes of Voltaire being carried past to the Pantheon. Voltaire had set down the implausible madness of the world and his comedy was to be played as tragedy.

The two lovers became part of the scene of these wilder times, making love in coaches, in passages with doors open all around, on the quays. (Freud had not yet appeared to hint at danger as part of sex satisfaction.) Lovemaking in a coach had its drawbacks, drawers for ladies were not yet popular, the fashion for a half dozen petticoats lay just ahead. Morris could be thankful wide panniers, ribbons and bows and lacings had been replaced by fashionable blouses and skirts under a redingote. But still a lover had to labor over knots and intricate, intimate garments in a musty interior on wheels while the coach horses *chomped* and the coachman snoozed. It is a ribald scene from Fielding or Smollett, both of whom Morris read with pleasure.

Now with the revolution fanning white hot Flahaut demanded the right to sleep again with his wife. Adele could have replied in the words of a popular novel of the times: "He wishes to take back all the rights he has scorned—*il voulait reprendre tous ses droits méprisés.*" All we do know is that she refused the husband entry and the lovers celebrated the rejection.

Lafayette resigned his command of the National Guard and proudly announced, "The Revolution is ended. The liberty of France is secured," proving himself the worst guesser of history until Chamberlain at Munich. Lafayette was called on to command the army, for on the borders the enemies of the revolution were on the move to choke the lovers of liberty, equality and fraternity.

Back home in America, Congress was in lively debate. Should Gouverneur Morris be appointed American Minister to France? A debate of Talmudic elaboration took place. Eighteen days of talk and Morris was confirmed, but in a close vote, sixteen to eleven.

In rage Tom Paine wrote to Jefferson that Morris' "appointment is a most unfortunate one." Actually Morris was the man for the job; tough, involved deeply in French life, and not too blind to the amorphous fury that the revolution could bring. Paine continued to insist the events were normal. "The riots and outrages in France are nothing at all." Until the revolution in the normal way of events threw Paine into jail and refused to release him.

The new minister from America, Gouverneur Morris, took a house in the Rue de la Planche, Adele approving of the new Embassy. Cost was 2500 francs a year. Morris' first official report said, "The best picture . . . of the French nation, is that of cattle before a thunderstorm . . . the end is beyond the ken of mortal foresight." There were petitions to suspend the king. The dark sources of chaos or the proclaimed champions of natural man—one could prove either side—were moving beyond demagoguery.

In June of 1792 Morris noted in his journal in his neat script that a group of citizens forced their way into the Tuileries and compelled the king to don the Red Bonnet of Liberty. Just a few days before Morris as minister from the United States had been presented to the king and queen, who "shews me her son." Morris was rather sorry for the poor badgered king. Meanwhile the American naval hero, John Paul Jones, residing on the Rue de Tournon, was dying. He called for Morris to come and draw up his will. Duty's Child—that done, Morris rushed off to an after-dinner party, somewhat later to be called cocktails.

With the American naval hero dead Morris thought it ironic that John Paul Jones who "detested the French Revolution and all those concerned with it, should have been followed to the grave by a deputation from the

National Assembly. Some people here who like a rare show wished him to have a pompous funeral . . . I did not agree to waste money of which he had no great abundance." At an auction of Jones' belongings Morris bought the sword Jones had worn in his famous sea battle against the English ship *Serapis* (the weapon is now at Annapolis).

Morris felt it wise to advise the king, through his former Foreign Minister Montmorin, that he better run for it before he was executed. Morris laid out a skilled plan of escape, but the king decided not to try to get away again. It was, of course, a grave abuse of ambassadorial protocol for Morris to mix into internal politics of any nation. We have made meddling progress since then all over the world.

If the king did not dare leave, it was time to move his money to safety. The numbered Swiss bank accounts did not yet exist. Morris and the keeper of the royal household, Monciel, on July 24 began to move the royal treasure and certain papers into the American Embassy. Morris officially claimed he only "would consent to take charge of it . . . in case His Majesty could find no one else to trust." It was again hardly ethical for an Embassy of the United States to harbor royal cash (a cardinal from time to time, yes), but Morris was, as pointed out several times, "more royalist than the king."

In time the Embassy held nearly a half million of the king's francs, most of it converted into gold louis d'or and stored in purses, each holding twenty coins. More kept coming in. In time it was all smuggled into England. Six years later, in 1798, Morris turned over this royal hoard to the king's daughter in Vienna.

One hot August day the mob moved to seize the king, and the murder of the Swiss Guard proceeded like a game of toy soldiers. Ambassadors began to pack. The American Embassy began to gather in its French friends and refugees. Adele and her child (he in worn clothes to look like a street boy) made their way to the Embassy. Her husband, now sixty-six years old, went off to help some wounded friends after street fighting broke out. Marat (not yet an historic painting) was shouting in the streets to all who would hear, "Up, up, everyone! May the blood of the traitors begin to flow!"

Lafayette, always prone to do the wrong thing in a crisis, had been lured off-stage—he was with the revolutionary army in Luxembourg. He deserted his command on the news from Paris and went to join the Austrians. They treated him like a prisoner of war and he was held for many years.

In Paris soon all the diplomats, ambassadors, and ministers were gone, all but Gouverneur Morris. He was in great danger hiding aristocrats.

CHAPTER 4

Morris and the Terror

Terror at any object is quickly taught . . .

FRANCES GALTON

A PERILOUS TURN of events came the night armed *Commissaires de Section* arrived at the Embassy with a paper permitting them a "search of the legation for hidden arms." Not many arms, perhaps, but certainly they would discover a full house of refugee aristocrats. Morris boldly went out to face the search party and the gathering mob. He refused to let them enter a house that by diplomatic right was United States territory. No, they could not enter to search! As he wrote, he was "obliged to be very peremptory, and at length got rid of them." He received an official apology in the morning. But already Paris could hear the cannon of the enemy, the Duke of Brunswick, hammering at Verdun. Soon there were proclamations that "the enemy is at the gates of Paris ready to rescue the king!"

The slaughter of the aristocrats, landlords, speculators, politicians began. A week of killing. Adele was taken ill at the horror of it and was nursed by Morris at the Embassy. Three hundred people died—mostly it was men who were killed. Robespierre, mythological, wraithlike, ruled. Adele forged a passport and sent it to her husband who was in hiding. Most likely Morris aided in the forgery, at least helped in this move.

Talleyrand, playing some sort of hanky panky with the revolutionary leaders, was given a passport by Danton. He suggested Morris and Adele join him in England. At the moment Adele was safe in the Legation but any moment the Commune could demand her as an enemy of the revolution. It was decided to move her. In the wintry chill of the end of the year Adele and her seven-year-old son were on their way to England, without Morris. Christmas day Morris wrote, "Our friend has gone away . . . I wait, hoping in a while or soon she will be back."

Morris, the sole ambassador left in Paris, was a busy, harassed man, representing not only his country before a changing series of people in power, but trying to attend to the needs of Americans, and also working to save lives, perhaps worthless, dissolute lives that had brought on revolution, but still lives.

1793. The revolution, ringed by invading enemies, was fighting for its life. That year they executed the preposterous king, and then the queen, that once dilettante milkmaid, the exquisite princess. There is a remarkable little sketch by the artist David of the queen in mob cap, arms tied behind her back, haggard and yet with dignity, on her way to the knife— she, too, a lost, once lovely, foolish head.

Morris did his work—suffering from the sleet and ice of winter. It was hard walking for a man with a wooden leg. Then the French declared war on England. Morris' love was there across the channel; he had to face pressures from the French. The United States was invited into the war to drive the Spanish out of the Mississippi Valley. Tom Paine was for it. Morris, a cooler head, was not. It was dangerous nonsense. He was sorry the king had been executed. It had been a close vote, to lose or save his head. The vote of the Convention was 387 yes, cut off his head, 334 no.

Meanwhile, hiding out in Paris, the husband of Adele, the Count Flahaut, was proving himself no Scarlet Pimpernel. Captured, he was offered his life and freedom if he would implicate a friend as an enemy of the revolution. He said no, escaped; but when his attorney was held as a hostage, the count gave himself up. His head was cut off in the best Sidney Carton style.

Adele as the widow of an executed enemy of the state would herself face the knife if she returned to France. These events did not improve Morris' temper, and his stump, as if in its own rage, began to pain him again. The revolution was in a state of idiocy, its victims incessantly foolish.

One problem for Morris was the American adventurers in Paris who wanted papers to arm ships under the American flag to serve the French by attacking English merchant ships. He refused papers to these American pirates. He helped keep us out of a war with England by this move. The early day Birchers and red-hot American jingoists proclaimed him a coward for that. He was called "a royalist, a voluptuary, debauché and an Anglophile." The London newspapers ran a false item that the Embassy had been burned down and Morris murdered. He hardly had time to make the laconic answer that he was unaware of such events.

Morris didn't mind Paine being in trouble; "I must mention that Thomas Paine is in prison where he amuses himself with publishing a pamphlet against Jesus Christ." Paine claimed to be an American citizen. But he had adopted French citizenship and Morris washed his hands of him. He wrote that in the best of time Paine "had a larger share of every other sense than common sense, and ardent spirits impaired the small stock he originally possessed." Cruel perhaps, coming from a man who ended an evening himself drunk at times and suffered from fearful hangovers. (It was Morris' successor who got Paine and Madame de Lafayette out of the prisons of the revolution.)

The revolution had sent a cocky French ambassador, one Genet, to America. A brawling, mediocre exhibitionist, he had made trouble and so his recall had been requested. (Actually Genet feared to go home and settled in the United States as a private citizen.) This recall talk meant the usual procedure—for the French in turn to ask for Morris to be

recalled. John Jay as Chief Justice was first picked to replace Morris, but in the end James Monroe accepted the position under pressure. Outraged, Morris wrote Washington suggesting the creation of a navy so that "with twelve, perhaps twenty ships of the line no nation on earth will dare insult us." It was one of the few times he lost his head.

Paris was still fermenting. The heads of Robespierre, St. Just, Cauthon, and other makers of revolution "sneezed into the basket," as one wit put it. The back of the Terror was broken. Anglo-American historians have much exaggerated it. Twenty-six hundred seven people had been executed, a minute number compared to the killings by the Soviets, the Germans, and the Americans in the twentieth century.

The Paris that Morris lived in during the years of the revolution was a city where food was often hard to get, bread was adulterated and became sour and indigestible, plague came. The warehouses of Corbeil and Nogent-sur-Seine were empty. Those who remained rich or held power ate Lucullan meals at the cost of ten livres each at Meots. The poor for ten sous could get by on beef, an entree, and a glass of wine. Sugar was in short supply. Queues formed and waited for hours, to end up being told everything was sold out. People began to mutter of the good old days of the *ancien régime*.

The street drama of the revolution was that rare moment when something exciting happened at the daily executions. Mostly they were dull, bloody events that soon wore out their novelty. Yet there were moments: a general weeping as his head is put into the knife's yoke, DuBarry, a king's tender fleshpot, howling in fear, Danton roaring. (Did he really say to the executioner, "Show them my head, it's worth looking at"?) And Robespierre with his bullet-shattered jaw, waiting his turn, yelping as they brutally tore off his bandages. But for such strident moments executions became like scenes of sacrificing poultry.

At first it all seemed to proceed along the lines of the American Revolution. But Morris felt the French lacked the American calm and often had (he was a bigot) an ingrown criminal nature. The Swiss Guards had been massacred and buried, the dead patriots strewn with flowers and spoken well of. The revolution did have a French sense of style. At the Assembly in boxes, Morris noticed (he had an eye for such things), well-dressed ladies ate oranges, ices, sipped liqueurs, wore tricolor ribbons. Visitors and travelers drank wine and brandy and listened to the revolutionaries make speeches.

Pleasures grew wildly—old games went on. Mademoiselle Lacour of the Place des Petits-Pères provided *rouge et noir*, besides "pretty nieces."

Bathing houses for erotic games, strippers, obscene shows were running wide open. Republican marriage and Republican divorce were simple by municipal order.

Morris noted so much was changed. August, 1792, became IX Thermidor of the Year II. There were lugubrious party politics, times of fall from high places. He noted so many of them in his journal. The fall of the king, the fall of the *Girondins*, the *hébertistes*, the followers of Danton, at last Robespierre. The revolution may have swallowed court and nobles, but it ate its own children with as much relish. Someone said it was a time of the sublime with the ignoble in power, in turn.

Morris was to make much of the Terror; like most Anglo-American historians and upper-class French writers he exaggerated. Was it 2600 guillotined in the Champs Elysées? Yet there were still phaetons with good horses passing, fashionable women on show, lovers in parks, and merchants making a good fat thing of it. Paris held 800,000 citizens and most survived.

For the condemned it was dreadful; delay, agony, often foul prison life. And many were friends of Morris, or people he had met at salons and fêtes. The Terror was at its worst from July to December of 1793, from March to July of 1794. The Revolutionary Tribunal in those periods went on with its work. The American Embassy was filled with French refugees Morris was sheltering from sure death. He moved them on to London if he could. In the streets executions had gone on, fifty heads a day fell, "like slates off a roof." For a time the tumbrels carrying the condemned became part of the daily scenery. The children no longer stopped their play to watch, the citizen shrugged or crossed himself and turned away. As Kafka was to write a little over a century later: "Yearly leopards broke into the temple and drank the wine from the sacred chalice on the altar; in time it was made part of the ceremony." So there was hardly a Paris day that someplace the iron wheels of the tumbrel did not echo.

But to balance all that there were still advertisements of needed produce for the survivors: MME. BROGUIN'S FAMOUS POMADE FOR DYEING RED OR WHITE HAIR CHESTNUT OR BLACK ON A SINGLE APPLICATION . . . 9 FRANCS THE SMALL JAR.

There were even a few panniered skirts and knee breeches of the *ancien régime*. Morris had worn them, wooden leg exposed. The embroidered coats and white stockings did vanish and soon there was the fashion for the round hat, English frock coat, cashmere pantaloons, riding boots, and the popular cry was, "No wearing of breeches, dress as the *sans-culottes* (no breeches)."

The people of the streets, the poor, dressed with what they had, but those in power, those with new wealth or traders in army supplies dressed *à la Circassienne*, often with red and white and blue shoes, cockade pinned to a lady's *fichu*.

As the revolution settled down to fight invading enemies and its citizen armies gained victories, women grew daring. Houdon cast bronze busts of Washington, Molière, La Fontaine, the actor La Rive. People came visiting the wonders of Paris life. From Angers to Paris it cost thirty-six livres by coach. There were the salons of Madame Helvétius, Madame de Condorcet and Madame Panchoucke, where Franklin had once walked, flirted, and sipped tea, and now Mr. Morris might drop in, if affairs did not drive him into a frenzy of work and rage.

Some must die—a revolution without victims was unthought of—but others must attend an Academy gala where an eyewitness report had it the women enjoying the revolution had "the patches on their faces melting with the heat of the hall, the ardour of their sympathy, cheeks on fire, eyes sparkling, applauding, delectable lips bursting with phrases like 'Ah, Bravo . . .'" Grafitti read: "Paris shopkeepers, scum of the earth! Look out! The good old guillotine is still standing!"

If Morris had hangovers or his digestion went wrong, the common remedy was infusions of Ventaury and purges of Seidlitz water for "purging the caked bile." Every house that didn't buy the best in bottles might still have a half barrel of Bordeaux. A light repast at which Morris often joined some family would be of six courses. Black pudding, sausages, *pâté*, a couple of joints of meat, two roast fowl, four kinds of sweets, two mixed salads. As the revolution proceeded the ordinary middle-class citizen found all this a bit hard to assemble.

Some things didn't change. There were still bourgeois walking their dogs in the early days, pushing protesting donkeys. Mountebanks pitched and grimaced at the Pont Notre Dame, the Quai de Gesvre. A German traveler reported on the crowds: "One hardly ever sees a single person walking slowly, phlegmatically, hardly one whose hands and facial features are not in perpetual motion . . . this gives a Parisian crowd a distinction that can be found nowhere else . . . the multitude of street vendors and small merchants trying to make their voices heard above the tumult of the streets."

He does not mention the *boue de Paris* (Paris mud), which in wet weather was a deadly glue. But there were no more Sundays or religious feast days, so at least one didn't have to go to church as a social asset.

There were times when bread and meat cards were issued, and someone began to doctor the wine, a mixture "of pernicious drugs, alum, brandy and litharge." This caused more anger than most executions.

In one way Morris was not a modern man. He could not accept official murder. One wonders what he would have thought of the brutalities of the Soviets in Hungary, the Germans of the Third Reich, the Americans in Asia with napalm and poisoned jungles, and the civilian massacres of Guernica, the London Blitz, My Lai. If we have learned anything in our study of him, it was his fears of the common man in power. He was happy to leave his post.

On August 10, 1794, Morris took James Monroe, the new ambassador, to present his credentials to the powers of the moment that ruled France. Paine, still in prison, addressed a note to Monroe accusing Morris of wishing "to prevent my return to the United States that I should not expose his misconduct." On the nineteenth of October Morris was across the Swiss border with 400 louis d'or on his person, an illegal act. So we leave him, his Paris days over. He was to try to take up his tangled romance with Adele, who had turned to writing novels in England. They met again, but their sexual relations seem to have ended. There were doubts now on both sides, outcries, demands. In the end Morris went back home to America, and Adele married a man named De Souza. The romance with Morris was packed away in memory scented with frangipani.

In December of 1809, Morris married Anne Cary Randolph. Most likely he thought back often to his Parisian past. Did he remember Dryden's lines: "The Lioness stalks and hunts her lover through the lonely walks . . ." In 1816, at the age of sixty-five, Gouverneur Morris died, a remarkable man of spirit, temper, some wisdom, and with an ironic outlook on life and its events. Adele died at the age of seventy-five in Paris, near Talleyrand's former palace where she had heard Talleyrand, the father of her son, say, "Love is a reality in the realm of the imagination."

All these sensual, sybaritic people passed from view.

Talleyrand, the most cynical and wise of this ménage of three (one forgets the husband) survived under three revolutions and passed from this earth as a most intriguing figure in 1837, at the good ripe age of eighty-four. He would have approved—as an eyewitness to so much—the remark of Leon Trotsky (whose company he most likely would have enjoyed): "Revolutions are always impolite because the upper classes have never taught manners to the people."

Gouverneur Morris today still remains partly hidden from our view by our too simple attitudes toward heroes of history. We overlook the labyrinth of half secret missions he walked, the man himself so full of life and lusts. Few read his splendid journals with their clear pictures and horrifying apprehensions, for they are not as glorious as the charge on horseback, the crossing of the Delaware, the final attack at Yorktown. As for his personal life—our Calvinist, guilt-ridden generations have been shocked by the extra-marital intimacies he sets down as if he were simply devouring a gourmet's meal. In our franker (and sicker) times, when the cant of a morality we never really had has been pushed aside, we can look more directly at this one-legged man and say: "So he had been at the Cena Trimalchio of Petronius." Yet admit, "There was a man . . ."

CHAPTER 5

Fulton's Folly on the Seine

A man must dare to be happy.
  GOETHE

Americans, baffled at home, often had a way of turning up in Paris—
and still do. Benjamin Franklin was not the only inventor from the
United States who worked on science in France. Robert Fulton was in
Paris in 1797, a handsome young man in his early thirties who was born in
Pennsylvania. Already known for his inventions and work on canal improvements, he was also a painter, the student of Benjamin West, President of the Royal Academy. Fulton was a charmer, witty, warmly
accepted by the sophisticated Parisian society who called him *Toot*. The
American ambassador, Joel Barlow, was pleased to show Fulton around.
Fulton had lived with Benjamin West in England for some years, worked
as a waterways engineer, and invented cast iron aqueducts and power
shovels.

He was a long way from his beginnings as a Pennsylvania farm boy.
His cherished invention of the moment was his torpedo. (Why inventors
seize on the delinquencies of legal mass murder needs explaining.) The
French Revolution was ardently warlike, or had wars forced on it; historians accept both views. The young American felt there was a future for a
deadly submarine weapon that could move under water, attach itself to
an enemy vessel, and blow it up.

Between the pleasures of Paris and meetings with French patent officers, he wondered, why not expand his idea, why not an actual submarine
with a crew inside and his time-bomb torpedo fired at an enemy ship by
harpoon? A particularly seminal idea that has killed hundreds of thousands since—after basic improvements. But like so many young men
bursting with ideas, Fulton was short of money, and just when plans for
an actual submarine filled his mind. To get money for the model he sold a
painting he did in Rome, a work of art called *The Burning of Moscow*. It
was a strange bit of crystal-ball prophecy, for the young Bonaparte, who
was later actually to be at the burning of the Russian city, was also in
Paris, back from a huge disaster in Egypt, the dream of the burning of the
czar's city not yet within his destiny. With the one thousand dollars Fulton got for the picture he began his submarine. He soon ran out of money
again, but as an American friendly to the iconoclastic rhetoric of the
French Revolution, Fulton turned to the Directoire for aid. However, the
revolutionaries were not too eager to help. Young Bonaparte had spoken
of a whiff of grapeshot to control the mob; political changes were taking
place.

Fulton, of course, did not actually invent the submarine. Leonardo Da
Vinci had sketched one to run on compressed air, some said, but he never
built one, and there had been diving bells. The first actual submarine had
been built by another American, David Bushnell of Connecticut, and
used in the American Revolution, with meager success by blundering
handlers.

Fulton's version was much more like the modern submarine. It had a
conning tower, ballast tanks to fill and empty for rising and diving. In the
first model he showed in Paris he had four men as the motor power,
cranking an endless belt turning a propeller shaft, the interior lit by
candles! Yet most of its basic principles are incorporated into today's
undersea boat.

Fulton, using the revolutionary calendar, noted: "On the third of Thermidor I commenced my experiments by plunging to depth of five feet,
and so on to twenty-five. I went no further as the machine could bear no
greater pressure of superincumbent water. My boat had 212 cubic feet of
capacity, contained enough oxygen to support four men and two small
candles for three hours."

When not involved in selling submarine ideas, Fulton found that life in
revolutionary France had its excitements. The Directoire was leading to
war with England, so they looked with more favor on Fulton's invention.

Napoleon became First Consul, and the French Admiralty was nudged into action with a kick. Fulton began to perfect the submarine *Nautilus* (Jules Verne was to use that name for his undersea boat in his famous novel *Twenty Thousand Leagues Under the Sea*).

Fulton was given money, an advance against a sliding scale for his promises to destroy British warships: 60,000 francs for destroying a ten-gun ship and up to 400,000 francs for sinking a thirty-gun ship-of-the-line. Napoleon, like so many continental leaders since Caesar and William the Conqueror (and the late Hitler), dreamed of invading England. So if the British fleet could be destroyed by M. Fulton, first England, then Europe was his.

Fulton had perfected a brass globe to hold air under pressure, and he had developed an underwater bomb to attach to the hulls of warships. No mere rocket on a harpoon. But he found two worlds in conflict: the hint of the Industrial Age *and* the afterglow of rebel philosophers.

It was a time of lively revolution in dress as well as inventions. Robert Fulton was a man who liked a well-cut coat and a proper tilt to his top hat. He, too, was a man on a transmission belt between painting and steam power. The artist David encouraged a near classical nudity, and Fulton as a painter had worked from the nude. But now the underclad girls and women invaded the streets, the balls, the dance halls in the mode of Ceres robes, Galatea dresses, Minerva gowns, Diana drapery. What mattered most was that it was transparent lawn or tulle, under a conical beehive of a blonde or red wig *à la Bérénice*. Callipygian Venus was the fashion and Fulton was young enough to be delighted.

A prominent Philadelphia Main Line family still has, in its attic, trunks filled with such styles (among clysters, bleeding cups, pillion saddles) bought by the wives, sons, and daughters of merchants who were in Paris at this time. The garments were never worn publicly on the streets of the City of Brotherly Love.

There is a painting of the elder male member of this family done in Paris at that time by a follower of Gros. We also see the proper, middle-aged, solid citizen walking on the Petit Coblentz and Frascati in drawings by Vernet. The family owns pictures of the son seen as a dandy with greasy locks hanging over his ears, hair teased up in back, a square-cut frock coat with huge lapels, neck hidden in a sextuple cravat covering the chin up nearly to the nose. One can imagine Fulton so attired with dragging breeches, a heavy walking stick, a low-crowned, broad-brimmed hat. Such is the still hidden picture of a Philadelphian youth in Paris. He does not wear golden earrings as some dandies did. As for the father, perhaps he carried a pistol in case someone threatened his ladies at the Glacier Velloni or the Passage du Perron. The ladies were friends of female Parisians who dressed in the style of the Merveilleuse. They were addicted to wigs, thin-soled pumps called buskins, Grecian tunics.

A daybook of their accounts notes they witnessed Robespierre's Festival of the Supreme Being, where the "sea green monster" sat on the Mountain of Champs-de-Mer. "He is not satisfied with being top dog, he also wants to be God Almighty," quipped one observer. Unfortunately, the family will not permit their own letters to be reproduced, though they have allowed them to be read. They tell us a great deal about the life of an average American in Paris, of how a merchant, a sea captain, a wine dealer, or a strayed inventor like Robert Fulton would live.

They drank white and red wine, they played the pianoforte accompanying the singing of the duet from *Oedipus at Colonus:* "Nay, forsooth, let us stray no farther, beloved." A list for a picnic party in the country, in a grove along the river, includes: a three-pound pigeon pie, a platter of *pâté*, baked cod and potatoes, three kinds of cheese, coffee and brandy. Everyone wore tricolor cockades for safety. Some guest recited Lebrun's poem, "Republican Ode on the Taking of Toulon" ("this chap Bonaparte, what's he like?"). They also sang "Blue Eyes and Dark Eyes."

We can imagine Fulton between his experiments at such an American picnic on the Seine. Or accompanying the Philadelphians to the Théâtre de la République in the Rue de la Loi to view the tragedy *Epicharis,* the *Two Brothers, Michel Cervantes.* Actually their letters mention Robert Fulton as being in Paris only twice, and both times spell his name *Fultun.*

Life was not dull as the times of the revolution changed to Napoleonic glory; society just shifted its patterns. The Café Flamande still had its fine beer, the *Journal de Paris* was on file at the Café de Valois. One wonders if Thomas Paine, in exile from America, living in poverty in Paris, came there to read it. Certainly he did not go to the Café Mécanique where coffee was the special item, piped boiling hot into cups through a hollow center table leg. Most popular with Americans with money were such cafés as the Café de Foy, the Left Bank's Café Zoppi, Café Charpentier (whose proprietor was Danton's father-in-law).

But Fulton's life in Paris was also practical. Before taking on the British Navy, in August of 1801, his submarine was bobbing about in the harbor of Brest. Some notables came down from Paris to see his submarine blow up a sloop with a twenty-pound bomb worked by a clockwork motor. The vessel went up in fragments, right on time, and there were cheers and drinking of wine at this breach of etiquette in the formal game of eighteenth-century warfare.

Now Fulton and his crew would go after the blockading British fleet so arrogantly flying the Union Jack in sight of French shores.

However the British knew of Fulton and his ideas, and while they were too hidebound to use submarine ideas themselves, they were aware that the young man in Paris had convinced the French that his inventions were practical. Orders went out. *Do not engage any submergible craft.* The British did not stand and fight. They bunched on sail and moved away from the four men in a wooden cigar cranking their endless belt. It was no contest. Fulton's man-motored shell could not catch a British man-of-war under sail, but he tried all summer.

By luck his last chance to attach a bomb to a seventy-four-gun man-of-war *nearly* worked, but the British vessel escaped. The French Navy shrugged skeptically—it was too bad, M. Fulton, but the idea of a submarine would have to be given up. Man was not a fish to exist under water, even in your strange aquarium.

Fulton, back in Paris, insisted it hadn't been a fair trial of his submarine. He needed an engine, not manpower. But the times were in change, confusion, disarray; no one would listen.

In Paris, taking his problems to fellow Americans, Fulton met Robert Livingston, a well-connected, rich New Yorker who had been sent by Congress to negotiate the Louisiana Purchase from Napoleon. Napoleon needed cash to fight the frustrations pouring in on him, and he had a feeling the British would soon seize New Orleans and all the Louisiana land anyway. He smiled at assertions of the fact it wasn't his—he had just taken it away from the Spanish and it was not actually his to sell. Mr. Livingston, never one to overlook a likely bit of real estate, was willing to buy in the name of President Thomas Jefferson of the United States. These Americans, it was whispered in Paris, would buy anything.

Robert Livingston was no empty-headed diplomat raised on astrology or palmistry. For some time he had been interested in the steamboat experiments of Fitch and Rumsey, American visionaries and inventors. But no practical vessel had resulted. In Paris Livingston earnestly talked the matter of a steamboat over with the handsome young Mr. Fulton. Livingston was a supersalesman, the first of a long line of Americans with the hard and soft, fast and slow sells. He permitted no excessive introspection. Fulton had done no steam engine work, but he was an engineer, practical and ardent. In the young man's ear was planted the idea of the

great future of steamboats in America with its great rivers, its planned canals. All that was needed was a practical steamboat—one of extreme simplicity as to parts and design.

Fulton was still involved with his submarine, but the idea of trying steam as a power plant appealed to him, and the picture of all those American rivers used only by rafts and barges and bull boats, Indian birchbarks, gave him thought . . . Invention is to perfect the unexpected, the untried.

Postrevolutionary Paris appealed to Robert Livingston, and he and Fulton enjoyed its delights, its social scene. It was not today's Paris. The Jardin des Tuileries lacked the Rue de Rivoli, and the city was a network of alleyways, yards, cul-de-sacs, gates, and stone stairs; all worn down by human effluvia before Baron Haussmann changed Paris. One walked carefully down one-cart lanes around Germain-des-Prés and the Pantheon, past scenes lit with torches echoing to cries of people for liberty and glory.

The revolution had made it a city a young or middle-aged American could connect with after the just finished war and battles in the former English colonies. The Parisian women Fulton knew wore earrings made of bits of stone from the Bastille. As were rings, medallions, pendants, and amulets some Americans bought and sent home with gifts of tortoise shell and feather fans. Few Americans dared wear the carmagnole rig—hip-length jacket, tricolor striped trousers, red waistcoat, wooden clogs, scarlet cap—the *bonnet rouge* of fashion. Fulton, while amused, pleased perhaps at the passing of kings, was no *sans-culotte* of the *faubourg*. He was a man of machines, not of politics.

Time was coming around to consolidating the French Revolution, "saving it." The *bonnets de laine* no longer carried pikes, often with heads on them (one, it is grisly to relate, the dissected genitalia of a notoriously sporting countess). Napoleon was moving toward a crown.

The Parisian women Fulton sometimes knew were the *tutoiement* blue-stocking intellectuals rather than the revolutionary amazons, pistols in belt, swords at side, riding whip in hand. He was no prude, his years in England had been part of the sporting roistering life. As a painter he saw there was a certain bohemian strain changing society. Monsieur was still *Citoyen*, Madame was *Citoyenne*. An American had to remember the Place Royale was now the Place des Fédérés, Place Louis XV the Place de la Révolution, Rue Bourbon the Place des Piques. And, of course, as one who came from the land of Washington and Paine, one should walk with

a ring of one's heels hard on the stones of Rue des Droits de l'Homme—
The Rights of Man Street.

Americans went to the new dance halls in Paris flowered by the revolution. The Tivoli, Paphos, Ruggieris. Some once holy halls were filled with sweating dancing couples; the former Noviciat des Jesuites, the Carmelites du Marais, the Filles des Sainte Marie. And when someone recognized an American dancing, he was cheered as a fellow fighter for *la liberté.*

Fulton, besides the big fancy halls, knew the places of the small bourgeois, of porters, soldiers dancing the quadrille, the polka in the full cry of violins and clarinets. Musicians got six livres a night playing dance tunes, wrote one American home, "but there are three free litres of cheap wine extra." He wrote that some macabre dances once celebrated the day's toll of the guillotine, but most people wanted to forget the Terror. "Some of the women still wear a red ribbon around the neck, on the line where the guillotine blade usually struck." So the carousers, parvenus, workers all whirled to the dance tunes; salesgirls, whores, ladies, soldiers, householders, wives and lovers, politicians and mistresses, *all* dancing. The letter writer recorded a song:

> Zig-zag, fork and spoon
> Dance to the tune of the rigadoon!

Fulton found most of the revolutionary officials fairly honest and hardworking. Perhaps a little too earnest for change, for power—power some saw as the true immortality. So those who led dull lives at home and were overworked at the office were in the majority. Only the Barras circle of opportunists had orgied with women like Josephine, Madame Tallien, relaxed at card playing, small fêtes, sometimes even skipped at children's games. It was this inner debauched circle that Fulton had to court to get money for his inventions, the group that had brought into focus the once shabby Lieutenant Bonaparte made over as General Bonaparte. He who would see the true value of the American's torpedoes and submarines.

Profiteers and speculators, as in all military-industrial set-ups, spent fortunes made in army contracts, stole more. But these men were not interested in submergible boats.

Mr. Livingston continued talking surface steamboats.

American schoolbooks and popular histories have no (or little) space for the fact that it was in Paris that Robert Fulton first built a practical steamboat that worked, and ran it on the Seine—and *not* on the Hudson—for all Paris to see. It wasn't easy. His first steamboat was sixty-six feet long with an eight-foot beam, three-foot draught, and it had a flat bottom. For a man with a head for figures Fulton had not done his homework too well. When the engine and boiler were put on board, the boat came apart and split.

Fulton built a second boat, and this time figured hull stress properly. The inventor's first steamboat to move by steam took easily to the Seine. Parisians cheered as the little ship chugged away at a full four and a half miles an hour. So it was Paris and not New York, and it was a flat-bottomed hull and *not* the *Katherine of Clermont* (never called just the *Clermont* except by history) that clearly showed the practical value of Robert Fulton's steamboat. The first expectancy and incertitude were over. Steam could move ships.

Robert Livingston was eager for Fulton to return to America with him and begin steamboating there at once. But Fulton was still full of the idea of his torpedoes and submarines. Who would buy them? In those casual days he had no difficulty in changing sides, going with his plans from the French to the British. The soul of the scientist—as Dr. Strangelove was to prove—usually lacks moral values and loyalties. At worst their work would mean the mass disposal of drones.

Again Fulton had, on paper, a practical deal to pay for his submarine idea. It read that the British Admiralty was to pay him one thousand dollars a month *and* one half of the value of all ships his inventions destroyed for the next fourteen years. As with most dealings of nations, it was a scrap of paper. When the war with the French ended, the English shrugged off the contract; it was clear it had been merely a scheme to keep Fulton from working with his devil tools for the French. It may have been Fulton who first said, "The sun never sets on the British flag. God doesn't trust it in the dark."

It was time for Robert Fulton to get to America and go to work on an American steamboat. The main problem was the engine. The only people making a practical steam engine were the English firm of Boulton and Watts, and there was a strict embargo on the export of machinery to any other country. Even trained mechanics were not permitted to emigrate because they could carry their knowledge of how to build engines and machines with them.

Only two Boulton and Watts engines had been permitted to leave England. Aaron Burr's water company had one, and the French had the other, owned by the government's Paris Waterworks. Fulton was out of favor with the French. He had changed sides during a war with too much ease. So the Paris engine was out of the question, and Burr was making money with his and not to be talked into putting it into Fulton's Folly.

The inventor, using his connections, diplomacy, friends in the British Navy Office, made it clear they owed him a favor for breaking their agreement with him. He managed to get an engine built and shipped to America. (It cost him $4,670 for an engine with a cylinder of 24-inch diameter with a four-foot stroke. To this he would have to add a 20-foot-long boiler, a 150-foot-long hull, with a 12-foot beam, a 7-foot-deep hold.)

We shall not follow Robert Fulton and his tenuous career to America. For many years an old Paris barge was, wrongly, pointed out as "*M. Fulton's le bon steamboat*," the very first of his craft to take to the water and move to the cheers of the Parisians.

In later years Fulton must have regretted leaving Paris, his friends, his painting, the fine living, the sights and sounds of the French city. His world contracted into problems and troubles after the *Clermont* steamed up river. The twenty-year monopoly he and Livingston held proved worthless. Other shipbuilders hastened to join the boom, and Fulton's plans and designs were pirated by everyone. Rivals in river wars wrecked his boats. The law courts were busy. Fulton spent more time facing judges than actually working on inventions.

He never gave up his visions for improved naval weapons and armament. The War of 1812 against the English was on. There was talk the French might help—for the French were also fighting the English (Moscow was truly burning now, not just in Fulton's painting). Fulton designed the first steam man-of-war. It was called the *Demologos,* or *Fulton the First.* Actually it was a floating fort with paddlewheels between double hulls. He never could collect from the federal government fully what was due him for this ship.

Fulton was a worn-out man. Law suits, rival steamship people, the failure to have the government meet its obligations plagued him. On October 29, 1814, *Fulton the First* was christened.

Napoleon's sun had set. Did Robert Fulton think of seeing Paris again? There was talk of building a steamship to cross the Atlantic. But he never saw transoceanic steam or the city on the Seine again. Never looked at the barge hulk they were saying was his first practical steamboat. He died in 1815 while working on plans for the world's longest canal, one to slice its way from the Great Lakes to New York harbor.

It would be called the Erie, *not* the Fulton Canal.

Book Two
MASTERS AND MISFITS

CHAPTER 6

Paris: 1800–1814
What the Americans Found

Let us endure an hour and see injustice done.

SHAKESPEARE

THE AMERICANS visiting Paris from the period of the Revolution to Napoleon found a busy, muddy, fun-loving city. With its grandiose facetiousness and its fine parks, it was a city able to excite and show its color to visitors, even as the map of Europe changed. Americans noted the frenzy for physical sensation, glory, and high fashion.

Conscripts were herded through the streets—young soldiers—at least 15,000 a year from Paris alone. In letters and diaries of the visitors we sense an attraction to war and its rewards in the hardened professional soldiers who had fought on a dozen fronts all over Europe. The city was full of grenadiers, hussars, cavalrymen, trumpeters, dragoons; dazzling sights in a day when uniforms were extravagant and beautiful. There was much gold and red, tight breeches showing off virile manhood, shiny boots, tassels, high and fancy headgear of fur, leather, feathers, and metal ornamentation.

The other side of the picture is also found in letters sent back to America, facts that lack the glory of Raffet's popular military prints. "Deserters run to a thousand a day, an officer in the Luxembourg told us . . . much of the army, he admits, is made up of drunkards, scroungers, rapists."

But there were still balloon ascents over Paris, and parachutists, and for the young American hunting sexual adventure, the Jardin des Capucines offered "shades favorable to the sweet effusions of love, confidences of friendship, the artifacts of passion." "French letters" (condoms made of fish bladders) sold by peddlers were on hand.

The American merchant and family, the sea captain, the student enjoyed Paris; the military ceremony on the Champs-de-Mars, the ornate warlike dramas on windy, rainy, or sunny parade fields for the Distribution of the Eagles to the regiments. When Marie Louise replaced Josephine as queen, the pageantry was more flamboyant but, noted one letter writer, "not much enthusiasm nor gladness . . . and as for the lower classes for them a feast was set out and one hears of 4,900 pastries, 1,200 smoked tongues, over 1,000 each of legs of mutton, shoulders of mutton, 250 turkeys, 360 capons, the like number of other fowl, and 3,000 sausages."

The visitors heard the twenty-two guns fired in 1811 to announce the birth of a prince, the tragic, ill-fated King of Rome. Stendhal notes of that event: "I was in bed with Angéline. The cannon woke her at ten o'clock . . . In the Rue Saint Honoré people applauded as they do at the appearance of a favorite actor."

Visitors and tourists did not feel the great bread famine that year or next. A drought had made a shortage of corn (wheat) and for the Paris family a loaf of bread had gone up in price from twelve sous to eighteen sous. There have been bread riots, Americans wrote home, the people refuse to eat the black bread available, they love the fine crisp crust of the white loaf.

Some Americans, still conscious of a lack of goods in the colonies, were impressed by furniture of mahogany, citrus wood, ebony, decorated with bronze details. The mirrors and couches, chairs and tables "were in a style said to be Egyptian and Greek, lit by argent lamps and candles"—often with a gilt harp and a polished piano added to show status. The fireplaces ate up too much wood and coal, and draughts were chilly just as back home. Madras nightcaps, gored flannel waistcoats, dressing gowns kept one warm in a Paris that did little to produce heat in winter. In 1809 American visitors had discovered the perfection of the match to start a fire. One could wear French boots with tassels to keep one's feet warm without being looked down on as a dandy.

Theater fascinated those visitors who overcame Puritan guilt about the stage. Curtain time was at six o'clock; only the Comédie Française began at seven. The curtain had to be down at nine-thirty by order of the Bureau of Police. Then came card playing on the Faubourg Saint Germain or joining the young bloods on the Boulevard des Italiens to ogle the courtesans or to become attached to some prostitute.

The city was not shocked at its vices, and many visitors would have been disappointed if they didn't exist. An English newspaper the Americans read said there were 75,000 whores in Paris, and although some found their way to the crowded prison of Petite-Force, little control of their way of life was attempted.

Gambling, too, depleted the pockets of many Americans. Letters of credit on New York, Philadelphia, Boston, were cashed to help support the fifteen licensed gambling houses and hundreds of illegal ones. Cards, dice were played, of course, but also games in terms the tourist had a little trouble understanding. *Trente et quarante, passe-dix, biribi?*

For the richest visitors there were high-class gambling places like the Club des Princes, the Club des Etrangers. Both places provided fine food

and ladies willing for any diversity of nature for those who could leave
the lure of the tables.

Homosexuals often held places of power in Napoleon's government,
and these patronized the young male prostitutes found in herds around all
places of amusement in the city. Not all Americans were baffled or im-
mune to their limp-wristed charms.

But mostly what we catch from letters home to Boston, Charleston,
Philadelphia are the simple tourist pleasures of walking in the fashionable
places, like the Petit Coblentz, or strolling to ices at Frascati, gawking at
the people passing the Café Jardin Turc. Noted were the color and sound
of the Boulevard du Temple, that street of theater where were found rope
walkers, tumblers, dwarfs, two-headed calves, a bearded girl ("no trick-
ery, I examined it very closely"). There was Jacques the live frog eater to
revolt the ladies, and Munito the Fortunetelling Dog and his cards to
predict a good and easy sea voyage home.

American women did not like the *fêtes galantes* as much as their men-
folk did, with the whores offering themselves, girls showing garters for
sale, sealing wax, scents, laces, and peddling themselves with their sales
items "so shameless that a well-bred woman cannot walk past."

There had been only two bridges crossing the Seine in the main city
area, over a river spotted with floating mills, laundry floats, and naked
bathers leaping from coal barges "without bathing drawers." One of these
bathers, "recovering an American lady's hat that had blown into the
water, returned it, facing her *en naturalibus.* 'Excuse me, Madame, for
having no gloves.'"

The visiting male like the female sometimes succumbed to the Paris
mode; a plum-colored tailcoat with leg-of-mutton sleeves, extra wide double lapels, tight breeches rather revealing at the crotch. As for Madame
and Miss America abroad, there were armpit waistlines, and even for a
few daring ones at the Embassy balls transparent Merveilleuse dresses.
One could go to watch the famous actors; even if the French on stage was
not understood, the actors were remarkable. There was the great Talma,
Mademoiselle George (when she wasn't bedding with the Emperor),
Mademoiselle Chevigny of the Ballet Andromaque, and the claques, on
copious bribes, making a great clatter. There was also censorship of
drama. The rigid rule was for edifying comedy, noble tragedy in the
theaters. As some wit wrote: "Keep virtue on the stage, because we have
to have it someplace."

It was a Paris recovering from the revolution, welcoming visitors, and
for the traveler, the tourist, a city marvelous and yet often crude. We can

catch a glimpse of it, as if through a door open a few inches, in the paintings and prints the Americans brought back: works by Bouhot, Grabizza, Nicolle, the fine genre pictures of Louis-Leopold Boilly; engravings of Parisian shoppers on the fashionable Faubourg Saint Denis, of the fiacres, cabriolets passing on the still miserably surfaced streets. A cabriolet cost 2,200 francs to own, a cab (there were few) cost twenty sous a trip, a fiacre, one franc fifty, and the drivers were as reckless and demanding of huge tips as through the ages. With so few cabs to be had, many walked and "charming women were accompanied to balls holding an umbrella, carrying their shoes in their pockets."

In 1810 protection—as in our large cities today—was not very effective for person or property. That year Americans saw the Austrian Embassy burned down, "cremating the beautiful Princess Schwarzenberg and ten others." Napoleon cursed the firemen. "Six firemen, several drunk, and the fire colonel not even present!"

One had also to walk with care to protect one's clothes, for the streets were often also the sewers. Butcher shops slaughtered there, so a visitor could see "the victims immolated in the sight of passers-by."

Paris at the start of the century in 1800 had 600,000 people; at least 50,000 were visitors and tourists, refugees—including Americans—who had settled down there for good. They lived in a city where alleys, passageways were of medieval narrowness, floored with decay and disjointed flagstones that caused Stendhal to cry out, "You barbarians, your streets stink aloud!" It would take a lesser Napoleon to create a modern Paris, the beauty we see today. And Americans of the day knew that pigs kept the streets clean in many cities back home. (Dickens found hogs running wild in parts of New York City a half century later.)

Water in Paris was sold at two sous for two pails, and often it was filthy river water. The streets were supposed to be lit by 4,000 Argrand lanterns hung on ropes, and *Te Deums* were again acted out at Notre Dame. Most Americans feared popery and Jesuit torture chambers but enjoyed the drama. They thrilled to the cries of *"Vive l'Empereur!"* the sound of kettle drums, the sight of Murat's cavalry, the carabineers, all part of that legendary *Grande Armée*, cheered now by returned émigrés, *cidevant* nobles, the *nouveaux riches*, and the famous Paris street mob.

"For once," wrote a Virginian tobacco grower, "Paris proves Pascal wrong in his talk of 'Man's most secret misery is his inability to endure the sight of himself.' The Parisian enjoys himself, and so did we."

CHAPTER 7

An American Count—
Benjamin Thompson

In the Beginning was hydrogen.
THOMAS HUXLEY

I N THE BLOODY yet often golden years of Napoleon's reign, in the first decade of the nineteenth century, there appeared in Paris a man of sixty, calling himself Count Rumford. He had a reputation as a distinguished diplomat, a brilliant scientist, inventor, publisher of some remarkable technical papers, former Prime Minister of Bavaria. He had been offered by the United States the position of first superintendent of the new military academy to be erected at West Point. He was also suspected by several nations of being a double agent and a rogue.

Today the name of Benjamin Thompson, Count Rumford, is unknown except to a few students of the history of science. Yet his achievements in invention and research were in many ways equal to Thomas Edison's, and he was the forerunner of men like DeForest, Michelson, Millikan, and Steinmetz. He is the father of the science of modern artillery and new theories of heat. On the side he invented the drip coffee pot and the first functional modern cooking pots and pans, and worked out the theory of how clothes keep the body warm by capturing air in tiny cells. Benjamin Thompson gave Napoleon the idea of a truly scientific mobile artillery, along the line to be developed later into blitzkrieg and the Panzer divisions. The French Academy of St. Cyr for training officers was modeled on Thompson's Bavarian military school. He was a member of the French

Institute, a rare honor for a foreigner. (A fellow member, admitted at the same time, was Thomas Jefferson.)

Combining his interest in science and women, he began to court the widow of the great chemist, Antoine Lavoisier (remembered today, if at all, by the mouthwash Lavoris, which he did *not* concoct). Madame Lavoisier was the hostess of one of the most famous salons in Paris, where the wits, the politically powerful, the philosophers, writers, and poets gathered to eat, drink, flirt, and recite to each other their virtues or brag of their vices. Madame Lavoisier was a countess and she was rich. Count Rumford was soon an intimate in the grand salons, and, always in need of love and money, paraded his ardor and his charm. He was a master of frivolous elegance when he had to be.

He was a charmer, even at sixty. There is a Gainsborough portrait showing him as a young man of disciplined splendor, with a long serious head, an aquiline nose, a mouth a bit cruel but witty, very fine lace at his neck, and a fashionable wig by Truefit on his head. There is also a famous print by the satiric artist James Gillray of Sir Humphrey Davy demonstrating to a room full of celebrated personalities of the day his discovery of laughing gas. As a test patient Sir Humphrey is inhaling the gas through a tube. The result, in the print, is a hideous breaking of wind blowing out the seat of Sir Humphrey's breeches. Standing composedly, but at a safe distance, Count Rumford is on the experimenter's right. Those were the years when Count Rumford had money. The year 1794 saw him give a thousand pounds to the Royal Society, another thousand to the American Academy of Arts and Sciences; hardly in keeping with his indulgent, ironic pose.

Who was this remarkable American and why has our history neglected him? How did he come to spend his last years in Paris? Let us first look at the Paris high life he knew.

The fashionable world of Madame Lavoisier into which Count Rumford fitted himself during his courtship was dominated by a semi-Grecian nudity for women, so that they were warned against standing with a light behind them. "The fair one thus lay open to profane glances at charms not intended for show." Madame Lavoisier lived in the world of the exaggerated *décolletage* of Josephine's breasts (but Josephine never exposed her teeth which were in bad decay). The count often accompanied Madame Lavoisier to Lerot, *couturier* to the empress, fashion oracle of Paris. The cost was 1,500 to 3,000 francs a dress. Madame could afford it, but not on the scale of Josephine, who in one year spent 143,311 francs for dresses.

From an early portrait it would appear Count Rumford was a good dresser, a dandy if not a fop. Studying the fashion pages of the *Messagère*, the drawings of Vernet, we get some idea of the well-dressed Parisian male. The writer Stendhal spells it out for us, describing his evening clothes as "a black waistcoat, black silk breeches and stockings, cinnamon-bronze coat, well-tied cravat, superb shirt front. I looked a very handsome man, of the style of Talma."

Men in the count's world wore three waistcoats at times, narrow shoes or slim boots, boxcoats with triple collars, so that the head was often hidden up to the jawline.

The American and English men in Paris were amazed at the barbers and hairdressers who serviced men's hair in the Titus look, the severe Caracalla-do, the stags' coquettish Alcibiades—all supposed to be very ancient Greco-Roman in source.

As one Anglo-Saxon recorded his trip to Paris, "Powdered queues were cut off, barbers produced the look of the young orangutangs—reeking of pomades and perfumes—for eighteen francs."

Most visiting American and British women protested the female style of breasts pushed up by short corsets—nipples often showing—but obeyed the fashion in the matter of baroque fantasy of hair, jewels, scents, and hats. And what hats the old prints show us! Preposterous hats *à l'Anglaise, toques à la Sphynx*, Minerva Helmets, poke bonnets; felt, straw,

satin, all worn when the count and Madame Lavoisier went walking in style on the Promenade de Longchamps or riding in a coach upholstered in blue silk to match the hat.

Madame Lavoisier's salon was high fashion as well as good talk. She liked the good life, the excitement of seeing and doing the town. Count Rumford at this period of courtship could only go along, among ladies in sequinned tulle, silk, and velvet for court dress, in their heelless buskins, faces made up with items bought from Martin, the fashionable perfumer: rouges, grease paints, powders, body scents to aid chemises trimmed with Valenciennes and Malines lace. The count, a man of scientific research, must have discovered drawers were now being worn by ladies, garments that soon became the fashion. Once only whores wore drawers, slit fore and aft.

The count, looking to marry money, wondered at the cost of gowns of lamé, tulle, and the work of silk mercers and embroiderers. And furs! Madame Lavoisier must have envied the only four chinchilla coats in Paris. Records do not show she owned one of these rare furs. But opened to her well-filled purse were lynx capes, Siberian lamb tippets, ermine, blue and silver fox, all at the smart fur shop, *A la Reine d'Espagne*.

One had to be seen. There were the grand public gardens for Count Rumford to take the countess to; the Tuileries for the fashionable set; a mere nod at the middle-class families at the Luxembourg; a visit to the Jardin des Plantes to be stared at by the animals. The fun-loving countess, escorted by the count, enjoyed the garden of the Palais Royal for the firing of the noonday gun to set one's watch by. If she was up by then.

There were uniforms everywhere to remind Count Rumford of the wars all over Europe. Officers hung out at the Café de Roy, moneymen and stock speculators, army contractors at the Café Chartres. At the Café Valois and Café Borel, Count Rumford met dandies, dragoon captains, whores, chess players, actors, actresses, brushed against pickpockets while he had his boots shined.

But moving back to his beginnings as plain Benjamin Thompson; he was born in 1753 in the small Massachusetts town of Woburn, a village of mud paths that did not even boast a coach. He never knew his father, who died when he was still a boy. Widows who were poor married if they could, and his mother married a poor man, making a destitute family group in a backwater town. Benjamin's education was catch-as-catch-can in a country school with the dull and torpid sons of local farmers. Yet in the boy stirred grandiose psychological yearnings.

He stood out from the crowd by his red hair, his already handsome looks, his ideas of how to make his fortune. He hoped to become a great soldier, a companion of great men he had vaguely heard of, men to be looked up to. The usual vapid generalities of youth had in him a solid core of purpose.

The town was too small for his hopes. By reason of his fine skill in making letters, a head for figures, he became a storekeeper's apprentice in Salem and soon moved on to the city of Boston. He made a poor store-keeper; his mind was not on dried cod, mule collars, yards of calico. It was on France, on Paris, the court of the French kings. At seventeen Benjamin was teaching himself the French language, aping the local gentry, wearing what finery he could afford. He took up fencing; no Parisian dandy could afford not to master the foils. Boston seemed provincial as he read more, and he read a great deal in science and philosophy. But how to become famous? How to walk the streets of Paris with the beaus, chatter with the hellrake bucks of London? His future seemed such a tangled arabesque of wishes, even sentimental falsifications.

At nineteen he was teaching school in Portsmouth, New Hampshire, at local fêtes wearing his one good gentleman's suit of tailoring. The richest woman available in the district was the widow of a Colonel Rolfe, the thirty-two-year-old Sarah Rolfe. He married the widow, ordered a proper gentleman's wardrobe, wore magnificent velvets and silks, fine shirts, and smallclothes, as underwear was then called. He got the best wigs, the most elegant walking cane; this nineteen-year-old bridegroom knew how to live. He was also the manager of his wife's thousand-acre estate. Through an introduction to Governor Wentworth, by his wife's family, he was appointed a major in the Second Provincial Regiment. He was beginning—as a later philosopher put it—to see the world whole and see it constantly.

But the forests were gathering against King George in England. It was 1774. The Liberty Boys were out tarring and feathering too ardent Tories. One day they went to tar, feather, and ride out of town on a rail Squire Benjamin Thompson. ("If it weren't for the honor," one rail sitter is said to have reported to Mark Twain, "I'd rather have walked.")

Why this rancor against him? He was accused of stealth, of being disloyal to the rising American cause, having, it was said, sent letters to British General Gage in Boston. Thompson later claimed to have witnessed the Boston Massacre, which wasn't a massacre at all until silver-smith Paul Revere did his imaginary genre print of it. He was also accused of turning back four deserters, "lobsterbacks," to British military justice. Such loyalty to "King Jarg" was dangerous.

The mob decided to burn down Thompson's house. He fled back to dismal Woburn, leaving his family behind. They were unharmed; the tar and feathers unused. The next year was a bad one for Thompson. He tried to get a commission with the British, then, with a bland indifference, one under Washington. He struck out both times. Neither side trusted him to follow their kettledrums and trumpets.

Yet all his life he had a way of recovering quickly. Moving behind the British lines in 1776, he was in time to be part of the English leaving Boston where they had been under siege by the Americans. A commission of four was sent to London by General Gage to explain the military situation to the king's men. Benjamin Thompson was one member of the commission. How and why? Charm, brains, a social climber. Insiders were not surprised that he had been a British agent from the start. The information did not reach American historians for 161 years, when the British War Ministry opened some of its files in return for President Roosevelt turning over fifty over-age destroyers to England in 1940.

In England Thompson's reports impressed Lord George Germaine, His Majesty's Colonial Secretary, in charge of winning the war. He sensed this handsome young American in his early twenties was shrewd and possessed a form of military genius too rare in any army. Lord Germaine was as amazing as Thompson; kicked out of the army for cowardice in the field, he moved into politics, supported a small army of spies, blackmailed his way into the power of Colonial Affairs. And still had time to follow a career as a notoriously degenerate homosexual, able to bow and curtsy in the formal court minuet.

Thompson became Lord Germaine's lover—the popular term was calamite. The lord was fantastically in love with this youth of twenty-two, making him undersecretary in the ministry of the Carolinas and Georgia. Thompson became part of the lechery, cuckoldry, the wild gay life of London high society, the drinking, brawling world one finds so skillfully pictured in Smollett's novel *Roderick Random*, with its scenes of homosexuals in power in Hanoverian London.

Thompson was still interested in science and in the art of warfare. He invented a machine to measure the explosive force of gunpowder, also firing a shot into a pendulum to measure a slug's momentum. He invented nearly the entire early system of ballistics. Among waxed wainscoting, Hyson tea silver, regimental gorgets, he was also science's child.

On the practical side, as a man of the world, making purchases for the army he collected bribes for the higher-ups, his own share coming to seven hundred pounds a year. By 1777 it was figured he had gotten what would today be a million dollars (in the days when a million dollars was real) and lived up most of it in drunken, transitory pleasures. It was "a fur bit" from the muddy New England village and a forgotten family.

Greedy, while cruising with the British fleets, Thompson made a deal to become a French agent (Paris still glimmered for him). The plot was to assist in the capture of an English fleet, and Thompson was to get his share, one eighth of the prize money. The brazen unconcern of even a London hellrake's morals is astounding. Two men employed in the scheme with him were captured. One turned state's witness; the other, a Frenchman named LaMotte, was hanged, disemboweled, drawn while alive, quartered, carved like beef, as was the habit of the time.

And the third conspirator, Benjy Thompson? He still held the protection of Lord Germaine, who had the goods on everyone in high places. Instead of hanging, Thompson went to America as a Lieutenant-Colonel of Horse Dragoons to fight the rebels. The war was drawing to an end, and Thompson soon returned to England, going back to his wild life, but also to his scientific research.

Adventuring to Bavaria, he was made the minister of war, minister of the interior, and royal scientist to the king. His career was as amazing as it was odd; he was one of the most brilliant scientists of his time. The king, fat George III, going mad at times, made Thompson Knight of the Garter for his work as a spy; for while in Bavaria, Thompson was acting for British espionage. However, double-crossing the English, he decided Bavaria was a good place to be a great man. Adaptability, he knew, is essential to survival.

Tired of the beggars who filled the small country, Thompson had the army move all beggars and unemployed into Houses of Industry to work for their keep by making uniforms and supplies for the army. Thompson, as army supplier, took his share and cut on everything produced there. In 1791, born a Protestant but godless, he was made a Count of the Holy Roman Empire (as the historian Gibbon, who knew Thompson, was to write, "It was neither Holy, Roman nor an empire"). He took the name Rumford from the early name of Concord, Massachusetts.

The Houses of Industry had some rare recruits. The Bavarian middle class and noble aristocracy were lusty and much given to adultery and sexual orgies. When girls became pregnant and were unmarried, the count had them cared for for several months at one of his offshoots of the Houses of Industry. He kept the children as wards, educated them well enough to become skilled workers in the Houses of Industry. He knew modern labor management. He created the first public schools in Bavaria, for he preferred efficiency to waste. To him all kitchens were wasteful; so he redesigned kitchen gear, pots, pans, fireplaces, stoves. He demonstrated that heat could not pass across a vacuum; he invented what is today called the Thermos bottle.

In 1795 he dared to go back to London to present his papers to the Royal Society. His baggage was stolen by the British Secret Service. However, he published scientific papers on the discovery of convection currents and why fabrics and fibers keep our bodies warm.

He was in trouble in Bavaria, so he appointed himself minister to Great Britain; but the English were having none of that. Over fifty years old now, Thompson got in touch with the American ambassador, Rufus King. He sold the ambassador on the idea of setting up an Academy for American army officers along the lines of his Bavarian military training system. President Adams had the United States War Department offer the count the job as the first superintendent of the military academy being erected at West Point. No writer of fiction would dare invent the strange turns of Thompson's life.

Asked the count, what was the fee and the living like? And would his rank be the equivalent of George Washington's? The boldness of this from a man who had betrayed Americans, served as a British spy, and fought with his dragoons against the Continental Army was amazing, unprincipled, and foolish, and certainly showed a dislocation of reality.

Meanwhile Rufus King was informed by the delighted British that Thompson was a double-dealing agent—triple-dealing even, having worked for them, the French, the Bavarians, and in turn betrayed even the Bavarians. The count told the red-faced ambassador the appointment would have to be made anyway. The United States would be the laughing stock of Europe, the count carefully explained, if the announcement offering him West Point, which had already been made, were followed by exposure of the fact that the offer had been made to a double agent.

CHAPTER 8

Salons and Courtship

I'll have my house the academy of wits.
JAMES SHIRLEY, 1637

T HE AMBASSADOR, trapped, suggested a face-saving plan for everyone. The United States would offer Count Rumford West Point and he would gallantly *refuse*, claiming his scientific work kept him too busy in Europe. It sounded like a potpourri of bad plots all mixed up. So the little diplomatic game was played out. The offer was officially made, rejected, and West Point was not headed by one of the great military scientists. But it did use Count Rumford's model of an academy for training officers.

Now England and America had soured for him. Bavaria had become for him a firing-squad country. So the count, at sixty, came to Paris. Here was Napoleon, a man of his own kind. Brilliant, wary, crafty, modern, without mercy, and completely untrustworthy; Napoleon, who dreamed of a United Europe, a dynasty. The emperor admired Count Rumford's theories of the science and use of artillery. They also shared a rational skepticism of Judaic-Christian morality and a belief in the worthlessness of most of the human race.

His courtship of the widow Lavoisier brought Count Rumford fully into the world of the Paris salons. It was a world dominated by brilliant women who in their mansions collected the bright and bored, the wise and the wild. It was a particular Paris game and a tradition. A shared solace with a dependency on wit and gossip.

These women were called the *salonnardes*. They were usually charming in person and dress, often great talkers themselves, but certainly at their best as grand mixers. They lifted French society from mere talk to part of the intellectual life of Europe. Of their salons the historian Gibbon wrote that they were "the perfection of that inestimable art which softens and refines and embellishes the intercourse of life." He also noted, "It has always seemed to me . . . in Paris, the women are far superior to the men." So the blatantly aggressive, the unctuous intellectuals, the wits, the radicals all mixed.

Certainly the great salons of Paris were unique, such as the salon of Madame du Deffand where Horace Walpole worshipped at her shoes. When she was sixty-eight, Walpole could still write of her: "She is delicious, as eager about what happens every day as I am about the last century." When she died she left Walpole her papers *and* her dog.

Madame Lavoisier's salon was a direct descendant of the great salons that ran from Madame Geoffrin and Mademoiselle de Lespinasse to after the revolution and Mesdames de Staël and Récamier. One could almost dedicate the week to the various salons and the various subjects that would be talked of. Madame du Deffand gave over Saturday to the political lions of the moment, Madame Geoffrin fed the artists on Monday, and celebrated philosophers and poets got Wednesday. Tuesday was scientists' day at Madame Helvétius's, Sunday and Tuesday Baroness d'Holbach had a mixed bag, and Tuesday Madame Necker showed her wit and wealth to the thinkers and doers. Subjects ran from carnal and spiritual affection to the German sculptor who carved Christ wearing a wig.

Lord Rumford, when it came his time to court Madame Lavoisier at the salons, proved his charm, distinguished manner, the complexity of his intellect, his superior tact and grace. Some of the salons were for flirting, for making the Gallic *double entendre*, some were for serious talk of republican ideas. Others were for gambling. It was expected that a man would have a mistress and a lady a lover, and they might with timetable care avoid each other at the salons. Talk could be wild, but within the range of good manners and good taste.

A proper *salonnarde* like Madame Lavoisier ran a distinguished house where men of science and men of the arts mixed without rancor and recalled the days of such Philosophes as Fontenelle, Montesquieu, Voltaire, the salon of the *Encyclopédie* of Diderot and his group. There were *petits soupers*, grand dinners for visiting Anglo-Saxons like Hume, Walpole, Franklin. Some of the hostesses were pious, and it could be said, "She had a pew in the church of the Capuchins, with as much mystery as

the *galante* women of that day had their *petites maisons* for their *amours.*"

Count Rumford wanted no secret love nest; he wanted marriage and a rich dowry, and so he attended the salons and continued his courtship. The lady was not displeased; she read from Henault's *Abrégé Chronologique de l'Historie de France* and asked the proper scientific questions of the count.

The salon would soon decline and decay as Napoleon brought closer the age of Balzac and Daumier. Madame du Deffand's salon began to fade as she aged, and she could ask of a favorite philosopher, "And you, Monsieur de Voltaire, the declared lover of Truth, tell me in good faith, have you found it? You combat and destroy errors, but what have you put into its place?" A young man asked Voltaire how to start a new religion. The answer: "Get yourself killed and rise from the dead on the third day."

We do not know of the intimate moments of Count Rumford's courtship. What has been written of love in the salons can only give us some idea. A Jeanne de Montsauge could write of a Don Juan of the salons: "The levity, even hardness with which he treats women comes from the small consideration in which he holds them. He thinks them flirtatious, vain, weak, false and frivolous . . . though obliged to recognize good qualities in some, he does not . . . value them highly, but holds that they have more vices than virtues." Of the same man Madame de Staël could say, "His conversation is the most varied, most animated, the richest I have ever known."

Did the Countess Lavoisier suffer from Count Rumford as did Mademoiselle de Lespinasse from another man? Her letters show us some of the agony of salon love. "Oh, my God, by what charm, by what fatality have you come to distract me? Why did I not die in September? I could have died then without . . . the reproaches that now I make to myself." Later: "You alone in the universe can possess and occupy my being, my heart, my soul can from now on be filled by you alone . . . So many contradictions, so many conflicting emotions . . . all true, and three little words to explain them: *I love you.*"

Perhaps, perhaps this was how the American Count Rumford affected the widow. There is no surviving evidence. All we do know is that they were married. One social historian put it this way: "Their marriage was the union of two of the most glamorous figures of the day."

It lasted, this marriage *à la mode*, for four years. The countess loved her salon, loved the gay life, enjoyed parties. Count Rumford was getting old. He had his science, his work on his caloric theory; above all he loved order. He was inventing at a great pace and the damn parties interfered. He was working out the standardization of light, the first protometer to measure light intensities. We owe to him the term *candle power* as a standard of measurement. He invented the steam-heat radiator and that delight of Victorian houses, the central heating system; he had plumbers install it in the Royal Institution and the French Institute. As a subject of conversation it made for dull salon entertainment.

The couple separated, and the laws, the *Code Napoléon,* were such that he left his wife with half her fortune, very well off indeed. The marriage was not childless; during the four years the count managed to have a son, but by Countess Lavoisier's gardener's daughter.

He had no intention of going back to America. He had a surviving daughter by his deserted American wife (there is some doubt that he was ever legally divorced by her, or had the right to marry the countess).

He lived the simple, well-cared-for life of a man with money and he had his work; while all around him in Europe raged the fury of the Napoleonic wars. It was the time when the modern world was being

born. Soon would come the world of Balzac's *La Comédie Humaine*,
those charts of lust for power, fame, and possessions, the rise of the
middle class. The old world of glory, of Napoleon, was setting out to die
in its wonderful uniforms, its fur busbies and shakos and its prancing
horses. The weathered soldiers with wild mustaches who had been in
Spain and who had retreated from burning Moscow with the *Grands
Chasseurs* would go marching to Waterloo.

The marriage of Count Rumford and the Countess Lavoisier failed
because of the kind of people they were, and on the count's side there is
the suspicion that it was a marriage for money. Yet they might have lived
out their marriage if their personalities and needs had been compatible.
The countess wanted the gay life, and the count as he aged wanted time
to think, to experiment, to write.

He still liked good food, was a gourmet, a man who, as we've shown,
invented the drip coffee pot, a more practical and scientific kitchen. He
had attended many a dinner with butlers in maroon coats, gold buttons,
announcing each dish, footmen serving, roast partridge being dissected.
"Which do you prefer, countess, the parson's nose or the merry thigh?"

For an aging man this stuffing with truffled turkey, red-legged ducks
must have been an ordeal. Grand gourmandizers were notorious in the
Paris he knew. Grimod de la Reynières encouraged them in his yearly
Almanac des Gourmets. A dinner at the Hôtel de Grimod could last five
hours, with rare wines in dust-covered bottles (yet Napoleon, who usually
gulped his meal in fifteen minutes, drank grocer's wine at six francs a
bottle). The true feeder, like the countess, could agree that "the leg of
mutton must be looked forward to like a lover's first rendezvous."

No doubt the count was as happy to get rid of the banquets as of the
countess.

From letters of American travelers we learn that grand gourmandizers
went beyond silver chafing dishes and footmen in livery. They knew where
to go for the best supplies. Cherbet's provision shop welcomed them;
Hyment's sold them fish and stuffed tongues; at Corcellet there were larks
and Toulouse pastries.

The count inspected many kitchens to work out his plans for moderniz-
ing cooking. He found the middle class lived well too. Eight pounds of
beef could be bought for five francs, good country ham, two francs fifty,
ten dozen oysters cost four francs, claret, brandy three francs. And always
a *déjeuner à la fourchette* at eleven in the morning. No wonder Americans were impressed.

Sugar was costly. The West Indies mills were mostly in British hands.
The blockade by Nelson's fleet and others was tight. So the lump of sugar

was often hung from the ceiling on a string and everyone took a turn with a quick dip in his cup of tea or coffee.

The count, growing old, wanted only candles and Carcel lamps for an early bedtime, a madras nightcap and a good book. The countess, freed of him, continued her visits to the *fêtes galantes*, the music of Madame Récamier's mulatto *chef d'orchestre*, the remembered gossip of the *ancien régime*, the brilliant conversation of Narbonne and Talleyrand. Also pastoral ballets under Bengal lights were enjoyed, card playing in houses on the Faubourg Saint Germain. So what if the Marshals Ney, Lefebvre, Murat, Angerean, Lannes were once sons of coopers, millers, innkeepers, bricklayers, hostlers and grooms! It was a new age. But of the count's science more than of final military victories.

Did the count care as the old world of past glories and kings came apart at the seams? He worked on, and such was the force of respect for quality in those days that even while he lived in Paris the enemy governments of England and Bavaria paid him his pensions. Business was business, and the House of Rothschild had banking privileges everywhere. Count Rumford established a Harvard professorship which is still one of the great honors available. He knew he was the father of the great researchers to come, and that he more than any man had done the most to advance human comfort, human living.

He was a strange and remarkable American. Dishonest, a double agent, a taker of bribes, a maker of graft into a science. He defied nations, hopes, and causes. Yet as a scientist and inventor we owe him a great deal of comfort, and his endowments and aid pushed forward the boundaries of the scientists who followed.

He died in 1814 with that bitter disappointment of selfish, lonely men, lamenting, wondering why all had gone wrong, why more honors had not come, while his worth, his intellect had been used to advantage by kings, dukes, dictators, national institutions. He belonged in the age of Stendhal. *"L'homme ne peut pas se fier à l'homme*, man cannot trust man."

There are many things in the life of Benjamin Thompson that are remarkable—the work of genius—contradicted by some nasty bits of business. Yet his virtues stand out clearly to this day. Take the matter of the potato being accepted as food, one of the great boons to the poor of the world and a pleasure to many gourmets. The early Spanish had found the tuber in Peru, but for 250 years it was grown only as cattle food by people who were afraid that it poisoned the ground it grew in and caused acute diarrhea. Even when King Louis XVI endorsed and gorged on it, and also an apothecary named Parmentier (potatoes were once called "Parmentiers"), it remained an uneatable food for most of Europe.

Only the Irish were forced to eat the tuber in their starvation plight, and they found it easy to raise, cheap to plant, giving a good crop on mean plots of land. It became the Irish potato, and because of the wretched facts of Irish life, the Irish were considered savages little better than swill-eating animals. This did great harm to acceptance of the potato by the French and Germans, who did not want to be classed in their food habits with the "Irish apes."

It was Count Rumford, head of army ordnance, who ordered all soldiers serving the Duke of Bavaria to plant a patch of the tubers, care for it, harvest it, and then, damn them! eat the potatoes! As the food historian Mark Graubard pointed out: "The duration of military service in those days gave a soldier more than ample time to learn the art of raising potatoes and developing a taste for them. After the men returned to their farms, potato crops appeared all over the country and the food of Europe gained greater security."

Soon the markets of Paris were offering potatoes and French chefs were inventing dishes for their *cuisines.* In an old handwritten French recipe book one finds *Pommes de Terre, Comte de Rumford*: "Boil peeled potatoes in salt water. Mash, add butter, a spoon of orange flower water, a pinch salt, a half glass water. Heat for four minutes. Beat in two eggs and roll into little balls. Heat oil, toss balls into boiling fat. Take care in removing and sprinkle with sugar when served."

Taking him as a whole, Benjamin Thompson was not a typical Regency buck, not just a romantic Paris salon visitor in satin and lace. Had he been born just a little later, he would have been a believer in the system called *le beylisme,* the doctrines that were seen as revelations much later by the followers of Stendhal (born Henri Beyle). Basically the philosophy was that knowledge comes from sensations, perceptions, a branch of empiricism; the pursuit of knowledge is in observation and experiment. This was a way of living Benjamin Thompson followed all his life.

A deeply involved thinker of this system can attribute the origin of all knowledge to experience. Stendhal was to explain all passion and love as an experimental method; only the exact knowledge of all the facts in an affair of love can bring true happiness. Certainly Count Rumford, from his various experiences in the passions, like Stendhal himself, never found the fulfillment in love he expected. They were both too involved with method (the curse of the centuries that followed them).

Benjamin Thompson, buried in a French grave, forgotten, was the sufferer of a complaint seen by William James, and hardly ever quoted completely: "The exclusive worship of the bitch goddess success is our national disease."

We have few texts of what other Americans of the period saw in Paris, but from surviving letters, journals, we find that high life and vice interested them. The gardens of the Palais Royal, they discovered, were haunts of gentlemen of pleasure, ladies of little virtue. It was a world of the senses and was self-contained. "If shut up for life in the Palais Royal, if one had the money, everything is available. Even the *Journal de Débats* while having your hair styled."

There were fifteen restaurants there in its best years, thirty cafés, seventeen billiard saloons, two dozen jewelers (and fences buying loot from criminals), six booksellers of literature and erotic volumes, wig shops, fancy food and fruit merchants, even a dentist-pedicure, who was said to do abortions on the side, and the ever popular silhouette cutter.

Its gardens were hemmed in by gambling houses (one had a priest in residence so that would-be suicides could be put in a state of grace and the dying receive the last rites). There were moneylenders' offices, bordellos where a Black Mass or an all-night orgy of perversions could be arranged for, also rooms to rent to lovers.

From letters and journals and memoirs it becomes clear that Americans favored as the two most popular items of Paris "the Emperor viewing his Guards, and a visit to the whores of the Palais Royal." Some wrote the prostitutes were Number One. Here were found the town flesh-seekers in top hats and kerseymere trousers, looking over the women, or talking a pretty nursemaid into leaving her charges for an hour or so playing by themselves.

The American traveler in Napoleon's Paris usually came, as in all periods of the city's history, for "amusement and fleshly delights." But the good citizens themselves were also sensualists. One third of all children were illegitimate, no matter how hard the *Code Napoléon* preached devout family life. Liaisons were matters of social status-making to the froufrou sound of taffeta petticoats. Licensing and medical examination of prostitutes were tried, but bribery made control impossible. Infection was common, as many a returning American discovered. Organized all-night orgies were rarely raided, but one raid picked up and freed three marquises, a member of the council of state, a barrister, an advocate of the court of cassation. Some left town singing, "*Adieu Paris, adieu petits pastez . . . Adieu m'amour, adieu douces fillettes.*"

Another raid picked up the defrocked Curé Bonjour during a full Saturnalia of the Black Mass, with a certified virgin for the obscene rites. Another raid was on a masked audience in a theater watching an erotic play. Once the prefect of police, needing something to entertain his jaded guests, raided a pornographic bookstore for material. "Paris respectability is a superstition rather than a fact."

Alfresco pleasures existed for all Parisian classes, complete with pickpockets, fireworks, dancing balls at the Tivoli in the Rue Saint Lazare. "Mothers, bring your daughters here. They run no risk of enjoying themselves at the expense of morality."

In one hall 300 people daringly danced the *waltz*, imported from Germany, then cooled off their frenzy by eating ices, and flirting with hussar or grenadier officers who had been to Spain and Italy, even to Egypt. Americans enjoyed it, but came home condemning the French as sensualists.

CHAPTER 9

Indians in the Louvre—
George Catlin's Show

I love people who have no jails and no poorhouse.
I love people who don't live for the love of money.

GEORGE CATLIN

IN 1845 special visitors to the Louvre were astonished to find an American Indian Gallery in place there, with a huge hide tepee erected on the floor of what had once been the palace of kings. The savages were armed with an assortment of weapons, leather furnishings, fur garments, feather headdresses, and drums, and the walls were lined by the paintings of George Catlin. He was the American painter of Indians and Indian scenes, in Paris with his wife Clara and four children.

In the 1830s he had lived on the Great Plains, the upper Missouri, the headwaters of the Mississippi, the southwest, painting the tribes and their life. Hard times had come to the artist who had spent so much of his life with the wild native culture of the west in *terra incognita*, painting the most remarkable scenes of Indian life and portraits of chiefs and warriors. George Catlin went against the grain of the art fashion of the time, and so, with desperate audacity, as he wrote: "In the fall of 1839 I embarked on board the packet ship *Rosius* . . . with my Indian collection . . . eight tons of freight consisting of 600 portraits and other paintings . . . several thousand Indian costumes, weapons, etc." His wife and daughter were to join him later with a child as yet unborn but expected, perhaps, on the high seas.

In 1848 Catlin was to publish his two-volume *Notes on Eight Years Travel and Residence in Europe*, so we can follow his trail from Liverpool where the *Rosius* landed him and his cargo, to London where he exhibited his paintings and Indian artifacts in Egyptian Hall, Piccadilly, leased at 550 pounds a year as Catlin's Gallery of North American Indians. When he opened the show of Indians in no rigidly stereotyped attitudes on November 1, 1840, the guests began to arrive—the Duchess of Sutherland, the Bishop of London, the Duke of Wellington—to see and wonder, all at the cost of one shilling each, with Mr. Catlin lecturing in the evenings. "I have viewed man in the innocent simplicity of nature."

Joined soon by his wife and *two* daughters, Catlin added *tableaux vivants*, setting up actors in costumes to play out Indian raids, warfare, dramatizing the wild with painted bodies, war whoops, and songs taught them by the artist. London found it all an incredible phenomenon.

When business fell off at Catlin's Gallery after the second season, a group of nine Ojibway Indians arrived in England, brought over by a showman named Rankin, who joined forces for a while with Catlin. A royal performance was given by the true Indians, in Catlin costumes, for Queen Victoria at Buckingham Palace.

Meanwhile the Catlins had increased their family by two more children. As interest fell off in Indians painted or living, even in an outdoor show with mounted Indians, Catlin decided to move on to Paris. He was a remarkably dedicated man, truly in love with the Indians and desperately short of money all his life.

In April of 1845 the Catlins and the Indians were housed at the Victoria Hotel in Paris, and he rented the Salle Valentino in the Rue Saint Honoré. He also unloaded eight tons of Indian gear and paintings. Louis Philippe, king of France (at the moment) had been in exile in America from 1797 to 1800, and had, in a small boat, royally floated down the Mississippi, in the manner of Mark Twain's Duke and King in *Huckleberry Finn*, but without the dramatic show of the Royal Nonesuch. He was a king trying to cling to a throne in the bitter sectarian bigotry of French politics.

The live Indians were Ioways now. Fourteen of them had been stranded in England by some other show, and they had run to Catlin for shelter and food. In Paris they were loaded into a great lumbering four-horse omnibus, and in paint and feathers were pulled through the streets attracting a great deal of attention. The Parisians went wild with joy at these monstrous apparitions chanting war cries. The streets were packed as the omnibus pulled up before the American Embassy. Mr. King, the United States Minister to France, made them welcome. There is no mention of peace pipe smoking, but he did invite them all in for lunch. And ladies in tippets of ermine, taffeta cloaks, and satin bonnets fearfully enjoyed the sight.

After lunch the party was taken to the prefect of police, perhaps to impress on the Indians the power of the white man's law beside the Seine. Catlin was showman enough by now to encourage the street crowds, the men in top hats, women in voluminous skirts, to follow the Indians through the city and have the Ioways from time to time utter war whoops and wave tomahawks.

The king gave the Indians and Catlin an audience at the Tuileries Palace. It was a grand meeting; there was an amazing naiveté in the French interest in *les sauvages*. The king and his queen, with the Count of Paris, the Duchess of Orléans, Princess Adelaide, Prince and Princess de Joinville, and all the members of the court that could crowded into the Salle de Bal. The king made a fine speech, which an interpreter did over into English: "Tell these fine fellows I am delighted to see them, that I have been in many of the wigwams of the Indians in America when I was a young man, and they treated me kindly everywhere . . . This is the queen, tell them these boys are my grandsons."

In this casual intimacy the Indians did their dances, beat drums, waved weapons. Catlin made a speech explaining what was going on and the white man's greed: "I have stood amidst these unsophisticated people . . . hunting grounds from which he has fled. . . ."

The public show at the Salle Valentino opened in June, 1845, and was a great success. The press gave it much space calling it, *de haut en bas*, the most extraordinary event ever seen in Paris. The list of guests was impressive. Among them were Victor Hugo, Baron von Humboldt, George Sand, and others. But the climate of Paris was not good for Indians. Two of the original group had died in England, now the doctors said the rest were getting "consumption of the lungs." The wife of Little Wolf, the chief, died; his son also had died. The Great Spirit was angry and deadly. The Ioways packed and left in July for America from Le Havre.

Catlin was stuck with an expensive lease on the hall, and his wife suddenly took to her bed with lung trouble. She died at the end of July. Clara was thirty-seven years old. Catlin sent her body back home for burial, a broken man, short of money, in danger of losing his collection, and with four children left motherless, aged ten, eight, six, and three, in a foreign city. He felt a sense of guilt, for Clara had begged that they give up their tours and go home, that Catlin forget the Indian culture he was trying to explain and show to the world. He was an artist, she insisted, he should paint, do nothing else. Beset by tensions, grief, problems of paying bills, he could not move.

A new batch of Indians from another failed show in London came to Paris to beg Catlin for aid. These new recruits were eleven Ojibways. Catlin put on a new show, but by now the Parisians had lost interest in the novelty of Indians; business was tapering off.

The king was entertaining the king and queen of Belgium, and he invited Catlin to a royal breakfast at the Palace of St. Cloud. It seemed the king of the Belgians had also been a visitor to America, and had even been a guest at George Washington's plantation at Mount Vernon, had listened to the general's farewell address. Indians at times were more interesting to the French in the nineteenth century than even Offenbach's *La Périchole*.

It was at this breakfast that the French king suggested—and a royal suggestion was as good as an order—that Catlin set up his gallery of Indian paintings and his Ojibways with a tepee in a large hall at the Louvre. A private show for the royal family, the royal guests, and their friends. There was also a hint that perhaps it would be a good thing for the French nation to buy the collection. Catlin would be delighted to sell the tons of artifacts, the hundreds of paintings.

So the king, the royal guests, and the court attended the Louvre Indian Gallery show, watched the Indians perform, and heard Catlin's lecture. Catlin was a handsome figure of a man and a fine speaker. The court people entered the wigwams, fingered drums. The Catlin children, even the youngest, little George, and his nurse, were presented to the queen.

The talk of buying the collection for France faded away, but the king ordered fifteen copies of his Indian portraits from Catlin, to be hung at Versailles. When Catlin at the suggestion of the king of the Belgians moved the show to Brussels, smallpox broke out among the Ojibways and three died. Hospitalization of the rest nearly ruined Catlin. He got the surviving Indians onto a boat bound for America. The failure in Brussels cost Catlin nearly two thousand dollars. His prospects were—as a frontier saying put it—"withering like Jonah's gourd."

In Paris his collection was put in storage, and Catlin painted the pictures for the king while he hoped for help from his own government. He was desperate for money; his four small children took up much of his time. The amenities and amusements of Paris society no longer seemed vital. The king of France might order pictures, but would he pay? Catlin doubted it. "What the emolument will be I don't know yet, probably like the *honour* . . . it will be a costly article."

Catlin tried next to sell the collection to the British Museum. Then he again addressed Congress in hopes of their buying his collection for the American nation. Meanwhile he painted, low in spirits. Only the children kept him going. "My house, though there is gloom about it, has a melancholy charm, its halls enlivened by the notes of my little innocents . . . My dear namesake, George, and my only boy, then three and a half years old."

Paris was not a healthy city. Europe had yet to accept sanitation, discover the germ theory. Fresh air was considered dangerous, raw milk healthy. Medicine was hardly out of the herb stage. Tuberculosis was the great killer in those days. Catlin's wife had died of it. Now the Catlin children in the Paris flat were all suddenly seriously ill. One by one they took to their beds with "lung trouble." Either the poor sanitary conditions of the time aided the spread of the white plague or, as some medical men now think, the strains of the disease were more deadly then. Whatever it was, whole families were wiped out in mass tragedies. Little George died. Wrote the grief-stricken father, "The remains of the little fellow were sent to New York, as a lovely flower to be planted by the grave of his mother."

In the sad studio, in the Place Madeleine, with his three daughters, the artist painted for the king. Catlin was past fifty. He knew he was not painting well. Art had once been a joy for him. Now in tragic exile, the

purpose, the pleasure were gone from it. His best work was behind him—
or rather in storage, unsold.

There was hope for showing and selling his art in America, where an
Englishman, James Smithson, in his will had set up a national museum,
the Smithsonian Institution. A report to Congress suggested that a gallery
be set up there for "the work of Mr. Catlin." But it came to nothing as the
Mexican war and Manifest Destiny were more important than "pictures
of red hostiles." No action was taken to acquire the Catlin collection. The
artist was left in incomprehensible anguish, locked in expatriation and
despair.

Catlin's continued efforts to sell his collection failed. And in Paris, the
king, liking the first set of paintings, ordered twenty-nine more. It took a
year to paint them. The price was to be one hundred dollars each. But the
king—as the artist feared—never paid him a cent or a sou. Catlin managed to exist, kept his children, went on painting; how no one knows.
Utter despondency must have engulfed him.

In 1848 the streets of Paris echoed to the mobs crying, *"Vive la Ré-
forme!"* and everyone was singing the *Marseillaise*, while the king and
queen, minds undisturbed by the intrusion of any original thoughts,
slipped away to safety and England. Revolution was a habit in Paris. The
cobblestones of Paris made great weapons, the barricades could be built
of carts and rubbish. For students, dreamers, street people it was a
change from taxes, disease, domestic problems—a free time for prophets
and prejudices. No matter who ruled, as Balzac saw, mob or king, the rich
got richer, the poor poorer. The dead were buried—and plans made for
another uprising. Hugo, Delacroix got material for literature and art; the
revolution made slogans, promises. 1848 saw all of Europe in ferment,
bitter hopes of a better time.

To George Catlin none of this mattered. The mob ran wild in the
streets as the court fled; they began to loot; the police, the militia often
joined in the games. Catlin's apartment was invaded, bayonets slashed
holes in some of his pictures; an obsession against authority doesn't spare
a painter.

Catlin had the quality of survival. He and the little girls, most of his
collection, managed to get away to England. But he was penniless there.
He was also going deaf. His vogue as the Indian artist had passed among
the mode-setters in London society. He was selling paintings there for ten
dollars each, with a two shilling charge for frames.

Back in America Congress again brought up a bill to buy the Catlin
collection. It was defeated by one vote, cast by Jefferson Davis of Ken-

tucky. The illogicalities of history amaze one. For a moment they nearly touch, an American artist in Paris and one of the fomenters of a most bloody civil war. Catlin had borrowed, begged; he was deeply in debt. One creditor, a Mr. Harrison, who made boilers in Philadelphia, paid off some of Catlin's debts and in return bundled up the collection and shipped it to America, where moldering in storage for years a great deal of it rotted away, turned to dust, fed the moths. Rare Indian artifacts were destroyed, marvelous paintings damaged.

In 1853 Catlin was living alone in a dingy room in Paris, at the Hôtel des Etrangers, on the Rue Tronchet. His little girls had been taken away from him by his wife's family and shipped to America. An old man, although only fifty-six, he wandered the streets of Paris, as he wrote, "destitute, despondent and deaf, but still without bitterness." One of the *déracinés*, the exiles Paris often housed. He spent his time in the *Bibliothèque Impériale* reading room. He began to study up on Brazil, its Indians, still mostly unknown. He would go there and paint a new kind of Indian, make a new reputation. But it would not be easy. He owed debts, even in his miserable life in Paris he had creditors demanding payments. So like a fugitive he disappeared from Paris. "I obtained a British passport . . . and an incognito cognomen, as kings and emperors sometimes do."

There were trips by Catlin to South America for painting and recording, but the great days for his art were over. The powerful strokes of his youthful style, the relish in paint tossed off at ease, the command performance before an English queen and a French king, a show at the Louvre, all that was past. But good or bad he was painting Indians.

He had read Thoreau: "I learned this, at least, that if one advances confidently in the direction of his dreams, and endeavors to live the life which he has imagined, he will meet with a success unexpected in common hours. If you have built castles in the air, your work need not be lost; that is where they should be. Now put the foundations under them."

The deaf old man at sixty-two came back to Paris after the last of his most dangerous trips to the wilds. But living could be even cheaper in Brussels. The American consul there who visited him reported: "His studio was in an obscure street near the Antwerp railroad station . . . scantily furnished. He lives in a frugal way . . . few acquaintances . . . almost a recluse."

There was no past epoch of sin, gaiety, pleasures to brood on. He was seventy-four, and so, after being away thirty-one years, he returned to America. He had an exhibit of his work at Fifth Avenue and 14th Street, at the Sommerville Gallery. But the show was overlooked, and those paintings, too, went into permanent storage.

In 1871, at last, Catlin's work was invited to the Smithsonian. Twelve hundred paintings and sketches. It was hoped Congress would finally buy it for the nation, but when Catlin died, aged seventy-seven, the next year, nothing had been done. In time the Harrison Boiler Company collection was accepted as a gift by the Smithsonian: Fire, insects, and water had ruined much, including the paintings, but the collection still remained a marvelous monument to a native master. As for the paintings done for the defaulting king of France, Catlin had recovered those from revolutionary Paris, and they in time became part of a collection that ended up at the Museum of Natural History in New York.

And never again did American Indians pound their gristle-heels and dance in the Louvre.

CHAPTER 10

The Butterfly—
James Abbott McNeill Whistler

It takes endless labor to eradicate the traces of labor.

WHISTLER

WHISTLER WAS BORN in three cities according to the pert eccentricity of his own statements. He could have made it four if he had added Paris to the legends of his birthplace. There is no discoverable reason why he told his first biographer, Theodore Duret, that he was born in Baltimore, or the bewigged judge in the Whistler-Ruskin trial it was the old St. Petersburg of Imperial Russia. He was actually born in Lowell, Massachusetts, but his mother (not yet the little, old, capped lady in the chair) recorded the wrong date, July 10, 1834. He was born on the eleventh, as his father's records show.

He was a cocky young man of twenty-one, already touched with bohemian venality when he came to Paris to study art. Just the year before he had been bounced out of the United States Military Academy at West Point. He claimed it was the result of some dissatisfaction about his marks, ending with his answering a chemistry teacher's question with "Silicon is a gas." As he later put it with his witty irreverence, "If silicon *had* been a gas, I could have become a general."

He had led his class (a dull one) in drawing at West Point, but the Point never produced an American art master, so no one took his sketching seriously. He drifted down to Baltimore, then into the drafting department of the United States Coast and Geodetic Survey. Maps were then engraved or etched on copper, and Whistler enhanced his time, when bored with the rigid rules of map making, by etching little heads and figures on the edge of the plates, additions which would have to be cut away when the map was printed. It did not help his standing with the serious department head. But Washington was also a social city, though moving in deadly earnestness toward the Civil War, and Whistler was a social success. Slim, slight, an impressive head, he was seen at the Legation parties in a frock coat of his own design, created to save money on his salary of a dollar and a half a day, as well as to express his feelings for a proper fit. When his rent was unpaid, he pointed out to his landlord the sketches that he had made on the walls. "I'll not charge you anything for the decorations."

He made no genuflections to his masters; when he reported late for work his excuse was, "I was not too late, the office opened too early." During January and February of 1855, according to records, he was present for work only twelve days. He sat among the fiddlers and flautists, not the workers. When he did work, he still sketched caricatures of his superiors on the margin of the plates. He acquired a professional skill as an etcher, but he preferred affectation and frivolity to dullness.

Paris was his goal, not government service. So at the end of February he was ready; told the family he was going to Paris, and asked for their blessing. And three hundred and fifty dollars a year in quarterly installments. He promised no ostentation, luxury, or extravagance.

Paris saw him, small, dapper in a white duck suit, his hair in wild black ringleted disorder, captive under a low-crowned, broad-brimmed hat— and as seen in a Du Maurier drawing—with a black ribbon falling over the brim in front of his eyes. He had come from London, first class, of course, where he had visited his half sister Deborah on Sloane Street. Deborah was married to Seymour Haden, who secretly hoped to become an artist and did in time become a well-known etcher and a confirmed enemy of Whistler.

The young man was in Paris, a Paris of a special time and with a special glow, a period which Whistler for some years was to be part of, and where he would become a kind of legend. It was the time of the Second Empire at its most addled golden glory, the apogee of Napoleon III (Victor Hugo called him "Napoleon the Little"). The fears of another bloody revolution in 1848 had passed, and now the people of Balzac, Guys, Daumier were busy working for goals of power, social status, property, money, an effort to rise from one class to another, the turmoil and drama that we see in the great novelist's books and in the genius of the lithograph prints of the artists. Daumier was to produce nearly 4,000 prints!

There was a kind of maudlin cry of prosperity in Paris, of gaiety, even if there was a war with Russia some place at the end of the world. Long lines of people fought their way into the Ministry of Finance to subscribe to the new Government Loan.

Whistler could see how well lit the city was. Gas lamps appeared all over the place. No longer was Paris to be in medieval dark. The city was now *La Ville Lumière*; an amorphous, ancient mass. Baron Haussmann had at last made over the boulevards, cut new ones through, made wide wonderful streets that came to focus at points where cannon could be mounted to blow to shreds any more ideas of precocious rebels setting up barricades. It was *le siècle du boulevard*. Whistler found the men in top hats, fashionable frock coats, narrow trousers, pants uncreased as yet (it was Victoria's son Edward who would make fashionable trousers pressed to a crease). The billowing fullness of the skirts of the dress coats were a ballet of mode and fashion. And Whistler was to love the cafés; how fine for a man who liked loafing as much as art, perhaps at that time even more. It was good—a *café fine* at elbow—to read the war communiqués in a cosy café, the horror and death and the dreadful winter of the Crimea far away; no radio or television existed to bring the true horror of war directly into the home. Only the news that Malakoff had been gal- lantly taken with French *élan*, and Sebastopol captured.

There was an international exhibition on orders from the emperor with his needle-pointed mustache and the little imperial scrap of beard, the roué's roving eye for women.

Whistler's entrance into Paris was unnoticed. His train brought him to the Gare de Boulogne, later to become the Gare du Nord. His knowledge of Paris consisted almost entirely of a reading of Murger's *Scènes de la Vie de Bohème*, already a generation out of date. He knew from it that one could only as an artist, or rather as an aspiring artist, live in the *Quartier latin*, the Left Bank, the *rive gauche*. Getting into a fiacre he ordered the driver to take him to a hotel near the Théâtre de l'Odéon.

"*Je connais ça*," said the fiacre driver.

Ah—as he later remembered it—this was the real thing, thought Whis- tler. Baron Haussmann's modernization had touched the south bank of the Seine. There were broken up facades, unpainted houses, weed-grown gardens near the Sorbonne, the Luxembourg; it was almost real green country at times. Streets went radiating out from the Place Saint Sulpice where an enclosure kept a wild boar on public display. There was as yet no Boulevard Saint Germain, "Boul Miche." For the young American it was *very* much like *La Vie de Bohème*, and the people he passed could be playing at Schaunard and Marcel in cold, artistic attics, in undisciplined pathos.

The Hôtel Corneille to which Whistler was driven was a dismal old pile, huge, ancient, with a hundred rooms or more, and a *porte cochère*. Even two café-billiards with loungers, sharpers, students (art and medical), *grisettes, modistes,* certainly no *grandes cocottes,* or the fancy courtesans one saw in the drawings of Constantin Guys or the fashion models of Gavarni. But Jimmy hoped they were full of vehement passions.

There was a huge courtyard, deep in litter and horse droppings, and a dining room that was no credit to French cooking. And everywhere dirt, insects, and dilapidation. The place was soon to go bankrupt. To the young American it was still romance! The beginning of the artist's life. It was an age more used than we to the mordant human stench of insanitary life.

The Hôtel Corneille was international if nothing else. Among its boarders was George Du Maurier, tall, thin, handsome in his grace, manly in his look, with the proper English shoulders and the hope of a mustache. He did not know it then, but he and others were living the world he was to shine up and present in his popular novel *Trilby* forty years later. (The characters: The Laird, Taffy, and The Greek from that novel were present in real life as T. R. Lamont, Joseph Rowley and Alec Ionides— three forgotten painters of little merit if they had not been immortalized in the novel.) Also the hotel was to attract Edward Poynter, later to be Sir Edward, President of the Royal Academy, and Thomas Armstrong, one day to be Director of the South Kensington Museum—now the Victoria and Albert. Hardly the types to remain lifelong friends of the rebel Jimmy Whistler.

The Britishers were out for art and fun and clean English sports. For them the life of faith and contemplation was not enough. All but the sports and the bathing they shared with Whistler. He disliked exercise and the tough metaphysical questions. Although an apprentice dandy, he was not yet too clean under the unique and hard conditions of being poor in Paris.

The English were serious and proper Victorians with ideas of duty and work, and a bit given to seeing all other breeds—"the damned nigahs and colonials"—as somewhat below them. They had decided as a group to study under Gleyre, who had a studio where he taught French and foreign students what one art historian called "all that was unimportant in the method of Ingres."

Whistler only took to heart the master's words, "Black, *mes enfants,* is the base of tone." That philosophy is the key to Whistler's color scheme in most of his paintings. It has resulted in much of his work turning dark and fading into the background. It gave his best work the sadness of uncommunicative forms.

He got little else from Gleyre for Whistler didn't attend classes very often. He wanted the life of the bohemian French friends, over which the English wondered: really old chap! The dirt and the sordidness Whistler saw merely as local color. His life was not neat; he was self-indulgent and full of sensibilities.

When his brother-in-law Haden came to Paris with the Thackerays and had him to dinner, Jimmy had already pawned his dress suit and so he borrowed one from T. R. Lamont. He wore shoes that fitted but were not elegant enough to please him. He had stolen them from outside a door in the corridor of the Hôtel Corneille, some unsuspecting guest having, as was the custom, put them out overnight to be polished. As for the proper gloves, the story is he got a pair by making love to the *vendeuse* of a nearby shop.

Whistler was Dr. Jekyll and Mr. Hyde socially during his Paris years. From the dives of the *Quartier latin* he would be invited by the American

Embassy to their polished social affairs because of his dead father's one-time splendid connection with federal projects. Whistler liked to mix with the people at fêtes and parties over which flew the American flag. He himself had no jingo interest in political affairs. However, pressured by Whistler, Hugh Moon, the American ambassador, got him invitations to the balls of the emperor at the Tuileries. Here, in his own dancing pumps, which he wore all the time on his dainty feet in street or studio, and in borrowed English finery, he trod the privileged dance steps of the Second Empire in its gaudy glory with Napoleon III, a *fine mouche*—crafty fox. Whistler saw no reason not to have the best of two worlds, the glitter of embassy and court life and the low-life experiences of the *rive gauche*. He was at this time notorious for vacillating in extremes.

When the Hôtel Corneille sank into bankruptcy and closed its rotting doors, he moved to share a room with a French bank clerk called Aubert. The expression was *manger de la vache enragée*—having a lean time of it. In a way Whistler's laziness was an escape. He couldn't stand much more of all that exercise the English painters practiced. "Why the devil can't you fellows get your concierge to do that sort of muck for you?"

Other forms of life the British led he enjoyed. Café life, storytelling, and songs of music halls, *tableaux vivants*, street singers. He himself would oblige with music using a walking stick or umbrella as if it were a banjo, and he'd offer up a Negro melody once heard during his Baltimore days.

> De world was made in six days
> An finished on de seventh
> Accordin to de contract
> It shoulda been de eleventh.

He is said to have had a good voice, and blackface minstrel shows so popular in America were beginning to invade Europe.

> But de masons dey fell sick
> The joiners they wouldn't work
> So dey thought de cheapest way
> Wuz just to fill it up wid dirt.

(Later, when on tour, a Negro group from Fisk University came to Paris to put on an Ethiopian Minstrel Show. They had to blacken up their faces and wear woolly wigs to be convincing in their roles.)

The Englishmen moved to a studio at 53 Rue Notre Dame des Champs with their dumbbells and barbells. Whistler still preferred the bohemian world of the students and artists called the No Shirts. Often they were just plain loafers and drinkers of the quarter, producing the trivial and transitory in the arts. Whistler still had evenings of socializing at the American

Embassy. When strapped for money he would announce, "But you know I bank with the Rothschilds." Such banking, however, merely consisted of cashing the drafts sent him from home.

His painting, in his rearrangement of attitudes, made little progress. It took effort and time in the days of true art training to prepare canvas, to mix paints, to scrub out and begin again, to pose models, to labor over compositions. Instead Whistler did much etching, being attracted to the copper plate on which he could quickly sketch his subject, bathe the plate in acid to bite his line into the surface, and then print it. He proposed an etching club to be called "Lawd" to the English, a sort of anagram of the initial letters of their names, the resulting etchings to be "sent to a literary bloke in England" to be made into a book. Nothing came of it, but there were always the wild gyrations of the Moulin Rouge and the Mont de Piété—the municipal pawnshop.

Besides the painters' life in the Latin Quarter Jimmy Whistler grabbed as much fun as could be found at student balls, where one rubbed literally against the *demi-monde,* the working girl out for fun, and the plain tarts. Also rumor was that often a lady was there looking for adventure. The Bacchanalia of the world of Baudelaire and Huysmans would soon give it all literary form.

Devoting himself to fêtes and café life, to some *petite amie*, Whistler slept late, hardly ever rising before eleven in the morning. Just in time to miss working at Gleyre's studio, so the rest of the day could be spent in the cafés with a few copper plates in his pocket, scratching an etching if in the mood, hoping the evening would produce a group *vernissage.*

Whistler was a sensual fellow who liked the physical pleasure and company of women. If not the *grande cocotte,* the famous horizontals of Paris, there were the *grisettes* that Murger and the Second Empire made famous, just as the later Hemingway made famous those dream lays in war hospitals, sleeping bags, and even in the gondolas of Venice. How much of the *grisette* charm was myth would be hard to deduce today. We hear so much of those lovely, hard-working, faithful, willing girls, such splendid sexual objects, often, in the most romantic manner, stepping aside for some better woman from the lover's own social class, and dying loyally, coughing out their lives in some attic like the consumptive Mimi of *La Bohème.*

Whistler moved among them, his charm in place, his ability to amuse and make love building him a reputation among the little hat trimmers, sewing girls, *modistes,* shop assistants, tobacconists' clerks. The two essentials for sexual gallantry he had: desire and a convenient bed.

Sunday saw the *grisette* free in a Paris more countrylike than now, a city smelling of the best horses, and the art student like Whistler, the law clerk, the medical scholar and the girls could all ride out by the horse omnibus, carrying baskets of food, *petits-fours* and wine, and lacy sunshades. They could ride to Ranelagh, to Belleville, and if someone were in funds, even stand treat to a fine meal in some café. There was boating on a river the Impressionists had not yet tried to capture in all its nuances. Life was a promiscuous naiveté to young lovers.

In bad weather there was the theater of heavy drama, and the audience had oranges and hot rolls to be eaten with tears over the sad fate of the lovers on stage. Whistler enjoyed circus acts, clowns, Japanese-trained balancing dogs. Daumier was painting it all but not exhibiting. It was fun to watch the fat rumped horses going round and round and tiny girls flipping in their tutus from horse to horse, leaping through paper rings.

The formula of student and *grisette* love called for only one dress on her part, one heart of gold, little pains suffered silently, and complete doglike devotion. At least that was the ideal. These sex-satisfying odalisques of Paris were actually more human and less docile than the fiction image, as Whistler was to find out, even if the girls could often quote Alfred de Musset, their favorite poet on *l'amour.*

> Poète, prends ton luth de la jeunesse
> Fermant cette nuit dans les veines de Dieu.

Whistler learned of the reality of relationships when he made an etching of one female reciter of poetry called Eloise. With her Jimmy set up a ménage in the Rue Saint Sulpice, and he called his love Fumette, not Eloise. In the Quarter she was called simply *La Tigresse* for her peppery and dangerous temper, her sharp, spurlike claws, her raging voice. The artist had indeed picked a tigress.

CHAPTER 11

The Tigress and After

*One's duty as a gentleman should never
interfere with one's pleasures.*

OSCAR WILDE

W HISTLER LEARNED of the volubility of women, the stormy seasons of
the menstrual cycle. If he stayed away too long at a café or
gossiping in a studio, he came back to their lodging to find *La Tigresse*
waving her arms and cursing. Once very vexed and enraged, perhaps jealous that he was with some model or slut, she tore up all of Whistler's
drawings, almost all he had to show for his artistic reason for being in
Paris. This would cure him of playing *boules* in the Bois, excuses to visit
the *bateaux mouches* on the Seine.

It was a blow, losing all those drawings—he took it badly, broke down
and wept. Then he took up his flat straw hat with its ribbons, went out,
met two friends, and began to get drunk. He got very intoxicated, and for
him the drink brought on a gaiety and desire for movement, color,
amusement, for moods beating themselves to bits in the night. Whistler
suggested a debauch in Les Halles, the great market that ran all night
and where herds of cattle marched, sides of beef hung rich gold with fat,
pigs slashed open, mountains of vegetables made still lifes. Counters of
lacquered, gill-stirring fish were brought, bartered, carried off to provide
the food of Paris for the next day. An all-night binge and feed was what
Whistler wanted in some little restaurant, an onion soup, some ragout, a
bit of tawny oil-fried fish. The problem was none of the three men had
any money. Poverty was a perpetual irony.

Whistler recalled he knew an American named Lucas. He ran there, woke Lucas, crying out he was stony, strapped, begged a loan. Lucas refused. The three friends went off anyway and ordered a meal and wine in a smaller eatery. Whistler, angry, was speaking of a duel to the death with that damn Lucas. What did Lucas know of artists, of fame and genius, the age-old dichotomy. As the story went around Paris later, Whistler's friends agreed a duel would serve that rotten American swine Lucas right. They ate and drank and fell asleep at table leaving it to Whistler to find a way to pay *l'addition.* The patron, too, was beginning to worry about it. Whistler again went out to try to find funds, leaving a patron no longer pleased and amused at the compliments to his cuisine. Whistler managed to get money from an American painter and came back in triumph to pay the bill. But, as he said to his friends, "The swine had the bad manners to abuse the situation. He insisted on *my* looking at *his* pictures."

His jaunty self-assurance soon returned. He forgave *La Tigresse,* but it was clear the situation could not last this life of travail and turmoil, even if she sang the street and café songs he liked:

> *Voulez-vous savoir, savoir,*
> *Comment les artistes aiment?*
> *Ils aiment si artistement,*
> *Ils sont de si artistes gens . . .*

And Whistler would sing out the refrain:

> *Ramenez vos moutons des champs.*

Neither was given to restraint. One last fight, one last panting outcry of voices, curses, perhaps blows, and the tigress was out of Whistler's life, she moving in with a friendly musician. Tradition has it that in the end she took the road to the brothels of Buenos Aires and died there. One suspects Whistler himself in later years supplied this dark, bittersweet ending.

It was lonely and melancholy for Whistler being without a woman. For all their depths of deviousness, Whistler felt they had a sweet incredibility.

His next ménage was with a cocotte and dancer who performed the lace-showing, crotch-tearing cancan at the Bal Bullier. Her name was Finette, and Whistler etched her; he never used a mistress merely for bed, but drew or painted them all. If Finette was a tart, she was also a professional dancer. In 1867 she was invited to dance the cancan in

London. In Victorian London she danced not in those fluffy drawers showing costume garters on naked thighs, but in male attire, which was approved by the London *Times* for "much of the objection which our English audience would have to the French dance was removed." This was the England—as Whistler was to remember—where when laws were drawn up against homosexuals, strictures on lesbians were left out. When a public office official was asked about this oversight, he replied, "Frankly, we just didn't know how to explain lesbianism to Her Majesty."

Finette was no mild little *modiste* merely loyal and willing to work her fingers to the bone for her man. She was an *artiste* and had a certain sultry elegance, a show-business sophistication. One French critic called her *"une créole de moeurs légères."*

Whistler's attendance at Gleyre's classes grew even more rare, but he did meet there an Alsatian named Dabo, and made another friend, a painter of no fame, Ernest Delannoy.

Whistler had bounce; even if at times squalor lighted by a three-sou candle took over. He avoided the Paris law courts and those men of justice Daumier set down in close to a hundred lithograph prints, in many drawings and paintings. Whistler ignored the great game of cupidity played in the courts, the pitiful mockery of justice, the cunning mask of the greedy lawyers, the wolf and fox faces topped by round hats of the decaying or indifferent judges in their black gowns, who were usually seated under a painting of the Crucifixion, indifferent to His suffering as to the mistreatment of the wretched people who came before them.

No, Whistler was the butterfly—not an agonizer over injustice. He sensed it was a time of change; people wanted to settle down, make money, and enjoy the easy pleasures. Whistler, moving through the medieval labyrinth of the Montagne Ste. Geneviève at a cheap *table d'hôte,* or asking a loan outside the Mont de Piété, the municipal pawnshop, saw the full drama of this new world. He observed and was amused at the *haut monde,* the sippers of aperitifs in the cafés, the charwomen, the *marchands du charbon,* the speculators, the frugal little government *fonctionnaires.* Balzac recorded it perfectly, this world of ragged *littérateurs,* strutting actors at *soirées,* dazed absinthe drinkers in the dens of the Rue St. Jacques, toughs dancing in the open air at the Closerie des Lilas, and Monsieur and Madame drinking a *marc de Bourgogne* to celebrate the new ribbon of the Legion of Honor on a fat shoulder. Whistler shrugged, drew, chased the girls. He saw life as a world of material success and social climbing; the poor begging, and the newly rich Second Empire army supply contractors arriving at performances of

Meyerbeer's *Robert le Diable*. Modern society was "a world seeking gold and pleasure," as Balzac defined it, adding, "Take these two words, *gold and pleasure,* for a lantern and explore the great stucco cage of Paris."

A hungry artist of Paris—if he had friends—could do portraits. Whistler did one of Captain Williams, also called Stonington Bill, who in plebeian cordiality also offered to pay Whistler twenty-five dollars for any famous picture he copied. In the days before color printing directly from photographs, some hungry artists earned a living at times copying famous paintings. Whistler did too. "I copied a picture, I cannot remember by whom . . . a snow scene with a horse and soldier standing by it, and another in the snow at his feet; a second of St. Luke with his halo and draperies, a third of a woman holding up a child towards a barred window . . . I have no doubt I made something very interesting out of them."

With two hundred and fifty francs earned copying pictures Whistler talked his friend Delannoy into a walking tour to Alsace. Whistler was ready in his fencing shoes, the wide-brimmed, ribboned hat, his pockets full of copper plates to etch. At first all went well. But they soon ran out of money and later claimed they sold drawings for food, played the drums in a traveling show. They staggered back to Paris looking like a pair of soiled tramps, telling Gargantuan lies of their adventures.

Whistler had his etchings of the trip printed at Delatre's shop and went back to copying at the Louvre the nude Angelica chained to a rock by Ingres. When he was told it was painted too thin, he explained, "What I'm paid doesn't run to much more than linseed oil at a hundred francs a copy."

As a copyist Whistler was bored, but watching a shy young man working on a replica of the Marriage at Cana, he was impressed. He praised the copy and introduced himself.

The copyist saw *"un personnage en chapeau bizarre"* and said, "I'm Fantin-Latour."

With no reticence they at once became close friends and went to lunch at the Café Molière. When asked where he was studying, Whistler admitted to Gleyre and to being *un jeune homme sportif.*

The young Frenchman shook his head. "You are wasting your time under Gleyre." He went on to speak of Gustave Courbet and realism, of painting the modern world clearly, brutally, not as bric-a-brac.

Whistler let him talk, this artist who mistook a monologue for conversation. He was interested. The artist Courbet was a wild, loving, drinking, brawling, political-minded, stout fellow. He loved the girls, food,

drink, and had good friends; Corot, Daumier, Baudelaire had all climbed the Louis XIII staircase, the pride of Courbet's studio, a vast loft in the Rue Hautefeille, once the chapel of the Praemonstratensian monastery. Murger of *La Vie de Bohème* had been there, even his hero Schaunard, under his true name of Schanne. They talked for total efficiency, for total anarchy, those esoteric fantasies of politics.

"Could I meet Courbet?" Whistler asked.

It was arranged, and up the unswept royal staircase went Whistler and turned on his charm, with what effect on the bulky realist we don't know. James Whistler did leave the studio crying out dramatically to his friends, *"C'est un grand homme. C'est un grand homme!"*

The meeting was intrinsically significant. Whistler hadn't been paying much attendance at Gleyre's studio, and now he formed a Society of Three with Fantin and the artist Legros. Courbet himself approved of young artists and visited the studio of the painter F. S. Bonvin to talk to the students, to look at their work, offer advice. Here *"le petit Vistlaire,"* as his French friends called him, settled down to work. He had passed lazy, amusing, irrelevant years in Paris and now he would prove to himself he was painting seriously. Bonvin worked rather poorly in the style of minor Dutch masters, but at least he taught Whistler how to put down paint properly, how to mix his colors. It was the only true art training he was ever to have and it was meager. He never was very sure of his drawing of hands and feet. His knowledge of human anatomy never went beyond his mistresses' bodies in bed. In the end his art expressed the ideas of the poet Mallarmé: "Exclude the real, the too precise, until all becomes completely vague."

Whistler began, with the wrong impression that he was now a realist, to draw and paint the world of the Bal Bullier, the cafés, the streets, La Mère Gérard, the old flower woman. His etchings of her are very fine, and from another model, a peddler of chamber pots in a nearly plumbingless Paris, he did up a picture, *L'Homme à la Pipe*, a tribute to Courbet's version of the subject.

It was 1859, and Whistler felt time brushing its wings on his unruly head of dark curls with one white lock artfully hanging over his brow. He was clever about his artistic failings and began to work from memory, and therefore he was able to do away with the hard-to-paint and unnecessary details.

A fellow etcher, Bracquemond, had introduced Whistler to Japanese prints, and Whistler recognized their splendid patterns, their nuances of form and color in Koryusai, Utamara, Hokusai, as what he had been seeking. There was a rage to collect Japanese prints, china and pottery, study Hana-ogi, the most famous courtesan, and even a cult to eat Japanese food. But the prints in their profound repose, their striking images of Kabuki gave the painters ideas.

The men around Courbet also were reintroducing Goya, his somber blacks and blood-reds, slashing brushwork, and the remorseless terseness, the firmness of Valázquez. Whistler was what in show business is called "a quick study," and the Spaniards' styles mixed with his pleasure in Japanese prints, Asuka teacups, celadon porcelain. He began to mold his style into a personal manner—smoky, tranquil, witty.

His visits to his brother-in-law and etcher, Seymour Haden, in London, became more frequent. Paris had given Whistler a wild, careless way of life which he now wanted to leave for a more elegant one. Was it as in Milton's lines, "Fame is the spur that clear spirit doth raise" but "to scorn delights and live laborious days"? Hardly likely, yet the bohemian was about to become a London dandy. All his life Whistler was to have no allegiance to any country, any social level, but only to be what he felt was his due as an artist.

The Paris Salon had rejected Whistler's painting of his sister, Mrs. Haden, at the piano. But the Royal Academy of 1860 had accepted it. And what was more, a Royal Academician, John Philip, had bought it. It was an omen. Comic incongruities, Whistler knew, make our destinies. Money and fame and social success lay in London. He invited his friends Legros and Fantin to come to England to battle the Puritan theocracy according to Victoria, to be led by happy insolence to taste roast-bif' and champagne and Dimitrios cigarettes. Even to face the Haden butler, sleep between clean sheets, and have their underwear sent out to a laundry. (Another French artist visiting them paled at the sound of a shower, which suggested that bathing was expected. *"Qu'est-ce que c'est que cette espèce de cataracte de Niagara?"*)

Strange, portentous feelings stirred in Whistler—intangible as yet as night music. After visits to London and returns to Paris, at last Whistler moved to London not to return to Paris until old age.

It is not part of our story to follow Whistler's fabulous stormy career in England, but just to relate those things that were to force him in the end back to Paris, after a great legal struggle with the critic John Ruskin. The costs of that affair in effect drove him from England.

John Ruskin was a defender of and admirer of Turner (when Turner no longer needed such help). A strange figure, this mutton-chopped Ruskin, overeducated, intelligent, a man who could not consummate his marriage, but was painfully addicted to masturbation. Ruskin is the first recorded English follower of the cult of Lolita. He was mad for very young teen-age girls.

Ruskin's bird's nest of a mind became unstrapped from time to time, and he was entering the foyer of one of his strange smoky mental periods when he revolted, in public print, against Whistler's Art for Art's Sake ideas. This was impiety to Ruskin. His monthly public letter *Fors Clavigera* was a mixture of social problems, furniture and art talk, and the "Companionship of St. George," a new order of chivalry to change modern morals and manners. He wanted nothing less than a regeneration of the world. A splendid, lively writer, his system of aesthetics was often nonsense, ideas almost worthless to the following generation. But he was a remarkably skilled word master, with a fine prose still worth reading. He hoped for some vague ideal called "beauty of subject," which turned him away from Rembrandt and other Dutch painters.

Ruskin had been hopelessly in love with a sickly girl child named Rose LaTouche, and wanted to marry her in the manner of his strange sex life with his long gone wife (she testified she left him a virgin). Rose was a strict Evangelical and Ruskin, loose-minded toward the true faith, found himself rejected. Sickly, rather moronic or numbed by her hothouse upbringing, Rose died young, in 1875. This further unhinged Ruskin's mind. He complained of giddiness and dizziness and in that condition went to view a show of paintings at the Grosvenor Gallery.

Of the vapid, glossy, Burne-Jones paintings, fortified by his faith in art Ruskin said, "I know these will be immortal." But facing Whistler's *The Falling Rocket* (called *Nocturne in Blue and Silver* by the artist), Ruskin blew his senses. It was an impression of the expiring of a sky rocket sent up from Cremorne Garden as seen from Chelsea shore; a splash of golden tone against a blue void, a luxurious glow, the splendid moment of a sky-sent frailty.

Ruskin's response to this phallic rocket exploding orgasmically in the sky—in a way denied to Ruskin—is a classic of suppressed sexuality, but an awful piece of art criticism: "For Mr. Whistler's own sake, no less than for the protection of the purchaser, Sir Cotts Linsay ought not to have admitted work into the gallery in which ill-educated conceit of the artist so nearly approached the aspect of wilful imposture. I have seen and heard much of cockney impudence before now, but never expected to hear a coxcomb ask two hundred guineas to fling a pot of paint in the public's face."

The review caused a sensation in art and social circles, and Whistler decided to sue for libel. What an insult to a dandy and a famous painter, a man about town with an eyeglass in place, a cane, one lock of white hair over one eye. And to be called a cockney, he a West Point man, a dancer at embassy balls. He had to sue; Ruskin was the major art critic, and the remark was ruining Whistler. He was always in debt, and just then he was having a house built for himself in Tite Street, Chelsea. He was notorious but not successful. He was a witty antagonist, braying for vengeance.

While waiting to come to court and bash Mr. Ruskin, Whistler worked with the architect E. W. Godwin on a house of his own, an arrangement in green and white, green slate, white brick. Godwin had been the lover of Ellen Terry, the actress, when she left her husband, the painter Watts. He was the father of her two children, one of whom turned out to be the eccentric genius, the stage designer Gordon Craig. Godwin, not always on the path of strict monogamy, was married at the time of the Ruskin affair to one of his pupils, Beatrice Philips. She was in her early twenties, dark-haired, "handsome in the French way." She worked in several of the arts, a clever girl, who admired in a chummy, unassuming way the art of paint and painters. Whistler began to give her art lessons and turned on his charm. The husband did not object. It was a tranquil friendship of three sensualists, enjoying life like the indigenous birds.

Whistler prepared for his day in court—polished his eyeglass and his wit. Ruskin did not appear at the trial. He had come through a fresh mental breakdown, a period of delirium. It was decided that his doctor should appear instead of the patient, although it was not apparent the medical man had absorbed any art knowledge from Ruskin.

Whistler v. Ruskin opened on November 25, 1878. The main attack by the attorney general was to prove Whistler was an eccentric, an unsuccessful, lazy craftsman, an artist who "knocked off" in a day or so pictures for which he was overpaid. The omniscience of proper English law destroying the idolatry of art. Whistler made a good appearance on the stand, defending himself, his work, and all artists against whiffling pedants and Counselor Snugnoses.

When asked—with a mild sneer—if for two days' work he demanded two hundred guineas, Whistler answered, "No, I ask it for the knowledge of a lifetime." As to the patronizing lawyer's question, "Do you think you could make *me* understand the beauty of that picture?" Whistler plunged for the jugular: "The attempt would be hopeless."

So it went, the mechanical mumbling of legal ritual, the sudden sword slash of the libeled artist. A puzzled, confused jury brought in a verdict for Whistler. "With damages, me Lud, of one farthing."

Whistler wore the coin on his watch chain the rest of his life. But as both sides had to pay their own costs, Whistler was ruined, and in the end Paris was to be the only solution for his debts and his mangled reputation. Buyers and sitters avoided the artist. He had borrowed large sums, owed hundreds of guineas to fishmonger, greengrocer, milkman, coalman, baker, wine merchant, house builder, frame-maker, tailor, bootmaker, music dealer. Even his dues to the Arts Club. His unpaid law court debts were 500 pounds. He had borrowed two thousand pounds and was to lose his new house when asked to repay.

Living with bailiffs in the house, on May 8, 1879, he filed petition in bankruptcy court with debts amounting to nearly 5,000 pounds. He was deep in his forties, and while he could smile and make jests, he was a badly hurt man. The power of the purse and the cost and greed of the law courts were as deadly as cannon.

Meanwhile the Godwins had separated, and Mrs. Godwin continued to see Whistler. He joined her at the deathbed of her husband, Mr. Godwin, for a last farewell. The three being, it seemed, strong in their various combinations of friendship.

Beatrice Godwin began to visit Whistler at his home, and fight with Maude, officially the mistress-in-residence. Terrible quarrels took place. Maude was sent on her way. In August of 1888 Beatrice Godwin and James Whistler were married at St. James Abbot's Church in Kensington. (She was a hefty person, and when Whistler was snide to Aubrey Beardsley, that artist drew her as *The Fat Woman*.)

It was the first step to the road to Paris. The bride was much younger than the aging painter, taller too, at five feet five and carrying forty pounds more in weight. Whistler adored her and called her Trixie. The womanizer had been tamed. He went out less, painted less. Whistler and Mrs. Whistler settled in, up six flights of stairs in Paris. He took a studio at 86 Rue Notre Dame. He was honored by the ribbon of the Legion of Honor. His wife kept house at their new apartment at 110 Rue du Bac.

Whistler's heart was weakening, though his hair was still black, some suggested with the help of dye, his eyeglass still in place on the aging, wrinkling face. It was not the same Paris. The Empire was dead at Sedan. The Impressionists were rising in a loud, gay style so far from his own nuances. Victor Hugo no longer led the romantics, but a down-at-heel tramp, Paul Verlaine. A strange boy, Rimbaud, had replaced the lush romantic poets of Jimmy Whistler's youth. Only the poet Mallarmé among the avant-garde admired Whistler's work. He saw in the artist a touch of *diablerie*. Whistler did a lithograph of the poet to be used in a book of his poems. Mallarmé translated and gave readings of Whistler's

"Ten O'Clock" lecture. Poets came to visit, but not many painters. Trixie didn't help, not liking "foreigners" very much, even on their home grounds. Her poor French was hardly a blessing. The old couple continued to shuffle along in their personal rhythms.

In 1894 Trixie's health began to decline. She died two years later. Running about wild-eyed in his grief, clothes in disorder, Whistler cried out to a friend, "Don't speak to me!"

To fight off age he began to paint his face like an aging courtesan. Visitors described him as looking "like an old conjuror," a puppet, some fantastic creature out of *The Tales of Hoffman*. At an inn he asked the landlady who she thought he was. "Lor' now, I should fancy you was from the music halls." One visitor found him nursing a cold by "inhaling eucalyptus from a steaming jug." He disliked the new genius of painting, Cézanne. "If a child of ten had drawn that on her slate . . . a good mother ought to have slapped her." In need of money Whistler opened a school, the *Académie Whistler*. It failed. Always a poor pupil, he was no better as a teacher.

Feeble, ill, not painting much, he returned to London to die among English-speaking people near Old Chelsea Church, on July 17, 1903, near the grave of Hogarth, who despised the French, or anyone influenced by the Paris scene.

The art historian James Laver said of Whistler, "He was not Timon of Athens, he was Cyrano tilting at the Academies, refusing to conform to accepted standards. The strange little man, half charlatan, half dancing master as he seemed to his contemporaries, is, in the end, a noble figure."

In Paris, at the Luxembourg, the most popular painting for the visitors is the picture they insist on calling *Whistler's Mother*, not the feisty little artist's own title: *Arrangement in Gray and Black*.

CHAPTER 12

The Original Tiffany Master

The luxurious and outré elegance of French design,
c. 1900, in furniture, pottery, metalwork and small
decorative objects is handsomely Art Nouveau, *though*
the accepted implications of the term in confining
it strictly to France, thus excludes Beardsley,
Mackintosh, Tiffany and Gaudi—that is, the
international nature of the style.

Times Literary Supplement, LONDON

C ERTAINLY we must not leave out Louis Comfort Tiffany, an American whose most noted mistress in Paris was one of the greatest and most notorious of the grand courtesans, Tiffany whose stained-glass lampshades, tree-trunk art patterns, and flower forms in metal and other substances were just a few years ago revived first with a minimum of gratitude as "camp" fun, and then as genuine American genre. His fame and décor were not merely American but international. Modern design of the turn of the century found him its most celebrated and most salable artist. His logical fantasy, his fine bizarre use of metal and glass remain his monument.

He was born in New York City in 1848, the son of Charles Lewis and Harriet Young Tiffany. Charles Tiffany, with nothing but a fine and honorable background, got together on loan a thousand dollars in 1837 and opened a tiny drygoods and stationery shop. There is no chronicle of frivolity or levity in his life.

From such beginnings grew the present-day, world-renowned Tiffany & Company. But young Louis wanted no part of that small, safe life of struggling, earnest shopkeepers. He was a red-headed child, wild, headstrong, and not easy to control. He was packed off to the Flushing Academy on Long Island, and there, somehow, he became interested in the arts. His parents, like good, middle-class climbers into society, decided

Louis should go to college. The salient characteristics of a degree would improve the family's image. But Louis had no desire for a formal education, no wish to enter the family business; he wanted to study art. The parents gave in and he went to the studio of George Inness, whose mild, genteel landscapes were a romantic feature of the Hudson River school of painting.

The youth Louis was eighteen, loved the cosy, paint-stained life of the studio, the painters and writers who came there to smoke cheroots, drink the rye whisky, and talk of Paris, of the artists' pleasant yet unquiet life, of the great collections of art on display there. Although Louis painted good landscapes, he was a poor pupil. Inness confessed: "The more I teach him, the less he knows." Louis was frivolous, complicated, changeful, and just then elusive.

Paris was Louis's goal, and somehow when he was twenty-one he got his parents to let him go there to study at the studio of Louis Bailly. Study is too strong a word; Louis loved and lived in Paris the way that Whistler and the heroes of *Trilby* ordered their lives, a sort of aesthetic delinquency with a denigration and condescension to ordinary existence.

Louis's teacher was no Degas, no Guys, no hunter of the audible, pulsating scenes of everyday life in Paris of the Second Empire. Bailly painted imaginary landscapes of North Africa and the Near East in his Paris studios. Louis was delighted with the subject matter. With another American artist in Paris, Samuel Coleman, he went to seek out the color and glow of North Africa, sample the women, the *couscous*, the *rafa* brandy, perhaps inhale the opium pipe. Certainly he delighted in the color and confusion of an Arabian Night's world. Islamic fabrics and design pleased him with their rhythmic structures that kept a decorative distance from nature. The artistic, social Paris of the time was ablaze with the pseudo-Oriental and the brass, beady, inlaid Near Eastern art. Mansions had "Turkish corners," Moorish rooms, divans from Arab harems, camel saddles. Americans brought back some of this; Turkish rugs, harem divans, and tents were found in Sioux City, in Chicago's bohemian studios, even among the followers of Mrs. Astor. The poems of Omar the Tentmaker (filtered through English genius) were recited with gritty lucidity by corn-fed hostesses.

Louis Tiffany, his head whirling with color and pattern, came home in 1870 with a cargo of his North African paintings. Sales were good at five hundred dollars each. But the young man was more interested in crafts, in industrial arts, in home decor. Exquisite detail delighted him, not acres of heroic canvas.

Back he went to Paris in 1875, and after a pleasurable time but with his eyes open to the production of decor, he knew which way his life's work lay. He said his way pointed toward "decorative work . . . I believe there is more in it than in painting."

He had made close friendships with fellow American artists in Paris who kept them informed of the mode, and in 1879 he opened up as Louis C. Tiffany & Co., Associated Artists, offices in Paris, main workshops in America. Their first big order was an embroidered drop curtain for the Madison Square Theater. Oscar Wilde, the dilettante, visiting America (he had said at U.S. Customs, "I have nothing to declare but my genius"), inspected the curtain and pronounced, "It has been executed by a masterhand."

But needlework was not Louis's major art form. Glass delighted him. He had experimented with it for years. The ancient stained-glass windows of French churches had inspired him, and also the special blown and colored glass of the *hôtels* of the grand courtesans and the often preposterous salons of French society. However, he wanted neither medieval forms nor techniques, nor the chi-chi of Marie Antoinette (there still exists as a vase a ceramic replica of her breast, nipple and all). Louis said, "I took up chemistry and built furnaces . . . and through

years of experiments I found means to avoid the use of paints; etching, or burning, or otherwise treating the surface of the glass, so that it is now possible to produce figures in glass of which even the flesh tones are not superficially treated—built up of what I call 'genuine glass.' "

In time he called his art Favrile Glass. Favrile, he claimed, came from the Latin *fabrile menin*—handmade. Students of Latin might argue the point, but society loved the results. Having exquisite Tiffany meant social status.

For the World Columbian Exposition of 1893 in Chicago, Louis put together over a million bits of mosaics, iridescent and opalescent glass, pearls, precious stones, all in a setting of black and white marble which he proudly called "a modern Byzantine Chapel." It was said to be the most sensational exhibition at the exposition, although the most talked about item at the exposition was the rotating navel of a belly dancer known as Little Egypt.

In Paris Louis's work was featured at Samuel Bing's *Salon de l'Art Nouveau*. Louis was the darling of the decorator set in Paris and a hero of its enervated sensual games. Bing became Louis's European dealer, and he commissioned special orders. Louis won prizes all over Europe at every major fair or exposition. *"Quelle élégance! Quelle distinction! C'est admirable!"*

High living in Paris was also part of his career.

To most Americans today the name of Louis Tiffany is connected, if at all, with a posh jewelry store of that same name, a minor novel by Truman Capote, and the Tiffany lamp. But in the Eighties and Nineties of the last century he was also known in Paris as the keeper of the notorious courtesan, Léonide Leblanc, better known as Mademoiselle Maximum, supposedly for her capacity for taking on lovers. Although around fifty, she still held "the most extravagant and generous protection of the rich American, Louis Tiffany."

Léonide belonged with the most famous of the grand horizontals, those courtesans that enlivened the nineteenth century in Paris with a sensual infection that comes to us in fiction in the form of Zola's *Nana*, Courbet's fleshy nudes, Chassériau's reclining figure of Alice Ozy, the drama, *La Dame aux Camélias* (the coughing courtesan in that play, by the way, was never named Camille).

But behind novel, painting, or play were real women, destroyers of fortunes, reputations, makers of suicides, bankrupts, and often infection beds of what one coy writer before penicillin called "the Disease of Venus." Blanche d'Antigny, Cora Pearl (real name Eliza Emma Crouch!),

La Paiva (Thérèse Lachmann) Marguerite Bellanger, Alphonsine Plessis, also called Marie Duplessis and known to fame as the original of Dumas *fils' La Dame aux Camélias*—in this exotic world and its next generation the name Louis Tiffany was well known.

Rich Americans competed with Frenchmen, Englishmen, Italians, a Papal Knight, a Russian prince, even a Shah, for the bodies and time of these grand courtesans. That Louis Tiffany would be enthralled by one near fifty shows the lure that Léonide Leblanc could retain until her final decline.

Léonide was born December 8, 1842, in the village of Burley, Department of the Loire. Her father crushed stones for roadmaking. When she was six, the family walked to Paris, Léonide barefooted, all being too poor to buy a ride. The family wanted Léonide to train to become a governess, but the headstrong girl of fourteen wanted to be an actress. She ran off and joined a catch-as-catch-can theater group. There, as one writer put it, a manager, M. Cogniard of the Théâtre des Variétés, "seduced by Léonide's beauty, and then by her talent, engaged her for three years." She appeared in vaudeville in an early comedy by Victorien Sardou. "How pretty she was, disguised as a man, smoking a big fat cigar which made her feel quite sick."

Acting was fine, but men were interesting and more rewarding. The pilgrimages to her bed seemed more lucrative than the stage. Yet she was aware of that precious moment in people when two experiences touch. She ran off to Italy with "some handsome and famous Italian," turned up in Rome, Florence, Milan; a grand tour for a courtesan. The Italian faded away. In Paris there were rumors she had entered the Great Turk's harem in Constantinople. Capricious, vivacious, she turned up in London (supported in style) drank pale ale, went to the races, took boxing lessons. One day in some stoical, fluctuating doubt, she said to her maid, "Have you noticed, Juliette, men and women are the same every place you go?"

"No, madame. In Africa they have black skins."

"Then let us go to Africa."

However Paris was her strongest tie, and in January, 1866, *La Vie Parisienne* reported, "Léonide Leblanc has returned."

Actually she began by marriage to a German photographer, and after losing him, she became the mistress of a *boulevardier* and journalist named Aurelian Scholl, who brought her to the famous keepers of a journal, the Goncourts, for them to look over: "the little wonder of nature and prostitution."

She grew rich from lovers' buying her bed. She hardly ever refused a man if he could afford her price. As poor Scholl put it, "If you put her away on top of Mont Blanc, she would still be accessible." She was mistress to Prince Napoleon (soon to be emperor), to Henri d'Orléans, the Duke d'Aumale. The *Grand Seigneur* of Chantilly filled her apartment with rare furniture, bibelots, *objets d'art*. In that rare and fascinating

book, *Le Demi-monde sous le Second Empire*, she is written of as "voluptuousness in flesh and blood." She met men at the Café Anglais in the private *Le Grand Seize*, entertained notorious womanizers, all eating, drinking, taking a hand at baccarat, not getting home till nine the next morning.

Americans were often her prey. We can catch only glimpses of these gents from the USA—male escorts and bed partners. *La Vie Parisienne* teased with an item, "She appeared . . . with a federal Yankee who was pretty well ballasted with dollars and the gold dust of California."

Léonide was a fantastic gambler, often, it would appear, with rich Americans backing her play. At the gambling spa of Homberg a Paris newspaper announced after she won a half million francs: "Just wait, she will want the whole million." It was at Baden she twice broke the bank. "Then she lit a Maryland cigarette with banknotes, laughing at the thalers and double thalers gone with the wind." In six months she spent all her huge winnings.

While Louis Tiffany may have been her biggest American catch, her most world-shaking lover was the great political figure of France, "The Tiger," Georges Clemenceau, who could be called part American, for he lived in the United States for some time around the period of the Civil War. As she was also sexually involved with the Duke d'Aumale at the time, and both men knew of each other's visiting hours, the Duke could ask, "And what has your *Communard sans culotte* friend got to say for himself?"

Louis Tiffany, when he was her protector, never put down in prose his impressions of her, but as he was a poet of metal and gems, and a wildly romantic dreamer, perhaps his ideas of Léonide were close to those expressed by Charles Diguet in his book *Les Jolies Femmes de Paris*. "This is the dream made flesh. This is the ideal which haunts the dreams of poets . . . the figure is a poem, all these curves are stanzas written by God to astonish the children of men." However, she was out of the price range of poets.

What was Léonide really like? Her photographs, those faded sepia replicas of early camera work, show little to fit that ecstasy written about her, but that may be the fault of the camera of that day. Or the fact that many sensual, fascinating women are not photogenic; the camera fails to capture them for various reasons. What the pictures show, and none feature her glorious body, is a head of fussy curls, eyes not too large, a pert nose, and a rather fleshy lower lip.

She faded fast. By 1883, when she was forty-one, she was listed in the directory of whores, *Les Jolies Femmes de Paris*, as "the remains of true beauty and grace . . . it is difficult to do justice to such a celebrated whore . . . Every notable rake has passed at least one night in her arms for a modern Don Juan catalogue would not be complete unless he could inscribe in it the honor of having 'had' Léonide Leblanc . . . hasten to enjoy her once, before it is *too* late."

She was fifty when Louis Tiffany broke with her, and over what? A young hairdresser who had attracted her. She was seen hurrying afoot along the Bois de Boulogne to meet the *coiffeur*, while Tiffany waited for her with a declining, outraged ardor. After her break with the American, since she had had none of the ant's sense for the rainy day but rather the indifference of the grasshopper to the future, her lot was hard.

As she faded from the scene, younger demimondaines replaced her as the great charmer, even if at times she appeared on the stage to cheers and whistles. She was only fifty-two when she died in a small hotel on the Rue Haussmann in February of 1894. There was a nun at her side who reported, as was expected in those days of deathbed converts, that she had become reconciled with God. Gide is said to have remarked in conversation, "Why not? God is a man."

As one admirer wrote, "The vanity of earthly things came home to me as I saw her thinly attended funeral going slowly toward Père Lachaise."

There is no notice if Louis Tiffany sent flowers.

Her epitaph as reported by a journalist wit: "It was said of Léonide that, unlike Napoleon's Old Guard, she always surrendered, and never died."

So between Paris love and his atelier in New York—he hardly would call it a factory—Tiffany was a very busy man. By 1898, he had a stock of five thousand art objects on hand for buyers. Favrile glass was social status indeed, for those who would support the passing modes of art.

By 1909 he was in business in a very big way, establishing the Tiffany Studios where hundreds of girls applied his decor. They were called *craftsmen*, these girls, rather than factory hands, although their pay was hardly more. Glass, bronze, ceramic, enamel, Tiffany used them all on lamps, vases, penwipers, pin trays, stemwear, lighting fixtures, art jewelry, tiaras, necklaces. The precious stone objects he sold through his father's store.

A born hedonist, a cheerful Silenus, his parties in Paris and New York drew international attention. He was a striking looking man with his flaming red Edwardian beard, his frantic gestures; a personality who knew his worth, and knew his desires. He gave great costume fêtes where the flesh of models, international harlots, society women, and the best of the men-about-town, lascivious viewers, rich collectors, and artists met and reveled. His style in all things remained a phenomenon of costly explicitness.

In 1913, aging but still vital and virile, he gave a great Egyptian costume party, turning his studio into the Valley of the Nile. It was not as naughty as his less discreet and private Paris parties, but it was a pleasure to the readers of the world newspapers. "Egyptian beauties, barelegged youths and Pinkerton men in Oriental costumes mingled with hundreds of guests . . . The most lavish costume fête ever seen in New York."

The years approaching the Great War didn't much diminish Tiffany's ideas. With Paris talking of war, of a war drawing close, he gave in memory of his wild times there a Peacock Dinner for his male friends, the rounders, sportsmen, sensualists of his set. Roast peacock was served—in its retrieved feathers—carried in by young girls wearing transparent Greek garments, with the trays of birds carried on their shoulders, all making a colorful procession as they paraded around the table. It was a farewell to the realm of dreams before the guns of August sounded.

He published his own memorial, *The Art Work of Louis C. Tiffany*, in 1914, when as a British statesman said, "The lights are going out all over Europe, we shall not see them relit in our time." His own light was going out as a pioneer maker of expensive decor. Tastes and times were changing in a world of incoherent anguish. He retired to his estate, Laurelton Hall, on Long sland. "A retreat for arists," he called it in 1918, the Louis Comfort Tiffany Foundation. There was, he announced, to be "no formal instruction"—he had been a poor student himself as a youth. He called for "art by absorption."

He was old now, no longer so impulsively engaged. The red beard was white, but well shaped, the sensual fawn's face still ironic as it stares out at us from his last pictures, wise to the divergent art of living. He was no moralist except about art. He had lived his life as he wanted. He had flaunted a grand courtesan as his mistress openly in Paris, with no nod toward respectability. It had not hurt him, he felt. Among his last public words were these: "The most helpful thing I can think of is to show people that beauty is everywhere . . . uplifting . . . health-giving."

Perhaps he was aware that the famous Tiffany shade—some made to hold twenty incandescent bulbs—would degenerate after he was gone into what has been called "a bland cliché for pseudo-elegance."

He would have liked best his Paris dealer Samuel Bing's remark after looking at the master's peacock-feather vase: "This was Nature in her most seductive aspects." Mr. Bing could have said the same of its maker.

Book Three
THE MIDDLE GROUND

CHAPTER 13

U.S. Minister to a Siege— Elihu Washburne

Paris is a sinister Chicago.

J. K. HUYSMANS

How MANY Americans can name Elihu Washburne, friend and confidant of Abraham Lincoln and General Grant, who served eight years as minister to France, who saw the Second Empire fall under Prussian *Schrecklichkeit*, and lived through the murderous Paris siege? He kept his head and emerged as a most heroic, level-headed American. He served his country with honor in a France in tragic and grotesque turmoil, war, revolution; saw the murder, the incredible slaughter of 20,000 Frenchmen by other Frenchmen. Washburne recorded it all in *Recollections of a Minister to France*, where in great detail he put down what it was like to be an American who went to Paris neither to escape American material crudity nor to seek some aberrant pleasure, some vague dreamland in which to create art. His words on leaving Paris give no hint of the dangers he lived through.

On the 10th day of September, 1877, I left Paris for home, going to Le Havre and then taking the steamer to pass over to Southampton where I was to take the German steamer for New York. After a reasonably good passage to New York we reached what was thereafter to be our home at Chicago, on the 23d of September, 1877. It was on the 17th day of March, 1869, that . . . Mr. Hamilton Fish as Secretary of State signed my commission as Minister to France . . . this made my term of service as Minister eight years and a half.

President Grant had appointed him minister in 1869, but not all America approved: "Minister to France, a post to which he may have some qualifications," said *The Nation*, "but *what* they are it would be difficult to say." Secretary of the Navy Gideon Welles wrote: "He may represent correctly the man who appoints him, but is no credit to the country."

Washburne came of a poor family badly served by a bankrupt country store, so that at thirteen he was a hired hand on a farm, then a printer in the style of Franklin. When Washburne developed a hernia, he studied law, a profession that called for no heavy lifting. Law in those days was little more than reading some books and putting up a shingle.

Elihu as a young lawyer opened an office in Galena, Illinois, and came to know—before they became myths—both Lincoln and Grant. Washburne was a Whig congressman and he served sixteen years in Washington. He also got the title of "Watchdog of the Treasury," but the thieves in office managed to pretty nearly carry off the nation anyway. Grant's friends would "steal anything but a red hot stove lid." Both Lincoln and Grant, Washburne's intimate friends, realized he was a man to be trusted. He knew one could abandon possessions but never oneself.

When Grant appointed him minister to France, it may have been to

get the watchdog out of the way. France's Second Empire was a setting sun; its glow and vivacity were fading. The splendor of life Washburne saw at the Tuileries, at Saint Cloud and Compiègne, was about to die in a war brought on by Bismarck.

The Empress Eugénie on her chaise longue, in coiffure and décolletée, dominated a world of fashion and art. The public monuments, the costumes by Worth were but a veneer for a cracking era. The fêtes to the sound of Offenbach and Gounod were to be dirges, the collections of Winterhalter portraits and Delacroix's romantic figures but fading colors. Baron Haussmann had made Paris over as an aesthetic delight, the most beautiful city in the world. He had given it broad boulevards, built the Opéra, landscaped the Bois de Boulogne, lit the streets with over 30,000 gas lamp posts.

Washburne saw the glitter created by a debauched and debilitated emperor and wondered:

The cry of "*Vive l'Empereur*," uttered by the courtiers and parasites, was often heard in the streets and was responded to by a goodly throng in Paris, which, flattered by the counterfeit consideration of the government, dazzled by the glitter of the court, or fattening on the wealth of royalty, abandoned itself to the falsehood of pleasant dreams, and bowed down before the false glory and the material strength of the Empire. . . .

It was on July 28, 1870, that the Emperor left the palace of St. Cloud to take command of the army in person. A gentleman belonging to the Court, who was present at the moment of departure, recounted to me that the occasion was a most solemn one, and that even then there was a prescience that the Emperor was leaving Paris never to return.

By cooking up a fake crisis Bismarck had sucked Napoleon III into a war by which Germany hoped to dominate Europe. Washburne sadly saw the foolish pageant for what it was—the snap of a trap. The Second Empire was destroyed in six weeks of modern apocalyptic fury. The emperor, a sick *bon vivant*, and over 100,000 of his troops surrendered at Sedan. A Republic was set up in Paris; people sang the "Marseillaise," cried "*Vive la République!*" The Germans laid siege to Paris for 130 days. An American dentist, Dr. Evins, practicing in Paris, got the empress out of the Tuileries as a mob came for her, and set her on her way to England. Gone were the *théâtres de société*, amateur plays, and *medianoches*, the midnight suppers.

Bismarck asked Washburne as American minister in Paris to protect German lives and property in Paris. All other ambassadors had fled (as in Morris's day). Every German who could came to Washburne to get a visa to leave France, for he alone represented the Germans now. Gendarmes tried to hold back the 30,000 Germans in Paris from rushing the Embassy. The minister, as he recorded, writing at his mahogany escritoire, was "literally overwhelmed." He took on mobs of 3,000 a day. He did a remarkable job of getting train transport for 10,000 Germans and gave financial aid to 3,000.

In September Washburne announced that the United States accepted the fall of Napoleon III and would be the first nation officially to recognize the new Republic. The Embassy was cheered by French crowds crying *"Vive l'Amérique!"* and Washburne was kissed by males and females alike. All this, he reported, made him weak "as an Indian's dog which had to lean against a tree to bark."

The Republic's reward for recognition was to plant heavy tax levies against American property in Paris, property then worth ten million dollars. Washburne, resolute and firm when it came to money, had that idea revoked. It was a time when even at home Americans took up arms against taxes.

The Prussians held Paris under heavy siege. A food shortage was the major problem (with the Germans bringing up the Krupp cannon against the ancient gates). The fresh meat ration officially was one sixteenth of a pound a day, but there was hardly any fresh meat except for the rich. The black market made millionaires, the weak began to die. Some people of means had pity and helped. The fine Rothschild coach horses were sold to make steaks and soups. Horse, mule meat at two dollars a pound was grabbed up. Cats, rats ("two francs a rat"), dogs dressed in French style hung in butcher shops. The Paris zoo was a meat mine as the city's famed cuisine changed to wolf, antelope, elephant, and kangaroo. All went into chops and stews, but no one could stand to eat the gamy lion and tiger filets. Camel Kidney was a specialty at the Boucherie Anglaise for a short time. The Café Voisin listed *"Chat accompagné de rats."* Debility, lassitude, great hunger stalked the city.

On January 1, 1871, the Germans, guns in position, began to bombard the city. The American Embassy was hit by shellfire, one shell exploding twenty feet from Washburne. He was unhurt and wrote: "Four months of siege today, and where has all this time gone? It seems to me as if I had been buried alive."

The secretary of the legation recalled, "If we heard of any part of Paris where shells were likely to burst and bullets to whistle, Washburne was sure to have important business in that direction."

The Republic had to get news of the outer world in by pigeon and balloon. (Two Americans manned a balloon, the *George Sand*.) Washburne got his daily London papers in diplomatic pouches, but he gave them up as mobs gathered, wanting to know the news from *outside*. A Parisian journal said, "We gave you Lafayette and Rochambeau, in return for which we only ask for one copy of an English paper." Washburne's porter was offered a thousand-franc bribe for a paper. The Minister felt that "it is too much to me to have the news for two millions of people."

On the one hundred thirty-first day of siege an armistice took place. Thirty thousand German troops paraded in proud mechanical step through Paris; Germans lack tact and feelings for a loser's heartbreak (Hitler was to reenact the tasteless, humiliating scene in 1941). Washburne observed Paris seemed "literally to have died out. There was neither song nor shout in all her streets. The whole population was marching about as if under a cloud of oppression. The gas was not yet lighted, and the streets presented a sinister and sombre aspect. All the butcher and barber shops in that part of the city occupied by the Germans were closed, and if the people had not provided themselves for the emergency, there would have been an increase of suffering. The Bourse was closed . . . no newspapers appeared on that day except the Journal Official. No placards were posted upon the walls of Paris."

The citizens of Paris rose in revolt against the hard terms and proclaimed a new government, the Commune. It was made up of most of the liberal political parties, from the moderate Republicans to the Jacobins and Socialists. Karl Marx, sitting on his boils and carbuncles in London at the British Museum, raised his hand in benediction. However, communism as we know it today did not exist. The Commune began as mildly socialist. The National Guard joined the citizens of Paris. The reactionary royalists called it rebellion. Civil war began between the people of Paris and the monied French who had moved their government to Versailles. Washburne was again left in Paris, as umpire now between two warring parties, doing his best to calm both sides as he hurried from one French government to the other. He saw that business, industry, labor, enterprise were

all buried in one common grave; and all was devastation, desolation and ruin. The physiognomy of the city became more and more sad. All the upper part of the Champs Elysées and all that portion of the city surrounding the Arc de Triomphe continued to be deserted through fear of the shells . . . In going from my residence to the legation, it seemed as if I were passing through a city of the dead. There was not a carriage, and hardly a human being in the streets. Immense barricades were going up. The great manufactories and the workshops were closed. The vast stores, where were to be found the wonders and marvels of Parisian industry, were no longer open. The cafés were closed at ten o'clock in the evening. The gas was extinguished, and Paris, without its brilliantly lighted cafés and with its thronging multitudes on the sidewalks, was no longer Paris.

Civil war is the most deadly, illogical war of all, where man is wolf to man, as has been proved in America, in Russia, in Germany, in Spain, in Africa. Hatred for one's brother was to become in our century more evil and deadly even than hatred for an outside enemy. The Versaillists began to brutally bombard Paris, their own magnificent city, killing French men, women, and children. The Communards—action creates reaction—began to execute hostages in retaliation. Four hundred eighty people were shot, including the Archbishop of Paris. As in the Dreyfus case the Church in France sided with the reactionaries. Magnanimity, compassion do not exist in civil war, as Washburne sadly knew.

When in May the Versaillists, who had lost France to the Germans, advanced on Paris, the city was put to the torch by the Communard fire squads. The Louvre was saved, but the Tuileries and the Hôtel de Ville were burned down. Martyrdoms were as easy to get as cobblestones. Revenge took over. The Commune, after seventy-two days, was destroyed with brutal directness. The terrible vengeance of what was now the government was bestial. Horror and anguish were witnessed by Washburne. Twenty thousand citizens of Paris, Communards or not, were seized and executed, including many women and children. As only officials of the Commune were supposed to carry watches, an army general ordered "any citizens of Paris seized with a timepiece to be shot at once."

The people were forgotten, the bullet holes filled in. By September of 1877, Washburne was going home. He refused the French honor, the testimonials the government offered for his services. Horror would serve to remind him of Paris. He was very tired of the use of terror as an effective instrument of action. At home the American Secretary of State announced, "Washburne is entitled to all the honor his friends may wish to confer upon him . . . No compliment can be paid him that I would not join in."

In 1880 it seemed as if Washburne would have a shoo-in for the Republican Presidential nomination. But Grant wanted a third term, why no one could understand. "He never used his other two terms in office." His term in the White House was a time of the most evil and corrupt looting of public resources and the Treasury until Harding came along. Grant himself did not profit personally by any of the disgraceful business of his two terms, but he knew what was going on and how his friends were using him. He was a great man, corrupted by his late success in life; he wanted social position and had the political sense of a sloth.

At the convention Grant could not get the delegates for nomination. On the thirty-sixth ballot, Washburne, left high and dry by Grant's delegates, was defeated by James Garfield. There was talk that Grant—in a dog-in-the-manger manner—had double-crossed Washburne. Grant's son, "a jackass," called Elihu Washburne a "liar and a fraud." A long friendship was destroyed. Washburne and Grant never spoke to each other again.

There was nothing left for the two old men but to retire and write their memoirs. Grant's is a literary masterpiece. Washburne's story of his eight years in Paris is a fine honest document, well worth bringing back into the light, the story of an American in Paris when the city, in terminal crisis, stood siege, was burned, saw civil conflict, and feebly recovered an unsteady political pattern which curses France to this day. Washburne had read Emerson: "Society is everywhere in conspiracy . . . whoever would be a man, must be a nonconformist."

Few Americans in Paris during the mid-nineteenth century and later ever saw the other side of the life of the city. An unsigned report gives us a picture of that world:

The galleries or *passages* running through the heart of old Paris . . . reconstruct a complete material and psychological inscape. In these galleries the *flâneur* had his privileged terrain. Here could be harvested the vast output of gossip, erotic and political innuendo, argo, of which the *feuilletonistes* created their new art. The display of goods in the covered arcades and in the new emporia of the Second Empire made of Paris an Aladdin's cave of mature capitalism. In the music of Offenbach Parisian society found the perfect expression of its own feverish, partly ironic, partly entranced pulse of life. Yet, at the same time, the shimmering Babylon, as so many poets and publicists called it, engendered new savageries of destitution. Under the opulent surface ran currents of hunger, of alcoholism, of sweated labour in great *ateliers* and factories. In the night world of *la ville lumière* during the 1860s, extremes of wealth and of desolation jostled each other on pavements made both magical and ghostly by the introduction of gas lighting.

It was the world of Hugo, Sue, and the naturalistic novels of Zola. Some Americans could read them in the original French. A young American, Frank Norris, studying painting in Paris was so impressed by naturalism in fiction he rushed home to San Francisco to write an American Zolaesque novel about a dentist, *McTeague*.

But the American artist, like the American tourist, in the main avoided the sordid side of Paris.

CHAPTER 14

Daughter of the Robber Baron

*France is the land where dalliance is so
passionately understood.*

ARNOLD BENNETT

J AY GOULD, frail, tubercular, was "one of the greatest thieves that America produced." He and Jim Fisk nearly wrecked the American gold reserves on Black Friday. They captured and ruined the Erie railroad system. Gould destroyed the savings of enough widows and other unlucky, foolish investors to fill a thousand melodramas as the evil mastermind of his time. He was without mercy, morals, or any prodigious human feelings.

Gould was one of the first to have part of his vast, tainted wealth fall into the hands of a titled European fortune hunter, to have a daughter exploited, humiliated by a titled *flâneur* (a time-passer) working at a leisurely pace.

Comte Boniface de Castellane was no ordinary parasite. He had a reputation as a womanizer among the courtesans and grand cocottes, the *petites femmes*, as a man whose pleasures in the boudoir were nearly his life's work. However, the mamas of respectable girls of good families saw him as the prince of the aristocracy, the prime matrimonial catch. But the count's eyes were on the dowry of Jay Gould's daughter, Anna. It came to a fine $15,000,000, no matter what liaisons and adulteries the count left behind him. "My ancestors exercised the prerogative of coining money . . . I thought it would be fascinating to complete her education in the best finishing school—marriage."

There was, of course, one blemish—the fact that Anna was not a particularly attractive girl. Contemporary reports pictured her as having a pallid, fish-belly white skin, features simple and plain with no hint of charm, abominable eyebrows, thick as caterpillars and meeting over an unattractive nose. It would be cruel to go on with this inventory based on those who knew her; but everyone noticed her stringy arms were covered with fuzzy hair that reached up to her shoulders. Poor Anna. She had already been rejected as a bride by a fortune-hunting English marquis of some aesthetic sensibility, with the report, "That girl will never be fool enough to marry anyone who'd be fool enough to marry her."

Count Boni was pure *Almanac de Gotha* stock, one of the handsomest men to walk the boulevards of *tout Paris*, a Castellane, a blond "Apollo in morning coat," on his head a topper called a *haut de forme*, a gold-topped ivory cane in well-gloved hands. A dandy coming from a wedding at Saint Philippe du Roule, sniffing his carnation in buttonhole, or from a baptism at Sainte Clothilde. Or more likely engaged with some courtesan on a chaise longue or at a gay soirée or delivering some Boissier bonbons to the ballerinas in the Foyer de Danse of the Opéra. His was already a busy life—and now to handle fifteen million American dollars.

"Beauty and the Beast," as one malicious witness put it, were married in 1894. He was twenty-seven, she eighteen. They settled in Paris with the American fortune. Boni was not a hoarder and he spent his wife's wealth lavishly, with grace and show. He had a lapidary glow in buying. He showed his merit as a party giver by throwing a fête hardly ever matched when the Countess Anna was twenty-one.

He took over the *Tire aux Pigeons* in the Bois ("The Bois is not a woods but a garden of women"), built a stage to hold the dancers of half the theaters in Paris. There were two hundred musicians to offer a score to the entire *corps de ballet* of the Opéra, hired for the event. The place was made light by eighty thousand Venetian lanterns, the ground padded by fifteen kilometers of red velvet (a kilometer is nearly two thirds of a mile).

To add more light six hundred lackeys in royal-red livery were hired, each to hold up a flaming torch. The birthday party itself was produced in two parts. First just a dinner *intime* for two hundred and fifty guests, then a big fête for three thousand people to enjoy a ballet at lakeside, grand fireworks, all climaxed by the release of two hundred frightened swans. These birds banged their way over the heads of the guests to splash into the lake.

Anna seemed numb and lost in all this jamboree, her looks not improved by a coiffure by Lentheric, a Pacquin gown on her wraithlike figure. She must have wondered, as one guest viewing the scene noted, "Why the French Revolution hadn't cut off more heads."

Boni, in the intoxication of money, lived high on the Gould loot. One valet woke him, another robed him, a blue-clad, gold-buttoned footman brought him coffee and brioche. A silent discreet barber came to scrape smooth the blond cheeks, and for that queasy feeling a masseur worked slack muscles back into firmness; after all, sometimes there had been husbandly ardors in the night—he was to produce two heirs from the stringy body of Anna. All this besides servicing his Paris harem. His toenails were painted a Du Barry pink by a Chinese pedicure, as if acting in a travesty of social satire. Waiting were his free-loaders, and the tailor, shirtmaker, bootmaker. Also a few sharklike art dealers; he was a sucker for their glib talk.

As there was gossip in salon and café that Anna was Jewish (not true), Boni also dabbled with the arch anti-Semite, the artist Forain (of whom Degas said, "Forain found his talent by picking my pockets"), in reactionary Catholic politics. He lacked any psychological depths; was the entire man when on parade or in bed.

When the count came to write his memoirs, he expressed his dislike of the world he had been forced to live in: "Faced with an uncomprehending middle class society, I went back to the past, and there made for myself a life of glorious pageantry consisting of beautiful women and splendid spectacles . . . so I consoled myself . . . out of an urgent need for beauty and a dislike for the world that surrounds me."

For some, resurrected ideals may turn sour, but the count did well in a distasteful world. He built a palace on the Avenue du Bois, the Palais Rose, of pink marble from the quarry from which the Sun King built the Grand Trianon. The Palais Rose was inspired by that structure. Boni's friends pointed out that the count's place was even more impressive, but then, "Boni has more money than Louis XIV." The fastidiousness of fifty generations marinated in noblity showed in daring taste.

There was to be only candlelight, not M. Edison's glaring Mazdas. Said Boni, "Between an electric light and a candle is the difference between a glass eye and a real eye." There was a private theater to hold five hundred, a railroad-station-sized ballroom, salons with Gobelin hangings, paintings of the count's grand taste, rare furniture that made collectors' mouths water. He showed it all off, pointing a cane with a meerschaum handle, gold ferrule.

Boni had his own suite of rooms, Anna her private quarters. There was set aside, however, a bedroom with a huge linen field of canopied bed, where Boni did his husbandly duties with tired facetiousness when he felt he had to contribute his mite to all those millions.

Boni's aunt, a harsh, wise old bird, was not impressed by all this show and grandeur. As the Comtesse de Bealincourt, she, seeing the palace for the first time could only remark: "My nephew and his wife must march up their grand staircase with peacock feathers stuck up their asses." Her comment loses nothing in translation.

Boni's not too discreet and subtle affairs with his odalisques went on. Women had spoiled Boni, and now the American millions gave him a sense of sensual fantasy. He grew to like not merely the good life but the fantastic, exacerbated life, as if trying to see how much of Jay Gould's treasure he could get rid of.

"Before I give a party, I just open the windows and toss out all the money I have." The remark is Baudelairean, but behind it is the scream of a man aware of the futility of all human endeavor.

Boni was a man who was to be seen at the elegant, exclusive clubs; the Jockey, the Agricole, the Travellers, the Cercle de la Rue Royale. He was a charter member of the world of dalliance, *galanterie*; and a pretty bodice or a gown cut *décolletée à la baignoire*, a face under a Reboux hat, aroused his sense of sex as a sport. The theologians of Freud would too easily label him a latent homosexual proving his manhood. He was the typical *boulevardier*, taking time out for a bit of fornication as easily as for an aperitif.

He paid no attention to the serious problems of the world, unless it was to the stock market to see if his father-in-law's money was safe. *Liberté-Egalité-Fraternité* he thought too vulgar to place on public buildings. He would as soon have supported the Third Republic as ride with the common folk in the Impériale, the double-decker omnibus drawn by three huge Percherons, the true friends of the city's sparrows. He might have been amused by Anatole France's line: "There is justice for all. It is just as much against the law for the rich as for the poor to sleep under the bridges of Paris."

Boni was a profoundly dedicated man, fully committed. He lived life as seen through a woman's garter, or the *flûte* of Veuve Clicquot. He had wit and the irony to see the comedy of all those American millions to spend for his amusement. He could agree with La Rochefoucauld's maxims: "If we had no faults, we should not find so much enjoyment in seeing faults in others" and "You can find women who have never had a love affair, but seldom women who have had only one."

Anna had to submit to the christening of their palace by the Curé of

Saint Honoré d'Eylau, assisted by two priests and a choir of thirty (Anna never became a Catholic). Candles lit up hundreds of chandeliers and that grand staircase that had annoyed the aunt now held on each step a lackey with a lit taper in a gold candlestick.

The guests—of ancient lineage or social caricature—marched up to be announced by the Swiss butler, Clement. At the top waited Anna and Boni, backed by a fifty piece orchestra and singers who gave out with laconic voice such Bourbon Royalist songs as *"Vive Henri Quatre!"*

Of the two children Anna insisted the first be named after her father, who even in Paris was "the notorious Jay Gould."

Boni shouted with an explosive hostility, "My heir will *not* be named after a thief!"

Anna replied logically, "Yet you don't mind taking the thief's money."

Boni could only shrug at the bourgeois answer. He bought two châteaux, a villa at Deauville, where his valet tested the sea water with a thermometer for temperature before Boni put a toe in. There was also a three-masted 1600-ton auxiliary-engined yacht, the *Walhalla*.

The lugubrious fall of the Comte Boni de Castellane from all this splendor was to be sudden. He had, of course, not given up his collection

of whores and courtesans, or the adultery with weak-willed wives of others. One wit suggested "his coat-of-arms should include the *penis erectus*."

Anna never really became a stylish *Parisienne*, even though she tried the new style of *le fif o'clock tea*, a fashionable British import, wore hand-kerchief-linen underwear embroidered with *fleur de lis* (the Castellanes were true blue Royalists down to the skin). With pathetic tenacity she donned feathered peignoirs for a husband who had dined late at Voisin's and spent the best of the night in a courtesan's bed or visited the Quartier Mouffetard for serious debauchery. She could not properly ride at the Rambouillet Hunt, or drive a tallyho like another American in Paris, the publisher James Gordon Bennett.

Doubts of Boni's conduct were with her as he and she rode through the Bois in a *calèche* Daumont (four horses pulling in single file), two postil-ions mounted and two footmen in cherry-colored livery seated on tiger seats behind. All eyes were on Boni—who held artifice above nature—in white frock coat, white top hat, gloved hand waving an ivory cane in greeting. For Anna no gentlemen rode as *escorte d'honneur* as they did for some other women. There were no lovers in her life from among the officers of the *Chasseurs à Cheval*. She sat, unhappy in her inflexible bastion of a corset, had her portrait done by Boldoni and by Helleu, tried to read the gossip of *Figaro* and *Gaulois*. She had, poor woman, no *panache*—as the *Parisiennes* called dash.

There were so many of these rich American heiresses in Europe, most of them unhappy, riding out in their coach or early Panhard, Dion, or Mercedes, wondering if perhaps the tattered tramps of both sexes—the *clochards*, under the bridges of Paris—were not happier.

Anna retained an untrammeled innocence on certain matters. She had held tight to that early American idea that a husband did not sleep with other women, but attended to his animal needs in the big family double-bed. This joyless doctrine, of course, amused fashionable Paris. In their ranks vice had become a social ritual.

Anna brought over a handsome young detective from America. She introduced him as a "well-known Virginia gentleman of fine family." (She had inherited Jay Gould's tricky ways.) Boni was delighted to show the Virginian the sin spots, the joy girls of a decadent reveler. He intro-duced him to mistresses past and present, even exposed some delightful love letters full of extravagant clichés as to his sexual powers.

The result of all the facts presented to her and her lawyers was that Anna got a divorce in 1906. Out of the pink palace went Boni with only a few bundles of clothes; the money tree cut down, all the châteaux taken from him. His high-flying days were over, and he was not one to settle for prudence and decorum. He became the tout for art and antique dealers, steering foolish or eager Americans and others into shops and galleries, and getting in return a small commission. He did have some capacity for stoicism in his shabby new situation.

As for Anna, she did not return to America, but married Boni's cousin, Duke Helie de Sagan de Périgord, in 1909. At least *that*—the gossip said— "keeps all that money in the family." At times Boni's friends would take the moneyless fellow to Maxims for a feed. Once when Boni was eating there, in walked his cousin, Helie. Boni shrugged, said to his friends, "Ah, yes, the Duke. We both did service in the same army corps."

CHAPTER 15

And a Few Others

To be able to fill leisure intelligently is
the last product of civilization.

BERTRAND RUSSELL

IF ANNA GOULD never enjoyed to the full *"Le Hig Leaf"* (as the fancy steppers of French society called the High Life) or marrying into French nobility of rigid social genealogy, there were American girls who did. Clara Ward came from Detroit, Michigan, where a mechanic named Henry Ford was soon to be tinkering with a motor car for the masses. Clara married Prince Caraman-Chimay, moved on to enjoy the demimonde set, went marauding about to hear the Montmartre *chansoniers*, was blatantly frank in admiring the courtesans called the *dégrafées*, the "unbuttoned." Clara was seen with the best top hats at Auteuil, or watching polo at Bagatelle, even reported on skates at the Palais de Glace or waving to the Prince of Wales eating lobster at Paillard's.

One would expect of her that a setting in the dizzy whirl of the *art nouveau* group at Maxim's with Boldi's orchestra playing *Frou-frou* would be a satisfactory, settled condition of life. Then suddenly Clara eloped with the gypsy violinist Rige, a wild, tempestuous affair. Still later Clara, the exhilarated Princess Caraman-Chimay, was featured in the Folies Bergères in daring "Plastic Poses," wearing pink tights.

The most exciting Americans Maxim's ever saw were a troupe of American Indians, Sioux and Apache, a Wild West Show, playing at the *Cirque d'hiver*, brought into Maxim's en masse by a Dutch Baron Paland.

They rushed in wearing war paint, feathers, and waving tomahawks. The Baron ordered cigars and champagne for everybody. Cornuche, the manager, had to ask them to leave; there was talk of taking scalps as the hostiles took on the bubbly firewater.

An American, known today only as Mr. L, used to perform a ceremony in Maxim's he called "The Liturgy of the Golden Calf," a blasphemous drama in which he lined up all the help of Maxim's, from captains of tables to the lowly bus boys. Then Mr. L, carrying high a ritual platter on which were stacks of gold coins, would march down the line with the solemn pace of a bishop or cardinal, and stop before each member of the staff. He would have him stick out his tongue and then would place a gold coin on it, making the sign of the cross with his free hand. It was the time when the mines in the American west were making millionaires in the last great goldstrikes. So perhaps Mr. L was a California agnostic, thinking of starting his own version of a godhead; one based solidly on the gold standard rather than on dogma and theology.

Mr. Todd (first name not on record) was from New York. But he lacked Mr. L's imagination. He merely tossed handfuls of *louis d'or* around the place like sowing Kansas corn, and laughed as the help, the *demi-castors*

(whores who, like beavers—*castors* in French—use their tails in their work) scrambled for the gold coins, kicking, scratching, and screaming as they dived and hunted. Some called all this the luxury of stylized despair, the breakdown of Judeo-Christian absolutes. Most just thought of it as foolish American fun.

Tipping was done with more manners and a touch of grace by some, or with a flashy "what-the-hell, they're only French" grin. James Gordon Bennett, owner of the Paris *Herald,* was known to tip a flower girl, if he was in the mood, five hundred francs for a bunch of violets. It was a reaction to a hard pioneer past, perhaps—of the memory of "Heavenly Father, bless us, and keep us all alive; there's ten of us to dinner, and only enough for five."

The most thrilling experience a raw, rich American male could have was to take an actress or *courtisane* to a *cabinet particulier*—one of those private, discreet dining rooms where low lights, sofas, candles, and a locked door made the finely honed Puritan sense of sin a sauce for the night's adventure. At the Café Anglais there was the notorious *Grand Seize,* a private dining nook "reserved exclusively for royalty," a divanned alcove with décor of white, gold, and red. But an American millionaire did manage to have it for a night with the grand horizontal, Caroline Otero, better known to the trade as La Belle Otero.

Of course, not all Americans in Paris hunted vice. Many like William Dean Howells and Mark Twain were in Paris with their families, and while they may have sniffed the ilang-ilang scent and studied chinchilla wraps, they went to see the museum pictures, taste new dishes in banquets, hire an eight-spring landau to go and admire the beauty of the chestnut trees on the wide boulevards.

It is perhaps to be regretted that the American newspapers had sensational Sunday magazine sections that featured with lurid illustrations the doings of rich Americans in Europe. Actually hundreds of thousands of Americans spent their most exciting moments writing postal cards, and their worst shock was to discover the natives spoke a different brand of French than that taught in Newark, New Jersey, high schools.

"All Americans in print are too gentle, too affectionate, too fulsome. The reality requires a satirist, merciless but just." So wrote George Santayana on Americans abroad. But he did not read Mr. Hearst's Sunday newspapers, and he was a snob about Americans, and a philosopher who saw contemporary history, at its peak, as merely the will to seek the renewal of ideas and patterns best abandoned.

The average American followed Mark Twain's readers' simple ideas:

the French talk funny, eat frogs, and don't bathe. One shouldn't trust the water, and all French women can become spectacles of depravity. The sheets were cleaner in St. Louis, and John L. Sullivan could lick Napoleon "one hand tied behind his back."

～

Almost nothing has been put into print about the close encounter of the very moral American philosopher, Ralph Waldo Emerson, with two notorious Parisian whores, the grand cocottes Caroline Letessier and Caroline Hasse. It was during the dying days of the Second Empire when the Franco-Prussian war had resulted in the dreadful siege of Paris, at the end of which the French middle and upper classes would execute 20,000 Parisians by firing squads.

The two prostitutes, escaping from the siege, went to England. In London they got in touch with a certain undergraduate of Magdalen College, Oxford, who had known the women and enjoyed their skill in Paris, where his parents lived. He felt a desire for their company and invited the two Carolines to visit Oxford, as two of his "French cousins." Settling in at the Randolph Hotel, the women were entertained at teas and lunches at Magdalen. An earnest young don, a divine, began to pulse with wild-eyed love for Caroline Letessier, declaring publicly his passion for one of the "dainty girls." A contemporary historian of the period wrote: "If he had seen her as I did a few months before throwing plates at the head of Lord Charles Hamilton in a *cabinet particulier* he *might* have hesitated."

Ralph Waldo Emerson was in Europe; he had been visiting Henry James and was the guest of the somber Dean of Christ College. The Dean also was charmed by the girls and he invited them to meet, among others, the leading professor of Greek, the father of the original Alice in Wonderland (how delighted Lewis Carroll would have been by this strange tea party had he known), and, of course, the Dean's American guest, Mr. Emerson of Concord, Massachusetts. At the lunch at Christ Church Mr. Emerson was delighted with the company of the bright and charming young whores, who knew how to entertain at table. Emerson escorted the girls to a garden party that followed the lunch. There on the Deanery lawn the girls played a polite game of croquet to the cheers of Emerson and Sir William Harcourt, among others. Sir William was very amused, for he had bought the professional services of the two girls in Paris at their going rate, and here they were in the citadel of the Church of England itself. The girls also recognized their dear "Sir Willie," but it seemed best for Sir William and the two Carolines to play out the game of being total strangers to each other—in true Victorian decorum.

Emerson left for America, never to know he had held the hands and exchanged table talk with two of the most notorious Paris whores of their time. As for the "somewhat tempestuous" undergraduate, who had invited his "French cousins" to Oxford, in later years he was "one of the most respected members of society, and identified with clerical and religious matters."

Perhaps Nietzsche was right when he wrote: "Emerson is one who lives instinctively on ambrosia, and leaves everything indigestible on his plate."

CHAPTER 16

The Shy Master—
Henry James

*The great thing is to be saturated with something—
that is, in one way or another, with life: and I
chose the form of my saturation.*

HENRY JAMES

I N NOVEMBER, 1875, there lived at No. 29 Rue de Luxembourg (now Rue
Cambon) a Mr. James, a balding, bearded American of thirty-two.
He was not yet the Henry James of the future London tea parties, a diner-
outer, nor the international literary figure of today, the favorite of professors and deep-thinking critics. He still saw himself as the child of fatality
and chance, as a writer of some small success. "Henry James writes fiction
as if it were a painful duty," said Oscar Wilde. Acting the part of enormous self-complacency, he was under contract to write a series of letters
of Parisian life for the New York *Tribune*.

The district where he lived was still at the time residential, with many
high garden walls and private, curtained-off family life. James had a third-
floor flat that consisted of a parlor, two bedrooms, a foyer that could do
duty with no qualms as a dining room, and a cosy kitchen with shiny
casseroles on the walls. The furniture was chosen with care, and the
assortment of clocks and drapes, mirrors, lamps, and romantic twisted
candlesticks showed that a sensitive soul was in residence.

Below James's windows the cab horses banged their hoofs to their
patron of the hackney cab, Saint Fiacre, as they waited for trade. James
would watch for the morning parade of the troop of cuirassiers clopping
by, breastplates polished, plumes high, as the riders trotted toward the
barracks set up by one of the ministries on the Place Vendôme. James's

rent was sixty-five dollars a month, the porter got six dollars more to do the little errands and duties needed by a bachelor-apartment-dweller. In the proper Jamesian style of pompous clarity he noted, "When I reflect upon my last winter's disbursement in New York, it is remarkably cheap." He was a bit hard up for funds, nothing to really worry him, but he had splurged a bit on his wardrobe in London (he disliked haggling with tradespeople). His woodpile, kept in the kitchen, would cost five dollars and his linens two dollars a month. He was meticulous in money matters and tended to panic (gracefully) when he thought of austerity that could become poverty.

He was writing a novel, *The American,* about a man from the United States in Europe, a sort of innocent with conventions of honor and morality, and James noted the magazine *Revue des Deux Mondes* had translated his story "The Last of the Valerii" (without permission). It was nice to be read in French; pride could be such an imbecile indulgence. As a writer of a series of letters for America, James was acting out the journalist seeking material, and he paid a visit to the noted Russian writer, Ivan Turgenev, living on the Rue de Douai. The house belonged to Pauline Viardot, a singer of some fame, who had borne the Russian writer a daughter. In the proper gloomy Russian mood the house held a ménage of lover, husband, and child, also mistress and other assorted characters. Turgenev's mature years were spent following the singer from city to city in one of those murky, tragic, over-romantic love affairs, not satisfactory, but yet not unrewarding.

Henry James, whose sexual conditioning and responses were to remain a bit mysterious, must have been intrigued. His story-seeking sense was on perpetual vigilance. James was attempting to make himself a serious novelist, and the short Mr. James and the over-tall, white-haired Russian met as artists of words. They spoke, James remembered, "on a variety of subjects." Most likely of other writers, for the Russian offered to introduce the American to the giant of French letters, Gustave Flaubert, and also to George Sand.

For a Russian, fifty years of age, Turgenev had a certain *penchant à la tristesse,* continually seeing life as a pack of Tarot cards. He could speak English, and the two men got along well for they were both sheltered sons of well-to-do parents, given to art. Also in a way James may have been searching for a European father figure, for he was one of those exiles from home, made so under strange conditions. He was seeking a place to send down roots. James at that time thought Paris was the city he could become a part of, which, with elegant precision, would fit his mood.

The two writers met at the café on the Avenue de L'Opéra for *déjeuner,* a place where dominoes were played and café habitués downed the deadly absinthe. The American came to one of Madame Viardot's Thursday musicals. Sunday was saved for charades and games. Madame was as "ugly as eyes on the side of her head and an interminable upper lip can make her, and yet also handsome." Yes and no; James, as always, was on the defense against women. For him the path of thought on women never led to action.

In December of 1875 the Russian writer took James to meet Flaubert and Guy de Maupassant who was in training as a writer. Maupassant was already one of the sexual marvels of Paris, moving to a syphilitic's short, mad life. There was also present dumpy, near-sighted Emile Zola, already on the first volume of the Rougon-Macquart series. The American was meeting with the giants of French letters, the first team, the realists. He was with the great Russian, and the talk was of naturalism, the science of mankind.

There is no doubt that James was shocked. For his pastiche view of life, of morals and manners, social settings, besides his own inner secrets, life just ran too strong and raw in the new circle of feisty, sensual men he

now found himself with. Their language was a penitential scourging to him. And of Edmond de Goncourt James had heard whispered talk of a journal with all its filthy, voluptuous tales and gossip about everyone. James's serenity was blurred by talk of *succès de scandale*.

These Frenchmen were charming talkers, James admitted, but what was one to make of young Maupassant, this Norman giant and notorious cocksman, who was talking of writing a story of a "whore-house *de province*" ("*La Maison Tellier*")? And what of Zola, who confided to James he was making a huge collection of street obscenities, grafitti, the *gros mots* of the filthy lower classes for his novel *L'Assommoir*, soon to start its serial run in a magazine. One of the remarkable features of that novel would be the true, sordid details of drunkards. Hardly a tale likely to bring comfort to the finicky, well-raised Mr. James, who was trying to be a stern and stoical moralist.

James began to wonder if the literary life he wanted was this Paris writers' scene. Would he enjoy, even accept, being a permanent part of it all? And what if these lusty gossips probed into his private life, these flamboyant, womanizing, sensual men with their stories of seductions, lusts, pronging of housemaids, governesses, the exchange of information on mistresses. Worst of all, it was no secret about the literary and art worlds' infection by venereal disease. Taints were clearly marked already in Flaubert, Daudet, and others, and Maupassant was to die a raving madman from syphilitic degeneration.

James considered places of refuge. Where to go next? Rome? Florence? the Low Countries? A search for German *Gemütlichkeit*? England? James had tried them all. He'd soon be forty, and he had not yet broken through into popularity, been accepted seriously as a writer.

What was he doing in Paris? Writing letters for a New York newspaper, hardly pleased with his results (nor were they). Where was the color, the fun, the elegant atmosphere, that flavor, like a herb sauce, of the inside life of the French? His editor was asking for something James lacked: skin-to-skin contact with life.

He had been born in New York City in April of 1843, a year after his brother William. The family was three generations away from Ireland and its fey Celtic charm. The father, after making a fortune, turned to Swedenborg's mysticism and the radical politics of Fourier. They traveled. The James family, children and all, spent as much time in Europe as in America; a consuming yet disenchanting passion for knowledge drove them. They were cosmopolites; Henry was educated in private schools in Paris, London, Geneva. He grew up a bit snobbish about Americans in trade, frontiersmen, fur traders, cotton merchants. At fourteen, pretty, soft, dreamy, a veneer of decorum, he began to write novels and plays. It was at the age of eighteen that a mystery, a scalding cataclysm entered his life. Helping to put out a fire at Newport, James suffered what he called, "Horrid even if obscure hurt." By that strange statement some have said he meant he had been castrated by the fire, or made impotent by scar tissue. Some have also seen this as the reason for ending so many of his stories with death. "Castration, or fear of castration, is supposed to preoccupy the mind with ideas of suicide and death." Certainly Ernest Hemingway, who admitted to periods of impotence and whose hero in *The Sun Also Rises* has lost a vital part of his genitalia in the war, fits the pattern by writing about death in many forms, and ended his own life in an extraterrestrial forlornness that the average man is spared.

There are, of course, other ideas of James's true injuries; one is that he developed a severe back strain, caused by a psychological and physiolog- ical trauma tied to his father image (his father also was not a whole man; he had lost a leg in a fire). Whatever it was it seems to have warped or curtailed James's sex life. It is certain he used the back injury, mental or real, to avoid fighting a young American's part in the Civil War. He was afraid of the physical side of life, looking as he did slightly effeminate before the beard grew in. He would avoid a confrontation of any sort if he could. He refused to sign a letter of American and British authors protesting the harsh legal and jail treatment of Oscar Wilde after his conviction by hypocritical Victorian morality.

James's wandering in Europe, after he escaped taking part in the Civil War, did not bring peace after all; he saw Europe as an earthly but most wicked paradise. Europe was to him in those early days "a place for the moral destruction of the innocent New Worlders who visit it, the returning puritans who have no idea of the world from which their ancestors have departed." As for his writing, "I aspire to write in such a way that it would be impossible . . . to say I am at a given moment an American writing about England, or an Englishman writing about America . . . far from being ashamed of such an ambiguity, I should be exceedingly proud of it." Some say this is nonsense; James was always a benign American talker among the teacups and the better gentlemen's clubs of England, a facsimile of those he aped. He hunted a haven, but had read Baudelaire: "*Quand partons-nous vers le bonheur?* When shall we set out towards happiness?"

James never married, although he made coy public gestures of no great strength in shy appraisals of his attitudes toward one or two women he was sure would reject him. He was actually a homosexual, who perhaps most of his life was not physically engaged, but as he grew older, became more and more passionately friendly with sensitive young men who were practicing homosexuals. Such a friend was the novelist Hugh Walpole, whom he touted as one of the coming masters of English letters.

James's stories of terror among children border on the perverted. Somehow James's timid reactions, his fears of life, led him to picture himself in his fiction as a small girl among more masterful males. He wrote of "emerging out of a personal healing process . . . the dear old blessed, healing, consoling way."

All this private squirming under the cover of the clubman, the week-end guest at aristocratic mansions he loved so well, was it the actor becoming the part, the tea-table mandarin? James as he aged had affectionate friendships with younger men, like the author and publisher, Woolcott Balestier, to whom Kipling also was emotionally attached. Some of them—notably "Beloved little Hugh" Walpole—were of acknowledged homosexual bias. There is a story by Somerset Maugham of an advance by Walpole to James, an advance repulsed, according to one version with "*Si vieillesse pouvait!*" For the most part these acolytes aspired to write and used bemused Henry James as an aid to getting into the literary scene.

The romance of his life was an aspiring young American sculptor, Hendrik Anderson. James and Anderson shared the same Christian name, were born in the same month. In James's conscious or subconscious was the fact that the middle-aged author and the youthful sculptor were both second sons, overshadowed by older brothers. James had written a parable, "The Great Good Place," about an author who dreams of retreat into a monastic community and is restored to life by an admiring acolyte. James conceived for the young sculptor an "affectionate friendship," a friendship expressed in letters: "Dearest, dearest boy, more tenderly embraced than I can say . . . lean on me as a lover . . . Your terribly tender old friend." However Anderson seems to have been a stupid dolt with only a beautiful body. The sculptor—"the heroic young master of the grand style"—appears between the lines of James's letters to have been no sort of intellectual companion for his admirer.

All that was still in the future as the younger Henry James brooded over his life in Paris; to stay or not to stay? His secret might become exposed to these passionate, keenly aware whoremongers of French writers. He had failed to crack the tight inner society of the French society he had wanted to meet. He noted: "The French are the people in the world one may have to go more of the way to meet than to meet any other." He eyed the great mansions in the Faubourg Saint Germain but didn't enter that aristocratic atmosphere. He did get into the salon of the Marquise de Blocqueville, but she belonged to the inextricable, lost world of Napoleon's marshals. The evenings of those salons he did crack drove him mad with the rhythmical wailing of parlor music. He claimed no sense of music, a stone ear, yet for social reasons he stood in the salons "in a suffocating room listening to an interminable fiddling . . . Gustave Doré, standing beside me, seemed as bored as myself." Another time, "I enjoyed the circle, but I had an overdose of Wagner."

James was snobbish about the Americans who lived in Paris—"the American village encamped *en plein Paris*." The few he felt it expedient to have tea with were those he sensed to be socially important, those now forgotten Mrs. Wisters, Mrs. Lockwoods, *and* Mrs. Charles Strong, a lifelong expatriate, the former Eleanor Fearing of New York, deep in conversion to the Catholic Church. She was not one of those tall, earthshaking goddesses full of the Life Force Bernard Shaw was soon to bring into life.

Like so many inclined to homosexuality, James usually cultivated older women, widows, divorcees. In jest he wrote his brother William of a Henriette Reubell: "If I wanted to marry an ugly Parisian-American with money and *toutes les élégances*, Miss Reubell would be a very good objective. But I don't." In his novel *The Ambassadors*, she became Miss Barrace, the perfectly adjusted American expatriate, devoid of any deep commitments.

James had written twenty Paris letters for the New York *Tribune*, and they were not what he or they wanted. Paris from the inside he had failed to penetrate, and his surface texts were the usual journalist fodder one got from American journalists writing from Paris. James was a bit more polished in style, a little duller than an experienced reporter. He wrote of Notre Dame all "pearly grays." It was not what the readers wanted. He never really understood the modern movements in art that Paris produced. His sense of painting was better keyed to the illustrators of the English school; charm, generalities, good taste. As a critic he fell back on Meissonier's *Battle of Eylau*. "The best thing, say, is a certain cuirassier, and in the cuirassier the best thing is his clothes, and in his clothes the best thing is his leather straps, and in his leather straps the best thing is the buckles," etc., etc. This inventory of trivia filled space. It was more like Gertrude Stein than Henry James.

In all he got 400 dollars from the New York *Tribune* for his twenty letters, and the newspaper called the contract off, to James's delight.

The Paris James lived in was that of the streets, the galleries of the rich Americans. He liked to loaf in the cafés after a morning of writing. He drank *bocks,* eyed the passing crowds, saw people dining on the Champs Elysées under umbrellas of trees, at tables set by ivied walls. Sometimes he would try a fried fish at a river-front *guinguette* (he was a martyr to constipation) or he'd take a lonely trip for a penny on a steamer to Auteuil. Instead of life on acres of parquetry, damask, Beauvais hangings, he rode on top of the three-horse public coach through the night air of the Bois de Boulogne after a late dinner. Infinitely complex, with a too subtle mind, we get the picture of an isolated man, locked into himself and his writing except for the evenings he spent with the French writers and the Russian novelist. But their style of life, their alcoholic gossip he now saw were not for him. He was also beginning to be shaky in his view of the natives. "The better I like the French personality, the more convinced I am of their bottomless superficiality." To enter French society he realized was *un combat perpétuel.*

He took a July trip downriver, and returning in September found his Paris apartment had been rented behind his back. For a few months he tried other quarters. Then the final no to Paris: "I don't remember what suddenly brought me to the point of saying—'Go to; I will try London.'" He had been a full year in Paris, and "it is rather ignoble to stay in Paris simply for the restaurants."

He would not go back to America. He was also unused to change, and as other Americans came to Paris, to Europe, he was puzzled by their daring (was it also envy?) and *their* reason for coming over. "A new generation that I do know not and mainly prize not has taken universal possession. . . . It is a wretched business, this quarrel of ours with our country, this everlasting impatience to get out of it."

Yet many were to become his admirers. Few would say with Mark Twain, "I'd rather be dammed to John Bunyan's heaven than read that [Henry James]."

So Henry James left Paris. Of this man with an internal immobility the saddest line in a journal he kept at that time must be, "I shall be an eternal outsider."

He crossed the Channel on December 10, 1876, from Boulogne to Folkestone. He would never shake off his stay in the French city. "Anyone who has ever lived in Paris will always have a corner of affection for it in his heart and will often go back."

Except for professors and Ph.Ds Henry James no longer speaks to most of us. He is walled off to the general public by his ponderous style, his limited canvas on which his narrow view of the human condition is painted. It leaves out too much of life—he was valiant enough to see that. And what of the Americans he wrote of? In our age of the jet set, the international way-out, wandering, anti-establishment student world, the economy air-conditioned tours of a dozen countries on the run, he is a dodo bird, or worse—unknown. His cultured, artistic Americans are gone forever from the earth. In a time of social climbers with their pads, avant-garde gimmicks, American swingers, and second-rate sex novels—an age which is the apotheosis of mediocrity—James's Americans with taste and leisure and fine manners are lost in a mist mingled with the smoke of battle of the Great War of 1914–1918. The last relics died in discreetly shuttered flats, great Louis XV beds holding their sick bones. We see the last public notice of them in little items: Walter Berry, Harry Lehr, Edith Wharton are dead. And of some of the other Americans, James said, "So much taste, and all of it bad."

James himself was the last of the greatly talented, stern and stuffy American literary men in exile, those who sat in soothed pride at London club windows. He became a British citizen during the war and died in 1916 at seventy-three.

Mary Cassatt, the tough-skinned, iron-hard maiden from Pennsylvania wrote once of him: "Henry James was a fine man, and he has improved since he first wrote; then he was inclined to be society, but superior people get over that."

He didn't, of course. He could seriously set down such a line as "a position in society is a legitimate object of ambition."

He left no epitaph, and he would perhaps have felt it in bad taste to have his words carved in stone. If his writing was his life, then what George Moore said of him perhaps fits: "His whole book is one long flutter near to the one magical and unique word, but the word is not spoken."

CHAPTER 17

Hedonist at Large—
James Gordon Bennett

The only paradise is paradise lost.
MARCEL PROUST

M ANY of the Americans who made their way to Paris to live were
writers and painters, often of tedious preciosity, or colorless folk
with mere money and some small social position, even *déclassé* derelicts.
James Gordon Bennett the younger, however, was a true original, a cock-
sure hedonist who made "the journey from Byzantium to Montparnasse"
in style. Lucius Beebe, who once worked on one of Bennett's newspapers,
called him "the great American expatriate and cut-up of the Paris boulevards." His excesses, his vulgarity, his drunken escapades, his strenuous
unorthodoxies, the limitless opulence of his one-million-dollar-a-year income (after taxes) permitted him to sneer at all social and moral conventions. He was the true voluptuary, preserved into old age in brandy. No
restaurateur or *hôtelier* failed to overcharge him.

His father, the fearful, stern maker of a great newspaper, the New York
Herald, raised young Bennett to anticipate a rich gold mine as publisher.
Later, when Bennett established the Paris edition of the New York *Herald*
(wrongly called the *Paris Herald* by most historians and writers), he was
to have two sources of power in two important newspapers. His life was
that of a man constantly endangered by his wild dashing about as a
sportsman, by overeating, by predatory games, by entertaining the
grandes horizontales. As a newspaper owner he was so mean a boss that

there were those who would cheerfully have murdered him, if they could have avoided the guillotine or the gallows.

Bennett was above the shrill *poseurs* of the arts, the imbecilities of the political minds; he was for the buoyant life of sensation and comfort. He was more than just a typical money king of the nineteenth century who was to spend most of his life in Paris. He was a true explorer of the domain of experience. Bennett was born in 1841. His Irish mother could not abide living with the original James Gordon Bennett, and so she removed herself and young James to France. Here the heir spent six months of every year; the other six with his unctuous old pirate of a father. There was no divorce. Separation by a wide ocean seemed to be enough, since it left each parent defiantly to live his own life. So James became one of those international children, part French, part American. His life could have inspired Henry James for a masterful study, a novel of divided Americans in Paris, of the power of the purse as used by ruthless exiles.

At fifteen James Gordon Bennett, Jr., not only spoke French with great fluency but was already drinking hard stuff and had early embarked on a sexual life direct and enjoyable without any unsophisticated nonsense about morality or willful eccentricity.

Bennett was a member of the New York Yacht Club, owner of the 160-ton sloop the *Henrietta* (named after Mama) when the Civil War boiled to a start. He offered his boat for US Naval service and was assigned to keep the rebels from taking Long Island, himself serving as a third lieutenant—a rank one wit observed "that may have been created for him." However the US Naval vessel *Henrietta* was too often seen at anchor at the New York Yacht Club, with club servants rushing the best food, wine, and brandy aboard the lucky warship. Bennett's philosophy was a sincere belief in the corruptibility of the world. While the yacht *Henrietta* was in the Navy, it actually served as a Federal Revenue Cutter. The boat was equipped with two six-pound rifled bronze cannon cast at Chicopee, Massachusetts, and later a brass twelve-pounder was added to her armament. Neither the guns nor Lieutenant Bennett ever saw action, but the fault was not his.

After the war Bennett took up horses and coaching as a sport; watching a Narragansett pacer, driving a team of four-in-hand or six was the proper social activity for a young blood with money. And he was a wild coachman, no matter who was on board, driving with mad ferocity while the attendant in red coat blew on his long golden horn. Bennett handled the reins with strength, and, some fatuous, complacent people felt, with madness. There was a report, true it seems, that after midnight, driving a coach, Bennett was often delighted to strip himself naked but for the white top hat and glowing cigar, and throw the whip into his straining, matched teams of expensive horses.

Papa was still alive, so James, Jr., cavorted and offended Newport, the social bastion of the upper *haute bourgeoisie*. Papa died in 1868, and James entered into his kingdom with the glee of a Bourbon king. He was nearly twenty-seven years of age, and the newspaper he inherited was making a profit for him of $750,000 a year, at a time when the money was worth six times what it is today and taxes hardly existed. For him life was capable of anything but a guilty conscience.

The companions of his youth were all fast young men, "blue-blooded New Yorkers": Heckschers, Howlands, Osgoods, Jeromes, and others. He had a great liking for showgirls, and was one of the main supporters of "Lydia Thompson and her British Blonds," who came to America to show off their hefty limbs and voluptuous curves, most exciting for the ribald blue-bloods. Bennett's favorite of the group was Pauline Markham. An admirer (not Bennett) had described her as possessing the "voice of velvet and the lost arms of the Venus de Milo." Bennett himself was more direct and not as lyrical about the women he conquered.

He was just as casual with his reporters, and when one asked for more money, Bennett replied, "I can get all the brains I want . . . picked up any day for twenty-five dollars per week." He told his staff plainly, "I want you fellows to remember that *I* am the only reader of this paper. *I* am the only one to please. If *I* want it turned upside down, it *must* be turned upside down."

Bennett had, however, a fine newspaper sense. He hired Mark Twain to write a series of travel letters from a trip to the Holy Land, the *Quaker City Letters*, which later were used to produce Twain's first best seller, *The Innocents Abroad*. Bennett also hired Henry M. Stanley to find (not to rescue as claimed) the missionary David Livingston in unknown Africa.

Stanley was a prima donna in his own right and he and Bennett did not get along after Stanley became world famous as a Bennett reporter. Stanley wanted the credit for himself, and the *Herald* began to roast Stanley's lectures on the African trip. Bennett growled, "Who the hell was Stanley *before* I found him! Who thought of hunting up Livingston? Who paid the bills!" Later, when there was talk of Stanley and his wife not getting along, Bennett sent a reporter to ask Stanley, "Do you beat your wife?" The reporter escaped with his life.

What sent James Gordon Bennett to Paris for good, what made him an exile from his native land, was one of those society scandals that today seem merely foolish, the miscalculation of a boozy caprice. But in 1876 it caused a social shock that sent Bennett eastward to Europe for good. It began with the idea that since he was a very rich young man with valuable properties he should marry, even if just for heirs. He found Caroline May, who came from one of those stiff and proper families, proud and aware of a coherent universe in their ancestors' world in Maryland. Caroline was beautiful, her family solidly entrenched socially in a grand house in New York City, upholding the highest social position in a society made up of descendants of former fur traders, slavers, whisky sellers to Indians, land thieves, and robber barons. However in "The Four Hundred," it meant something to be on top in this society where gossip, scrutiny, and pride were always busy.

It seemed as if Jimmy Bennett, with Caroline May at his side, would stop being the playboy, taper off his drinking, settle down with his beauty to breed heirs for the New York *Herald*.

The Mays, on New Year's Day, 1877, were holding open house in their Manhattan town house, the festive seasonal decor properly gay, with eggnog, old wine bottles, tidbits of sea life, and solid game birds and sliced beef ready to welcome in the New Year with its excruciating clangor of the city's bells. The men were in claw-hammered dress coats, the ladies in their marvelous gowns with long trains and the proper lacing to give them those wasp waists, magnificent shoulders and breasts, then so much the fashion. Standing by were the English butler, the footmen, the maid servants who saw to things between the walls of walnut wainscoting, among the groups of the best people.

There was snow in those days at New Year's, and Bennett arrived at the May's in a two-horse cutter on thin steel blades. He was enveloped in buffalo robes, and it was apparent that he was already filled with a great deal of New Year's cheer, his favorite brandy. He managed to get into the house and greet the guests, his bride-to-be, her parents, Caroline's bored brother. Bennett continued drinking. A good fire burned in the ornate fireplace. Bennett seemed only vaguely aware of what was going on around him, or perhaps he mistook it all for that male retreat, the Union Club, and the fireplace for a urinal. Whatever he thought—if he thought at all—he opened his fly ("took his best friend in hand") and proceeded to piss on the leaping flames. (One untrue bit of gossip insisted he used the Steinway grand piano, *not* the fireplace.)

The reaction of the guests may be imagined as horror, panic, revulsion. Just why, we don't know, as most of the mature ladies present were producing from six to a dozen children, and were aware of the male organ of generation. As for the younger women, "they could have covered their eyes." But suddenly the New Year's celebration at the May's came to a silent end. Four men quickly helped Bennett through the front doors to his cutter; overcoat and hat were added, and the horses started on their way. Never had there been such originality to social disgrace.

There was wildfire gossiping around town in the best circles, raffish and bawdy comment, and shock in others at what had happened at the May's on New Year's. Bennett, lunching the next day at the Union Club ("on a broiled Southdown mutton chop and part of a bottle of Pommery Brut") felt the worst was over. He had little memory of his hectic moment of natural gaiety. However, in front of the club, as he left, his way was barred by Frederick May, the twenty-five-year-old brother of Caroline, his once intended bride. Frederick began to flog James with a horsewhip, and they progressed from there to a rolling fight in the snow. Club members at well-placed windows watched and enjoyed the sight. A rival newspaper, *The Sun*, stated, "Blood stained the snow from sidewalk to gutter." Hardly honest reporting. The fight was stopped before any serious damage was done and Bennett with grimaces of pain and howls of outrage was sent away in a horse cab.

Rekindling his rage with brandy, Bennett decided to resort to the *code duello* and call out young May to meet him on the field of honor. As his second he picked Charles Longfellow, the son of America's favorite poet, who had sailed and jollied and chased *jeunes filles* with him. Charles called on young May and a duel was arranged in all the formal convention of man-to-man face-offs.

The duel was a little out of date in America. Ever since Aaron Burr gunned down Alexander Hamilton in Weehawken, dueling had been frowned upon in the north as too murderous a game of what the Greeks called *tyche*—chance. So the two parties in this duel-to-be went south to ill-named Slaughter's Gap, Maryland, with all the proper dramatis personae—seconds, surgeons and their kits in attendance.

Twelve paces separated the two protagonists as they lifted their dueling pistols. The signal to fire was given. Young May fired into the air. Bennett shrugged at this gesture of disdain and also wasted his shot. Honor had been satisfied by the gesture of a duel. People who record such things claim it was the last formal duel on public notice in the United States.

With the duel over, his affianced lost, there was nothing for Bennett to do but to go into exile in Paris. The city would be his home, and what visits he would make to the quibbling United States were merely to lower the pay of his journalists and to see that his newspaper prospered. (And to write of Saratoga as "a seraglio of the prurient aristocracy.")

In Paris James Gordon Bennett began to attract attention by his horses and carriages. They were marvelous examples of the carriage-maker's splendid but slow art, and the matched teams were of the best breeds, fit for this modern Petronius, steeds reined by the most ornate of coachmen in voluptuous livery. From time to time Bennett himself took over the reins to show his skill as a coach handler. The auto age was just dawning, producing the ornate Victorian machines, heavy with brass and some still carrying a dashboard holder for a buggy whip. Bennett expanded into a fleet of Dion Boutons and Renaults, but took his time about retiring the horse. He had an eye for fine coach work, the patterned cloth with which the tonneaus were trimmed, the glitter of harness fittings. No lover of wheels ever lost his love for the carriage and the scent of the best horses.

Bennett was now a Parisian with a town house, a permanent resident on the Seine. As for the American society there, he remarked, "It consists of people who don't invite me to their parties."

He was not lovable, some hinted, with his trigger temper, his mad moments, a voluptuary embracing soufflé Armagnac, brioches, brandy, mauve-gowned expensive public women, the grand courtesans of the day.

If Bennett did not trust the human race, he did have a full faith in dogs. He owned many, Pomeranians, Pekinese, and cocker spaniels. His impressions and reaction to an employee was often taken from how the dogs reacted to him. To James dogs were the best judges of human character. When an Irish editor was summoned to Paris by Bennett because he was out of favor, the man attached a slice of liver inside his top hat and poured anise on a handkerchief he jammed into his coattail pocket. As he entered with his hat held against his chest, the dogs greeted the man with joy, frolicking and leaping around him with barks of pleasure. The man remained on the Bennett payroll.

Bennett was not above being engaged in fist fights. Once in Delmonico's he got snippy with a stranger and was knocked out cold on the floor. The stranger was Billy Edwards, a light-heavyweight boxer. Bennett was delighted he had been knocked out by a pro. The two men became friends.

In his playboy days Bennett often tangled with the police. Driving a four-in-hand wildly through Manhattan, he got into a match with a tough police captain, Alexander Williams, who had said, "There is more law in the end of a nightstick than in all the courts in the land." Bennett felt that club when the captain gave him a few bumps, and later he went after the captain in the *Herald*. Williams was a noted grafter and died a millionaire. In time the two men became friends. Bennett respected direct action, even if he were sometimes on the receiving end of it. After his duel with Fred May, there were those who said Bennett feared May still would go to Paris and take a shot at him.

One of Bennett's discarded mistresses who called herself "Camille Clermont" wrote that Bennett had "a coat of mail which for the last few weeks he wore underneath his clothes . . . He feared Mr. May would probably shoot him . . . on sight. Mr. May declared he had no homicidal intentions, so to his great relief JGB discarded his cuirass." Hell hath no fury like a discarded mistress who can write a book (as Picasso was also to learn). Camille wrote, "Beneath his thin veneer of civilization JGB was in reality a Barbarian . . . he has never learned the precious maxim: 'Never hurt those who love you . . .'" But Bennett apparently agreed with Napoleon, "Women are all right in bed and on the bidet but nowhere else."

He was banned by the smart hostesses, the old families of the Faubourg Saint Germain, the people who were to fill the pages of Proust; they wanted no part of this gourmandizing rich American. His income, it was whispered, was nearly one million dollars a year, and he was trying to spend it all. Those who flocked to his spending sprees were the usual international free-loaders, moochers, confidence men and their women. The art dealers and junk sellers came too, to provide those exotic things a millionaire with no brake on his appetite would desire for grand or petty gratification of pleasure.

Bennett was a big feeder, and in Paris Maxim's and Voisin's were his grazing grounds; also the Ritz, where under the monocled eye of Olivier, the *maître d'hôtel*, he managed usually to curb his wild ways, that ecstatic, blasphemous way of life. Often when he entered a restaurant in a well-oiled mood of *folie de grandeur*, he would walk down the place between the tables pulling at every tablecloth, smashing glasses, overturning silver dishes full of food, bringing flower vases and silverware into clattering disorder. It was the needed fulfillment of a gross, perverse child. Then sated, Bennett would calmly pull out wads of money and pay for everything, even the cleaning of garments and replacement of those that never again would be wearable. There is no record that anyone impervious to wealth ever punched him on the nose for his outrageous habits of play. The *maître d'hôtel* would usually smile and slide off some thickness from the packet of banknotes held out to him to pluck off like artichoke leaves.

If James wasn't in the mood to wreck a place, he might instead decide to have a military inspection of the entire staff of a restaurant, all the personnel standing at attention, from wine stewards to sauce cooks, busboys to vegetable scrapers. He would hand out to each francs worth one hundred dollars. Some of the staff, seeing Bennett's condition, smelling of the best brandy, would hurry to the end of the line after getting their reward and accept an added payment. Bennett remained enigmatic, exuberant, convinced of the power of money all his long life.

He established the Paris edition of the New York *Herald* just to have a public voice in France where such an irreconcilable type as he could get even with people, become a power in a city where journalists were bought and sold, bribed and entertained by one side or the other in any public crisis. Bennett gained social status; he was a rich publisher and Paris began to see James Gordon Bennett as a man of stature, backed by immense wealth. In time the newspaper earned its way, but for years it cost Bennett $100,000 a year. On both his papers he was a mean man, making editors into office boys and office boys into editors at a whim, and in general making life a squalorous hell for whoever worked for him at miserable wages. However, he was not fool enough really to harm his newspapers by his shenanigans. He appears to have been a capable and cunning publisher, and could have been the equal of Pulitzer and Hearst in debasing the national media if he had tried. Unlike Balzac's Rastignac, looking down on the city from above Père Lachaise, he never cried, "Now you and I come to grips!" There was no fun in that.

CHAPTER 18

Mr. Bennett and the Owls

One can mislay oneself.

RIMBAUD

As a sportsman and yacht owner, James Gordon Bennett, in 1899, had his newspaper set up a deal with Guglielmo Marconi, then struggling to survive and make the wireless accepted, to report to Bennett the results of the America Cup Races. This cost him five thousand dollars. We don't know if his favorite yacht won. His hostility to his employees, however, remained; there was talk of his throwing his cane at some of the journalists.

No true *arbiter elegantiae*, he drank, ate ortolans stuffed with smaller ortolans, knew his way with a *contrefilet à la Clamart* or *quenelles de brochet Nantua*, but his favorite dish remained mutton chops. Jingling hard gold louis in his pockets, he dined, drove his coach, picked his women, inspected his yacht wearing a bum-freezer claw-tailed coat. He owned the 900-ton auxiliary steam and sail yacht the *Namouna*. But he was dreaming of something "more roomy." In time he had designed for himself the steam yacht *Lysistrata*, named, he assumed, after "a beautiful Greek lady, and very fast." The yacht cost $625,000 (a sum equal today to four or five million dollars). It was built at Dunbarton by Denny & Brothers. The result shocked the rich and brought pleasure to the poor and middle-class newspaper readers who read of its incredible fittings, its wild parties, its vice-rich trips. Bennett had three suites, one on *each* of the yacht's three decks, in case he did not care to go up or down stairs.

There was a large Turkish bath, hot and cold bathing rooms, and a masseur always on duty.

In Paris under his own mansard roofs Bennett had butter from his farms nearby, on shipboard there was a padded stall for a fine Alderney cow, rich in butterfat, so the commodore could have his reviving brandy-and-milk punch on arising. Electric fans kept the ship's cow cooled, and it was hoped she did not suffer *mal de mer.* In his train travels he kept another cow in her own baggage car to service the Bennett private railroad coach.

At sea Bennett insisted on clean-shaven crews, and guests must not play cards, but must eat their fill of grouse, plover eggs—his favorite among eggs—wine which was always on hand. His greatest idea of a practical joke was to kidnap some important guest who had come on board in harbor for an afternoon tea or cocktails. At Villefranche one day he carried off Lady Lily Bagot and the Countess of Essex, two former American girls who had married into nobility in England. They did not find the piracy amusing, and there were dour faces at the games of this fellow when next morning he brought the ladies back and they went ashore looking ridiculous in their crumpled evening gowns.

It looked like duel time again. James made deep and formal apologies to the fox-hunting, grouse-shooting peers and husbands, and a visit to Cartier in Paris resulted in the sending of a diamond tiara and a pearl necklace to the ladies, thus soothing the irked pair.

Some claim that jokesters express a blunted despair, a torpor of the mind.

Brillat Savarin was no hero to James Bennett, who, although a best paying guest and always welcome at the Café de Paris, Voisin's, Foyot's, Maxim's, was no specialist or adorer of exotic food. His idea of gourmet food remained Southdown mutton chops, a dish almost no American had heard of or would order if he had. This simple, rather gamy item placed around a grilled lamb kidney was Bennett's standard test of any restaurater's promises of good food. The chops had to be well aged and done *just* so. In Monte Carlo he once bought a restaurant when he found the place usually reserved for him had been taken by others. Heads were shaken; "So sorry, Mr. Bennett—*but*—" Damn and double damn. James paid forty thousand dollars for the place right then and there, and ousted the people at his usual table. The chef, who knew his man, had the mutton chops on the fire, just coming to crisp perfection.

A mutton chop story that can be checked is of the year he came over on a liner (the yacht was in drydock) to New York to inspect the new

quarters for his newspaper, designed by Stanford White in Herald Square. But first for lunch at the Union Club, where the mutton chops were to his taste, if memory held. The chops came to table overcooked. James called a meeting of the club staff, ordered the whole kitchen fired at once, the head waiter, the dining room group—everyone. Everyone. But the club's house rules did not permit a member to hold a rump court of one. James left, took a cab to the North River (now called the Harlem River), and found a ship just leaving for Europe—but space was all booked. He paid five full fares to take over the captain's quarters, and never got to his newspaper's new setting in Herald Square or saw the fourteen-thousand-dollar desk set in silver that had been ordered for him.

James Gordon Bennett, in his staccato, authoritative manner, had a few estates scattered around in France. There was the fabulous apartment in Paris in the Etoile section, where the footmen got five dollars extra a month if they wore powder in their hair for parties. At Versailles he had a country place, where coaching, hunting, and other sports could be played out with horns, braying hounds, and stirrup cups of apple brandy, and mutton chop dinners. His Scotland shooting box he neglected, but they shipped him grouse and plover eggs, fresh salmon, and some of the heather-fed local mutton.

Bennett also had a residence at Beaulieu on the blue Mediterranean, so as not to be too far from his yacht in good sailing weather. He was certainly an asset to the French economy; someone interested in the facts has figured out James Gordon Bennett spent in Paris and the rest of France forty million dollars in good living, good times, and a full and long life as he fought the ignominy of aging. When annoyed by too bulging pockets stuffed with *mille-franc* notes, Bennett was known to improve the fit of his tailoring by tossing the offending money into a burning fireplace. He refused to submit to the irreconcilables others accepted.

Few could believe his big tips. A new valet was shocked when on the *Blue Train*, Paris to Monte, Bennett gave the *wagon-lit* conductor twenty thousand francs (about four thousand dollars). The valet took back all but a hundred francs. But Bennett went into a temper fit when given this refund and ordered the valet to give the conductor back the rest of his tip. Some claimed the conductor resigned from the *Blue Train* and opened a hotel and bar in Boulogne.

We know very little about James Gordon Bennett from the inside, the anguish of the heart if any, what coherent idea of identity he had. We know nothing of his true emotions, his private sentiments and attitudes toward the world, beyond the public displays and the crudeness which might have masked a great deal, or nothing. He did seem to have a poignant sense of things passing. So play, play. A rich alcoholic and sensualist is always taken at his face value. But with Bennett we have one odd clue that there was something more, perhaps much more than met the eye. Perhaps some unreal Marvellian garden with birds in it.

Not a man given to any organized religion, Bennett was dedicated to the images of owls—an owl, he claimed, saved him once from shipwreck! Bennett held there was some mystic, shaman-like quality to owls. He covered his material possessions with images of owls, when there was space. When the New York *Herald* building was erected on Broadway and Thirty-fifth Street, the roof line showed two huge bronze owls with electric eyes that blinked off and on, and two giant figures beat hammers on a bell to announce the hours to the citizens around the town. The facade cost two hundred thousand dollars. It is re-erected today near the Hall of Fame at New York University's Washington Heights campus.

Owls gave him some extraordinary substantial relief, an affinity with nature. The image of the owl—we have no clue as to what it actually meant to him (he was not a man to think of it as the Greek symbol of wisdom)—clung to him to the very end.

Bennett even wanted to enter eternity with an owl as the bearer of his remains. He would, he decided, be buried inside a huge, 200-foot-tall, stone bird, hollowed out. A staircase would lead up to the eyes of the owl, eyes serving as windows and observation balconies. From chains hanging from inside the bird's head James Gordon Bennett's casket—he inside it—would be suspended to hang free of the malevolent rot of earth burial. It was a plan for a mausoleum that dwarfed anything any other rich American had yet thought of. So, too, the founder of Islam was supposed to remain suspended between heaven and earth.

From Paris Bennett commissioned Stanford White to draw up plans for the burial owl and to hire the sculptor Andrew O'Conner to create the entombing bird in glazed Vermont granite. Between Paris and New York Bennett kept the letters to White flying; long, involved, intricate details were worked out. He wanted no pretty hoot owl looking for a mere barn mouse. He wanted a really ferocious bird, one that would menace the landscape of the Washington Heights family property where it was to roost for eternity. Work was to start as soon as the final plans were completed.

But Bennett had time for other thoughts besides death. The impression most people had was that Bennett died a bachelor. Actually in September of 1914 he left the Catholic Church of his mother, became an Episco-palian, and married the widow of the Baron de Reuter, née Maud Parker of Philadelphia. The baron had been related to the founder of the famous newsgathering organization, Reuters. Bennett thus kept his personal life in touch with some form of journalism.

But his major project remained the plans for his owl tomb. Bennett wanted to supervise its progress himself, domesticate himself as it were to the owl's interior, its roominess, view, and comfort. And the price? Stan-ford White said it would cost one million if all of Bennett's ideas were to be worked out. Bennett did not bat an eye but said one million dollars would satisfy him. It was a portentous *idée fixe* and he held to it.

But the project never got past the planning stages. Stanford White, a notorious womanizer, was shot down one night in full public view by Harry K. Thaw in the Madison Square Gardens roof restaurant; Thaw was the playboy husband of a woman White was once entangled with.

James Gordon Bennett in a clairvoyant moment predicted he would die on his seventy-seventh birthday. In 1918 he fulfilled his prediction. No owl tomb existed. Bennett was buried at Passy, across the river from Paris. There is a pair of owls—like emblematic devices—carved on his grave-stone.

Bennett was a man who was a vessel of assorted loosely affiliated desires and greeds, desires sexual and visceral, and he remains one of the wonders of the *belle époque*. He was the hero of the bar habitués and supporter of available beautiful women. For all his idiosyncrasies, to Paris James Gordon Bennett was a typical American millionaire, swinging with the social pendulum, but not giving a damn if he were accepted or not; he knew the ironic truth that with little expenditure of effort his money always would be there to buy the visible world. He left America when he felt it lacked something his pagan being craved—unrealized assumptions, luminous freedoms. He would have agreed with Gertrude Stein, speaking of the place she grew up in in the United States: "There is no there there."

CHAPTER 19

American Madonna Painter— Mary Cassatt

America is the country where philosophy is
the least studied.

ALEXIS DE TOCQUEVILLE

I F THE AMERICANS in Paris we have treated of up to now have seemed foolish, sensual, amusing, wise, with some uniqueness, they have mostly remained human and often lovable. If not all are to be graciously approved of, we can sense in them an affinity to the human condition, the human comedy. But when a long-chinned, stern-faced Miss Mary Stevenson Cassatt, aged twenty-two, came to Paris to paint seriously, she was more provocative than lovable. She had been to Paris as a child several times. She was already the rude, outspoken personality that hardened even more as she aged and became an acid-spitting, nearly blind old lady, still poor-mouthing, demanding service, insulting friends and foe. But painting, until her eyes failed her, the best Impressionist paintings done by an American. As a French collector put it, *"Le grand peintre américain est Mary Cassatt."*

She was not, as most people imagine, born in Philadelphia, but in Allegheny City, Allegheny County, Pennsylvania, on May 22, 1844. Her family was Scotch-Irish with claims to French Huguenot connections by a Jacques Cossart (original spelling), born in Normandy in 1595. Her brother, Alexander, was the president of the great Pennsylvania Railroad System. The family were Episcopalians, attended the Church of the

Epiphany, treated God as a neighbor in good social standing. The Cassatts traveled often to Europe, and in the early 1850s had an apartment on the Rue Monceau, later a larger one off the Champs Elysées on the Avenue Marbeuf. They witnessed the coup d'état of 1851 that began the Second Empire of Napoleon III. The Cassatts approved, for the French king gave an illusion of permanence. Mary at eleven attended the *Exposition Universelle* of 1855. But at this time it is not likely she met Degas, Pissarro, and Whistler, all of whom also attended; later she knew them all well. She felt artists were a privileged class, even if mostly fools.

A young American painter, Stanley Haseltine, wrote to his mother in Philadelphia of the visit of Queen Victoria to the French fair. "On Sunday the Queen entered Paris. The streets from the depot of the Chemin de Fer to the Palais de St. Cloud were thronged with people . . . I had a very good look at the Queen; for this satisfaction I had to wait six hours in the crowd." Perhaps Mary did too. (There is a photograph of Mary Cassatt as a very old lady in which she is a leaner image of the old Victoria.)

The Cassatt family was to stay five years in Europe in gentility and affluence.

Back in America, in 1861, Mary at seventeen became an art student at the Pennsylvania Academy in Philadelphia, one of the few art schools in the country. It stood on Chestnut Street between Tenth and Eleventh. Wrote a fellow student of Mary: "We have several new students, both male and female, but Miss Cassatt and I are still at the head." Four rather dull years followed for Mary at the doddering, strangling academy. Seeking escape, she set out for Paris, only to run directly into the Franco-Prussian War, which she waited out in Philadelphia, until she became bored and went to Spain and Italy to paint. She was in the Paris Salon of 1872 with a Spanish scene, *Pendant le Carnaval*. She is listed officially by her middle name, as Stevenson (Mlle Mary). Now she was in Paris for good, advising the rich Havemeyers to buy a Whistler, Degas, Pissarro, Monet. Degas had not yet met Mary Cassatt, but seeing one of her pictures, he exclaimed: *"C'est vrai. Voilà quelqu'un qui sent comme moi."* A pithy, rough-barked bigot and wit, he was not given usually to such praise.

Mary also met a young American art student, John Singer Sargent, and disliked him; she disliked most American artists of merit, and many French ones. She was not a loving personality. Love she saved for never ending pictures of mothers and babies. She had no use for children when they reached their early teens. She sensed a scabrous antagonism in them that resembled their parents.

In 1877 Degas came to her studio to invite Mary to join the group known as the Impressionists. Degas, the sour misanthrope, clever and sharp-fanged, was forty-three; Mary, direct, ruthless in her opinions, harsh on her equals, in self-imposed exile from home, was thirty-three. These two carnivorous personalities were no doubt attracted to each other by their low opinion of the human race, by their use of cutting remarks to people they did not like. She lacked Degas's rapierlike wit, but had his snobbish idea of the worth of race and class. Like him, she, too, was to go almost entirely blind. Dressed in aigrette plumes, ornamental hatpins, batiste waists, froufrou sounding silks, she felt she helped add decor to Degas's life.

Not much research has been done on the intimate life of these two humans. Both disliked society, high or low. The American books done on Mary Cassatt are usually by some pedantic curator who lists paintings and tells us everything about her but what we really would like to know. Were they lovers? Did their intimacy reach the point of body contact— some felicitous zone of mutual pleasure? Paris gossip says yes. As for documented facts, one may shrug it off with a "who knows." Did she help Degas with aid from her wealthy family when he was in need? We do know she helped sell many of his paintings to rich Americans who were not too keen on Impressionism but didn't dare refuse *the* Miss Cassatt.

What is clear is that Mary's harsh and brutal frankness, her decisive, often reactionary opinions pleased Degas. All his life she held a great appeal for him, yet at times he could set even her back on her heels with his teeth-gnashing comments. He and Forain were the leading anti-Semites among the artists. Yet it is to Mary's credit that she supported Alfred Dreyfus in the crisis that split France over the railroading by the French Army and the Church of an innocent man to Devils Island "for the good of the service."

Degas neither liked nor tolerated women artists. Of the marvelous Berthe Morisot he said, "She makes pictures the way she makes hats." Only of Mary, and Utrillo's mother, Suzanne Valadon, could he say: "I will not admit that a woman can draw so well." There is a good chance he was Utrillo's father. Suzanne, when asked, "Was it Degas, Renoir, Lautrec?" answered, "They are all such fine artists, I'd sign any of their work."

Mary Cassatt did not splash the family wealth around in Paris, and there are hints she played at being the poor artist. A letter of her father's tells us that Mame (the family's name for Mary) "is working away diligently as ever, but she has not sold anything lately and her studio expenses with models from one to two francs an hour are heavy . . . the studio must at least support itself." This reminds us not of a French queen playing at milkmaid, but of a certain Philadelphia banker who was seen the day after Thanksgiving rescuing the skeleton of the family turkey from the refuse bin and handing it to his cook: "There is a good soup to be made out of this yet." And the Cassatts were Philadelphians by then.

There is no doubt that Degas helped her paint, and many Cassatt paintings of that period may have been done in part by Degas. In a letter she wrote about a painting of hers she states, "I sent it to the American section of the big exposition of '79; they refused it. As Mr. Degas had found it to be good, I was furious, all the more so since *he* had worked on it." She also objected to the rejection because on the jury "one was a pharmacist!"

She showed her most charming and important picture at the fourth Impressionist show in 1879. *La Loge* is a design of a red-haired girl in a pink gown seated in an opera box. Degas could not have done it better. Paul Gauguin, at the show, liked the work of two women painters. He said of Mary, "Mlle Cassatt has as much charm (as the other) but has more power." (*"Mlle Cassatt a autant de charme, mais elle a plus de force."*)

Degas did some etchings of Mary, slim and elegant, visiting at the Louvre, corseted, seen from the back, staring at ancient sculptures. Degas caught her best in his seated portrait of 1884. She is at ease, in one of her hats, leaning forward, looking at some photographs. She is long-chinned, wears an ironic smile, almost a leer on her face, the eyes already appear odd, as if the cataracts were forming. It's a stern picture of a not very attractive woman, for all of the fine brushwork, the skilled, candid kind of pose Degas had learned from the camera and the Japanese print. We sense a woman not easy to know, not easy to like. She was already started on her race to the world's record for paintings of mothers with young children. It is *too* easy to say, even if true, that she ached in some not too subconscious way for motherhood, for a child. Yet, as noticed by many, she lost interest in children once they began to move toward puberty. She shared with Lewis Carroll this desire for closeness to the undeveloped child, but would have been horrified at his perverse emotions. Nor is there in her any of the leering, sick attraction of a Nabokov hero toward the innocent female child.

It is interesting to follow Mary's image as it changes in the photographs we have of her, from the long-chinned young woman, so sure of herself, to the over-tailored Mary caught at the Cloisters of St. Trophime in 1912, with a Reboux hat, sunshade, Russian sable (?) scarf, lace at her throat. She appears a proper Dean Howells' character abroad—as seen in one of his novels. (How deceiving images are; she had a bite like a cobra.) In a 1914 photograph we see her with heron feathers spread on a large hat, hands tucked into a fox muff, long jade beads in place. Her mouth is a surgeon's slit, the eyes viewing the world with mistrust. Saddest of all is Mary at her Château de Beauxfresne in 1925; the Queen Victoria picture, a very old lady in nightcap and robe; the thin mouth is the same firm slit. She is wearing the jade beads. There is no relaxing into calm, tranquil old age, no giving the world the benefit of the doubt. The defiant stare remains petulant—our reaction is of the cruelty of nature to women as they age.

We do not know enough about Mary's private life, and most likely never will, unless more letters and journals exist in some Philadelphia attic to reveal her secret core. Was she when young disappointed in love? Was she savaged by a man? Was she appalled by the pale version of the gentlemen available to her set? Or had she no regard for anything much but paint and canvas, the etching needle and the copper plate? Yet how explain the countless women and children, the fetishlike consistency of the repeated *and* repeated theme. Diverse conflicting levels of consciousness must have existed in her—of these we know nothing.

There is little new that can be said of her paintings. They have the power of draftsmanship, a good sense of color, an ability to make pictorial statements of a subject of much general interest. They even have charm; for her, astonishing charm. She is at times nearly as good as Degas, with a sense of color nearly like Monet, almost as facile as Renoir. *Nearly* and *almost* seem to be her destiny and her limitation. For all their skill, and even signs of genius, her paintings seen in large numbers numb one. Though admitting their splendid merits, if we stay too long before them, the character of the cold woman somehow seeps into the warm tones.

Some of her anger at life was physical. "Mame is not well at all—dyspeptic." Another letter states, "Mame has got to work again in her studio, but is not in good spirits at all, one of her gloomy spells."

Like Jonathan Swift she preferred horses to the human Yahoos. As a horsewoman she had some falls and a bad one nearly destroyed her, so she was forced to give up horseback riding from then on. No wonder she gave the impression of a dismounted Amazon. Although she loved horses, she spared no birds—their plumes decorated many of her hats.

She traveled badly over water and realized it, but her father knew her well and wrote of a sea trip: "Mame was very sick . . . had to be carried off the boat . . . She is dreadfully headstrong . . . experience is lost upon her."

Mary had invited Sargent to join the Impressionists. She never forgave him when he said a polite no. When later he called on her as a visitor, she refused to see him. It was said she resented his success. She could carry a grudge like a dagger all her life. Mary lived on the Rue Pierre Charron, in a very fashionable apartment near the Trocadéro. She no longer rented a studio outside, but made over one of the rooms. To aid art, even her art, she was not above subsidizing galleries. When Durand-Ruel got into financial trouble, near bankruptcy, she lent them money and most likely saved them from closing.

It was never easy to find out just where she stood in relationship to her native land. Yet she did write in a letter: "I am an American definitely and frankly an American." She hardly acted that way. As for Americans in Paris, she and her family detested Mrs. John W. Mackay, whose wealth had come from the Comstock Lode, and all like her. Mary Cassatt's mother defined the attitude of both herself and her daughter toward Americans in Paris: "We jog along as usual and make no acquaintances among the Americans who form the colony, for as a rule they are people one wouldn't want to know at home."

Seeking permanent roots, in March of 1887 Mary moved into an apartment on the Rue de Marignan, and she kept it as her Paris address until her death. She also added to the household a maid, Mathilde Vallet, who was to become housekeeper and companion and was to stay until the end, serving Mary forty-four years. The Cassatts as a group, while in Paris, had cooks, maids, even a coachman until World War I. Then they hired a chauffeur. When horses were still in the family, there was a groom, or *tigre*, whom Mary painted into a picture with a mother and child.

It was in the summer of 1888 that her love of riding nearly killed her. Degas wrote: "Mlle Cassat has had a fall from a horse, broken the tibia of her right leg, dislocated her left shoulder . . . she is getting on well . . . she will be immobilized for weeks this summer, then deprived of any activity, and most surely of her passion as a horsewoman . . . The horse most likely put its foot down a hole made by the rain."

Accident-prone or not, horses were bad luck; in 1890 she was tossed from her carriage onto the stones of the Rue Pierre Charron and "as I alighted on my forehead, I have the blackest eye . . . anyone was ever disfigured with." The carriage was splintered nearly to bits by the kicking horse, the coachman fell off his perch, and the dogs that happened to be in the carriage were injured. Mary escaped with bruises. Paris traffic was getting worse.

After her father's death in 1891, Mary bought the Château de Beaux-fresne north of Paris, a dilapidated seventeenth-century manor house that needed lots of American money to put it in any kind of order. She was happy to announce that the costs of the house and repairs *all* came from sales of her paintings. Repairs, in the leisurely manner of French work-men, took until 1893. The country place and her Paris flat were Mary's two points of existence from then on.

The manor house was a forty-five-acre estate with vast gardens and lawns and many well-cared-for trees. It was a pink-red brick house of three stories, with white marble trimming. There were towers, hexagonal open belfries, a circular drawing room, and two tin bathtubs. For decor Mary added Japanese prints, Venetian glass. The furniture was Empire, left behind by the last owners, stuff then out of fashion. Mary painted a lot of it green. The house gave her pleasure but did not charm her out of her taciturn view of life.

She grew and served such American delights as corn on the cob, also eggplant and tomatoes. Transport was modern. In 1906 she owned a Renault limousine driven by Armand Delaporte, her chauffeur. Mary Cassatt died in his arms, one respectable obituary stated, so it must have been a completely innocent relationship.

Mary loved to shout at her guests, carrying the point of her argument —whatever it was—nearly to insult. Only Degas could stand up to her, demolish her with his annihilating verbal punch and wit. One of the guests at the château, who wrote under the name of Vernon Lee, gave Mary the English brush-off. "Miss Cassatt is very nice, simple, an odd mixture . . . the almost childish, garrulous American provincial." This is hardly the picture we have of Mary, and how she would have howled had she seen it in print. She never grew senile and remained always the martinet.

She ran a tight ship at the château and at the flat. Mathilde was *gouvernante* (or housekeeper) and hairdresser. There was also a cook, a housemaid, a chauffeur, the valuable Armand, and in the country there was added an extra maid and three gardeners. Mary worked, until her eyesight failed, a full eight hours a day at her paintings, and nights on her drawings. She was a very skilled draftsman, drawing magnificently but without any insatiable dash or spirit. There is no adventure to her fine drawing, no scream of agony as with Goya, no comic hilarity at life as with Hokusai (imagine her accepting a title like Old-Lady-Mad-About-Drawing).

For all her setting up shop in the midst of the fashionable, artistic world of Paris, she remained in many ways the Philadelphia old maid, whose values and bigotries were that of the Main Line. George Biddle visiting her saw her as one of the most vital, "high-minded, dedicated and prejudiced human beings I have ever known." Her intolerance, friends claimed, came from some insatiable, clamorous hunger for something missed—perhaps love.

She could curse "in the broadest profanity" with the jargon and argot of the Paris slums, the world of Zola's language at her command. Like so many who find the world a crushing despair full of innocuous cant, she took pleasure in fine food. As a gourmet Mary knew the value of sauces and seasonings, of Aylesbury duckling, truffled *foie gras*. She had a nose and a palate for fine wines; a good Musigny, the proper Sauterne. She kept a live trout pond and a guest could catch his own dinner. César Ritz could produce no finer poached turbot than her kitchen. At the best restaurants of Paris they knew the old tigress who demanded the secrets of their kitchens. Mary did not smoke, and while men could "sneak a cheroot or seegar," women were not permitted to put the weed to their lips in her presence. Her servants she controlled with a cold look, and they toed the line or got the spiny, rasping side of her tongue.

She believed in folk medicine, yarbs and pioneer brews and messes like any Pennsylvania hill jasper. Mary was a splendid Paris dresser, without being flashy. The dressmakers Doucet, Redfern, La Ferrière, the best in Paris, knew Mary Cassatt and were proud to serve her. Reboux hats with aigrettes and plumes delighted her. She dressed her studio models in Pacquin creations. In an age of the corset, hers were tight and firm and kept her body erect and ramrod stiff. Her lorgnette for her failing eyes hung on an amethyst chain. She appeared so regal that French royalists sometimes confused her with the Comtesse de Paris; which must have delighted Mary, who had no doubts about her superiority over the barbarians that populated the world.

No one dared cut her roses but herself, and while she herself never drove a motor car, she had once driven two frisky horses in tandem.

The *Philadelphia Ledger*, which went into the best homes of the best people, found her news in 1898, during a visit: "Mary Cassatt, sister of Mr. Cassatt, President of the Pennsylvania Railroad, returned from Europe yesterday. She has been studying [!] painting in France and owns the smallest Pekinese dog in the world." World famous, maybe, but still a *student* to Philadelphia.

On returning to France she announced, "I have some more plumbing, another bathroom . . . my French neighbors think I am demented." The French upper class in the country still frowned on unnecessary bathing.

Mary was called "The painter of the modern Madonna" by the *Chicago Inter-Ocean*. She made no public reaction. In 1904 she was made a *Chevalier de la Légion d'honneur*. She had turned down the offer earlier when the Luxembourg, with French frugality, had offered to trade the red sliver of ribbon in return for one of her paintings. The ambiguities of her character did not include primitive bartering.

In addition to her Renault landaulet, Mary's family came over with a White Steamer, and toured Europe with her in clouds of vapor. She had no ear for language, could not learn Italian, and her French had a gamy American accent. She began to dabble in spiritualism as many skeptics do as they age. By 1911 she had cataracts in both eyes, but "Dr. Borsch, he is a Philadelphian," she wrote, would operate. The operations were not very successful. The war of 1914 forced her to live out the fearful times mostly in a villa at Grasse.

In 1917 Degas died. "My oldest friend, I see no one to replace him." The times were out of joint for her. She had raged when one of her paintings was sent by a dealer to the famous 1913 Armory Show in New York. She despised her great contemporaries. Matisse's work she found "extremely feeble . . . commonplace . . ." Scorn was all the Cubists were worth, Monet's remarkable paintings of waterlilies looked to her "like glorified wallpaper." She spared hardly any avant-garde artist. She didn't change. *Mens cuisque id est quisque,* "the mind of each man is the man himself," or woman.

As for Gertude Stein and her ménage, really, Mary said, they were just buying the decadent stuff for their own vulgar sensationalism. In 1908 she had been lured into meeting Gertrude Stein at the Rue de Fleurus. She looked over the place, the Cézannes, Picassos, Matisses, since so famous, said to the woman who had dragged her there, "I have *never* in my life seen so many dreadful paintings in one place! I have never seen so many *dreadful* people gathered together and I want to be taken home at once." Out she marched to her car waiting at the curb.

She had little respect for Henry James, and detested Edith Wharton, felt Edith was a dismally bad writer and her husband "a wretched *parvenu*." There was no pleasing Mary. Perhaps physical suffering, the eye operations that went on in series and did not improve her sight, made life unendurable.

She used her foulest street oaths when speaking of Woodrow Wilson, and as one prim art historian wrote, she called him "an unprintable name." As for American students in Paris, she felt they were just "café tramps."

She had developed diabetes, and could no longer eat her gourmet foods. So soon eating at all became a waste of time. She took to rushing her guests at meals. "Hurry out and get lunch and hurry back."

The end came at last at eighty-three as a release; although she clung to life, dreaded the thought of dying. The date was July 14, 1926, *"Mary Cassatt est morte!"* She had left orders to open a vein when they supposed her dead. She was buried as a Protestant in a family vault set up at Mesnil-Theribus. She rests there (could she really rest even as a ghost?) with her father, mother, sister, and brother.

There were full military honors at her burial due to her Legion of Honor, and lots of roses, also a good turn-out of mourners, or sightseers. The day had begun grim and rainy, but the weather, perhaps fearing her wrath, cleared at the final moment. On the tomb are the words of an American family in final exile:

SÉPULTURE DE LA FAMILLE CASSATT

NATIVE DE PENNSYLVANIE

ETATS-UNIS DE L'AMERIQUE

CHAPTER 20

Yearners and Climbers

*What does God think of money? Just look
at the people he gives it to.*

MAURICE BARING

S OME RICH AMERICANS who settled in Paris were just seeking acceptance in the best French society rather than the affections of the
courtisane or the *flâneur*; rather the proper table than the exciting bed.
Lonely or disconsolate, already the American woman at the turn of the
century was beginning to gather in much of the nation's wealth as her
short-lived husband worked himself to death, leaving her rich and empty
of purpose or direction. Often a trip to Paris, the renting of some *hôtel*
mansion, suggested hope for the days ahead. Balzac called hope "the
only sin."

Hunting not for depravity or art but for social ritual was Mrs. Kate
(not Catherine) Moore, who had the millions, had the social itch. Even if
"trop vulgaire" she had a love of people, though considered a bit on the
foolish side with a pathetic tendency to prove it. She gave magnificent
dinners, tried to have a salon. Every French free-loader of any social
standing exploited her. If the Italian Opera at the Châtelet gave a series,
Kate Moore would buy out thirty grand tier boxes for the whole season.
Everyone whom she suspected could help her socially filled the boxes as
her guests. The wits of Paris were mean to her, but attended her parties
and dinners. She lived in an atmosphere of gossip produced by heavy
feeders and drinkers.

One of her tormentors was Comte Robert de Montesquiou-Fezensac, a rather too handsome snob, too lean and graceful, his waved hair, the proper stylish aristocratic mustache always in place. He fought a frustrating aesthetic struggle against the common world. He was a welcome talker in the salons of Paris. Poor Kate was not aware of La Rochefoucauld's remarks about talkers:

One of the reasons why so few people are to be found who seem sensible and pleasant in conversation is that almost everybody is thinking about what he wants to say himself rather than about answering clearly what is being said to him. The more clever and polite think it enough simply to put on an attentive expression, while all the time you can see in their eyes and train of thought that they are far removed from what you are saying and anxious to get back to what they want to say.

Full sensibility is not to be articulated, and the quality of the Paris salons had deteriorated by the time Americans came over in great numbers to taste the better life. Henry James had pointed out "Europe was good to the Americans," but he spoke usually as if Americans in Europe had come over little better than the savages they had battled on the frontiers. The theme of so many of his stories and novels was of the American lacking style or purpose, discovering in Europe a world recreated for them. He, too, was unaware that everything changes but the clichés; and he, like the most simple or vulgar traveling American, was devoted to personal clichés. He avoided Kate Moore's fêtes, preferring his own artificially tranquilized world—a world as false as hers.

Count Robert de Montesquiou, who tormented Kate, today is best remembered because three writers used him as models in their best or most flamboyant works. He is the source of the fascinating yet revolting Baron Charlus in Marcel Proust's novel, *Remembrance of Things Past,* as well as the hero Des Esseintes in J. K. Huysmans's *A Rebours*, and as a bird, he is the Peacock in Rostand's *Chantecler*. But none of these works could capture all the nuances of this snob, royalist, interior decorator, Symbolist poet, pederast, and *boulevardier*. He kept a pet turtle, its back set with rare jewels, diamonds, sapphires, amethysts. His bed was a carved black dragon, his sitting room contained a polar bear rug on which stood a full-sized Russian sleigh—use not given. He was a collector of the incongruous and the odd; the bullet that killed the Russian poet Pushkin. (He had inquired about the one that killed Lincoln; was it available?) He owned a hair from the beard of the historian Michelet, also Napoleon's bedpan at Waterloo. He published his own books; his *Le Chef des Odeurs Suaves* ("The Chief of Subtle Smells") was bound in blue satin with gold griffon wing designs. He advocated and endorsed the discrepancies between appearance and reality. He sensed only the artist and the criminal had the full power to express themselves.

When an American hostess asked Count Robert to introduce her to an exclusive salon, he shrugged, "Madame, that would be impossible. You see, the moment you appeared there it would no longer be exclusive."

But Kate Moore did not give up courting him and Robert de Montesquieu would sometimes accept a dinner at her house. At one of her large dinners she suddenly began to weep. When she was asked what was the matter, she explained, "I've swallowed my tooth. I've swallowed a tooth."

The guests found this very amusing; there was muffled laughter as they held napkins against their mouths full of the food she had served them.

However, the *maître d'hôtel* remained calm, waved off the idea of the loss as he bowed over her and said, "Madame can rest assured that madame has *not* swallowed her tooth. No, she has only forgotten it, left it on the dressing table in the water closet." With the proper gesture he presented her with a golden platter and on it was the porcelain tooth . . . Robert de Montesquieu maintained a good *maître d'hôtel* is always calm, always prepared for special crisis.

Kate Moore did manage to get to her table assorted dukes, duchesses, even a prince now and then. The biggest catch was King Edward VII, a jolly vulgarian, high liver, and womanizer. He found Kate Moore amusing as the typical American social climber. He agreed with her at the lack of kings available to invite for dinner. "But, my dear Mrs. Moore, you should have lived in the days of Louis XIV. Ah madame, in those days there were kings *everywhere*."

Kate was courted by art dealers, those born thieves, people who had objects, artifacts, furniture to sell at fabulous prices. She accepted them if such people could introduce her to some salon, a select *soirée*. She was kindly with her use of money, and spread the wealth around among many patch-pants noble French houses and their enthusiastic accomplices. When she died, her will remembered many people who had helped boost her a bit into some of the upper circles. When Robert de Montesquieu heard of her legacies and rewards, he shrugged his well-tailored shoulders. "Ah, Mrs. Moore, she has departed from us, as she always did from the Ritz. Handing out tips."

Kate Moore never married into French nobility. One who did was Winarella Singer, an American girl with the vast wealth of a sewing machine company behind her; machines which—no fault of hers—made possible the miserable sweatshop hells for hundreds of thousands of women. She became, through the needle trade, the Princess de Polignac. She, too, courted Robert de Montesquieu as a dinner guest. The Singers were reported to have some Jewish background, and Montesquieu followed the fashion of the Catholic upper class in supporting the Army and its dishonoring of Dreyfus as a needed ritual; he was violently anti-Semitic. (Degas, who suffered from syphilis, refused to take a Wasserman test because the Wasserman had an Israelite sounding name.) However at one time Montesquieu did bend enough to ask a Jewish banker to lend him some jewels for a costume ball.

The banker excused himself and shook his head. "Not those items, my dear count. You see they are old family jewels."

Montesquieu made a *moue* with his ironic lips. "I knew you had jewels. I didn't know you had a family."

The Princess de Polignac, née Singer, should have taken notice that the count had a sharp and acid tongue. Still one day she invited him to a supper "at little tables," as it was then labeled. Robert de Montesquieu sent word he would be delighted to accept: "How charming it will be, I know, your serving of supper on the little sewing machines."

So season after season Americans with money and social hopes bat-

tered at the gates of the best houses in Paris, trying for the drawing rooms of the Palais Monceau, the salons of the Comtesse de Greffulhe and of Madame de Caillavet, who had Anatole France on a leash.

Americans measured their dollars against these well-guarded ramparts of the old houses of the Faubourg Saint Germain; the world that Marcel Proust was to bring into larger life in another time, a life that held fast the doors against the American attacks. In his indiscreet journal, salacious, always well written, Edmond de Goncourt wrote of his fears of these pushy Americans. "These men and women are destined to be the future Conquerors of the world . . . Barbarians of Civilization who will devour the world."

CHAPTER 21

Society's Historian—
Miss Wharton

*Some people would never have fallen in love
if they had never heard of love.*

LA ROCHEFOUCAULD

IN THE YEARS just before World War I (the Great War as it was to be called for about a generation) Paris saw much of a pretty, middle-aged woman, Mrs. Wharton, with just a bit too much chin and a great deal of character, most of it stern. Her social conduct was stately—at least in public. "Poor Edith Wharton," was the whispering, leading around a husband, Teddy, who was slowly losing his mind. Edith Wharton had a reputation as a gifted novelist (deserved) and of being the mistress of Walter Van Rensselaer Berry (some were not sure if they were lovers or merely, as in her own words, "soul mates"). Certainly she lived by the stone age psychiatric advice of her time: Adapt and cope.

Edith's last name had been plain Jones when she married Teddy Wharton, a man who never had a profession, but had a great deal of money. Edward Robbins Wharton, twelve years older than Edith, the same dozen years out of Harvard; a fly fisherman, figure skater, hunt rider. She was twenty-three when she married, an intellectual, deeply bedded in the social aspic of her times, still set in Victorian *mœurs*. Yet the marriage was a failure, and she went to the noted neurologist, Dr. Weir Mitchell, about her frustrations as a wife to the brainless Teddy. Dr. Mitchell was a pretty good novelist himself. *The Red City*, a novel of the French Revolution, is still worth reading. He advised Mrs. Wharton to turn her mind to writing. It seemed a private niche to live in, and so she wrote.

Edith had sharp literary teeth—she attacked her society with ironic fury and fine style. Her prissy friend, Henry James, called her "the angel of devastation." Her literary adviser and close friend became Walter Berry, a man-about-Paris. "Pussy," as Teddy called his wife, fell more and more under the influence of Walter Berry in the immutable course of events. Her novel, *The House of Mirth*, made her literary reputation, and Walter Berry moved deeper into her life as the senses left poor Teddy.

Berry was one of the Americans in Paris who had left behind them any idea of permanent settlement in a crude United States. He was a New Yorker, a Van Rensselaer, the bluest blood Dutch-America had yet produced (of course there were *also* the Roosevelts). He had actually been born in Paris and had a mild career as consul to our French and Italian embassies. He was a lover of books and gossip, took solace in dependency on his own good taste. To use a vulgar expression popular at the time, Edith was "starved for love."

As the feeble brain of Teddy grew more foggy, Edith led him—almost in reins—in travels all over Europe. What passed for psychiatric consultation then did not help. As for Walter Berry, no *homme primitif*—he was a lifetime bachelor. Marriage was farthest from his mind. If Edith adored him, he could only shrug and accept her good taste. It was not until Teddy's third major breakdown that it was said Walter became her lover. She pursued him for years for marriage, but he managed to avoid that knot with this determined woman. For all her rational skepticism, she was deeply in love. As for Berry, no one was ever sure. Cultured, a lover of the fine things of life, his friendships with Henry James and Marcel Proust have been cited as proof of his ability to mingle with the best literary masters. A taster and not a creator of life and art, he was a man respected by people of talent.

Berry had been trained as a lawyer and had a cold logical mind. Many of Edith's friends claimed it was a selfish mind, that their relationship was *un amour impossible*. Being rich, Walter did not have to work at his profession. He was not popular with Edith's friends and admirers, who disliked him with a fury hardly at all in keeping with their upbringing. They did not think he was "good enough" for her personal, emotional life. His influence on her, outside of literary advice, consisted of belittling her true worth. His views of life were narrow, if rich in detail. He was an admitted snob. As a private letter puts it: "proud of his Dutch bloodline that had begun as farmers, fur dealers and various ways of cheating Indians when not slaughtering them. His snobbery was of a petty nature to most; a sneering at people wearing the wrong tie, not being able to order a wine or a proper meal, being seen in the company of people not in any social register, or members in a good club, or involved in the official arts of salon or academy."

His insolent but firm influence on Edith was bad and stunted her outlook. He was a Tory reactionary, what we would today too easily call a fascist. Edith let a great deal of his prejudice and bigotry seep into her, so that some people began to find in her qualities that were unattractive, qualities that she had absorbed from Berry and loyally accepted in dimensions beyond her own reason and experience.

For all her stern control of herself, Edith respected Walter Berry as a wise man of affairs, a full man of the world. Others saw merely a *boulevardier* in high collar, London-cut tailoring, top hat; the man who knew what was "right." Edith shouldn't have been so blind. She was more limber mentally, an interrelating intellect in her books, the writer of moods and emotions touching the mystic rim of life and its fortuitous play of chance. Berry had no deep philosophical core; he was a shallow surface creature for all his reading. He saw as unrewarding nonsense any attempt to probe religion, mysticism, or the point of intersection of materialism, the Aristotelian world of absolutes, and the poetry of things; those facades that could not be dragged into daylight and explained by an accepted logical or chemical report.

Edith herself, therefore, because of Berry's attitudes, never went deeply into the spiritual or the non-Aristotelian world. She might well have been a greater personality, even a better writer, without Berry at her side talking always in his drawling drawing-room voice, dialogue like something out of a London society play. It was too true that she expended her emotions—those womanly feelings of belonging to someone —on an unworthy clubman in spats and top hat, twirling a gold cane and gossiping in the bar of the Ritz, testing a goose-liver *ballottine* in a fashionable restaurant. It was clear Berry could not return her feelings, her insatiable hunger for close understanding with one human being.

She never admitted he was a selfish man, isolated in pride, smothered in the cotton wool of his background, his ideas of society and his own worth. People who knew Berry in Paris, and disliked him, spoke of his massive selfishness. Her doubts—she must have had them—affected Edith to a point where she took on the surface of his brittle veneer in an act of loyalty. With her it may have been a veneer, but to Paris it looked like a cold snobbery set in the aridity of her social position.

She was in an anomalous position; while she knew what people thought of Walter Berry, she never stopped loving him, never admitted that he would fail her when she needed him. Yet when she was at her most desperate, Berry slipped off to Egypt for some embassy post, escaping, some said, his responsibility to Edith with a few desultory platitudes as to her character.

Edith was not happy in their relationship, strong as it was on her side; on his it was too fluid and flowed away from her. Perhaps, like so many writers, she dreamed of a continual happiness, a great happiness that sometimes they gave to their characters, or thought of giving them. In her stories there is more than a hint of this difficult business of happiness. And in her fiction we find sometimes the cultured dilettantes, *boulevardiers*, selfish men about town, portraits of Walter Berry. Her friends saw Berry in the character of Anson Wavley in the story "After Holbein." It is sharp and bitter and draws blood. She could agree with Baudelaire: "The role of the artist is full self-abnegation."

Paris was at first strange to Edith; she had hoped to penetrate French society, the Parisian literary scene. Teddy, before he faded out, could not adjust to the new life in the French city. He remained an *américain pessimiste*. He and Edith fought over houses. He cried out she had de-

prived him of the management of their house back in America in Lennox, the Mount, and also of control of their money. There was little left of his mind.

The year 1911 was crucial for the Whartons. In September Teddy, back in the United States, was taking a cure at Hot Springs, and Edith sailed for Paris alone. He had promised if given control to hold on to their home, the Mount. But as the ship sailed, Teddy, in that spitefulness of the mean in spirit and the feeble in mind, sold the place.

Humility and forbearance came hard to Edith. She had been friendly with Henry James since soon after her marriage; at that time she had been invited to dinner in company with Henry James. Edith in those early days had been excited at meeting the Great Cham of polite, subtle society fiction, and had gotten a special dress to impress him. It was old-rose pink, embroidered with shiny beads. He had not been impressed by either the young writer or the dress. And she was too shy, in his aridity of public feeling, to enter into a conversation. The dinner for her was a failure. A few years later, again in Paris, she tried to say to James what she felt about his writing. It did not come off. But with time and many meetings their intimacy grew. He visited her in America. Edith flirted with him a bit, knowing she was safe with what Frank Harris (at the bar of a London club) had called "the capon in exile."

Now that Teddy was sinking into blankness, the marriage destroyed, Edith, with that determined upper lip often mistaken for snobbery, turned to James, explaining her dilemma. He tried in those bloated, overweight sentences of his to console her. James was a kind and generous man, in many ways admirable *if* his dignity and comforts were not disturbed. He had an almost female intuition under his hard-shell carapace of esteem and pride. He knew how Edith suffered.

By 1912 Teddy was locked away—he entered a sanitarium of his own free will, what was left of it, at the urging of Edith. It was in one of those luxurious private sanitariums of care and bland diets in Switzerland, on Lake Constance. "Those who are weak eat herbs," said St. Paul.

As for Edith, she gained a divorce in 1913, it being whispered among her friends it was done only "for her own protection." Perhaps Teddy, mentally destitute, did have violent moments when he was free to wander at her side. There was no hope of his ever recovering; he only grew worse. Edith told some people Teddy was hardly a living thing for the last twenty years of his life. He stayed on Lake Constance until after World War I, and in 1918 he was carried back to America. He died in 1928. Edith was to outlive him by nine years. Such is the story of her addled and tragic marriage. She would not be human and a sensitive artist if it deep down did not leave her with some rancor.

James was a friendly and portly shoulder in time of trouble. But he never saw Edith's merit as a writer. Her writing was clearer, crisper than his own involved style, expressing a much broader knowledge of life and sex—of which James almost all his life was as innocent as his walking stick. James did not grasp her remarkable abilities as a novelist. He thought her writing second-rate, but then he often thought much great writing second-rate (his praise was spread on a young literary gunzel, Hugh Walpole, a popular hack). When forced to say something to Edith of her work at a gathering, James said, in that bumbling clubman, half-stuttering style which made him a conversation piece—and a bit of an actor—"Admirable, admirable, a masterly little achievement . . . [a swishing of shoulders, a harump harump *harump harump* in the Jamesian style]. Of course as accomplished a mistress of the arts would not, without deliberate intention . . . [pause, a play of fingers, fluttered while flexing them] have given the tale so curiously conventional a treatment. . . . which conceivably, my dear lady, on further consideration have led you to your subject as—er—er [a bit of dramatic stumbling for effect] in itself a totally unsuitable one . . . harump *harump*." And reached for the teacup, having failed to impress his audience. Instead shouts of laughter went up.

This was the actor James. No wonder H. G. Wells was to say, "There are three Jameses in history. James the First, James the Second, and Henry James the old Pretender." Actually Edith saw James as a bristly mastiff with no bite.

By 1913 Edith Wharton had reached her literary peak with her novel, *The Customs of the Country*. Her great creative cycle was over although all the later books would merit attention. She was also free. With Teddy put away there was nothing to face now but Walter Berry and the Great War. Her mother was dead, having died in Paris. She had a brother Harry, also living in Paris, but they were not close, and he remains shadowy and insubstantial to us. There had been another brother, Fred, who after thirty settled years of marriage had "run off with another woman." It was not a romantic elopement, but something that led to much scandal and a legal mess. Edith sided with her deserted (and finally divorced) sister-in-law. She and brother Freddy broke all communication, one of those dreadful silences and hatreds so common between sisters and brothers in American society, chiefly caused by the scent or loss of money. Fred—as a footnote in a book—"died obscurely in New York," still, in 1918, unforgiven. However Edith was enough of Society's Proper Little Girl to buy black bordered writing paper as proper respect for the departed Freddy.

Harry, her other brother, living in Paris, was going a bit off his trolly, and Edith shivered, thinking of Teddy's collapse. Harry Jones was certainly an eccentric with infinite aspects, and he, too, like poor Fred, fell in with a woman who seduced him away from his social position. The family, the relatives, all shook their heads; Harry was much disapproved of in his new ménage. Sister and brother were both living in Paris, yet they never saw each other. Harry refused to have any visit from Edith, and went into great rages when it was suggested they should meet. There may have been latent family antagonisms at work; we shall never know.

Harry's end is clouded in the mystery of a horror film. According to some who claim to know, his wife was a twisted pathological case who felt that no matter how much money was on hand or banked there was a dire and dreadful poverty ahead. In that miserable manner of eccentric neurotics, she began to economize on heat and food. One sees these strange types sometimes in Paris markets, eyes swiveling from side to side, often muttering to themselves, wearing outmoded, uncleaned clothes, and often clutching to their shabby sides some net bag full of tainted meat or overripe food, as they hurry along a bit sideways, like a crab. One can picture them returning to an overcrowded flat, an ill-lit place, smelly, with the remains of fine furnishings, *objets de luxe*. It was believed Harry led such a shabby, sick life in his last years, and that his wife, as Harry grew feebler, already a disembodied person in 1922, starved him to death.

It is no wonder that Edith, cut off from family, found in Walter Berry something solid, even if cold, someone she had known for many years (there is a rumor he had courted her before she married Teddy). What was left of life she wanted to live fully. As the war of August moved up in 1914, Edith still had twenty years to fill. But the war—that stupid, foolish, murderous assault on the sanity and decency of the twentieth century—was to change not only her world but the condition of the society she knew. Lawn parties at Lennox, at the Mount, were to be replaced by a world dominated by formulas of Marx, Freud, and Einstein —leading to the ticking of the Doomsday Bomb. But first Edith was to see the society of pink-coated riders at Meadowbrook becoming fliers of Sopwith Camels.

Everyone talked of war coming during that 1914 spring and summer. No one knew it would destroy the leisure and manners of a calling-card age and that Mrs. Astor's Four Hundred's grandchildren were some day to come to Paris as Charleston-dancing flappers, as Gertrude Stein's Lost Generation, calling themselves Fitzgerald's "all the sad young men." As the war came nearer, Edith was to be no transmission belt to the future. She lived to nearly the end of the era of the Americans in Paris in the Twenties, but she could not leap into their lives as their historian or be their interpreter.

But she would not desert Paris when the Germans came to the mansions on the Rue Jacob, the old Saint Germain quarter—or even when Ernest Hemingway came with the kind of novel she could not have imagined possible or desired. She did not live to face Henry Miller.

So as the war maniacs of 1914, kings, kaiser, czar, social democrats, the parliamentary leaders of western civilization all rushed together in a clatter of telegraph keys roaring ultimatums, Edith was in a fine modern apartment on the Rue de Varenne. She had the eternal English pair: White to butler, Mrs. White to cook. A chauffeur named Cook, a personal maid, Gross, and spoiled yapping little dogs that came snarling and barking at visitors and often cocked a limb at a trouser leg.

In the entourage there was even that overused literary figure written in by second-rate novelists, the old, crotchety nanny. Anna Bahlmann was Edith's governess, a lone survivor from her childhood, red-scarfed, aged, getting deaf in poverty and coaxed back into Edith's home to survive. *What* service was the problem. Anna was one of those deaf people who will not admit their loss of hearing, and she disliked Paris as so many German-Americans did. With her failing memory, whatever business letters or bill-keeping she took on for Edith was a mess. So Edith lived in a diverse, conflicting manner, trying to bring order into disorder.

When war broke out Anna Bahlmann—with good luck—was in New York. Edith, free of her overripe nanny, no longer had to moan out loud at her burden, "Oh Lord, Oh Lord." It was not a prayer asking for aid; Berry had long since brought Edith, never too strong a church woman, around to his agnostic doubts. So nanny was out of the war, and the problem put away was *should* nanny eat in the servants hall? (No, nanny was *not* a servant.)

Then came the crisis with "dear old Grossie," Edith's maid, who became senile and had to have private nursing. Always there were servants on Edith's mind. Her old cook in America, Bagley, was to die, to Edith's horror, in a public charity ward. From all this one sensed in this sensitive, ironic writer the fact that perhaps she was at home and comfortable only with her servants. They formed a kind of family where she could drink her tea, pamper her smoke-and-amber-colored Pekinese dogs, and brood over her precarious situation with her lover. He did not desire to share her apartment permanently or invite her to his.

Dear old Grossie was replaced by an Elsie, and meanwhile the dismal war raged. Edith had to do without those things she had grown to like. Many things that came from New York, usually from Minnie, the sister-in-law deserted long ago by the wandering Fred. Edith missed that special soap, the good Peko-India tea, the toilet waters, the new novels and histories. Also with the war on Minnie could not correct the proof sheets of Edith's books, a task Edith found irksome and often handed over to Minnie. And furs were hard to get. Edith had a weakness for hairy pelts of animals stylishly tailored. Paris, the war-gray, brooding city, was alive only in the orgies of its officers and soldiers back from the front, the oaths and cries of the happy whores, and the gatherings of Allied majors and captains, seeking drink, women, and music, from the Ile de la Cité to the apartments of the Place Blanche.

The war had at first caught Edith off base. She had expected to close her flat and spend the fall in England, close to Henry James. But the banks had snapped shut, no checks were being honored. Edith had only a mere two hundred francs on hand. Berry gave her some money, but he, too, was pressed for cash. Black market exchanges were operating in the open air *pissotières*. Edith wired London for aid, and got back the answer, "HAVE NO MONEY." A cable to her New York bank brought the one word, "IMPOSSIBLE." A quivering palsy overtook Americans stranded in Paris, then an outcry and a mad rush to get home. Edith merely went to her empty flat. The servants had preceded her to England. In a cataleptic calm she looked at the linen shrouds on the furniture. She was alone. Berry had failed her again.

She was balanced in a war, in a perilous equilibrium. The Germans were at the Marne. There were ways of getting money for 100 percent interest—all against her Protestant ethic of thrift. Her first five hundred dollars on the money exchange cost her a thousand. Paris was drying up. Shop signs read, closed, *Pàur cause de mobilisation*. She applied for a permit to get to England, and waited, as the first days of August burned on the horizon and the gray German war machine tramped in dusty boots toward Paris, via the Schlieffen plan. The panic of the Americans to leave packed the shipping offices. Some few American college men planned to serve as ambulance drivers. There was to be talk of an American airplane unit. But for all the diverse, conflicting talk, the war would be over in six weeks—that was the general agreement. Meanwhile this made chaos of one's social plans, those laid-out tours to Italy for Michelangelo, to Baden Baden for the liver, to North Africa to see the Sphinx.

There was sudden unemployment in Paris as men went off to war in blue hammertail coats and red trousers, and the lack of demand for costly gowns, perfumes, carriages, splendid motor cars, furs, jewels, also threw many out of work. The great munition factories would later take up this slack. Edith was asked by her friend, the Comtesse d'Haussonville, president of the local French Red Cross, if she would aid in opening "a workshop for the unemployed" to roll bandages. It was clean romantic work.

Edith leaped at the chance. She got an empty flat, filled it with ninety women, and instead of rolling bandages, she set them to work making underwear. Winter would soon be there, and short war or long war a soldier likes clean underwear. Edith called on rich Americans still trapped in Paris by lack of transport and got funds to carry on her workshop.

The French by the thousands went out to die before 1915 came, singing, "*C'est l'Alsace et la Lorraine. C'est l'Alsace qu'il nous faut. Oh oh Oh!*"

The rest of the war Edith spent mostly organizing French-American Relief, writing letters and articles for American publications for aid to a Europe tearing itself to bits. In 1916 she got the Cocarde of the Legion of Honor, also a Belgian honor.

The French Red Cross asked her to report on conditions at the front and the people behind it—that sinister, deadly, Western Front in which a couple of million men were dying under extravagantly stupid generals—ordered to advance to gain a few feet, a mile or so, then dig in and live like poisoned rats expiring in a wall. Edith no more than most was aware of the insanity of the war. Her head too was filled with slogans, noble-sounding nonsense. Edith was aging, moving toward her sixties, but still she went to the front lines, peeked at the enemy barbed wire through a spyhole, smelled the dead, was trapped once by a small enemy attack. She would not don pants or boots, but in skirts tramped through the mud of the front, a filthy, liquid glue mixed with horse litter and the remains of hundreds of thousands of horses that had died. Edith came by in her tight, stylish skirt, on a mule, or treading the duckboards of some supporting trench. A far way from the dignity of the society she had written her books for and once been part of. She gagged at the rot and decay of the fearful field hospitals, ate lunch in a field rimmed with rusting guns.

Like those most vocal on both sides, she spoke not of the horror, but of "final victory, a shiny victory."

Edith was the organizations' favorite darling, so her novel in process was put aside. She could not write of the war as an artist. Her writings were shrill, often foolish, her idea of the right and wrong of events too simple. Like so many searching, unique persons, she saw the war as a crusade and not a power game. Many flags waving were enough of a cause for her. She retained a strong streak of fidelity to already lost values, even if she was finding the world at war an abomination; yet also an oversimplification she shared with Woodrow Wilson. Somehow the world would be "Made Safe for Democracy" if the United States did its duty and came into the war.

CHAPTER 22

Edith's War

The deed is everything, not the glory.
J. W. GOETHE, *Faust*

EDITH WAS AWARE that French democracy was a tradition, never a fact. She was for the beauty, the culture, the grace of France. It was a France she hardly knew beyond the fringes of boulevard society, a few salons in Paris that Berry had entry to—and for Edith a polite bow to some noble names. She had early found her own America vulgar, pushy, had fled to Paris. But in war in the abstract, Americans were suddenly clean and vigorous, a people who would repudiate the evil forces and die gallantly with an exquisite sense of what was right.

When America at last fell into the trap and came into the war, she wrote a letter to a New York woman about how proud she must be in having "two sons fighting in France." Then the son of a cousin, Newbold Rhineland (how the very name suggests one of her frivolous characters in an early novel), came to France with the United States Air Force. He flew in one of the canvas falcons, spiraling down to earth in an aerial combat. Was he dead or taken prisoner? Edith, as the Armistice came, began to pressure the Allied officials—was Newbold alive or dead? She badgered the American negotiators to find out the boy's destiny. Sadly came the report—Newbold was dead—concluding with a short response of official sympathy.

Edith was tired. Paris was tired and drab, neglected. It needed some moments to catch its breath before moving on toward the coming peace conferences. It was a time of decline, with hopes for resurrection, but Edith felt a need for withdrawal.

Edith's heart was acting up. But there were for Duty's Child some jobs to be finished. There were refugees to be sent home, bodies to be buried, potatoes to be found to feed the war's victims while the captains and the replacements of kings sat at Versailles, ate the cuisine of Paris.

Edith didn't write—she built sanitariums for the ill. But now money was hard to come by. The war was over, everyone who had wanted to give had given. Edith's income had shrunk. No new books of hers of any deep merit had appeared. Taxes were higher, so the apartment on the Rue de Varenne would have to go. And the auto? No—she would "hang onto my motor till the end."

She had bought in the spring of 1918 during the war an eighteenth-century house and garden, just beyond the northern fringe of Paris, at St.-Price-sous-Forêt.

The world was becoming lonely for her. Henry James was dead. And so many other antiques. In 1920 Edith Wharton produced *The Age of Innocence*, not a novel of the new age but a recall of her own childhood in the 1870s, an exorcism of old ghosts. It saved her motorcar by earning her the Pulitzer Prize.

Actually the prize had been awarded to Sinclair Lewis for his attack on the dullness and bigotry of village life, for *Main Street*, by a committee vote. But the Pulitzer Prize headmen, as was often the case, played politics; they felt Mr. Lewis was vulgar, and after much intriguing, politicking, and skulduggery, they picked Mrs. Wharton, a lady they preferred. It did not make the award sweet to Edith—not in this manner of giving it—or add to her admiration of the new America emerging.

It all added to Edith's aversion to the new America of bootleggers and of gangsters corrupting judges and buying up whole states. She heard of the permissive sexual revolution, of virginity mocked by the flapper and of country-club fornication in the backs of parked cars. She began to feel irritable; she was repelled by a changed America, by the rejection of the League of Nations, the scandals during Harding's Presidency, the Teapot Dome oil steal, the middle-class murders of the Halls-Mills, Judd-Snyder type, the whoopy era of speak-easys and bathtub gin. So the mood of Timon of Athens hovered over her in her isolation.

And Paris, what had happened to it? Those hoards of Americans were now pouring in, so crude, so vulgar, so loud; drinking, copulating with the new women, "American teen-age nookie." And divorcées driving fast cars, Stutz Bear Cats and Marmons, Americans attending brothels and

parties on the Left Bank, infesting the Latin Quarter with their harsh Midwestern accents, their money, so plentiful at a favorable rate of exchange. And their talk of Dada, *Anna Christie*, Gertrude Stein, *The Green Hat*. There were young roughs like Hemingway, drunks and party-busters like the Fitzgeralds. Scott and Zelda on the loose in Paris were the ideals, symbols of things ritzy, snazzy, the cat's pajamas.

Scott had sent Edith a copy of his novel *The Great Gatsby*. She had written him a letter saying good things about his work. When he was in Paris, she invited him to tea at the Pavillon Colombe with some literary friends of hers. Fitzgerald started out for the party in the suburbs, stopping from time to time to take on alcohol. Scott was a natural exhibitionist, with a glancing scrutiny, a defiant stare. When drunk he was a boor and a fool. He always felt a bit inferior because of his middle-class Irish background; he felt touched among the rich and successful he admired. Yet he was a graceful and singularly talented stylist.

Scott arrived primed at the Pavillon Colombe, and after greetings and the teacups were in hand, the guests sat waiting for the talk to begin between this new young talent and the old professional.

According to the story that went around Paris, Fitzgerald crudely began the attack. "Mrs. Wharton, you know what's the matter with you?"

"No, Mr. Fitzgerald, I've wondered what it could be."

"You don't know a thing about life, about living. When my wife and I first came to Paris, we took a room in a whorehouse, that's what we did. And you know, we lived there for two weeks."

The guests leaned forward with interest. Edith remained expressionless. Then her old irony came to service. "Mr. Fitzgerald, you haven't told what you did in the brothel."

Fitzgerald, flustered, on the verge of being nearly sober, beat a hasty retreat back to his Paris hotel. He told his wife Zelda he had been a real success at the party—he had really impressed Edith and her friends. But as he talked, he took drink after drink while reciting his success. Suddenly he broke down, pounded the table, and cried out, "They beat me, beat me!"

He would have been even more upset by the comment Edith put down in her journal concerning her odd contact with F. Scott Fitzgerald: "*Horrible!*"

Edith was bitter over the change she found in Americans. She could write, "Since the Americans have ceased to have dyspepsia, they have lost the only thing that gave them expression." A witty, but uniquely bizarre line.

She stood now for the permanent society of Europe as against the American barbarians. In exile, Edith lived in the past, and in her decline, in her anger, grew almost vulgar. She had her house, the Pavillon Colombe, her lily pond, roses, elms, many neat and lovely rooms, her flower paintings (not by one of those fearful moderns).

In winter she moved back to Paris proper. Reports pictured her as a chain-smoker, wearing gold-rimmed glasses, a grandame in her sixties. She still saw Walter Berry, tall and thin in old age, still the dandy with a head of white hair and a white mustache, now not too evocative or human, a cartoon rather than a living being. Both of them belonged to a Paris now gone. His great nose was larger, his collars higher, the striped trousers still as Edwardian as his top hat. His creed was never betray the self, nothing else matters. Paris still thought Berry handsome and wondered what he saw in old Mrs. Wharton. She had lost her trim figure and was what is politely called plump; her hair had lost its sheen. She tried the newer fashions, the hair styles, but with that sharp jawline extended by age the effect was grim. If only she could live serenely without remorse.

Berry, of course, was not faithful to her. For what vitality he had for pleasure he preferred young girls, dancing the Toddle to the music of

"Stumbling." He paraded them in public, these John Held, Jr., models, and before Edith's friends. She had always made him welcome in her world; he never brought her over into his. Proust, a good friend of Berry's, died without ever meeting Edith.

Berry, for all his high collars and mink-lined overcoats, had ties with the new young Americans in Paris—ties Edith lacked. Harry Crosby, a young cousin of Berry's and a nephew of J. P. Morgan, came to Paris with his wife, Caresse. They became some of the leaders of the wild young set in Paris. When Caresse began to act as Berry's hostess, Edith took a great dislike to her, but Caresse only sighed and smiled. "Mrs. Wharton doesn't like me, Uncle Walter."

But the old lovers were too tired to strike sparks on each other in anger. Walter Berry and Edith both went into major illnesses at the same time. He had a stroke, was left speechless; it affected his writing and reading. The alchemy of his personality disintegrated. Edith came to help him, meanwhile worrying over leaving her dogs. A vet attended and treated the dogs with caffeine, camphorated oil, and as a doggie reward each got a teaspoon of Edith's best champagne. She hurried from dogs to lover, held Walter's head in her arms; just once he answered her devotion by pressing her hand. A last stroke killed him on an October day in 1926. Edith went back to the role of the outsider. The Crosbys carried off his ashes and the dead man's fabulous collection of books. He is said to have left behind a bit of advice: "When emotional, never speak frankly to a woman."

Edith still had eleven years to fill in. The stock-market crash of 1929 merely singed her income. She still had two houses and twenty-two servants at work or out to pasture. Somehow she could never get rid of an old retainer. They clung like barnacles. Some of the servants died: Grossie, Elsie, very old friends.

She had a heart attack—an effect like a bird striking a wall—and she lingered in near coma for two months. She had divided what would remain. Money, minks, chinchillas, jewels, necklaces, her Renoir painting all were left to friends. Her own wish was to lie as close as she could be planted to the ashes of Walter Berry in the cemetery at Versailles. Her casket was large and ornate. With her inside it could not be taken down the stairs; it had to be lowered out of an upper window.

Her advice to young writers had been: "All that matters is that you should be free to finish the job."

Book Four
JE N'OUBLIERAI JAMAIS

CHAPTER 23

The Perfect Eye—
John Singer Sargent

If one cheats the world only to laugh at it,
the sin is already half forgiven.

GEORGE SANTAYANA

A YOUNG, CLEAN-CUT AMERICAN, with no thought of conscious revolt, raised by a decent mother and father who lived in Europe in respectable domestic contentment, exhibited a picture at the Paris Salon of 1884 that caused one of those sudden scandals and impassioned shouting matches. The twenty-eight-year-old artist was John Singer Sargent; the painting, the cause of it all, was a splendid portrait of a flashing American-born beauty named Madame Pierre Gautreau, but it was listed at the Salon as *Madame X*

By today's permissive standards the painting would hardly cause a blush, unless one were moved by the skillful handling of paint and a picture of a very beautiful woman of poise, with a kind of purring animal vitality. Sargent was no stranger to the Salon. He had been accepted and had shown paintings there for seven years. Now, no sooner had the doors of the Salon opened than an uproar over *Madame X* took place. The angry outcry was compared to the fury, turmoil, and rage set off by Manet's *Le Déjeuner sur l'herbe*, in which a nude lady lunched casually with some fully dressed gentlemen in a forest; a like furor had arisen over Manet's *Olympia*, in which he painted a Parisian harlot in a pose copied from a painting of a courtesan by Titian. Sargent's painting was not that bold. It had taste, showed painterly skill, and respected the proper decencies. It suggested no lechery, just a desirable woman. How had the innocent young American and his shocked parents blundered or wandered into this storm of artistic and social abuse?

John Singer Sargent was born in 1856 in Florence, Italy, the only son of American expatriates who were running out of money but still felt America was too crude, too much addicted to making fortunes for its own material ends, to bring their darling little John home to native shores. They were the kind of Americans one was to find in the novels of Henry James and Edith Wharton, a family who felt a need for "the better things" and who wandered over Europe with their furrowed, pensive faces, dragging children after them, children who never developed an American accent or any permanent roots. Vulgar America was *terra incognita* to these darlings.

The founder of the Sargent's once satisfactory shipping fortune, one Epes Sargent, had been painted by John Singleton Copley. John's own father had once been a doctor and surgeon in Philadelphia. The artist's mother was an amateur water colorist, a dilettante in music, and a snob about the vulgarity of anything from the United States except income. When she inherited some money, she got her husband to give up his practice and cross to Europe, where she and her husband and son wallowed in culture, in reduced circumstances.

Sargent was a handsome, well-built, blue-eyed youth. Once able to hold a brush, he joined his mother in painting wherever they were: the piazzas of Florence and Rome; long stays in Switzerland; rootless people gossiping at dusk to the sound of cowbells. The south of France saw them with camp stool and water colors. John did some fine work, but none of it strikingly new or exciting in mood. He studied at the Florence Academy, learning little there except how to prepare a canvas and mix paints and respect a copy of the painting of La Fornarina, Raphael's mistress. It was clear the boy needed to complete his art education in Paris, where there was such great talk of art and painters, and the new wild men attacking canvas in new ways. Sargent was eighteen when he came to Paris to study, shy, awkward, sheltered under Mama's sketching umbrella. Modest, too, yet speaking fine French. He dressed well, stylish but without arousing the feeling he was a dandy of the boulevards or the gross, fashionable cafés. He did stand out against the sloppy, careless dress of the usual art student seen in *boîtes* and dance halls and their transitory pleasures with the women of the studios.

As a painter Sargent did not enter the rising though scandalous school of the Impressionists but went into the atelier of the portrait artist,

Carolus-Duran (originally Charles Durand). Duran was a sleek and fast-working portraitist whose patrons were rich and opulent. He had no great originality or artistic merit. He painted the *haut monde* with suggestions of the styles of Franz Hals and Diego Velázquez, but without their breadth and spaciousness. He passed this flashing style on to his young pupil, John Singer Sargent. However in Sargent's skilled hand the paint was manipulated with the application of a Houdini doing card tricks.

Sargent was to become one of the most flashing geniuses of paint handled for the joy of paint itself. He added to this brushwork a skill in portrait-making that was to render him a success in the world of society, a connoisseur of dressed social flesh. Later in life he would prove himself one of the great water color artists of modern times.

Outside of his great talent for portraits, Sargent had certain grave faults as an artist. His drawings are weak and unexciting, his landscapes in oil too literal and detailed, his attempts at a mural style a disaster. But he was able to catch depths of expression, innate possibilities in well-cut clothes in his portraits. For what he is, a master of paint and surface, no modern press-agented handler of pigments is his peer. His portraits have a spacious tranquillity with a mild suggestion of a sneer.

If Henry James appears too often on these pages, it is because he is the historian of the well-off American migration of the late nineteenth century, seeking art and culture and social success in Europe along calculated, polite, and formal patterns. Studying Sargent's paintings James wrote of the work as "the slightly uncanny spectacle of a talent that on the very threshold of its career has nothing more to learn." James as a critic of both music and art was a bit of a fumbler who was always behind the times. So we have here an indication that Sargent was painting away in old accepted styles but with dashing rhythmic arabesques.

Sargent stumbled into his *succès de scandale* by his very innocence, in painting Madame Pierre Gautreau in his full-length portrait for the Salon. Yet there is more than a suggestion that she fascinated Sargent's young libido and troubled his sleep. Madame Gautreau was an aggressive, original, and beautiful American girl from New Orleans, who like so many Americans who yearned for culture and life abroad had married in Europe, in her case a French banker. Her reputation was notorious as the wearer of revealing gowns on a magnificently rounded figure. She wore lavender-tinted make-up in days when only whores used exaggerated make-up.

Sargent worked for eighteen months trying to capture this fey

woman's features, this bizarre beauty who lacked any demeanor of decorum. She was well-curved and plump in the taste of that day, and he had painted her and painted her. In the end he produced a smashing silhouette with serpentine curves and that magnificent *décolletage*. Wrote Albert Woolf in *Figaro*: "One more struggle and the lady would be free of the garment."

To capture the actual sound and image of the jibes and scandal the picture caused, here is a letter by Sargent's friend and fellow artist, Ralph Curtis, writing to the folks back home:

My dear People, Yesterday the birthday or funeral of the painter Scamps (John Sargent). Most exquis. weather. Walked up Champs E. Chestnuts in full flower and dense mob of "tout Paris" in pretty clothes, gesticulating and laughing, slowly going into the Ark of Art. In 15 mins. I saw no end of acquaintances and strangers, and heard every one say *"où est le portrait Gautreau?"* *"Oh allez voir ça."* John covered with dust stopped with his trunks at the club the night before and took me on to his house where we dined. He was very nervous about what he feared, but his fears were far exceeded by the facts of yesterday. There was a *grand tapage* before it all day. In a few minutes I found him dodging behind doors to avoid friends who looked grave. By the corridors he took me to see it. I was disappointed in the color. She looks decomposed.

All the women jeer. *"Ah voilà la belle!"* *"Oh quelle horreur!"* etc. Then a painter exclaims *"superbe style,"* *"magnifique audace!"* *"Quel dessin!"* Then the *blagueur* clubman—*"C'est une copie!"* *"Comment une copie?"* *"Mais oui— une peinture d'après une autre peinture s'appelle une copie."* I heard that. All the a.m. it was one series of *bons mots, mauvaises plaisanteries* and fierce discussions. John, poor boy, was *navré.* We got out a big *déjeuner* at Ledoyens of a dozen painters and ladies and I took him there. In the p.m. the tide turned as I kept saying it would, It was discovered to be the knowing thing to say, *"étrangement épatant!"* I went home with him, and remained there while he went to see the Boits. Mme. Gautreau and *mère* came to his studio "bathed in tears." I stayed them off but the mother returned and caught him and made a fearful scene saying, *"Ma fille est perdue—tout Paris se moque d'elle. Mon gendre sera obliger de se battre en duel Elle mourira de chagrin"* etc. John replied it was against all laws to retire a picture. He had painted her exactly as she was dressed, that nothing could be said of the canvas worse than had been said in print of her appearance *dans le monde,* etc., etc. Defending his cause made him feel much better. Still we talked it all over till one o'clock here last night and I fear he has never had such a blow. He says he wants to get out of Paris for a time. He goes to Eng. in 3 weeks. I fear là-bas he will fall into Pre-R. influence wh. has got a strange hold of him he says *since Siena.* I want him to go to Seville and do the tobacco girls with me in Nov. Says he will—*nous verrons . . .*

In *La Revue des Deux Mondes* Henry Houssaye wrote:

We should go, to forget, the grand success at the Salon; because there is success and success: the portrait of Mme . . . by M. Sargent. The profile is pointed, the eye microscopic, the mouth imperceptible, the skin made-up, the neck corded, the right arm badly articulated, the hand bony, the *décolletage* is not part of the head and shoulders and appears to avoid contact with the flesh. The painter's talent is found only in the mirrored reflections in the black satin skirt. To make of a young woman justly renowned for her beauty a kind of loaded portrait seems to be the set purpose of this shamefully executed work, and the praises given without any standards.

In *L'Illustration,* art critic Jules Comte wrote:

What a bitter disillusion waited for us before the work of the painter . . . Doubtless we shall find grace in the bones, especially in that of the neck, which is delicious, and the pose does not lack suppleness. But how could he dream of painting thus Mme X, dry, rough, angular. One would say facing this profile without line, that it's a paper cutout, and what a cutout. Not the shadow of design in the mouth, the nose is neither modeled nor drawn; no planes in the flat face, and what a complexion, what color. Never have we seen such a disgrace from an artist who seemed to hold out such hopes. But here we are, one hasn't time to reflect, one wishes to get away quickly, one can no longer stand his artistic influences.

Madame Gautreau's French relatives wrathfully demanded the painting be withdrawn from the Salon. The title *Madame X* hid no secret. News of the model's true name was café gossip . . . what grace with lasciviousness Madame Gautreau projected.

Sargent had hoped to become a successful portrait painter in Paris. He liked the city; he liked his life there. He had just made for himself and furnished a Paris studio. Luxurious could be the word for it. It had used up most of his funds. And now no woman would dare come and have her picture painted by the author of *Madame X*—no society women who could pay big fees. The laurels and myrtle of his honors were turned to weeds.

Paris lost John Singer Sargent. He moved to England, penniless, borrowing five pounds to pay for his stay at Bournemouth, a grim seaport where Aubrey Beardsley had coughed out most of his last short days. Sargent was seriously thinking of turning to landscape painting when a friend arranged for him to do a standing portrait of Robert Louis Stevenson. Thank the Lord, not another woman. He painted the writer as a strange and wonderful kind of Chinese-faced, lean skeleton of a man. Stevenson said of the artist's picture of him: "He represents me as a weird, very pretty, large-eyed, chicken-boned, slightly contorted poet. We lost our hearts to him . . . simple, bashful, honest, enthusiastic, and rude with a perfect (but inoffensive) English rudeness. *Pour comble*, he gives himself out to be an American." Unmasked as an American—how his parents must have felt let down.

It was the hope of many Americans living in France or England to be mistaken for Frenchmen or Englishmen. None ever did succeed in France, although a crude English mask did work for a few. Someone was sure at one time or another to blurt out, "The chap's really an American, you know."

It is of interest to record Sargent's fellow American art students in Paris, all unknown to fame or rememberance today. What became of the young hopefuls delighted with Paris? Where did Paris—or art—fail Walter Gay, Templeman Coolidge, Ralph Curtis (wish we had more of his letters), Charles Forbes, Robert Hinckley, Stephen H. Parker, Elliot Gregory, Chadwick and Harper Pennington? The list is endless; thousands of Americans had, with talent and great hopes, gone to Paris to study art, and almost none survive as recognized painters.

Whistler is almost the lone exception. Winslow Homer visited Paris on a hurried trip, failed to be impressed by Impressionism, did several marve-lously skilled drawings of wild cancan dancers and fêtes that anticipate Toulouse-Lautrec by thirty years. Otherwise, the young Americans come and go, pack up or desert their dried paints and rolls of canvases, mostly go back to farm and city, a father's business, a Ford agency, the law office. The years are littered by the defeated artists sponging drinks, painting signs, decor on coaches, fire engines, talking of just-gone days and nights of Paris, when you could touch Courbet, see Degas sketching, buy a drink for Gauguin.

After his Paris years John Singer Sargent went on to become the most highly paid, most sought after portrait artist of his time. Henry James, who boasted of dining out in the *best* houses in London three hundred nights in one year, took the young artist with him to many dinners at homes of those people who were born to ride to the hunt ("The unspeak-able in full pursuit of the uneatable," Oscar Wilde had written) or to arrange their lives and themselves for family portraits against waxed wainscoting. In time Sargent was getting fifteen-thousand dollars a portrait—the real old-fashioned dollars of the turn of the century. He was a jolly, hedonistic liver, a feeder and lover.

In the Louvre there is a painting he did of his wild gypsy mistress, the dancer Carmencita, the full-bosomed, wasp-waisted sensation, dancing at Koster and Beal's 14th Street Music Hall, where Sargent found her on his 1889 trip to America. While they were lovers her screaming rages, her passionate sexual moods, her high arched feet banging in anger and temper held him. It was infatuation and wonder for four months. He gave her gifts of "bracelets and things" as he put it, "that cost over $3,000."

He is said to have chased Mrs. Isabella Gardner ("Mrs. Jack") through the rooms of her Boston palace—and caught her. Hardly the image his prissy biographers give us.

John was no longer the innocent, well-raised, polite boy of stuffy Amer-icans settled in Europe. In 1897 he met Mrs. Charles Hunter, who was the American wife of a Pennsylvania coal baron. She preferred Europe to the smoke of Pittsburgh, was a sought-for hostess at her London mansion, and made trips to Paris for shopping. She and the painter became lovers, and John spent a great deal of his time in her social circle enjoying the mild bacchanals, playing the piano, reciting, doing comic take-offs on the most pretentious of his portraits' originals. (When Mr. Hunter died, there were rumors the lovers would marry. They never did. In her declining years, money slipping away, Mrs. Hunter lived by selling her Sargents.)

For us Sargent is the image-making Boswell, the guide to those upper-middle-class Americans, the social climbers in Europe who came to his studios to be painted for posterity. They stare out at us, a bit too elegant, a nose straightened here and there, a chin tucked out of the way—but all are so alive, so much a parody of their haughty poses. American strangers, far from home, hopeless in their quest for a new world unless overweight with money, they stand or sit on chaise longues, in their silks and satins, in hunting pinks, their overbred dogs at their feet. The lost Americans. If Sargent painted the entire family of some vulgar international art dealer, the live cigar smoldering in a fat hand is painted like the mocking eye of the Day of Judgment. Vanity, vanity, all is vanity, the paintings recite. He made sly justifications for his amusement at American faces and figures in a greedy Europe. Otherwise he painted what a most sophisticated eye distilled for his fingers to model. His Americans stand, presented just a bit too well for him not to have known he was mocking them, in some ridiculous contrition, as if they were trying to forget that only two or three generations back they were fur traders, washerwomen, forest runners, and transported Newgate thieves.

The portrait of Madame X, by the way, may be found these days in the Metropolitan Museum in New York.

CHAPTER 24

Mr. and Madame Butterfly In Paris

To speak of love is to make love.
BALZAC

I
N THE EARLY YEARS of this century there lived within the sight of the tower of Notre Dame, within walking distance of the Egyptian obelisk of Rameses II in the Place de la Concorde, in a well-kept private house, a still handsome young American and his small doll-like Japanese wife. They entertained almost not at all. They were not part of the social set of either the American colony or the French intellectuals. They collected neither Matisses's odalisques nor gossip about Gérard de Nerval, who caused a stir in artistic circles by hanging himself wearing his top hat.

What was clear to the few who noticed them, or those fewer people who knew their story, was that they were very much in love, a love for which both had made sacrifices, and that they were solidly of the *haute bourgeoisie*, with money to live well. The lady played the piano, not ragtime or popular songs, but classics; and when some celebrated stuffed shirt was given a public burial, the two stood with respect while the *Garde Républicaine* band played the "Funeral March" by Beethoven.

The road, or rather, the sea-way that brought them to Paris, began a long way off, in a chance meeting in a place as exotic as turn-of-the-century Paris. One could, and some did, call it a modern version of *Madame Butterfly* in which the girl marries her American lover and leaves her native setting.

This true *Madame Butterfly* story began in 1902 when the American, George Morgan—a close relative of the great womanizer and multimillionaire, Pierpont Morgan—landed in Japan. He was fleeing a busted romance in New York City, and Japan offered a change. At a performance of the geisha theater, *Myako Odori*, he saw the twenty-two-year-old Oyuki, a geisha since the age of fourteen, a serenely radiant beauty.

George was suddenly madly in love again. Using an interpreter he declared his passion. But Oyuki—herself in love with a student named Kawakami at the Imperial University—made George a polite "no-thank-you-so-much Morgan San." He was to her, no matter if a Morgan, still "a white devil barbarian," a foreigner of a race that had forced Japan to face the modern world.

George, indulgently amorous, didn't give up, but kept declaring his passion, even learning some Japanese love talk, a few poems. His uncle, Pierpont, never had such trouble with women.

But Oyuki with feminine elegance was firm. She would not be his kept woman, and please, would he stop coming around, it was most annoying. Politely but firmly she gave her answers.

Meanwhile the parents of Kawakami, her student boyfriend, hearing gossip of his interest in a geisha, cut off his allowance, and the boy had no other resources. Events seemed headed for a popular romantic suicide pact for the two lovers.

But Oyuki was practical, and sacrificial. To save the career of the student, George Morgan was fully admitted into her life as her official lover; and George was unaware, it is claimed, that his gifts and money passed on to keep the student Kawakami in school, in fine clothes and well fed—and, one suspects, well loved.

In 1903 Kawakami, now a graduate of the university, not even bothering to say good-bye to Oyuki, left town. Oyuki tried to find him, to plead, to beg, to be allowed to be his love slave. But it was no good and she went into a decline.

However her duties as a Japanese woman called her, and now she transferred her affection to George Morgan. She had used him, played the love act with him, been unfaithful to him, and now she saw her stern duty—the geisha code almost—was to make up for past errors. Modestly curtsying she accepted George's offer of marriage, an offer he had tediously kept repeating for some time

There was, of course, a catch to a hasty wedding. Oyuki was a slave girl. She had an iron-clad contract of agreement with the geisha quarter for her services for years. It cost the House of Morgan 40,000 yen to buy

Oyuki out of professional bondage. Feelings were mixed among the Japanese at this White Devil's ostentation, and Oyuki gave up her Japanese citizenship. In January, 1904, George and Oyuki were married by a flustered official of the American Consulate in Kobe. Etiquette forbade full official approval.

Bride and groom still had difficulty communicating, but no interpreter went on the honeymoon when the couple left to sail to New York. A bit of table training and house-breaking, American style, took place on the slow boat to the United States. Oyuki possessed an instinctive adaptability.

The House of Morgan on Wall Street, the Astors, Goulds, Vanderbilts —all the social circles the Morgans moved in—rejected the mixed couple, although they themselves were of lowly peasant and cheap-jack peddler ancestors, a society founded in America by fur traders, tin-wear tinkers, scow and barge folk. Oyuki was not invited to Mrs. Astor's balls, and George was dropped from the *Social Register*. In a year the couple, living no idyllic life, were back in Japan.

It was 1905—the war with Russia was on—white barbarians were not popular. Antiforeign feeling caused riots in the streets of Japan. Oyuki was bitterly attacked as one lower than a prostitute mated to a dog.

A few days showed them the temper of the Japanese toward their marriage. So sadly they wandered away and ended up in Paris where eventually they settled in their own house. It seems they had ten happy years there. Oyuki faced the horror of corsets, of rare steaks, of isolation when the "best people" cut the Morgan ménage dead. The look of expectancy left their faces. They were happy alone. Oyuki mastered the piano, but there is no full record of her favorite music—certainly *not* the *Mikado* or *Madame Butterfly*, one hopes.

The year 1914 blew up their private world. The Hun stood at the Marne; World War I changed the money markets George's fortune was based on. He had to go to the United States to attend to urgent business details. Oyuki, demurely alone, waited in Paris, in the big lonely house, staring at her piano. The German U-boats ruled the Atlantic, and George, once in New York, found it difficult as a civilian to return to his wife in Paris, in a France at war. Determined to get back, he spent months in strange zig-zag journeys. By 1916 he got to Spain. But he was not to be reunited with the waiting Oyuki. George Morgan, weary traveler, died suddenly of a heart attack in the capricious drama of events over which he had no control.

Oyuki in tragic forbearance had the body cremated, and, when the war ended, she set off on a sad pilgrimage to return the ashes to George's honorable family—as was only fitting and the duty of a widow.

The war had changed many of the attitudes of society. George's will made Oyuki a very rich woman. She sent for her piano and settled into a fine New York apartment. She gave recitals at many social gatherings—and those who knew said she was a most skilled performer, graced with a provocative poise.

The years passed, even World War II came, went, with it Pearl Harbor, two atom bombs dropped on thousands in Japan by Harry Truman. The call of home came to Oyuki—like the lemmings for the sea, she wanted the sights and smells and language of her childhood, her youth, her geisha days and nights; not the voluptuous flamboyant times but the color and forms of her childhood.

She decided to try to regain her Japanese citizenship. She returned to her birthplace, saw burned-out Tokyo, ravished cities and towns.

She was deep in her seventies—nearly half a century had passed since her last sight of Japan. And here, packed in so many layers of memories of places, of love lost with the student, Kawakami, and found in George Morgan, she—the geisha—waited for the final embrace from time.

So life copies in part Puccini's opera and its sentimental tear-jerking.

CHAPTER 25

Harry Lehr and What Followed

*It was wonderful to discover America but
it would have been more wonderful to lose it.*

THEODORE DREISER

WHEN WHAT PASSED for society in America in the late nineteenth century chose to escape what it thought of as the crudeness and dullness of America, it set up beachheads in London and in Paris. Money was the keynote, and some sort of social standing back home, which could be improved by buying a Corot ("something with trees") in a very heavy gold frame at Jacques Seligmann & Fils on the Rue de la Paix. Or later being dressed by Paul Poiret or Captain Molyneux. One attended the American church on the Rue de Berri, wore a Bengal straw hat in season, even spoke of the return of a French king and converting to Rome. And one ordered from Fortnum's, who exported food to expatriates and sent grouse all over Europe, insisting on birds "that have been shot through the head."

Sometimes this society brought with it its favorite clown. In the first decade of this century there appeared Harry Lehr, who was to spend twenty splendid, gay years as a Parisian. He was youngish then, and had a liking for the best society when he first appeared on the Paris scene, but he lacked the money to move about properly dressed, entertaining the best people. It was arranged for him to become an agent for a good brand of champagne.

He was the pet of such social battle-axes as Mrs. William Astor, Mrs.

Ogden Goelet, Mrs. Stuyvesant Fish. Harry was handsome; though later he grew stout, he still used his comic voice to good effect and kept a wide circle of friends in those American circles in Paris that didn't paint, write, or try to intellectualize the world. If he was superficial, Harry was amusing, and if he liked a copious, extravagant way of life, he worked hard for it. He was always on, a court jester, outranking the French fortune hunters with their chin beards shaped like *mons pubis* by their barbers.

Harry's friends had yachts, and on Joseph Leiter's boat there was a monkey called Jocko. Harry decided to give a royal dinner and sent out invitations to honor "Prince Jocko, of the Siamese Royal Family." It was a feeble jest, but the guests didn't expect much—they came and were amused. (Harry repeated the idea with a jackass called "Señor Burro.") He had certain problems in public. For years he carried around a little doll made of rags under his arm, and often there was a parrot that traveled with him on wrist or shoulder. Friday the thirteenth was a very unlucky day, Harry felt. He never left his house on that date, even if his patrons called for amusement. He had an extraordinary resilience and recovered quickly to clown again.

In 1907 Harry married one of the rich Drexel family, a widow, Mrs. John Vinton Dahlgren; he no longer had to push champagne or act the fool at the snap of someone's fingers. In Paris the couple lived first on the Rue de Lille next to the German Embassy, then in the Rue des Saints Pères. Harry gave all the servants such impressive titles as "Charles from Bordeaux," "Paul from Lyons," "Henry from Rheims." His favorite was "Pierre, footman of my godmother, the Duchess de Bassano."

As Harry aged and grew more portly, his gauche jests still convulsed his aging group. But his wife warned Olivier, the headwaiter at the Ritz, she would not be responsible for any bills her husband signed in the restaurant. The good life, the too good life, was ruining Mr. Lehr's health through Pouilly Fuissé, Courvoisier, and Noilly Pratt. The headwaiter sent word *he* himself would pay M. Lehr's account. Of course, he never had to.

In 1926 Harry Lehr was ailing, his health breaking down; the man was on the periphery of the grave, people hinted. His friends decided Harry was not to die in Paris but back in his home town of Baltimore. It was noted that no matter how much exiles disliked their native soil, most of them managed to get back to be buried at home under an American God, a perfect god for whom the rich practiced charity, the poor humility. Harry went back to Baltimore and died there in the fall of 1928.

Harry Lehr was already a memento from a fading era. An age of

elegance, the top hat, the twirling cane. The new generation of Americans to appear in Paris were mostly indifferent to what was called society. They read the sports paper, *L'Auto*, slept, if rich enough, with Peggy Hopkins Joyce, the most expensive American whore of her day, and bragged they could afford her icy blond charms. Friends of the new Americans were not Walter Berry or Henry James but the ragbag shaggy Harold Stearns, seated at the Select, who was the racing expert on an English-language newspaper and might pick a winner in the Grand Prix at Longchamps. And Alexander Calder, not yet the inventor of the mobile but a cartoonist drawing covers for Erskine Gwynne's English-language Paris magazine *The Boulevardier* and exhibiting his bent wire figures and circus games. The new Americans, sure of the Twilight of the Absolute—"the world is going to hell in a basket"—went neither to church nor to embassy dances but to the Bal Blomet dance hall, the headquarters of the Negro pimps, drug peddlers, sports figures and their women from France's African colonies. The Americans in those less bigoted times called the Bal Blomet "Nigger Heaven." They drank *menthe à l'eau* with the *café au lait* customers and tried an African girl for luck. The American Negro entertainers worked at La Plantation. It was a long long way from the polite five o'clock tea at the Ritz.

The whole Negro scene in Paris in the Twenties was jumping, with Lew Leslie's *Black Birds* running at the Moulin Rouge, and Josephine Baker still the rage. John Dos Passos painted the curtain when she appeared in *Les Ballets nègres* in 1925. She came to Paris when she was just eighteen, danced nude with only a string of bananas, was feisty and loud and sure of herself, claimed to have come from St. Louis and was a star of the Folies Bergères. In time she married a French count and had a château where she raised orphan children. From time to time Josephine returned to the United States to raise money for the count, the château, and the children. Jack Johnson was still a hero in French boxing circles. American jazz, the Dixieland classic, New Orleans and Kansas City style, was popular, and French professors wrote books on *Le Jazz 'Ot*.

The younger set of Americans ignored the old-line American society in Paris, preferred the Marquise (Gloria Swanson), La Falaise and Bébé Daniels to Mrs. Fish, the *Bal des Quatre Arts* to the old dying crowd that had loved Harry Lehr. ("We freely forgive in our friends those faults which do not affect us.") One heard in the *boîtes de nuit* such names and titles as Gershwin; Graudes, the shop for such things as the best permanent wave in Paris; Swann's Anglo-American Pharmacy on the Rue Castiglione for toothpaste; the lesbian play *La Prisonnière* at the Femina for a giggle.

A gay nihilism was expected on landing in France. The *Ile de France* was the fashionable boat to travel over on, having pushed aside in its popularity the grand Cunarders, the *Aquitania* and *Berengaria*. Smart New Yorkers used to turn out for the midnight sailing of the *France*; Libby Holman, Robert Sherwood, Philip Barry, Connie Bennett, in top hats, canes, white tie or backless evening gowns, bobbed hair, to drink the boatleg booze and Dutch Schultz champagne. They sometimes failed to get off in time (the bar opened at the twelve-mile limit), when it was announced "Last call for all those going ashore." The ship's lists carried such names toward Paris as Robert McAlmon, Grace Moore, Ralph Barton, the popular cartoonist of *The New Yorker* and *Vanity Fair*. (Ralph's wife Carlotta Monterey was to go off with Eugene O'Neill, and Ralph was to put a bullet through his own head.) There was also Jules Brulatour with his shiny wife Hope Hampton in tow, whom he was going to treat as an opera star, arranging for her to sing Manon in Paris at the Opéra Comique; Miss Fanny Ward, called "the oldest flapper in the world," who went in for chin and face lifts; Mrs. Charles Schwab, trying to revive society on Mrs. Astor's level and failing. Names, not abilities, began to matter, and so the gossip columnist was invented.

Few missed poor old Harry Lehr when news came he had died in Baltimore. But there was a High Russian Orthodox Mass for Sergei Diaghilev, who died still the controlling genius of the fading Ballet Russe, for whom Pavlova, Nijinsky, and others had danced, and Chagall and Picasso had painted scenery. The Americans were ballet mad, and Zelda Fitzgerald, starting near the age of thirty, drove herself deeper into madness by trying to become a prima ballerina, thumping and banging about in her Paris apartment.

Fashions, too, had changed. They had become direct and youthful. For costuming Worth was out and Coco Chanel, trailing a long line of jaded lovers as a legend, was in. The young American college students came over for vacations, delighted to hear the Rue de Lappe was "the wickedest street in the world," and it had to be explained to them just what the newspapers advertised as "*Suzy Masseuse*," and "Les Poses Vivantes." Their naiveté was found charming and rewarding by the French, and meanwhile writers sat at the Dome debating that only man says the universe is chaos—the universe says nothing.

Americans who had money in Paris soon fell into the proper routine. Sherry's for lunch, or the Tienda Oyster Bar, Ciro's for dinner, a midnight supper at Le Perroquet on the Rue de Clichy, Harry's for midnight music, and the last drinks with friends at Jimmy's. If one was of a literary or artistic nature (and with good introductions), on to Gertrude Stein's, or Picasso's studio, or Jean Cocteau's little gatherings, perhaps to smoke opium or have fun with a homosexual group. But it wasn't all that sinful for most of the Americans, writing so many postal cards back home, and if hung-over, plastering their brows at morning with cold wet towels, and being cautious about disease and overdrawing their accounts, or cabling home for money, "care of American Express."

The poet Hart Crane was raising holy hell in Montparnasse, breaking glasses, wrecking bars, getting jugged fighting the *gendarmerie* of the *République*. Some compared his poem *The Bridge* to *The Wasteland* of T. S. Eliot, who appeared now and again with his guide, Ezra Pound, in Paris. Eliot was pale as a fish belly, snobbish, a revolting Jew-hater in conversation, but *The Wasteland* became part of the instant intellectual culture of Americans in Paris. (That poem and H. L. Mencken's green-covered *American Mercury* bore evidence that the American in Paris wasn't just a goddamn Babbitt, bible-belt boob, or a mere wowser. When an unpublished writer recited, "We are all drowning off Dover Beach," the intellectuals knew he wasn't reporting a mass boating accident.)

There were already signs and hints that the world of Mr. Coolidge and Mr. Hoover was coming apart at the seams. However not just yet. But the Americans of the Twenties were not as settled in as the friends of Harry Lehr in their Paris. It was not the Paris of John Singer Sargent or of George Santayana. The survivors of that earlier era were dying slowly—reading the Paris *Times*—dying in their ornate flats with the good Louis XV furniture, the Millets and other Barbizons on the walls. Feeble old bodies, walking about a bit as they leaned on gold-headed canes, with their molting, mangy old lapdogs too weary to bark or piddle. People were still sending cards to mansions of marquises, whose children had long since closed the old houses, and were in Juan-les-Pins, Le Touquet, or Deauville. One could say of these earlier Americans that they had patterns of rich consistency. They didn't die in poverty at the Lavboisière Hospital, or entertain Texas Guinan or Mayor Jimmy Walker when those *outré* people came to Paris. The older Americans in their dislike of the newer Americans forgot their own first view of Paris.

CHAPTER 26

Student from Kansas

Paris is an immense hospitality.
VICTOR HUGO

J UST WHAT were the American students like up to World War I? In 1906 a young Kansas art student came up from Italy to study painting in Paris. In his six years in the city he learned among other things that he would never become a great artist, the world would survive without his art. Back in Kansas he studied law and in time became a respected judge. This section of A.D.'s memoirs are used with his permission:

Paris. I saw it beyond the umber-green fields the train was moving through; the little silly train, its speed cut down, aiming itself for the city some place ahead, past the old stone walls and the small houses and the dusty chickens running, mouths open, wings held high. The train was going past the estates wrapped in protective layers of trees and hedges, and then *there* it was—*Paris* —beyond the first scrap heaps that a city pushes around its edges. What did it matter to me, at seventeen, the hint of the complexity and difficulties ahead? *Paris!*

I rubbed on the train window, dusty from traveling over the Italian plains and the high mountains, across the overworked fields, French fields, so many of them. I hadn't thought there were so many fields in the world. Ahead I saw the spires and lofty shapes of the city coming nearer, yellow-orange in the fine, sunny weather. People in weary amiability were collecting their bags and bundles, children were growing shrill all around me, and the thick-set, amorous German couple were stretching and grunting—she fixing her tow-colored hair, he looking like any dark, unshaved Wagnerian stagehand, scratching his crotch, rubbing his teeth with the back of a stubby finger.

I felt jumpy and keyed high. My chest hurt with the excitement. I did not want to show it to these travelers. The slim knowledge I had gathered of Paris' new art, studio gossip in Florence, reading of magazines, all merged in my mind. And in the dust ahead of the train were names I had heard; the Invalides, the Esplanade, the Café des Deux Magots, the Printemps, the studios of artists on the Rue Odessa, the figures of Cécile Sorel, Henri de Rothschild, Cézanne. No—Cézanne must be dead or very old and still in the country—Cézanne, who had shown that to perceive the world, the external world, by the senses is not enough.

I pulled out a little blue notebook and with a thin pencil wrote: *Paris, May 18, 1906.*

I put away my notebook as the train began to shiver, the brakes took grip, and a voice thickened by apple brandy shouted, "Paris! Count your bundles."

A fragment of Italian poetry came to me. *Quivi era storiata l'alta gloria.*

Under the great glass roof of the station the train had come to a halt and was sending up clouds of steam and smoke, that for me seemed colored by Claude Monet; there was no other way of looking at it. The porters in horizon blue with good heavy carrying straps slack over their shoulders, awaiting the descending passengers, looked at me lugging my straw suitcase. It was a real spring day, and even here among the smells of hot iron, pigeon droppings, and dusty trains there was—I was sure—the odor that could only be Paris. I felt frightened, elated, a hell of a way from Kansas. I pushed past women in their large picture hats, the foam of lace showing at the bottom of their street-touching skirts, past fathers carrying soiled babies, sticky with sugary rewards. The porters left me alone; I looked to them, I knew, like one of those raw Italian workers that came in herds every year to become waiters, dish washers, gardeners, cutters of paving stones, none of whom could spare a sou to carry their one shabby bundle.

I plunged into the street. The traffic was formidable. Carriages and drays pulling loads of piled-up trunks stuck with fancy labels of Egypt and Chicago, autocars with red running gear, mostly chain driven, making a great blue stink of petrol to mix with the fragrance of the open-air *pissoirs*. I couldn't believe it—taking a leak right in the street, feet and head *showing!*

I set down my suitcase between my legs (one had to be careful in strange cities my uncle Willard had warned me). Girls hurried past in their shirtwaists and long sweeping skirts; they were more beautiful and some more ugly than the girls in Kansas City, Chicago, Florence, and Rome.

I saw a young man wearing a brown velveteen jacket and basque cap. I was sure he was an artist, a real sixteen-jewel Parisian artist. I smiled and put a hand on the man's arm.

"*Pardon.*" My French sounded weak and I knew the accent wasn't right yet. "I want to go to Montmartre."

The man shrugged. He had a half circle of ill-trimmed tawny mustache around a mouth of broken yellow teeth. "Ah, *il connaît son monde!* You go to the right and you get there in time. You want to get to the Butte?"

"Yes, the Rue Caulaincourt."

He took a tattered cigarette from a pocket, twisted its ends closed, and lit it, explaining all the time how I could get to Montmartre from the station. I understood only part of the sharp street jargon—*c'est selon*—but I had the direction. The French was too fast but I was sure with a little more time I would have no trouble with it.

"Thank you," I said, picking up my suitcase.

"Near the Bateau-Lavoir, and be sure to turn right at the bistro with the blue roof and keep going up hill."

"You're an artist?" I dared to ask.

The man pulled on his mustache. "That I am, in my craft. You ever need a truss, an India rubber stocking, a wrist strap at *bon marché*, you try Hugo's on the Rue de Saules." He waved his smoldering cigarette and moved into the crowd crossing the street between two drays carrying loads of coal. What the hell I figured, everybody has a right to look an artist. I smiled at my mistake; so many people dressed as artists in Paris. I'd have to get one of those jackets. I walked slowly toward Montmartre, dodging the omnibus and its huge horses, the elbows of hurrying Parisians. Yes, I kept thinking—the real Parisians. These were the genuine things, *froides mains, chaud amour.* And yet they

looked just like everyone else except for their clever look, their well-cut tailoring
—when they were well dressed. I felt at home already.

I knew I was as human looking as they were. I'd liked to have been a few
inches taller, but my massive forehead made up for it with my shiny black hair
(must get it cut before the duck tails grew much longer). As I looked in a
passing shop window I saw my Kansas face was pale as a white-washed barn,
dappled with blue jowled shadows that I'd scrape off with my father's long
razor.

The warm city air felt soft as a feather in my lungs. The large stone slabs of
the sidewalk seemed to bounce against my worn heels. A group of drinkers in a
café eyed me as I passed. I shifted the suitcase to my other arm, wondering if
they were thinking me a dolt. A small shop window attracted my attention:
GALLERY OF THE ARTS.

A tiny place, the window no bigger than a kitchen table. A fat man with a
spotted nose stood in the doorway picking his teeth with a wood match. He
wore a red waistcoat and across it a gold watch chain, thick enough maybe to
hold a small ship at anchor. In the window was a painting, very slick under too
much varnish, of a milkmaid with her pink-tipped breast escaping from a rustic
dress, and overpowering her in love play was a young man in a feathered cap,
wearing a tight eighteenth-century costume so that the muscles of his ass stuck
out in rather detailed anatomical correctness. A brown cow and a spotted dog
watched the scene.

I turned to enter the gallery and the fat man stepped slowly aside. I was no
buyer, his casual expression said.

"Do you have anything by Cézanne?"

"What do you take me for?" he said.

"An art dealer."

The man pointed the spitty end of the match at me. "I don't handle any of
the crazy stuff, that *succès de scandale* junk. You want a really good school of
Boucher? Or maybe a little dainty saint on wood for your mother?"

"Lautrec, Renoir?"

He waved a hand in disgust at the sound of these names and turned back to
lean in his doorway. "You'll find them up on the Butte, Rue Lepic—and I
wouldn't give you a lead franc for the lot of them. Buy old masters and stuff
tested by time, auctioned at the Hôtel Drouot."

I said thank you and pushed my way out into the sunlight, past the big gut
of the gallery owner. I saw now the gold chain was only brass, lightly plated,
the gold mostly worn off.

"How far am I from Montmartre?"

"The next square, turn left and you're on it."

I grasped the suitcase handle and moved on. Toward Cézanne, toward the
crazy stuff. As my high school teacher had said: "The difference between the
fine and the finest is infinite."

To help my European grammar, I remember I had bought a copy of *L'Ultimo de Mohecanni* by James Fenimore Cooper. I already had a copy of *La Vie de Bohème*. It looked pretty easy that day that I was going to become the goddamndest painter that Paris had ever seen. I was sure of it as I lit my first Gauloise cigarette and went hunting a studio that would some day have a bronze plaque out front saying *I* had lived there.

CHAPTER 27

La Stein

*It is the fate of every myth to creep by degrees
into the narrow limits of some alleged historical
reality, and to be treated by some later generations
as a unique fact with historical claims.*

NIETZSCHE

Paris was where the twentieth century was.

GERTRUDE STEIN

Too MUCH has already been written about the Paris of Gertrude Stein
and Ernest Hemingway, recorded with almost a paranoiac ferocity
dipped in old-rose nostalgia. A great deal more will be written. Ph.D.
theses are in the works, and professors by the dozens are staking out
rights to certain sections of lives—lavish and discontented—claims in the
manner of the gold miners of 1849 cutting up the goldfields. Much that
has been written is hasty journalism or pedantic autopsies by the university presses. A great deal of the material is made of myth and legend.
Survivors have added their faulty memories to take part in the action;
much of their histories is suspect. No one appears to be inarticulate. A
Dostoievskian gloom hangs over the survivors who were there, once, not
so long ago.

The setting of stage and roles has been hindered by the habit of the
two protagonists, in their autobiographical volumes to sink into operatic
fiction. Neither Gertrude Stein's *The Autobiography of Alice B. Toklas* nor
Hemingway's *A Moveable Feast* makes much effort to stick to the facts.
Insensitive and egocentric, they enjoyed cruel jests.

Perhaps because it is closer to us in time than the American Paris of
Franklin or Louis Tiffany, their Paris has produced much recent furore
and some readable texts. Paris was the exile base of disillusioned groups

of romantics at a time we too often regard as the most interesting of the eras when Americans went to Paris. Their publicity has been splendid. Both Gertrude Stein and Ernest Hemingway were types that were long ago best described by Lord Byron: "One half of the clever people of the world believe they are hated and persecuted, and the other half imagine they are admired and beloved. Both are wrong, and both false conclusions are produced by vanity, though that vanity is the strongest which believes in the hatred and persecution, as it implies a belief of extraordinary superiority to account for it."

He also saw clearly the burden the artist must bear: "The great object of life is sensation—to feel that we exist, even though in pain."

Both Gertrude and Hemingway, before fame—or notoriety—overtook them (hers long delayed), were to know the pain of forcing themselves onto a world indifferent to them. In Hemingway's case he placed himself early in his career beside the hero in Greek tragedy, whom he saw as a true hero because of his conscious acceptance of an inescapable fate. In Hemingway's credo he was to pervert this to a cult, perhaps rejecting natural death, a rejection which was more natural to him, some claim, than his famous definition of courage as "grace under pressure."

Paris, the 1900s to the end of the twenties, Gertrude, Hemingway, a postwar world of the Lost Generation (let us remember the mood was presented as romantic rancor), all came together at the proper time in the proper proportions. Elliot Paul, in a café, was to say of the American writers in Paris of the Twenties, "A table of people seated as if aware it was the Last Supper."

We see it as a period of the ossification of genius, of lost good times. When Hemingway could look back and say, "If you were lucky enough to have lived in Paris as a young man, then wherever you go for the rest of your life, it stays with you." And we can see them as recalcitrant children, drinking and loving, with the healthy glow of young carnivores.

"The Mother of Us All," they—and she repeated it—began to call Gertrude Stein, this strange, remarkable woman. As her writing became more obscure, as her detractors trampled on her work, she grew in public stature; to a few she became a cult, a symbol, until the real person is almost impossible to see in the clouds of myth-making incense that circle her life and times. She was a great myth-maker herself, one of formidable tenacity, never letting fact confuse her ideas of what the world should see as *La Stein.*

She seemed to preach, "Don't go home, and all is forgiven." Paris as a modern American cultural outpost owes much of its popularity to her.

"So Paris was the place that suited those of us that were to create the twentieth century art and literature, naturally enough." (No susceptibility to modesty ever stood in her way.) A remarkable statement by a personality who is known to the general public by a few nonsensical catch lines, "A rose is a rose is a rose" or "the pigeons on the grass alas," and perhaps by her best, in exuberant, amazing gaiety, "Toasted Susie is my ice cream."

While most think of her as San Francisco born, Gertrude Stein actually arrived among us on February 3, 1875, in Allegheny, Pennsylvania. The Steins were a well-off merchant family, but not multimillionaires, and

most of the family money later came from street car companies. They held some interest in the San Francisco Cable Car Company, and one of Gertrude's unintellectual, low-life brothers, Willy, a bit of a drunk, spent the major part of his adult life in the open, on the platform of a cable car, as a jolly, well-liked brakeman.

The Steins, like the Jameses, the Sargents, the Smiths, were a traveling American family. Vienna and Paris saw them, sightseeing, learning the languages, but their growing up was done in San Francisco. Besides Willy and Gertrude, there were her other brothers, Leo and Michael. All but Willy were to enjoy Paris. Gertrude claimed to have become a great reader, from "Shakespeare to the Congressional Record." But this erudition was hardly borne out by her conversation, which was mainly about the works of G. Stein. With a shrugging smile she ignored or knew little of the world's literature. As for music, she seems to have had a stone ear; her favorite piece of music, she admitted, was "The Trail of the Lonesome Pine."

Audacity and verve were her best points. At nineteen Gertrude was at Radcliffe where she claimed later to have been "the favorite pupil of William James." No proof exists of this statement. However she did study experiments in automatic writing and was co-author of a paper "Normal Motor Automatism." She was twenty-three when she entered Johns Hopkins to spend four years studying medicine but never taking a degree. When young, Gertrude was short, dumpy, a solid-featured young woman, already aware that emotionally and physically men had no attraction for her. She was inquisitive, bohemian, defiantly arty. Her personal sensibilities were toward girls not boys. Her knowledge of herself is shown in an early novel she wrote about a lesbian trio on a ship's crossing —a book that was not published during her lifetime. Once across the sea, Gertrude tried London, but by 1903 Leo was already in Paris. It was hard for her to admit that he found their first place in Paris, not she.

Leo had rented the studio at 27 Rue de Fleurus, and Gertrude joined him in September of 1903. (Alice Toklas didn't get to Paris until 1907.) Leo and Gertrude settled in. Their costumes, when they were dress-alikes, were the brown corduroy outfits and Greek sandals made by Isadora Duncan's brother, Raymond. He lived across the courtyard from the Steins and milked goats, spun and wove cloth, and grew his hair long. Otherwise, out of costume, the two Steins did not resemble each other. Leo was tall and thin, and he had a red-gold beard and the dashing stride of a Georgian roisterer. Gertrude was to remain short and dumpy, and to flatter her someone said, "She was like a block of granite."

Leo was a hypochondriac, full of traumas and neuroses, before those terms were known and became popular. Leo wrote, "I said I couldn't write. This was before I knew of Freud, so I could not tell them about inhibitions. If I had been living some place else, I would have known about Freud . . . but he was late to arrive in France." The French do not rush into innovation.

Self-analysis was Leo's life work just as Gertrude's was self-advertising. Leo had begun to paint, but as with writing, he kept getting in his own way with his self-incrimination. He was a brilliant art critic, having remarkably clear ideas on values of poetry and prose, much beyond Gertrude's oversimplification and sly games with short words. But little of Leo's ideas got onto paper. One catches a true glimpse of a splendid failed talent in a book of his letters, *Journey into Myself,* published after his death. Leo was a romantic figure; women flocked around him. The winner in 1905, or was it loser, was the beautiful model, Nina de Montparnasse (or was this her *nom de pose?*). Leo felt sex was a gateway, a deliverance of the burden of individuality.

In the spring of 1903 he had bought his first Cézanne, and when Gertrude joined him in the autumn, it was already hung on the wall. By the time the nineteenth century ended in 1914 (it did not end in 1900 as most claim), the walls of the Rue de Fleurus studio held Renoirs, Matisses, Picassos, two Gauguins, Manguins, a nude by Vallotton, a Toulouse-Lautrec, a Daumier, a small Delacroix, and an El Greco (suspect).

Leo was the driving collector and Gertrude tagged along; but in her book, *The Autobiography of Alice B. Toklas,* this fact is clouded, often blotted out. Certainly it was at the Rue de Fleurus that Matisse and Picasso first met. There came Rousseau, the odd-ball primitive genius, Braque, Vlaminck, who was also a professional bike racer (he even wrote good novels), Pascin, born Pincus, who was to become an American citizen during the Great War when he came to the United States. Marie Laurencin also came, she whom Gertrude was to present as a bit of a fall-down drunk, getting her eye blackened by her lover, Guillaume Apollinaire, the writer of pornographic books who was to become one of the great modern French poets. He wrote the first critical book on the cubists and coined the name for another art group, the *surréalistes.* He hinted his father had been a cardinal at the Vatican.

There were whole clusters of American painters digging away at the mountain that was Cézanne, taking from it the discoveries of the first cubists. Many Americans were just painters of no school at all. Gertrude and Leo fed and entertained Alfred Maurer, Maurice Sterne (who was to marry Mabel Dodge), Marsden Hartley. There were other American painters in Paris. Max Weber, a major second-generation cubist in those days, and two Americans who worked at what they called Synchronism, Morgan Russell and Stanton Macdonald-Wright. Russell loved to dress in women's clothes, Wright turned toward Buddha's navel.

The American closest to Gertrude's idea of attracting attention was Man Ray, but he did not get to Paris until after the war. However, there was, as usual, a latent hostility toward one another among the avant-garde.

The Steins' Saturday nights became a Paris tradition, and the food was good, and free. The talk may have been confusing, but the new painters were on show there and it was claimed it all helped their sales. Indolence and egotism mixed neatly at the Steins.

The Stein family was well off, but not filthy rich, as was the terrible tempered Dr. Barnes (the inventor of Argyrol, a prophylactic) when he came to Paris to buy up in his lordly manner (at canny prices) Soutine and a great deal of Matisse.

The Steins paid 5000 francs for their first Matisse ($1,000) and 150 francs ($30) for their first Picasso. Gertrude expected the shine of gratitude in their eyes.

Soon there were four Steins in Paris. Michael and his wife Sarah were to settle in on the Rue Madame, just around the corner, a cup-of-sugar borrowing distance away from Leo and Gertrude. At the death of the father, Michael was head of the family and the only surviving Stein who had a head for, or gave a damn about, figures. All the Steins had good incomes, and as they all collected the best of the School of Paris early, at bargain prices, when a bit of hard times came to them after the Hoover depression, they had the paintings to fall back on—art today worth millions.

The Steins became one of the sights of Paris, even when out·of their robes and sandals, yet they were more than lugubrious caricatures. The art dealer, Ambroise Vollard, remembered them: "Every time I went to an exhibition I saw the Steins, the two brothers and the sister." It was in the Autumn Salon that Leo bought Matisse's *Femme au Chapeau.* Gertrude claimed she did. Sarah said she *and* Leo did. Matisse, who owed Sarah a favor (she had aided him in setting up his school when times were hard, and helped him survive), said it was Sarah. For the thirty years the Michael Steins lived in Paris they were buying Matisses red hot off the easel. The Michael Steins also claimed it was *they*, not Gertrude, who brought the Cone sisters, Dr. Claribel and Etta, to the Quai Saint Michel to buy Matisses. But they bought when the artists needed sales— the Steins' unabashed desire to own was welcome. They encouraged others to buy art instead of Fabergé cigarette cases or a suit from Creeds.

Certainly the Cone sisters came in time to own in their collection of paintings works by Matisse valued at three million dollars at the time of the last sister's death; some say worth thirty million, inflation being what it is. Unlike today's big paying collectors, the Cone sisters at the turn of the century each had an inherited income of around only $2500 a year. Later it grew larger and larger, but they never had millions to invest in art as did recent peddlers of tomato pulp (Simon) or clap cures (Barnes).

It was Leo who actually discovered Picasso for the Stein family, but Gertrude was to claim she was first; she claimed to be first in everything the family did. In November of 1905 Leo had written to a friend he had found "a young Spaniard named Picasso whom I consider a genius of very considerable magnitude and one of the most able draughtsmen." He was right to go on record, as he did after Gertrude made her claims. He said: "I was the only person anywhere as far as I know, who in those early days recognized Picasso *and* Matisse."

Picasso was then still almost unknown, painting away in the old building known as *le bateau lavoir* because it looked somewhat like a laundry barge on the river. (Today a wreck—it is a national monument to art.) Leo, a seer prophesying greatness, bought his first Picasso from an old ex-clown named Clovis Sagot. It was of a family of *saltimbanques* with an ape. Another work he bought was of a nude girl holding a basket of flowers. Gertrude claimed she was shocked by the drawing of the legs and feet of the nude, and Sagot, hungry for a sale, offered to chop them off for her. The story is doubtful.

When Gertrude took up Picasso as a cause, she was stepping on the toes of Guillaume Apollinaire, the pioneer defender, historian, and advocate of Picasso and cubism. In fact Gertrude and Apollinaire resembled each other in some ways: stout, solid figures. Apollinaire had a tiny mouth and a pear-shaped head. Gertrude was the more masculine looking. A drunken American once called her *Le Belle Gonzesse,* "the beautiful babe."

Gertrude had a great yearning for fame. She got Picasso in 1906 to begin a portrait of her. There were, she claimed, eighty or ninety sittings, which, considering the speed with which Picasso worked (he painted *Guernica,* his huge mural, in less time) hardly was typical of his way of work. He left the face unfinished for a long time. And as he was working toward his Negro period, inching toward full cubism, when he did take the portrait up again, he did a revolutionary picture. Gertrude did not pose for the final head. Picasso did it from memory, so the rest of the picture, the body and hands, are in a sort of Renaissance style, dominated by the almost Negro styled carved head, a mask, not a person, with the archaic eyes left blank—a face as if ironed free of wrinkles every day. There is no attempt to make it a picture of a living person. The eyes do not match in size, the scale and perspective have been distorted. What we have is a precubist masterwork of great power, virile, without finesse—leading directly into his huge *Les Demoiselles d'Avignon* and from that into the revolution of the cubism he co-invented with Braque. One writer who dislikes Gertrude calls the portrait "a squatting frog."

CHAPTER 28

Gertrude in Glory

There is no there there . . .

G.S.

G ERTRUDE was the only one of the Steins who remained loyal to
Picasso when cubism began to dominate his work. Leo announced in disgust the Spaniard had "gone wrong when he began to have
ideas." Of synthetic cubism Leo wrote a mocking refrain, parodying his
sister's oxidizing style of writing: "But when the analysis is only a kind of
funny business, the synthesis will be only another kind of funny business.
With this kind of funny business analysis, anything can be analyzed . . .
any elements can be synthesized into any form . . ." Leo could do overtures, but grew sour over epilogues as he deserted an early love of the
painter.

From the above parody we see a Gertrude Stein was lost in Leo. Picasso
owed Leo a debt and so Leo got his last Picasso in 1910, but he had long
since moved away from supporting the artist. Gertrude on her own didn't
buy a Picasso "until 1911 or 1912." She bought a cubist Picasso, the first
picture for which she was responsible to come into 27 Rue de Fleurus.

The sister and brother act was breaking up, a chasm too wide for
jumping was developing. In 1914 they parted for good, each going his
own way. They were never actually to meet and talk again. They did
bow to each other once, meeting by accident on the Boulevard Saint
Germain near the Church of Saint-Germain-des-Prés. Leo took off his hat
and politely walked on. Gertrude rushed home to write a story, "How

She Bowed to Her Brother." As she put it, "Leo still had his beautiful walk, which was not historic but mythological." Some saw their parting as a love quarrel. Alice Toklas and Leo's mistress, Nina de Montparnasse, had come between brother and sister. Alice wanted sole rights to Gertrude. Even in death she hoped for reunion—becoming a Catholic when promised a future life with Gertrude. Gertrude, however, claimed, "As a Jew doesn't believe in an afterlife, I can be perfectly frank to everyone here on earth."

Hutchin Hapgood, an American journalist who knew them both, wrote, "She liked her brother Leo, but was by an inner necessity compelled to be conscious of her essential superiority . . . when the critical Leo could not follow the direction of her writing nor the direction of her emotional life, she seemed to feel herself spurned and insulted."

Alice Toklas's lifelong romance with Gertrude did seem to break up friendships. Hemingway in *A Moveable Feast* claims to have been shocked to discover their true relationship; which is nonsense, as he must have known about it as all Paris did for some time. He was merely putting pins into the image of his by then dead teacher, who had called him "yellow, fragile and a ninety percent Rotarian." ("Can't you make it 80 percent?" she claims Hemingway asked. "No, I can't.") She felt he had failed to live up to his promise as an artist, and had begun to mock all she had done for him as a young author. It was also galling for her to see a disciple become a headliner in the literary world, while *she* had great difficulty getting anything published and was looked upon by the major publishers in America and England as a freak and a fraud. She felt time going, irrevocably lost, and she was still not accepted.

Even so fond a Gertrude fan as the eccentric Mabel Dodge, a flitting figure in Paris and other bohemian settings of the world, when writing in praise of Gertrude at the time of the 1913 Armory Show had said, "She has taken the English language and according to many people has misused it, has used it roughly, uncouthly and brutally . . . madly, stupidly and hideously, but by her method she is finding the hidden and inner nature of nature."

While many serious critics never have accepted Gertrude's own high opinion of herself as an original genius, she had written from 1904 to 1906 a book of stories called *Three Lives*, which she published herself in 1909. It was a work in her own idea of style. She had no respect even for Henry James. Of him she wrote: "His whole paragraph was detached what it said from what it did, what it was from what it held, and over it all something floated not floated away but just floated, floated up there."

She was dangerous when crossed and saw only herself as the true

American genius in Paris. All others either bowed to her or were cast out into darkness. She could give the back of her hand rather than the offer of a handshake to a rival. George Moore, who knew the infighting of artists in Paris, summed it up perfectly: "A literary movement consists of five or six people who live in the same town and hate each other cordially."

With *Three Lives* Gertrude boldly announced she was "the first to write in the twentieth century manner." The book is of interest as it is written in her first-time-at-bat experimental style of simple words repeated and repeated so that a numbing mood is set up, often boring to many readers. One can see in the stories the strong influence of Flaubert's famous short story of a servant's life, "*Un Coeur Simple*." Gertrude, for a writer of fiction, was handicapped by an almost total lack of imagination as to the creation of character and plot, and a great deal of her method and style was forced on her, Leo claimed, by these missing talents. She made a virtue of her failings. One story in the book, "Melanctha," is a masterwork, the best thing, many readers feel, Gertrude ever wrote. In a circling, spiraling use of dialect and tempo it tells a Negro girl's story. There is a clue to Gertrude's final way-out style in her study of Baltimore Negro talk and voice pattern when she was at Johns Hopkins. The repetition and the rhythm of wandering speech is pure Stein. She never did anything as good or as close to a work of art. She made the encumbrance of simple talk a key to method. Her story of her family, *The Making of Americans*, is nearly unreadable, and one could take bets no one but a few literary personalities has ever read it completely through. As she was to write: "One of the things I have liked all these years is to be surrounded by people who know no English." Her work shows this harmed her.

Gertrude's one desperate stroke to seize popularity was in 1933 with the writing of *The Autobiography of Alice B. Toklas*. It is a book of appealing and wacky charm and is delightfully readable. It has a primitive, prattling style that fools one. Like some fake childish styles, behind it we find a clever, eager mind at work. It was her one book that was a popular success with a vast reading public that didn't give a damn about avant-garde writing. They accepted it in innocent assurance as fun reading. Its appeal was based mainly upon its sense of gossip, Gertrude's ability to retell stories about important names, at the same time making each sly little anecdote seem bland while she slipped a dagger into someone, keeping her pleasing smile. The *Atlantic* magazine published sections of it. It was not written, the reader discovered, in the teeth-twisting

Stein style but flowed along, if not like wine, at least like well-iced cola. Many Paris intellectuals laughed at its success, dubbed her "The Mother Goose of Montparnasse." Gertrude didn't give a damn. She loved the fame, the glory, the interviews, the pictures. For her, after so long, *so long*, anticipation had turned into achievement. The book's cover held a circle made up of the words *a rose is a rose is a rose*.

It was, of course, a work of a simple imagination, and the tales in many cases were often myths. Some people came right out and called her a great liar. She loved the word *great*, no matter in what context. Leo, who came off badly in the book, saw his wit, his skill in discovering art, all taken over by Gertrude as her own. He was outraged. He called the book a "farrago of rather clever anecdote, stupid brag and general bosh." He pointed out the lies, the wrong dates, the cracks in her memory. And such a liar. "God, what a liar she is! If I were not something of a psycho-pathologist I should be very mystified . . . Practically everything she says of our activity, our ties before 1911 is false both in fact and implication . . . her radical complexes . . . made it necessary practically to eliminate me . . . I simply cannot take Gertrude seriously as a literary phenomenon."

There were others who were distorted and lied about. The Paris maga-zine *transition* (all lower case, please) issued a booklet, *Testimony Against Gertrude Stein*, in which Matisse, Braque, Tristan Tzara, the Jolas's pointed out the mistakes, the untruths. Tzara, one of the founders of Dada, showed Gertrude and Alice as makers of "fraud, egomania, publicity seeking." Braque shrugged off her claimed art influence in Paris as nonsense. "Miss Stein understood nothing of what went on around her. But no superegotist does. She never knew French really well, and that was always a barrier . . . she has entirely misunderstood cubism, which she saw simply in terms of personalities . . . she never went beyond the state of the tourists." Others joined in the act of exorcism.

Hemingway revenged himself on her in his last book on Paris, attacking her and Alice's emotional life together—in very bad taste, as has been pointed out—and omitting altogether how much her teachings had influ-enced his style and his success. He had a tenacity that amounted to genius when he belittled all those who had once helped him.

The Autobiography became a best-seller, and Gertrude gloated over it. It was accepted as a masterly written, popular book. She now was reach-ing the Book-of-the-Month-Club type of reader, the deep core of the *Readers' Digest* crowd. None of this should overlook the fact that the book remains a remarkably amusing put-on, seriously erected by a woman in search of public acclaim.

How original was the book? Some feel it was inspired by the memoirs

of Picasso's former mistress, Fernande, *Picasso et ses amis.* It had begun appearing in *Le Mercure de France* in 1931. Some of the same stories appear in both volumes. Fernande's book is perhaps the truer history, but she lacked Gertrude's commercial touch, the facetious, deadpan levity in writing a popular book. *The Autobiography* is vivid, amusing and entertaining, while *Picasso et ses amis* is historic. Its worse sin was that it didn't sell well.

The material, hearty and sometimes insensitive, wasn't new in either book; the jokes were often old and worn to Parisians. Gertrude knocked out her book in a creative burst of six weeks. She handled a *bon mot* with the skill of a television comic. She could stab and needle a celebrity with a sudden dash and a roar of laughter. As she once told a pupil, "Hemingway, remarks are not literature."

Gertrude didn't give a damn what the critical intellectuals said, as her fame spread and more Americans came to Paris to see what it was like and perhaps to meet "Lovey" and "Pussy." Later Alice published her own story, *What Is Remembered,* and it could have been Gertrude writing both books. The style, jokes, and japes are the same. Alice and Gertrude, as if by the process of osmosis, sucked up each other's styles and shared absurdities. The anecdotes in both books are of the same kind, and the needlepoint epigrams have the Stein-Toklas touch: Alice's father, when told San Francisco was burning after the earthquake said, "That will give us a black eye in the east."

Alice, once tasting authorship, also produced the *Cookbook,* in whose pages one can find a candy recipe in which one of the ingredients is hashish. However Alice as an author didn't sell as well as Gertrude in the *Autobiography.*

With the success of Gertrude's book there was much written in major magazines and the press about her poetry and wilder prose. The newspaper columnists had their banal fun with her. But people did begin to wonder at such a text as *Tender Buttons* (was the title of the best-seller of the sixties, *Naked Lunch,* an echo of La Stein's way with two unrelated words?).

What could the reader make of "A Sound"? "Elephant beaten with candy and little pops and chews all bolts and reckless reckless rats, this is this"; or "A Cutlet": "A blind agitation is manly and uttermost." One wit in Harry's Bar said, "Sounds more like hamburger than a cutlet."

In her own heavy marching order with words Gertrude could sound profound until one analyzed what she had said. "Nothing changes from generation to generation except the thing seen and that makes a composition." She was an original, no doubt of it, but the end result, many find, is often hardly readable, not of much interest. To professors or experimental writers in quest of undiscovered patterns she is often a classic. The loyalty of her followers has lasted. She was early surrounded by sensitive young men from America, many of them homosexuals who saw in her The Mother of Us All, "the Hebraic bosom," as one put it, "of the Matriarch." They have defended her, written of her, analyzed her, sung her texts, put her to music, staged her, dramatized the works, made recordings. One can only repeat Stendhal's line: "Courage is the fear of appearing ridiculous or a coward in others' eyes."

Gertrude's cult in college circles is safe, but to serious literature most critics feel she has given little. As for her interest in painting, it was the Stein family, her brothers, who actually were the true pioneers. By the time she came to write of Matisse and Picasso, they were already world famous, and some of their fame rubbed off on her, rather than hers on them. She claimed to write the way Cézanne painted—some think this an indulgence impossible to bring off.

After Leo left Gertrude, she never made a major discovery of an original artist, even a fairly good artist. For years she plugged what critics found to be a second-rate little artist named Francis Rose, whose work is poor by any standard. One wonders, was this a Gertrude put-on? But she was deadly serious about the wretched painting. She lacked the clear eye of Tristan Tzara: "The true Dadaist is *against* Dada."

There was no contemplative torpor about her; her ego was never deflated, at least in public. When her friend Bernard Fay said to her that the three people of genius he had met were Picasso, Gertrude, and Gide, Gertrude claimed she asked, "Why include Gide?"

Seldom do we have more than Gertrude's word for many of the stories told by her and about her; it is always best to put that fact on notice. Sometimes even the avant-garde did not regard her with favor. William Carlos Williams has stated: "Stein's pages have become like the United States viewed from an airplane, the same senseless repetitions, the endless multiplications of toneless words." The Stein cult accepts this as an appreciation. Gertrude was always best when talking of herself and Paris. "I am an American and I have lived half my life in Paris, not the half that made me but the half in which I made what I made."

Few Americans really penetrated the true French artistic circle as Natalie Barney and a handful of others did. Gertrude hardly made a dent in the inner French world of literature and music, nor was she noticed by the great patrons of the arts, Misia Sert and Etienne de Beaumont; the playboys, Boni de Castellane and Montesquiou; famous hostesses Madeleine Lemaire, Madame de Rohan, Laure de Chevigné (Proust's Duchesse de Guermantes); Anna de Noailles (Cocteau's first Muse), the Guitrys, the Rostands *père et fils*. She wasn't with it for the Princesses Bibesco and Polignac; or the connoisseur of young exquisites, Jacques-Emile Blanche. She got no nod from Stravinsky, Joyce, "the Six", nor felt the impact of Diaghilev and his Ballet Russe, or of American women like Loie Fuller and Isadora Duncan. Proust, Gide, Mauriac failed to light her candle. She was not part of the scene in the Cocteau collaboration with Picasso and Satie in *Parade* during the First World War; the sponsoring of "Les Six" in *Le Coq et l'Harlequin*; the challenging avant-garde of *Les Mariés de la Tour Eiffel*.

There is (at times) a feeling that Gertrude Stein was isolated from much of Paris, as if she were living in Oklahoma City or Newark, New Jersey.

The jury is still out on Gertrude, on the group that surrounded her, on the Paris groups that worked independently of her. Did their work seem strange visions? George Santayana, a not too innocent bystander could write: "Why should one be angry with dreams, with myth, with allegory, with madness? We must not kill the mind, as some rationalists do, in trying to cure it. The life of reason, as I conceive it, is simply the dreaming mind becoming coherent, devising symbols and methods . . . by which it may fitly survive its own career."

But that was not "moral" American thinking. Somehow those who remained at home felt the Americans in Paris in the Twenties were making a damn easy, lazy, good thing of being rebels and having a hell of a time doing it. All those laments and agonies of romantic pain and sad love— "making love to dry thighs"—and lost, lost youth.

Alfred Kazin, who would have been unacceptable to the insiders as too square, wrote of them, "Lost and forever writing the history of their loss, they became specialists in anguish. They had the charm of the specially damned."

Which, in the end, is what so many of them were proud of being—"the specially damned."

CHAPTER 29

Stanton Macdonald-Wright— American of the School of Paris

Art is not nature. Art is nature digested.

GEORGE MOORE

As THIS BOOK is being prepared for publication, Stanton Macdonald-Wright is eighty-one. He is one of the two Americans who contributed directly a new style to the School of Paris painting. With Morgan Russell he developed an abstract colorist form of painting called synchronism. Samples of his work were featured in the great cubist exhibition at the Metropolitan Museum of Art in New York in 1971.

Macdonald-Wright's Paris, the art student days from 1907 to the opening guns of the Great War, was a Paris that was to prove that the nineteenth century lasted until 1914. Paris was to enter the twentieth century after the war as a different city.

Sitting with the artist in his Pacific Palisades studio, where he is still painting, I asked him to set down his version of that Paris.

My Paris of 1907 bore little resemblance to the Paris of today. Stately buildings, beautiful avenues remain, but the buoyant spirit of the people has changed to a bitter and mournful pessimism, a hard-edged greed for money, a lack of pride in its tradition of gaiety, fine food and wine, blithe spirits—and, yes, its treatment of women. In 1907 Paris was wine itself. In memory it remains the only place I ever felt wholly at home—*chez moi.*

At least three times a week the uniformed guards, called *piupiu,* in their shining helmets and cuirasses rode through the streets on their prancing horses, the band playing *Sambre et Meuse* or other marching songs and always the citizens stopped to admire.

The first day I enrolled at art school and fell at once to work. There were four schools on the Rue de la Grande Chaumière and art material shops close by. George Moore, who had once studied painting in Paris, came to give a talk every spring at the Sorbonne. He began: "Gentlemen, there are only two subjects a man of intelligence can dwell on—art and women." And those were our only interests. The *croquis* classes cost 50 cents, lasted two hours, and provided models (but no instruction) and were always full of students. We missed these night classes only for special events like the *Concert Rouge*, the Russian Ballet with Nijinsky and designs by Bakst, or Mary Garden in Strauss' *Salomé*.

Art engulfed us during working hours, and after that there were only the ladies. I knew a dozen Americans who had jumped their Methodist barriers and were enjoying double *ménages*. But the French girls could cook, clean, and speak to the tradesmen, and since they also helped us learn French, it was cheaper in the long run than living alone. Few Americans spoke French when they arrived, and so the language barrier prevented friendships with French painters. I was fortunate to have spoken French from childhood. In those days the French looked upon Americans as wealthy barbarians, incapable of producing art, or even of benefiting from French culture.

There were plenty of studios to rent cheaply (no bathrooms, no tubs), but there were public bathhouses, or one could drag out an oversized fingerbowl and your girl would fill it for you so you could sit in five inches of tepid water. The girls were always perfumed and dressed with great chic. They addressed each other as *Madame* when sharing a ménage.

Restaurants and cafés resounded with noisy arguments about art, and cliques battled cliques over Fauvism, Intimism, Cubism. One might tussle with a *copain* in a dance hall or café, shouting threats (thumbs in eyes—not too hard, pulling beards—softly) but it was all in fun and friendships remained. The only lasting dislike among artists I remember was that felt by Matisse for Othon Friesz. A number of Americans were protégés of Mrs. Harry Paine Whitney, among them my confrere, Morgan Russell, who did her proud. Unfortunately there were many who were bums and came over to live the life of Bohemians, or were merely incompetent.

The Café du Dôme was the gathering place of most American and German artists; André, the waiter there, lent the boys money and treated many as a father would. At the beginning of the World War the French police raided the Dôme, herded all the Germans out (many were summarily shot without trial, I have heard). The Rotonde was then a small zinc bar, a long narrow room with a terrace, where we drank our grog *Américain* in the coldest weather, warming ourselves at great porcelain stoves. Russell and I were its first artist patrons, and now it outranks the Dôme.

We caroused gaily on holidays, Bastille Day, July 14, and New Year's when we danced with everyone in the streets and went from café to café. We were

always in costume for the *Bal Julien* and the *Quatzarts*. Entrance was strictly guarded and by ticket only. The girls had to pass a mock jury by lifting their skirts above their waists to show in a *"concours de beaux culs"* they were eligible to grace the gathering. But costumes were discarded before long and we revelers went home on the subways—naked—or danced around the statues of the Opéra and the Madeleine. It was all just pure fun and gaiety, youthful exuberance. In these "immoralities" there was a spirit of humor like that to be found in the Japanese erotic *makemono*. Boys and girls came together to hold hands, not because they had been conditioned by political credos.

There were no political activities, no political patterns. I doubt if one of us in fifty knew the name of the French president. We were dedicated only to art; the problems of society did not touch us. Art was god, and churches were only to hold great paintings. We did not even read the newspapers except the extras put out at the yearly exhibition of the *Salon des Indépendants*. Anyone could exhibit for a fee of 25 Fr, and practically everyone did. But the hanging jury was astute—the finest works by important artists were in the last six rooms and you passed through miles of abortions to see the art of the day. You went many times for the sake of comparing what was done by others with your own work. It was in the *Salon d'Automne* I saw a painting by Matisse called *The Dance*. I still remember it in detail; possibly it was the door that opened for me into modern art and my own development.

Each day brought a fresh joyousness; no day was ever long enough for all we hoped to do, and if it hadn't been for days of pure physical enjoyment we would have worked ourselves crazy—candidates for Charenton. We'd take our current girl on the *bateau mouche* up the river Seine to St. Cloud, perhaps lunch at the Pavillon Bleu, then climb to the Lanterne of Diogenes where we could see the blue Seine far below winding past the Eiffel Tower, under the bridges past Notre Dame to disappear in the blue haze. Down again at twilight, and as the boat neared Paris, the lights, the smell of cooking, the deep violets and purples of the waters. I remember the Luxembourg gardens with the many "*petites veuves*" for conversation and light-hearted lovemaking, dinner with a bottle of wine, then singing as one walked home, preferring that rather than a fiacre with its old nag clop-clopping on the rough stones.

> *Je me souviens, je me souviens*
> *Des heures et des entretiens*
> *Et c'est le meilleur de mes biens.*
> *Dansons la gigue!*

CHAPTER 30

The Cone Sisters of Baltimore

It's pretty, but is it art?
RUDYARD KIPLING

I n 1905, beating their egos together like cymbals, there first appeared in Paris two sisters, fortyish; in size *large* and *larger*. Unwed Amazons dragging in their train a rather mordant but ineffectual brother named Frederic. The sisters were Dr. Claribel Cone and Etta Cone of Baltimore, Maryland. (The family origin seems to have been Tennessee, the family name originally Cohn or Cohen. Most likely the family were at first country peddlers, as so many now sacred Jewish family dynasties were in those days. The Cones progressed to become wealthy cotton-mill owners.)

The Cones, making melodious talk with a Southern accent, had come to Paris to visit their friend Gertrude Stein. Like her they were bright, given to public display—in appearance wide and formidable. Gertrude's oldest brother, Michael, introduced the Cones to Matisse. Gertrude, who ruled friendships with a manly hand, called Etta "a distant connection," and said Etta found Picasso "appalling but romantic." Etta did practice small charity, buying Picasso drawings at his studio to help the artist out. It cost her about 100 francs a visit, about twenty dollars at the Edwardian rate of exchange. Etta, who had no profession, was spending the winter in Paris. She began to help Gertrude by typing the manuscript for a book Gertrude was writing called *Three Lives*. Feeling she hadn't been given permission to read it, she typed it one letter at a time, desperately avoiding catching the meaning of the text, the meaning often hard enough to fathom even if one is permitted to read a Stein MS.

Etta was the sister who preferred sweet and pretty Picassos and Matisses, rather than their more experimental work. As Etta spread herself in the Stein circle, she said to Alice Toklas, "I can forgive but never forget." Alice, always knowing an opening when given one, answered, "I can forget but never forgive."

Dr. Claribel Cone, who had a deep and powerful ram's horn of a voice, enjoyed reading Gertrude's more exotic, experimental prose out loud to guests. She would read with gusto, then whisper to a baffled guest, "I don't really—ho-ho—understand any of it." But both sisters at this time were enthusiastic accomplices of the Stein ménage.

Dr. Claribel, with an insatiable appetite for glitter, was demanding of life, and Etta followed her wishes. Dr. Claribel liked good food, comfortable rooms and enormous beds, regal service. In Paris she could demand and command like a field marshal. But when she and Etta left Paris for travel, she would howl if the room were not ecstatically comfortable. If Etta pleaded, "But, Claribel, it's only for one night," Claribel would shake her head as if betrayed to torture, "*One* night is as important as any other night in my life. I *demand* to be comfortable!" A friend of Logan Smith identified them as "two huge, middle-aged, spoiled brats."

It was Etta, as a house guest of Gertrude in 1906, who bought the sisters' first Matisse painting, *The Yellow Jug*, the first of the sixty-six Matisses they were to leave to the Baltimore Museum of Fine Art, a splendid institution.

Picasso called the two formidable sisters "The Etta Cones." He did a stern, solid, iron-jawed portrait drawing of Dr. Claribel. She is a two-sided image in his drawing, with no discrepancies between appearance and pride.

Picasso told the Cones he was a fan of American comic strips, or "funny papers" as they were then called, before they degenerated in our time into sadistic adventure stories and soap operas. His favorite was "The Katzenjammer Kids," the wild, slapstick Sunday adventures of a shipwrecked German family marooned on a tropical island. There was Mama, Der Captain, Der Inspector, and two bad *bad* boys, Hans *und* Fritz. The Cone sisters kept Picasso supplied with bundles of these colored comic cartoons, which delighted the artist. More than likely the Cone sisters mailed the comic strips to Gertrude for Picasso. They were pack-rat types, but also gave gifts. When Michael Stein lived in Paris in his Le Corbusier house, Etta always brought to Europe for him perforated rolls for his player piano.

Dr. Claribel Cone was born in Tennessee in 1864 and arrived in Baltimore at the age of six. Already growing up to be massive, she decided in a man's world to become a doctor. The only medical school below Washington that would take in female students was the Baltimore Women's Medical College. Claribel, already vigorous and with androgynous features, was graduated from there in 1890.

The family, opulent bourgeoisie, owning the Cone cotton mills, did not force Dr. Claribel into general practice. She preferred pathology and studied under the renowned Dr. William Henry Welch at Johns Hopkins, then worked with Metchnikov in Paris and with Ehrlich at Frankfurt. (She published a few articles on gross and cellular pathology and physiology, usually too late to claim an innovation.)

After Dr. Claribel and Etta, their brother Frederic was dragged to Paris in 1885 for the first time, and the Cones became infected by life *à la française* and the charm of the city. The two sisters were to make thirty visits, often for long stays. Unlike the Strausses, Warburgs, Lehmans, Guggenheims abroad, the Cones enjoyed a bohemian side.

But mostly Dr. Claribel played the *Grande Dame*, demanding service and respect in her booming voice. Traveling in Germany, one night at the Munich Opera House, Dr. Claribel, a gaudy spectacle in feathers and an embroidered gown of bespangled black (her favorite color for clothes) was mistaken by Kaiser Wilhelm II for a duchess and he offered her his arm, which she took. *Eine Hand wäscht die andere.*

The Cone collecting of as yet unfamous but already notorious artists was more often charity than art appreciation, at least at first. But their collecting, if indolent, gave them a sense of elegance. With the passage of time, as the sisters aged and broadened, art became for them, as it often does with collectors, a disease. They never married, never showed any interest in men. In all, their collection of major works of art, leaving out drawings and prints, came to 180 items when it went into a fine museum. Besides the major collection of Matisses and Picassos, it contained Renoirs, Van Goghs, Cézannes, and Manets. At that as yet uninflated time it was valued at a paltry three million dollars. Today in the vastly overvalued, dealer controlled and manipulated international art market the collection merits that misused world *priceless*. No one knows the millions that the 180 major masterworks of the Post-Impressionists and School of Paris would

bring at auction today from the rich, social status collectors, if available
to their tax evasion foundations.

Etta was given to baggy, comfortable clothes, but Dr. Claribel pushed
boldly toward fantastic costumes. A theater lover—mostly for display of
herself—she would appear hung with ornaments running from Hindu
pins and Near East hangings, a set of remarkable, large breasts festooned
in Renaissance jewelry, her built-up *coiffure* stuck with geisha pins and
the contents of curio shops. To this were often added colorful fringed
shawls from Spain, enveloping capes made from Chinese mandarin or
Japanese Kabuki robes. Etta felt not too comfortable in public, even
precarious, but Dr. Claribel loved to astonish the crowd at an opening of
a play, opera, or art show. (There were rumors, unproved, she smoked
cigars in private, the finest H. Uppman's from Havana.) She is remembered as monumental, wrapped in vast Iberian or Oriental yardage, hair
jewel-studded, the great bosom trimmed and ornamented by the decor
once the favorites of Medici popes, or from Cellini's workshop. *Le moi
profond,* the real inner self of Dr. Claribel is a mystery to us.

Dr. Claribel's taste in art widened. Etta was always a bit flushed at her
first sight of some aberration of the art of the nude offered her. The
sisters had the run of Picasso's studio, for they provided him with funny
papers the Baltimore *Sun* published. While he looked and chuckled, they
nosed around, picking up sketches from the not too clean studio floor,
and paying very little for what they carried off to an indifferent, paro-
chial Baltimore. Picasso permitted his friendship for Americans to go only
so far. Henri Matisse, on the other hand, was warm and friendly and they
took his advice as to which of his paintings to buy.

From Paris, loaded with antiques, peculiar fashions, art, the sisters
would return to their overcrowded Eutaw Street apartment in Baltimore
to plan other trips next year. Besides the great paintings, they bought
trash; glorious junk also had their love. They were the eager victims of
many shady dealers, and buyers of an endless procession of furniture that
was labeled "Queen Anne," and "Renaissance," and sometimes was. It
crowded the flat. There were Oriental rugs, always described as "priceless," paid for with a lot of Cone Mills solid cash. Primitive or ritual
bronzes stood by Persian metal cloth, a great deal of Baroque, a gathering
of minor Asian artifacts, and even some African ritual items.

It was the early days of Freudian popularity, and the good doctor of
Vienna would have been interested in Dr. Claribel's major fetish: her

collection of boxes and chests, beyond reason. Intricate boxes within boxes, drawers, exotic secret compartments, baskets, chests, all were her joy, her passion.

In Paris in time the relationship of the Cone sisters to Gertrude Stein cooled. They were not, as many thought, closely related; as Gertrude explained, "Only cousins of theirs were related."

Dr. Claribel felt Gertrude was pushy at times. Both of them were monolithically selfish. Dr. Claribel felt she, too, had become a mover and forcer of ideas and art. Back in 1890 she had run a salon in Baltimore called "Claribel's Saturday." The sisters may have worn high button shoes and skirts that swept the floor, but they had an intrinsic sense of their worth and an awareness of their uniqueness. The town, however, thought them slightly cracked.

Dr. Claribel was never small or thin, so when she went to the theater in Paris she always tried to reserve two seats, one for herself and one for reticule, magnificent fur coat, and a rather unbecoming scoop hat. She was logically contrary—walking or seated a Fauve exhibition.

Dr. Claribel was not one to live on credit. Picasso, doing her portrait, stepped back and said, "It is finished." Dr. Claribel pulled up her skirts, petticoats, showing a stout, oaklike leg, and from a secret pocket among the lacy froufrou produced a thousand-franc note which she handed to the artist. "In payment, *cher maître.*"

Gertrude could no longer manipulate the Cone sisters as they matured into collectors and Lady Bountifuls. Around 1925 Gertrude announced that Etta Cone could have the high privilege of buying the manuscript of *Three Lives*, which Etta had typed. Etta declined the honor. The frost was on the friendship, and it grew colder. When Gertrude came to Baltimore in 1934, Etta managed to be out of town.

Before it ended, the friendship between the Gertrude Stein household and the Cone sisters had its ups and downs. For Alice Toklas, herself built on the lines of a breadstick, these large, Jewish, matronly, upholstered types were not the stuff of comrades. They maneuvered around each other demanding respect, and in the case of Gertrude an eagerness for worship and admiration of herself as a yet undiscovered genius.

Alice, the "Pussy" to Gertrude's "Lovey," was jealous of anyone who might come intimately closer to Gertrude than herself, so the Cone sisters continued to worry her. Alice was small and dark, with hatchet-sharp features; the pink, large Cone sisters, she felt, had to be kept in their place. Alice had acquired a certain prose skill from Gertrude's style of writing, the use of the sly stab. "Dr. Claribel was handsome and distin-

guished. Miss Etta not at all so. She and I disagreed about who should pay the lunch bill." Beyond that Alice had no kind word to say about the Cone sisters.

When in Paris the Cone sisters usually stayed at the Hôtel des Saints Péres, and from there like ocean liners leaving their docks, in their finery and Dr. Claribel's ornate body decor, they sailed forth onto the Paris streets to visit, to look at paintings, go to the theater and the opera. As time passed they depended less on Gertrude Stein as guide and art critic; and as many others discovered, the Stein-Toklas ménage never forgot *or* forgave.

As the sisters grew older, dipped deep into middle age, they became more legend than part of the American scene in Paris of the Twenties. The Cone sisters during those golden Twenties, as they added to their collections, felt the lure of Paris. Journalists' clippings give a taste of the worship of Paris:

The brilliance of her culture . . . radiated around the world like a beacon, drawing the most creative talents to Paris from all corners of the earth. In Tokyo Seritzawa wrote . . . *I Want to Die in Paris*, Nagai composed his modern Japanese classic, *Tales of France*. Chinese scholars and young revolutionaries came to study in Paris, capital of two masters of philosophy, Lu and Man—the Chinese pronunciation of the names Rousseau and Montesquieu. Picasso, a Spaniard, and Modigliani, an Italian . . . make the *Ecole de Paris* the greatest since the Renaissance.

Reading the memoirs of those who came and remembered how it had been (Hemingway was to say, "We all had a girl and her name is Nostalgia") one rarely comes across the names of Dr. Claribel and Etta. Their need for the arts was mainly visual but for the reading of Gertrude's texts. In all that has been written about those times they cast only shadows among the overused names of those Americans who fled the times to Paris. "From the Right Bank of Hemingway and Fitzgerald—the Ritz and Harry's New York Bar—to the . . . home of Gertrude Stein on the Left Bank and Isadora Duncan's Montparnasse studio . . . an extraordinary galaxy . . . James Joyce, John Dos Passos, John Steinbeck, E. E. Cummings, W. B. Yeats, Kay Boyle, Ezra Pound, Djuna Barnes, Glenway Wescott, and Eugene Jolas, editor of *transition*, which proclaimed 'revolution of the word,' Sinclair Lewis, Santayana and Sherwood Anderson . . ."

Names, names, *names* fill old press clippings.

In 1929 Wall Street laid the famous egg, and Dr. Claribel Cone died at sixty-five, impressive, ornate in the welter of that esoteric apartment on

Eutaw Street in Baltimore, among the paintings from Paris, the Oriental rugs, the Turkish scarves, the Renaissance furniture. All recalling the Paris of red walls, elderly waiters carrying wine buckets, Pompeian Art Nouveau mixed with Blue Period paintings.

The collection was shown to very few. It was almost impossible in the apartment's welter of uncontrolled collecting to see the color of Paris; its shapes and its atmosphere created by Picasso, Matisse (who said "Art evokes the same sensation as a good armchair"), Van Gogh, Manet, and others. Only the special, the discerning people were allowed a look.

The year after Dr. Claribel died, Matisse was in America, bringing with him some huge murals he had painted for the eccentric Dr. Barnes, "the mad collector of art" at Merion, Pennsylvania. Matisse, after a not too happy time with the strange Dr. Barnes, came on to Baltimore to visit Etta. In that Southern city he enjoyed the sight of his work on the walls of the apartment—those that were not in storage. He promised to make a posthumous portrait of Dr. Claribel, but he did not get around to it until 1934, when he also added one of Etta in charcoal. In Etta's portrait she is wide and aged, but in serene exaltation. It shows her seated in a stiff-backed chair with her solid face and an extra chin, an old-fashioned hairdress. She is wearing a sort of all-covering gown, a ruff around her plump chin. She resembles nothing so much as her one-time friend, Gertrude, before La Stein cut off her hair and grew gaunt.

The year of this Matisse drawing was also the year Etta bought the huge interior by the artist, *The Magnolia Branch*. It was five feet square, and perhaps the most important Matisse in America. (Etta bought a picture from the artist every year, and *always* mailed him a yearly birthday cake. There is a claim she baked the cake herself, but that is doubtful.) She also published a catalogue of their Matisse collection: thirty-two oils, eighteen drawings, seventy studies for the artist's Mallarmé etchings, and eighteen bronzes.

In August of 1949, twenty years after Dr. Claribel, Etta died. The Cone sisters' bequest to the Baltimore Museum of Art was an impressive one.

As one magazine writer put it in an unsigned story: "By the time Miss Etta and her brother died, the 'odd Cones' in Eutaw Street had become owners of one of the most fabulous private collections of modern paintings in existence, and once stuffy Baltimore was miraculously endowed with an art gold mine."

Book Five

WISH YOU WERE HERE

CHAPTER 31

The Sea Trip of H. L. Mencken

There is no use trying to be more spiritual than God.
God never meant man to be a purely spiritual creature.
That is why He uses material things like bread and wine
to put the new life into us. We may think this rather
crude and unspiritual. God does not:
He invented eating.

C. S. LEWIS

T HE CONE SISTERS were not the only citizens of Baltimore known in
Paris. In the fall of 1929 most Americans were coming home from
Paris except for a few old die-hards, deeply rooted there, or those who
were unwelcome to their families or society, a society already reeling
from the fall of the stock market.

One traveler, though, H. L. Mencken, was sailing east, headed for Paris
as a first stop. He was "a roly-poly little beer barrel of a man" with a too
simple face, fine blue eyes, bland limp hair parted in the middle and
buttered down on each side like a frontier saloonkeeper's. A talkative
little man given to cigars and red suspenders. He had a corrosive sense of
publicity and seemed to lack any introspection or repose.

The Seventh Day Adventists had said in an apocalyptic warning that
the end of the world was at hand, as called for by Luke XXI, 25-8. The
traveler announced that he was in agreement with the Adventists, that
for sure, "on some tomorrow, maybe next Tuesday, possibly even Monday, the heavens will split wide open, there will be a roaring of mighty
winds, shock troops of angels will come fluttering down to earth, the
righteous will be snatched up to bliss and the wicked will be thrust into
Hell."

H. L. Mencken was one of the "roaring winds" of the Twenties against
liberal truth and liberal cant, against the boobs' democracy. It is hard for

us now to recall his great reputation as the American crackerbarrel atheist, champion of German *Kultur*, flogger of political slobs, Babbitts,
wowsers, and boosters: All officeholders were thieves who could milk a
cow without waking her up. It was foolish to articulate the vague hopes
of the people; the Artful Dodger should be our patron saint. Mencken
was, with such ideas, the idol of the intellectual young, the unsophisticated readers of his magazine in its green cover, *The American Mercury*.
He was a fancy Dan of a writer whose prose today seems virtuoso corn.
His epigrams no longer sing, his wit is vaudeville jesting. But he was the
national iconoclast.

Now in 1929, he was fleeing, some said, a woman he had been courting
for many years; the teeth of marriage were snapping at his Baltimore
heels. The excuse to get away was a desire to see Paris—the natural prey
of Prussian generals—and officially, to cover with an admonitory eye, the
Naval Arms Conference to be held in London. It was another one of those
facetious and cant-filled meetings where the nations sat down to talk of
disarming, meaning hardly a word of it. In politics, Mencken had
preached, honesty is an unjustified extravagance.

Behind him was Sara Haardt, whom he had thought of marrying for
seven years now, and the bride was getting a bit shop-worn and angry.
He was forty-three years of age; she was years younger, one of those
dowdy, opinionated Southern women, from Alabama (and a good friend
of Zelda Fitzgerald). Sara was a bit of a blue-stocking, a low-key minor
writer. And an ill woman, whom the doctors, checking the X rays of her
lungs, offered only a few more years of life. Mencken, actually fearful of
women, had preached all his life, "Love is the delusion that one woman
differs from another." He had quoted Schopenhauer on women "as cunning, frivolous, childish, gifted in dissimulation, weak in reasoning, intel-
lectually inadequate, lacking a sense of justice. Only the man whose
intellect is clouded by his sexual impulses could give the name of the fair
sex to that undersized, narrow-shouldered, broad-hipped and short-
legged race." Mencken advocated the Nietzschean method, "Take a whip
when you approach a woman."

Yet he was actually a melon-soft cartoon of the revolting, iron-jawed
Prussian he claimed to be. He proclaimed a love of beer and Brahms, kept
a callow and jejune eye on the American democratic process as admin-
istered by Coolidge, Harding and Hoover. His hatred of Franklin Roosevelt was to be as great as his fear of bad cigars. His life style in print was
heavy wit, aggression and hate of American ideals.

Paris meant little more to Mencken than Offenbach's music and the cancan girls showing their lacy drawers. Yet perhaps in some fear of the Adventists' warning, he had gotten rid of his collection of pornographic books before sailing. Like so many feeble sexual performers, he talked loudly of lust and was excited by dirty pictures, while fearing actual body contact.

Mencken was a lonely figure as the boat pulled past the Statue of Liberty. His vogue as a prophet was passing with the flaming Twenties (roaring or not as the journalists were to call them), that decade of fame was all behind him. He was soon to be an anchorite with no pillar to perch on. He would be only a sideshow to the main attraction: the

Depression with its Dust Bowl, the agony of want and fear among millions of unemployed. His texts of rococo journalism would seem banal and dated.

On board ship he found lawyer Dudley Field Malone, another roaring boy of the Twenties and an old drinking partner, and *his* bride-to-be. They were to be married in London. It brought back Mencken's own problems of love and marriage, but the bar was open on the high seas, and he could taste the real *Münchener* beer. By the time the ship had docked at Cherbourg, he had taken on a great deal of beer.

Soon he was in Paris, and in the Gare St. Lazare the French reporters, in the proper gaudy dress of the press of the time, surrounded him, some wondering if they should treat him as a Hun or as a comic book American.

We can still read Mencken's interview in back files of the Paris newspapers. He scolded the French for "letting the Normandy countryside become disfigured by nasty American-styled billboards." He also said he would "at once dress like Paris journalists." He admired their purple spats, checked waistcoats, and bat-winged ties. A Jewish-American friend, Phil Goodman, led Mencken, still talking, to the Hôtel La Tremoille to check in, then to trot out to the Café de la Paix to drink Pilsener. The truth was that the great alcoholic swiller he claimed to be in print hardly ever drank hard stuff beyond one swig, and could not properly hold his whisky or Scotch. He did brag, as the waiter stacked up a pile of beer saucers so high, they "had to be secured with guy ropes." Most of the rest of Paris seemed to remain inscrutable to him. It failed to resemble Baltimore.

Another self-created legend was that Mencken was a lady-killer, a cavorter with wild girls and native American whores with a gold tooth well placed in front. However, Phil Goodman, an expert on venery, said his friend, a bachelor in his prime, ignored the girls for the food and drink. Mencken's pleasure in the sights of the grand city mostly consisted of walking the boulevards and reading the posters on the kiosks. Mencken took pride in having no taste for the visual or graphic arts; he considered painting an overrated art, and "no picture is worth more than a few moments' glance." He had no fastidious reticence about his art opinions, matching those of the Babbitts and boobs he flogged.

Nor did he mix much with the Left Bank bohemians, the doers and movers of the little literary magazines, the avant-garde prose makers. On his one visit to the Café du Dôme he sipped beer, watched the crowds move in and out of the cafés and bistros. This led him to make his one profound statement about Paris: "The cafés of Paris certainly dangerously outnumber the *pissoirs*." (Hemingway, in conversation about this remark, said, "Well, it beats all hollow saying 'Lafayette, we are here.'")

Mencken met Régis Michaud, who had translated the *Prejudices* into French and written *L'Ame Américaine*. They went on to meet a reporter from *Les Nouvelles Littéraires* in the Montparnasse apartment of an American exiled writer, Ludwig Lewisohn. The interview was planned to be a hell-and-brimstone attack on the stupid Americans of both political parties, the Bible-belt fundamentalists, the Pilgrim Fathers, the blue-nose Prohibitionists, and all the God-thumpers and fat cats in power, north, south, east, and west.

Ludwig Lewisohn, a German Jew, had in his youth emigrated to Charleston, South Carolina, and had boasted, "At the age of fifteen I was an American, a Southerner, and a Christian." He claimed native bigotry had driven him to Paris, to recant and to begin to think of a Jewish homeland. In truth there had been a Lewisohn failed marriage, sex problems, and an unrelenting wife to escape.

The interview with the two Americans blasting away left the United States with no shred of honor or reputation as they pointed out how indecent were the fundamental decencies of the United States. It even shocked some of the French, and one wrote, "If the official greeter of New York, M. Grover Whelan, were sent to welcome Mencken home, he most likely would order the tug boat to meet M. Mencken at the Battery to hustle him all the faster to jail."

Attacking American stupidity, materialism, and greed was wearing thin as newspaper material, and Mencken was one of the last dancers to that tired tune during the years of the Depression while the Dust Bowl and the Okies blew away. The Germans cheered him, the *Berliner Tageblatt* compared him to Heine and Voltaire, "younger and more lusty and free from all poison and maliciousness." Reading this, one reporter on the Paris *Herald* suggested the Germans couldn't read French if they missed the Mencken-Lewisohn attack on their native land, the United States.

Hitler and his Nazis were already aiming for power and a new attack on the French. Mencken was to continue to admire the new German spirit, its nationalism, even the Nazi way of doing things. Because of his unctuous, dangerous bigotry, in time his Jewish friends were to drop away as he began to sound as fully bigoted as the Klan.

Except for the convenient and frequent use of its *pissoirs* due to the pressure on the kidneys from his beer drinking, Paris made little impression on him. For all his bombast Mencken's writing was actually Edwardian journalism, and the avant-garde writing of Paris and London meant nothing to him. For painting he had no eye, and music for him was German. He had only hard words for Debussy and other French composers. It was clear to the French reporters Mencken was an occupying force rather than a friendly visitor to Paris. He moved on, having chilled some of his admirers among the French.

In London he saw the conference was a bad joke: "The Naval Conference turns out to be the usual tedious horror. The frauds meet all morning, and then issue idiotic statements, meaning nothing. The French always upset the apple-cart by telling the simple truth. It shocks the British beyond endurance. As for the Americans, they sit around vacantly, learning to drink tea. . . . Next week, I'll probably go to Oxford for a day to see Robert Bridges."

Bridges, in a later visit to New York, said Mencken was "the only American" he wanted to meet. Then he shut off *all* interviews with reporters. A tabloid therefore ran the headline: KING'S CANARY REFUSES TO CHIRP.

In February of 1930 Mencken was back at sea on the *Bremen*, bound for home. On landing in New York he outfoxed the other celebrity on board, the film star Richard Barthelmess, by producing a five-gallon beer glass, filling it with beer, and having it drunk up by the reporters who had come for interviews aboard. In August, with no more hiding place, he married Sara Haardt, after the press reported MENCKEN RECANTS JIBES AT TENDER PASSION. He made a good, considerate husband and a successful marriage.

In 1935 the Menckens went on a Mediterranean tour. They managed to crowd in Paris. As one reporter put it, "The Menckens had very little time in Paris. Sara decided to spend it in shopping, Henry [Mencken] in eating. Consequently, on his return voyage . . . he suffered from seasickness. By the time he landed . . . from the *Europa*, he was in a gloomy mood."

"I am convinced," he declared, "that the majority of people don't want liberty . . . I think most people would prefer to be ruled, governed, and directed. It may be that the ordinary man doesn't have to worry about so many things when he has no liberty."

The image of Hitler and the stupidities of Americans were to color the rest of his life. He noted, "History will accord the Nazis at least one white mark for having thrown Freud out of Vienna." Collecting Nazi postal cards, in heavy jest he wrote on one to a Jewish friend with relations dying in concentration camps: "This proves that Der Führer loves children." Another comment that lost him friends was, "Hitler's New Deal seems to be working better than Franklin's."

If he celebrated with poor American beer when the Germans marched into Paris, that fact has been removed from the records. When Mencken died, someone quoted Edna St. Vincent Millay, a poet he didn't care for: "And life goes on forever like the gnawing of a mouse."

CHAPTER 32

Barbette—Texas to Paris

There is a goal but no way.

FRANZ KAFKA

SOME EVENTS were accepted as great sensations in the Paris of the Twenties, sensations caused by Americans. But these things rarely caused excitement beyond the Anglo-American colonies, the literary folk, the drinkers at the Ritz bar, the fornicators, the horse-bettors, who gathered each in a kind of cluster around their specialties. They did not penetrate *tout Paris*— the true French life of the city. A few French literary figures like Gide might show some interest in American or British writers, or an attempt would be made to translate Joyce into French. But in the main the French society dazzler or literary figure over his vermouth aperitif or Calvados stayed in a world of his own kind.

One rare American did become the idol of French intellectual and social circles—the very inner core—and entered fully into the best society. The creature was Barbette, who was a high-wire performer, a dainty acrobat who came on in a Chanel gown and an ostrich-feather hat and stripped down to reveal a slim body in tights.

Jean Cocteau became the greatest admirer of the swaying, swinging little darling of the high wire. In many letters to friends he expressed his excitement, his admiration, again and again:

A music hall act called "Barbette" . . . been keeping me enthralled for a fortnight. The young American . . . the wire and trapeze act, a great actor, an angel, has become the friend of all of us. Go see him, be nice to him, as he deserves, tell everybody he is no mere acrobat in women's clothes, not just a graceful daredevil, but one of the most beautiful things in the theater. Stravinsky, Aurie, poets, painters and myself have seen no comparable display of artistry on the stage since Nijinsky. You won't be wasting your time . . . both a great acrobat, discriminating reader, in close touch with contemporary writing . . . The god of friendship has punished you for never being in Paris when we are. Your great loss for 1923, Barbette—a terrific act at the Casino de Paris . . . Ten unforgettable minutes. A theatrical masterpiece. Angel, flower, bird.

One forgot Apollinaire's *Calligrammes* or the gossip of the Saint Germain Quarter to talk of the amazing performer Barbette, who was what is usually called "the rage of Paris." Barbette was actually a young man from Texas named Vander Clyde. He was a mortal and born near Austin, Texas, in 1904. Living in a small, horse-littered town called Round Rock, as a boy he practiced wire-walking on his mother's iron-wire clothesline. His mother had a millinery shop where people rarely bought more than a yearly hat. There seems to be no mention of a father in any stories Barbette told of his life. Of his mother he said, "She was artistic, very much admired culture." She did take him to a sun-baked circus in Austin, and as the boy watched the spinning and tumbling wire-workers, he knew he, too, would someday be up there. He picked cotton with field-hands to make money to attend circuses. At fourteen he answered an advertisement in the show-business paper *Billboard* (he was already reading show-biz trade papers), an ad placed by a surviving member of the Alfarette Sisters, "The World Famous Aerial Queens." There was need for a partner, a swinging ring and trapeze worker to replace a dead sister of the act: in such odd fashion the universe is made conscious to some men.

Vander Clyde was told the job was his if he would take over the missing sister's costumes and play her role on the wire and trapeze. There was no moment of doubt or withdrawal. Vander did just that, dressing in a girl's costume and performing well. In time he went on to the "Whirling Sensations," a group that hung by their teeth on a revolving wheel and fluttered huge butterfly wings—a constellation whirling in space with mechanical and toothy ease.

Vander Clyde was an *artiste*—and knew it—not the common circus type. He began to work on his own act, a single, in woman's dress, presenting a trapeze performance of grace and skill. He claimed to have been a great reader of Shakespeare and explained he based his character of Barbette, as he now billed himself, on Shakespeare's heroines who were always played in Elizabethan times by boys in female attire. To descend from his perch was like a move from the sublime to the prosaic.

At the end of his act he would pull off his wig and reveal himself as a slim, handsome young man, to the great amazement of the audience, who could not believe this charming figure was not a girl. His grasp of their attention delighted him—power he saw as an end to itself and an art.

Barbette's success in the United States caused William Morris, the theater agent, to book him first in England and then in Paris. It was in Paris that as Barbette—a pre-Nabokovian nymphet—he really came into true being. "I felt I had found it, my city, my Paris."

He was at the Hôtel Moderne, and he opened at the Alhambra Music Hall. The audiences delighted in him—an attraction to rival the *Cirque d'Hiver*—and he was booked for the revue at the Casino de Paris. There he was a sensation again, and the best people lined up to visit him in his dressing room; to find Barbette close up a young man of great charm, a personality beyond the opulent razzle-dazzle of the stage.

American society appeared, and through Helen Gwynne, who led the best of the rich expatriates' circle, Barbette met Walter Berry, the Harry Lehrs, the Elisha Dyers, and a Vanderbilt or two—the beginning of café society. He also attracted Princess Violette Murat, and through her he moved like a splendid little Greek god into the best, the most exciting French high life. He entered, with poise and a precocious charm, the salons, the country homes; was greeted by literary figures, stage directors, actors, masters of newspapers, magazines, reviews. The Southern effusiveness of Barbette's accent was delightful as his French improved. He chummed with the Noailles, Georges Geffroy, Radiguet, and his greatest press agent was Jean Cocteau, poet, artist, playwright, novelist, film director, opium smoker, and most of all homosexual egotist, with an ability for self-publicity that would bring him at last in gold braid and sword to the French Academy.

La Nouvelle Revue Française ran a rave review by Drieu la Rochelle, in which the beauty of Barbette's performance was praised over and beyond the mere art of show world life. Barbette enjoyed the luminous, pulsating social whirl. One day, while nude in his hotel room, his face and arms covered with a skin bleaching cream he used to remove the last color of Texas, Barbette's beauty ritual was interrupted as a reporter walked in on him. He reported, "Barbette comes in two colors at home."

Paris was to be Barbette's home base; every year he returned to meet his French friends and admirers, playing his art at the Empire, the Moulin

Rouge, the Medrane Circus; and, of course, the Alhambra, where he had first come into Paris's view with the miraculous intensity of his art.

Cocteau never tired of analyzing Barbette and the magic of the performance of this *"drôle, jeune diable."* His impressions of the subject still retain the excitement, the near frenzy of his reactions:

Imagine the letdown it would be for us if Barbette were simply to remove his wig . . . after the fifth curtain call he does that; the letdown takes place. There is a murmur from the audience, and some people are embarrassed, some blush. Yes . . . having succeeded as an acrobat, causing some people nearly to faint, he now has to have his success as an actor. Watch his final tour de force. Simply to become a man, to run the film backward is not enough. The truth itself is translated to convince us as forcibly as did the lie. So Barbette, the moment he has snatched off his wig, plays the part of a man . . . The poet "de-classes" everything, becomes a classic. Barbette mimics poetry itself, that is his fascination . . . his acrobatics are not perilous. His affectations ought to be unbearable. The principle of his act embarrasses us. What is left? That thing he has created, going through turns under the spotlight.

Barbette toured Europe—was well known on the Compagnie des Wagons Lits, Express Europeans, Arlberg-Orient Express. He appeared in Warsaw, Madrid, Barcelona, Rome, Berlin, Copenhagen. Always to be taken up by the best people, who entertained him, took him around to historic spots and gay parties. He traveled in style with twenty-eight trunks and a maid "and a maid to assist the maid."

Barbette took great care of his makeup, spending hours to show him-self just right, appearing in a leather girdle, dressing in the proper gowns and tights, adjusting his wig, hairpins in his mouth as he looked into the mirror, turning himself into a young girl with great skill. Beyond the wire and the trapeze gear there was a white bearskin covered sofa in his act. Here Barbette did a kind of striptease as he got out of his long-trained evening gown. As Cocteau reported it:

A scabrous little scene, a real masterpiece—pantomime, summing up in parody all the women he has studied, becoming himself a woman . . . we are in the magic light of the theater, in this trick where truth has no currency, anything natural has no value. . . . So the only things that convince us are card tricks, sleights of hand of difficulties unknown to the audience . . . Thanks to Barbette, I know that it was not just for reasons of "decency" that great nations, great civilizations gave women's roles to men.

Cocteau wrote of his friend as a *leçon extraordinaire du métier théâtral*, as one above "incongruity, death, bad taste, indecency, indig-nation."

To the Cocteau set Barbette was a cause, a crusade to permit the sexes to cross each other's borderline. The poet reported: "He pleases those who see him as a woman, and those who are aware of the man—not forgetting those aroused by the supernatural beauty of sex."

Barbette led the life of the senses, remembered Princess Murat sniffing cocaine, going to a Marseilles bordello with Cocteau to see pornographic films. In 1932 Cocteau, directing his film *The Blood of the Poet*, included a scene in which the real Vicomtesse de Noailles, his patroness, played a small part seated in a theater box. When she saw the final version of the film, the vicomtesse objected, finding it too broad and shocking. So Barbette, dressed in the vicomtesse's gown and jewels, substituted for her, no one the wiser.

By the mid Thirties the world was deep in its great depression. Spain was committing suicide in a murderous betrayal, a civil war. The great wild days of the best society of Paris were passing, even as its members were aging on brittle bones. Barbette had taken several bad falls and had the scars to prove it. At a performance at the Moulin Rouge a curtain had fluttered, throwing him off balance and he had fallen, injuring himself so badly the rest of the season was canceled. The excruciating pain would go, but somehow his great days would not return.

Back in America in 1938, Barbette was working at Loews State—a vaudeville grind house—in New York City. He caught a chill in the drafty backstage and developed pneumonia. Something also happened to his joints; his bones "went wrong" and he needed surgery. He spent nearly two years in hospitals and when discharged he could not walk. He had a painful time teaching himself to use his legs again. The butterfly would flutter no more. The limbs were pinioned. Barbette was no longer a youth. Was it the time of *La Mort de Quelqu'un*?

The great days were over. A war roared in Europe. Hitler was in Paris. Barbette's friends were dead or in hiding or starving. A few were even collaborating. Barbette went back to Texas, to Austin. Gone forever were the fashionable days and gay nights of fame, the best French society of Paris rising to applaud, enchanted with him as he recited Rosalind's speech from *As You Like It*, in the role of the boy actor playing the part: "If I were a woman I would kiss as many of you as had beards that pleased me, complexions that liked me, and breaths that I defied not; and I am sure, as many as have good beards, or good faces, or sweet breaths, will, for my kind offer, when I make curtsy, bid me farewell." Or that moment of exhilaration as he came out in his best gown and hairdo to commence the strip before mounting up over the heads of the best people to begin his act.

He became an old man with a limp in his walk, assisted by a cane and memories, marooned in Austin, Texas. The person remained—the shell of a disembodied artist who had set the poet Paul Valéry, after seeing him as Barbette, to wondering about a Greek myth, "Hercules transformed into a Swallow."

CHAPTER 33

Caresse, Born Mary

*It was not so much what France gave you as what
she did not take away.*

GERTRUDE STEIN

S HE WAS BORN Mary Phelps Jacob and claimed such ancestors as Governor William Bradford of Plymouth Colony, the steamboat's Robert Fulton, a general in the Civil War, and an ambassador to the Court of St. James. Through her first husband, named Peabody, she could call J. P. Morgan uncle. Mr. Peabody was replaced by Harry Crosby, the nephew of Walter Berry. He called her Caresse, and as Caresse Crosby she rode to fame in Paris on a sea of money and a naked megalomania for attention.

One way of making a noise in Paris in the Twenties was to become a publisher of the avant-garde. The Crosbys established the Black Sun Press. Caresse found a wedge into the literary life of Europe through Walter Berry. She dropped names about like a tree does ripe fruit. In concupiscent times she flourished.

The Black Sun Press put out editions of Caresse's and Harry's own poetry, collections of letters from Marcel Proust and Henry James, and some texts by D. H. Lawrence. Lawrence and Frieda, visiting the Crosbys in Paris, got into a family fight, smashing Crosby china and records.

The Crosbys lived on the Rue de Lille, and gave huge parties just outside the city at Chantilly, where they took over the Jean-Jacques

Rousseau mill as *Le Moulin du Soleil*. Doings were lively. Caresse walking down a Paris boulevard was a Dada fantasy; gold necklace (solid gold, of course), varnished gold toenails and a lean nervous whippet on a jeweled leash. Parties at the Mill became famous. Lucky was the American who received an invitation: *"Mrs. Crosby vous prie d'assister à un country supper and dance."*

Harry Crosby's poems about his wife never ran past an itemized admiration and inventory of her "slender legs . . . girlishness . . . wayward eyes. . . ." The legs remained slender, the girlish loveliness grew with passing time a bit pug-dogged as to features. When Harry killed himself Caresse's "wayward eyes" turned toward a genius she had discovered, a young novelist whom she carried off to the Mill. Truthfully she could claim, "When I helped writers and artists, I benefited more than they did. I think everybody should chip in and do whatever can be done."

However the first young genius failed to produce a world-shaking second novel (what was the first?) and Caresse drifted into marriage with a new husband and went back to become the hostess of Hampton Manor in Virginia, "designed by Thomas Jefferson." Here she boarded and fed publicity-seeking geniuses like the exhibitionist Salvador Dali, often photographed perched up a tree, perhaps to escape the bad cooking at Hampton Manor (he insisted that he and his wife Gala eat out). Henry Miller, historian of Americans in Paris during the Thirties, once came under Caresse's wing; "he didn't write but *painted*, while Dali didn't paint but *wrote* his memoirs."

When Caresse came back to Europe, Paris was only a stopping-off place for her. She finally came to rest in a mountain lair, an eagle's nest of a huge castle in Italy's Rieti province, a place of over 350 rooms, and she called it Roccasinibalde. From twelve to thirty geniuses-in-training were often in residence, but the money was running out and some guests were asked to pay. Nonpaying guests had included Ezra Pound, the poet without a country. Max Ernst had been taken in when he was put out into the street, unable to pay his rent, and there was also a lady writer having somebody's baby, "she wasn't sure whose."

The charm of Caresse was her love of people who submitted to her domination.

But the old gay times, the wild freewheeling fun of the Paris days, of the Crosbys at the *Moulin du Soleil*, were gone. As one of Caresse's guests at Roccasinibalde put it (asking to be unnamed):

What the hell, once we were young with Caresse in Paris—and there was all the boozing and screwing, and talking about the Surreal, and Picasso's latest lay, and what six months' sensation of a novelist was dying of drink, and who had blown his cork and been put in a laughing farm. Now here, with Caresse's sour wine and goddamn *pasta* our breath doesn't hold out, our livers ache, and even Caresse has forgotten all her crystal chandelier background. Let's face it—here there are no folks around like Jo Davidson, Paul Valéry, Isadora Duncan, Ottoline Morrell, Harriet Weaver, or John Reed—not here at Roccas-inibalde. Her new crop of geniuses are mostly all phonies, freeloading fags and poets trying to make it to television.

What drove so many Americans like the Crosbys to stay in Europe, to feel lost and lonely, to become patrons, publishers, setting up places to nest down their geniuses? Some stated it was that strain of Puritanism from which most Americans suffered who went to Europe, up until World War II. They often defied the pilgrim's way, cursed that Calvinism had been ingrained in them by their culture, their prep-school chapels, by attending such "a Christers' college as Yale." The more they rebeled, the more they fled from Puritanism, somehow in the end they felt their Christian duty—even when the dogma and theology were gone. They, including Catholics and Jews, had to set up culture foundations if they could, or print little magazines, feed, clothe, make love to what they felt was the artist—if lucky, *perhaps* a genius. They helped Joyce, they bought Henry Miller meals, got lawyers for Ezra Pound, sent him birthday cakes, found him awards, even honors, while he was locked up by his government as a traitor.

Americans, turning away to exile, to art, free living, to secret desires, remembered not only the material dullness of Main Street and Babbitt and Mom's apple pies and silver cord, but also their childhoods, based for so many of them on the gloomy creed that there was sin and punishment and little more. Calvin sang it loud and clear as did the little white churches, the Elmer Gantrys, the Fundamentalists: "God is our only hope. Without His grace we are guilty and corrupt; Adam's fall a disaster felt by man until Judgment Day. After his fall, we are heir to malice, corruption; because of man's fall we all deserve to be condemned before God, sentenced to Hell."

The lapsed Puritan in Paris, the betrayer of his father's God, came often to the point when he was disillusioned. A failed artist, a broken love affair, unhealthy stimulants, and it was clear the toughness had been stripped away a generation or so back. In many cases they came to alcohol in larger and larger doses, drugs, a pointless wandering existence, sanitariums, suicides—they came even to going home.

As Karl Menninger pointed out, "Calvin Coolidge is alive in contemporary America, no matter how antireligious or sectarian our culture.

Under the libertine, under the pleasures of the mind, the body, we remain within reach of Calvin, Knox, Cotton Mather and Jonathan Edwards."

A world at the end of its tether drives us toward tasks of hope; we fight off the existential absurdity and feel the heavy collective responsibility of a sense of duty. So that, in Paris, the Americans pointed out the failed purpose of café loafers, who weren't painting or writing or composing or publishing. Many were feeding or supporting some work in progress, literary crusade. Anything, they felt, but a moral numbness; give us a cause, no matter how depraved.

I remember standing in Harry's Bar with Elliot Paul, when he was one of the editors of *transition*. "A hand is again writing '*Mene, mene tekel upharrsin*' on our wallpaper. Only we Americans really care for a translation."

CHAPTER 34

Jack Johnson of Paris

Mon âme vers d'affreux naufrages appareille.
My soul sails towards dreadful shipwrecks.

PAUL VERLAINE

*I pack my trunk, embrace my friends, embark
on the sea and at last wake up . . . and there
beside me is the stern fact, the sad self,
unrelenting, identical, that I fled from.*

EMERSON

IN THE INDIAN SUMMER of 1913, a group of three sailed for Europe from
Montreal, Canada, on the *Carinthia*, bound for Le Havre, France. A
huge Negro, his second white wife, and his nephew, acting as his manager. The black man was Jack Johnson, a fugitive from a United States
jail term, on what many called a frame-up. He was the first Negro heavyweight boxing champion of the world, and so was resented by the
bigoted whites.

"The cable's cut," said Jack, as the ship left the dock. He was a man of
no excessive introspection, but he felt sad.

Lucille, his wife, said, "We are now the three musketeers."

What the manager, Jack's nephew Gus Rhodes, said, if anything, is not
on record.

The ship's chief steward, on the purser's orders, told the party, "There
might be *some* difficulty about seating arrangements in the dining saloon." So in disciplined outrage they ate in their cabins. It was not a
happy trip.

When the ship got to Le Havre, Jack was amazed to find the pier lined
by a mass of French police. He wondered, had they come to arrest him
and turn him back to the American authorities to serve his prison term of
one year and a day? But it was only a sort of honor guard to keep back

the unaggressive crowd who were welcoming the black champion of the world. Not only because of his title, but the fact that he had been brought to trial in an American court by the federal government on strange charges—violation of the Mann Act—all this, because he was a black man, made him a hero to the masses of Europe. Jack and Gus had been in Paris before, in 1911, when Jack had toured as a music hall attraction in London, Paris, Berlin, Budapest, and St. Petersburg.

Now a fugitive, what Jack Johnson needed was money to live on. He planned to exhibit himself again in the theaters, the fairs, the music halls, and nephew Gus would see if a prize fight could be arranged in Paris, a real fight and with anyone who seemed able to stand up before the giant's skill and blows.

In Paris again, Jack remembered past parties, drunks, and smashed hotel suites. The three travelers went to see the Folies Bergères. Jack was called to the stage and cheered. But then there was a street fight that made Jack doubt his welcome. Someone had made a slurring remark about Jack's white wife, Lucille. Frenchmen had taken sides for and against the insult and a free-for-all took place. Jack struck a few controlled blows as the crowd grew wilder. The police came into it, banging

heads, as the Paris *flics* will, with billy clubs or lead-weighted folded capes. There was also a great deal of fancy kicking—a French form of combat—which amused Jack who had never seen French street fighting *à l'imprévu*.

The police did not blame Jack for the riot, and he went on to London to see what his chances were there for some stage appearances. The London *Times* had been kind to him when he became champion. It had looked him over in its tight British way: "He sported rather more gold teeth than are worn by gentlemen in the Shires, and enough diamonds to resemble a starry night, but he was on the whole a far more pleasant person to meet in a room than any of the white champions of complicated nationality whom America exports from time to time to these unwilling shores."

But bigotry exists in every place. In the fortuitous play of chance there had been some white slave scandals in England: kidnapping and holding captive girls for export to brothels. Jack was a notorious lover of white women, according to press reports that checked his wild living past. The newspapers began to print stories about his flight from American justice. As a result in some places there was a tight-lipped, back-of-the-hand attitude that added up to: "We don't want Jack Johnson in England." He was to get for his music hall appearance what was announced as $5,000 a week (most unlikely). The Variety Artists Union objected.

The *Times* wrote, "There is a general desire to make it clear that this is not a question of color. It is a question of maintaining the standard of music-hall art. That Jack Johnson should appear on the stage of a London music-hall is regarded as unthinkable, and those who hold that view do so without in any way wishing to prejudice any issue which may be pending or decided in America concerning the pugilist."

But Jack knew the truth. It was because of his victory over a white man in the ring. "My real crime was beating Jim Jeffries," he would announce from the music-hall stage. But what he wanted was to fight again.

He went back to Paris to fight, but his first ring appearance was against a huge Russian freak called Al Spoul in a wrestling match, which Jack with primordial skill ended by knocking out the Russian with his fists. However what he wanted was a real fight, a boxing match.

There appeared on the scene an Irish-American sharper named Dan McKetrick, who called himself "an international promoter." He had been staging fights in Paris under the fancy title of *La Société pour la Propagation de la Boxe Française*. Dan had an insatiable desire for putting one over, on anyone, and a painful accumulation of resentments. He had found an American fighter—an ex-navy man from Pittsburgh. He was red-haired, a "white hope"—the name given hopefuls who wanted to defeat Jack Johnson. Francis Charles Moran had some reputation for a hard right punch, called by sportswriters (a notoriously cynical lot) "The Old Mary Ann." It looked like a great fight for Paris: Jack the Black against Francis the White. Contracts were signed for the fight with great ceremony in the Bois de Boulogne, with bottles of wine on the table in front of press and cameras. The fight would take place early in 1914. Times seemed dull and the fight between a black man and a white man for the heavyweight championship of the world should put the year on record with some sort of sporting violence.

Who was this huge Negro, where were his roots, the French sports lovers asked. And what crimes had he heally committed to be a fugitive in Paris? Jack Johnson had been born in Galveston, Texas, in 1878, just fifteen years after Abraham Lincoln as a war measure had freed the slaves in America (actually only in the South) by his Proclamation. He was named John Arthur Johnson, but was always called Jack. Jack was a strong boy, a powerful, graceful figure, and to protect himself from the rough and tumble life of Negroes in a tough Texas town, he became a remarkable puncher. He had little schooling; he was in turn a milk-cart driver, horse-handler in a stable, a bakery worker, a longshoreman on the Galveston docks. Fighting as he had to on the waterfront against white bigots, black bullies, he soon made a reputation as a man with a remarkable punch; he had a great capacity to punish the other fellow. Jack worked at Professor Herman Bernau's Sporting Gym as a clean-up porter. Soon he was working out and boxing around town, but not yet in any ring as a professional. He went touring in the tank towns of the South, fighting wherever anyone would put up a small purse. He traveled with hobos, at times under trains, in boxcars, saw the inside of jails as a vagrant. In time he became a professional boxer, married a Negro wife, who didn't last long. Jack was getting no place, but his interest in women, white or black, grew. He drank, ate, and liked fast motorcars. His ambition was to survive, exist, amuse himself. He had a huge zest for life in a country where he was denied most hotels, eating places, public rights.

Jack was a magnificent fighter, and national boxing needed something to bring life to the so-called sport. In time, in mean halls with foul-faced men, Jack made his way. On July 4, 1910, Jack Johnson stood in a bear pit at Reno, Nevada; the heat was over 100 degrees. He was to fight the world heavyweight champion, Jim Jeffries. It was a slaughter. In the fifteenth round Jack knocked Jeffries down so hard the man could not rise. Jack's gloved hand was lifted as "the new World's Heavyweight Champion!" With moral imbecility the mob resented it.

Jack's troubles had begun. The nation was bigoted against a Negro in such a high position; filthy, dishonest, revolting though the fight game was, with its double-cross, setups, thrown fights and dives. In Chicago Jack opened a popular saloon, drove fast motorcars, took on a harem of women. He had already lost his first white wife, Etta Duryea, by suicide. Like J. Pierpont Morgan, Theodore Dreiser, Stanford White—all hedonists of the period—there is no denying Jack Johnson, too, liked the good life, the sensual delight of pleasuring willing women.

But he was black, so his Café de Champion in Chicago lost its liquor license, women he had been intimate with were arrested and questioned under pressure. Plans to ruin Jack were officially afoot. The press went over to the attack on "a lippy, sassy nigger stud." The federal government, dominated by Southern reactionaries (Representative Rodenberry of Georgia: "In Chicago white girls are made the slaves of an African brute") brought charges against Jack for violating the Mann Act. Using the testimony of a whore, one Belle Schreiber, who had been intimate with the fighter, the Department of Justice threw a foul punch. Bail was set at $30,000 for Jack when he was arrested. But Judge Landis announced, "I will not accept a cash bond in this case. There is a human cry in this case that cannot be overlooked." (This is the judge who kept Negro baseball players out of the big leagues for years.) Jack was handcuffed and jailed, but a writ of habeas corpus got him out. He was learning to walk *la strada dolente*. Wilson Mizner, the wit, said at a bar, "Jack was tried on charges on which half the men with balls in America could have been picked up somewhere along the line."

The formal charges read: "That Johnson brought Belle from Pittsburgh to Chicago, October 15, 1910, for the purposes of: (1) prostitution; (2) debauchery; (3) prostitution; (4) debauchery; (5) unlawful sexual intercourse; (6) committing the crime against nature; (7) prostitution; (8) unlawful sexual intercourse; (9) to induce prostitution; (10) unlawful sexual intercourse, and (11) crime against nature."

Only a law professor can explain why the same charges appear two or three times. Judge Landis threw Jack into jail again, for four days, then had to take bail. It was at this time that Jack Johnson married Lucille Cameron, a school girl from Minneapolis who had fallen in love with the fighter. Two Negro ministers attended the ceremony, a white saloon owner was best man. There was dancing and music; Jack agreed with Muhammed, "Man is closest to God in the embrace of a woman."

The Federal Justice Department trial was a joke, a sinister one. Judge George Albert Carpenter charged the jury with the happy fact: "A colored man has just as much right to be convicted under the Mann Act as a white man." One wonders if the judge ("Though no mental giant, Carpenter was a superior type of man as federal judges go") had ever read Anatole France's famous line: "The law is fair to all; it is just as illegal for the rich man as for the poor man to sleep under the bridges of Paris."

Judge Carpenter opened the proceedings by denying a motion for a new trial. "It is always an unpleasant duty for me to say what will compensate the government for violating its laws. The crime which this defendant stands convicted of is an aggravating one. The life of the defendant, by his own admission, had been such as to merit condemnation. We have had a number of defendants found guilty in this court of violations of the Mann Act who have been sentenced to severe punishment, from one to two years in the penitentiary. This defendant is one of the best-known men of his race, and his example has been far reaching, and the court is bound to consider the position he occupied among his people. In view of these facts, this is a case that calls for more than a fine."

In little over an hour the jury was back. "Guilty." The judge sentenced Jack to one year and one day in Joliet prison, adding a fine of $1,000. The one day would lose Jack most of his civil rights. There was a stay of execution for Jack's lawyer to appeal. It was then Jack and his wife and his nephew made for the Canadian border and took ship to France. It was a mistake. The year in prison and the small fine would have been less punishment than the years in sterile exile, often in dire poverty. All the mean years that began with his fight in Paris with Francis Moran. Sixty years later in Chicago many federal judges were even worse bigots about citizens' rights.

Dan McKetrick, the Paris promoter, was too sharp for his own good. The planned Johnson-Moran fight was running into trouble. As usual and as was expected by the French press, Dan passed out nearly $4,000 in bribes to the French reporters in order to get good coverage for his fighters and his fight. This was ritual procedure, as French as good, crusty French bread. But the cry still went up, "*Qui est Moran?*" The press gave little space to the fight, and Dan began to push out more bribes, gratuities, hundreds of free tickets. The Paris journalists, always underpaid, sold these tickets on the open market, damaging the box office sales.

Jack had broken a small bone in his left hand in exhibition boxing and the hand could not be used in the fight. He was not training very hard, if at all. He had found the cabarets and night dives a balm to his uncertainties. Dan McKetrick, as always finagling, insisted Frank Moran sign a contract with him as manager, expecting Moran to knock out Jack Johnson, flabby from his faked training. He figured Moran to win, and so *he* would own the next champion of the world. But Moran refused to sign, and Dan, claiming expenses already paid out for Moran, got his French lawyer to tie up the entire money collected at the box office the moment the fight was over. Of course this included Jack's share as well. Dan McKetrick wasted no lachrymose tenderness on fighters. He was sure Moran was his future, not the black man.

Jack, driving a good fast car late at night, would pass marching columns of French troops out for summer training. There was trouble in the Balkans, but there always was. Jack was more interested in working out the unrealized dreams of his adolescence.

On the night of June 27, 1914, the championship fight took place (next morning in the Bosnian town of Sarajevo the assassination of the Austrian Archduke Ferdinand and his wife was to lead to a bigger, more prolonged fight). At ringside for the Johnson-Moran fight were many Americans in Paris, fleshed out with such celebrated Parisians as Mistinguett and Maurice Chevalier, the tantalizing, willful Dolly sisters, Gaby Deslys, who was to bring back to Paris a Negro jazz band after the war, the Princess de Polignac, and other names, famous, notorious, androgynous, that the press liked to feature in reporting any event.

Jack's left arm was no use in the fight; he was out of training, out of shape. But with his speed and skill he managed to stay out of any real danger. When Moran got one punch home, Jack smiled, stepped back, bowed. "Congratulations, Frank."

Jack then smashed Moran's nose flat and proceeded to win the fight. His only worry throughout the bout had been that of getting his money. He had heard rumors of lawyers and legal papers that would act to attach the gate. He was right. The police seized all the assets as the fight ended and carried them off to the vaults of the Bank of France.

Johnson shook his head at the bad news. "Good-bye, money. You're goin' to be a long time gone." Nevertheless he gave a victory banquet for himself and his group: lobsters, chicken, Toscana cigars, whisky, and native champagne (French). Jack signed for the meal, having no cash to pay for it.

McKetrick, however, had outfoxed himself and was caught in a thickly woven web of his own making by having his lawyer seize the fight money. As war neared and the nations of Europe drove forward toward mass insanity, the lawyer was called into the reserves and marched to die with a million other Frenchmen. He left no orders or legal papers permitting his client to take over the money held in the Bank of France, an institution not overfriendly to Americans. The bank officials merely shrugged. They had no proper authority to turn the money over to anyone. If the Paris lawyer got furlough and came to them *en passant*, then we will see what we shall see. The lawyer did not have long to await his destiny; he was slaughtered in one of the first battles, spared the agony of day-to-day survival.

The money, *en fin de compte*, is still in the Bank of France. No one, the promoter, the fighters, or their heirs, if any, has seen a *sou* of it. In 1927 an American visitor to France was the charming rascal, Mayor James J. Walker of New York City, a dishonest rogue fleeing both an angry wife and an investigation of tin boxes containing graft and boodle from his terms in office. He acted as a lawyer for McKetrick, appealing to the sportsmanship of the Bank of France to release the money to McKetrick. The bank was amused but shook its collective head and hoped *M le maire* was enjoying Paris—which he was.

Jack Johnson's lost share in the fight came to $14,400. He was deeply in debt, owed many people, being a fancy liver even on credit.

By July the Great War was only a month away. Jack, needing money and an escape hatch from his creditors, went on to St. Petersburg with wife and nephew Gus. There he appeared in vaudeville shows and outdoor fairs. One night he got into a vodka drinking bout with a hairy priest with a long dirty beard and gleaming feline eyes. Some sports historians—taking Jack's word for it—insist the monk was the notorious Rasputin. Jack lost the drinking bout to the pious fellow—whoever he was—and got back to his hotel near morning as drunk as he ever had been. Even for a drinker of tenacity he was badly crocked.

He was rousted out a few hours later by the Russian Imperial Police and told to dress and come along. Jack, though suffering the king of all hangovers, managed to make the trip, and was told at the police station he and his party were to get out of Russia at once. As Rasputin was a favorite of the too simple-minded czarina, this turn of events lent some credence to the story of the Rasputin drinking contest.

As Jack told it later: "They invoked the five-and-ten law on me. That means you have *five* minutes to pack and *ten* minutes to git out of town." Royal bum's rush or not, it was a rough journey out of Russia across

Germany; troop trains were everywhere, soldiers, cannon, supplies were clogging all rail lines as Europe moved with mad absorption toward the guns of August. Jack and party got to Paris and he went to find his car. With wife and nephew packed in he raced off for Boulogne. The car was wrecked going off a fifty-foot embankment; however they were only bruised and went on. They ran into 4,000 cavalry horses blocking the pier at Boulogne. Jack was to remember the British troops coming ashore, the kilted Scots and the bands playing, "It's a Long Long Way to Tipperary." However he had no atavistic desire to fight in a white man's war, then or later.

In London the war was taking over; there was not much interest in Jack's music-hall act. But he managed to attract attention by just walking the streets—wearing a soft crushed canary-yellow hat, a tobacco-brown silk suit, red silk kerchief in breast pocket, 'gator leather shoes, and swinging a silver-headed cane like a swordsman. His Benz car was upholstered in leopard hide and he drove as usual as if escaping the deluge. All of this high living was mostly on credit.

Jack was down on his luck, and when promoter Jack Curley called on him to arrange a world championship fight between Jack and Jess Willard, the best of the "white hopes," Jack, his eyes still pinpointed with the hard light of ego, lit his cigarette in its lengthy tortoise-shell holder, puffed slowly, and asked in a French accent, "Who is thees Weelard?"

Curley wasn't put off by this kind of talk. After some back and forth conversation Jack agreed. "All right. I will take thees Weelard for you . . . just let me know in *which* round."

Curley then added—or so Jack claimed later—that the Mann Act conviction against Jack would be disposed of. The fix would be taken care of, but Jack *must* throw the fight to Willard as part of the deal. Jack, in his not too trustworthy memoirs, wrote, "We reached an agreement, as far as I was concerned, which would give Willard the championship and permit me to return home."

At last after much hassling the fight was set for Havana. Jack was thirty-seven. He was out of condition, living the easy life, eating and drinking as if famine were just around the corner. Only some personal moral fiber seemed firmly in place.

In April of 1915, 16,000 fight fans were on hand under a deadly Cuban sun. While no sadomasochist, Jack was in for a hard fight, and poorly prepared for it. Willard was six feet six, 250 pounds of hard muscle in fine shape. He came into the ring wearing a ten-gallon Stetson hat of a West that never existed. Jack was paunchy and flabby and looked it. But he was perky. He said to Willard, "I devoutly hope I just don't happen to hurt you, Jeff."

The fight began in the boiling heat. Jack had a hard time of it; the heat and his poor condition, it was soon clear, were doing him in. By the twenty-fourth round he told his seconds, "It don't . . . look . . . too good . . . right now." His wife was led from the ring to spare her the slaughter. Willard finally nailed Jack with a solid blow to the chin, and Jack was done for.

It was no fixed fight as so many claimed and still claim. Willard in basic English said, "If Johnson throwed that fight . . . I sure wish he had throwed it sooner . . . It was hotter in hell there."

As for a fix on the Mann Act charge against Jack, if it had been promised him, it never took place. Jack wandered for years before giving himself up in 1920 and serving his year and a day in the federal penitentiary at Leavenworth, Kansas. In 1924 his wife divorced him. Next year he married a beautiful blonde, Irene Pineau, who met him at a racetrack and got a divorce to marry Jack. At forty-six he fought a ten-round fight in Canada and got the decision. He continued to give boxing exhibitions and sparring matches until he was sixty-eight. Jack lectured at Hubert's Flea Museum on 42nd Street in New York . . . He still liked fast cars.

In June of 1945 he was at the wheel of a Lincoln Zephyr. At 3:30 in the morning, outside of Frankinton, North Carolina, trying to avoid an oncoming truck, he rammed the Lincoln into a pole. He was dead in a Raleigh hospital at 6:10 A.M.

CHAPTER 35

The Perils of Pearl in Paris

Every girl is sitting on her fortune if she only knew it.
NELL KIMBALL

THE WORLD of the Americans in Paris in the Twenties—full of fallible human nature—took in many strange figures. One of the most interesting and tragic was the first great film serial queen, Pearl White. Her *Perils of Pauline,* made in 1914, had been among the founding forms of what was to become world-wide motion picture entertainment, if not art. She had been—on the screen—thrown from trains, dropped into wells, shot at, blown up, left each nerve-racking week (before my own childish bugged-out eyes) hanging on a cliff, dangling over a pit of alligators, or tossed alive into a flaming building. Her face at all times was a white, non-comprehending, melancholy plumpness.

By the end of World War I the film industry, if not mature—it would never become that—was at least expanding its ideas of drama so that it might have some subtle relationship to human behavior. It was also putting younger actors into its serials.

Pearl was deep in her forties, at loose ends when she came to Paris, already drinking hard. It was difficult to separate her life into those parts that were fairly true and those sections of her existence invented by lurid journalists. But she was in Paris now, moon-faced, a gourmand if not a gourmet, and between too much food and drink she was losing her figure. There were also sordid love affairs of which the sensational press reported Egyptian pashas and the smell of opium pipes. The war was over. Her part of it had been the serial *Pearl of the Army* (the titles of her film serials were always simple, almost to the point of kindergarten texts: *See Pearl. Pearl is in danger. Pearl is brave*). What she had hoped to find in Paris in the Twenties she herself could not have expressed in her decline.

In 1924 the director of *Pearl of the Army,* Edward José, made his last film with her in Paris. With a French crew and mostly a French cast— Robert Lee was her leading man—he made a film called *Terror,* released in America as *The Perils of Paris.* There were some backgrounds of Paris streets, but in the main the Paris of the title was filmed in a not too richly endowed French film studio of plaster and paper, dusty walls and dark passages.

Pearl White, in the hallucinatory state of alcohol, made no more films after 1924. She became a wreck slowly, retaining the baby stare of her smoky, luminous eyes; living on into the Paris Thirties, in decline, forgotten by most. There existed a photograph of her in 1937, a year before she died, a frowsy, overplump woman, eyes unfocused, sadly matronly, middle-aged, wearing her frayed leopard coat of better days. Few remember her last days. She lived beyond the fringe of the two American colonies; neither of the writer-painter clusters nor of the café society, smart set groups. Pearl's haunts were the dingy world of once good hotels and run-down apartments, with a scattering of North Africans and Parisian Arabs, a milieu of opium, of shoddy affairs and *amours* with second-rate rogues and international types looking for unattached women.

Pearl White lacked a proper historian for her role as a pioneer of motion pictures. In 1938 she died in Paris. One florid text records the event with a line worthy of her film titles: "Pearl White was dead, like the white petals that lay on the floor beside her body."

CHAPTER 36

"Little American Girl"—1916

Screw art, it puts me in too many binds—
it's an asshole trade, being an artist.

ERIK SATIE

F OR HIS SHOW, *Parade*, in 1916 Jean Cocteau created as one of his
characters the "little American girl," and to orchestrate her he gave
the composer, Satie, some notes, part of which read: "The Titanic—
Nearer My God to Thee—The New York Herald—dynamos—airplanes
. . . the sheriff's daughter—Walt Whitman—the silence of stampedes—
cowboys with leather and goatskin chaps—the telegraph operator from
Los Angeles who married the detective in the end . . . the Sioux—bars—
saloons—ice-cream parlors—roadside taverns—Nick Carter . . ."

Cocteau was a great fan of Hollywood movies, it was clear.

Satie wrote back: "I've received the manuscript. Very astonishing!"

Cocteau got Picasso to do the sets and costumes. It was to be about an
America which none of the three had ever seen. Picasso took over, and
Satie liked that. "*Parade* is changing for the better, behind Cocteau.
Picasso has ideas that please me more than those of our Jean!"

"The Little American Girl" became in the show a superhuman cubistic
design. It was planned for the curtain to come down on the ballet with a
sign reading:

The drama
which
didn't take place
for those people
who stayed outside
was
by
Jean Cocteau Erik Satie Pablo Picasso

The "Little American Girl" gives us a good impression of what these Europeans imagined America and Americans to be. She wore a sailor jacket, white skirt, white knee-stockings. The music was ragtime—*Ragtime du Paquebot*—and she did a sort of series of impressions of Charlie Chaplin and Pearl White, the movie serial queen, swimming, driving a car, aiming a pistol. The rest of the material—the three Managers, the Acrobats, the Chinese Prestidigitator—do their stuff, and at the end the "Little American Girl" breaks into tears.

Along the way there are good solid whacks at America: the American Manager wears cowboy boots, chaps, an Uncle Sam hat, a body made of

skyscrapers; the violin music is badgered by the *click click* of the American Tool, an Underwood typewriter.

The show had competition; outside in the real world the Russian Revolution was beginning, the Germans began to bomb Paris from ninety miles away. At Verdun a million men were dying. And in America, the true America, Woodrow Wilson was being sucked into the war.

The critics felt *Parade*'s choreography was inept, and the music critic of *Carnet de la Semaine* had dreadful things to say of the score. Satie sent him a fan note on a postal card using his favorite term of insult:

> SIR AND DEAR FRIEND:
> You are nothing but an asshole, and an unmusical asshole at that.
>
> ERIK SATIE

The composer's range of insults seemed limited, but like Gertrude Stein, he didn't mind repeating himself. The critic sued and Satie got a sentence of eight days in jail. Cocteau slapped the court prosecutor, and the police dragged him off and roughed him up—an art the Paris *flics* are expert at.

It all made news in a Paris needing something to numb the agony of war. And soon a great many Americans would be in Paris, in uniform, but *Parade* would not be on view with its "Little American Girl."

CHAPTER 37

Elsie Janis—"The Big Show"

A NOW FORGOTTEN entertainer, singer, song writer, and poetess, Elsie Janis, in 1917-1918 during World War I, wrote what may be the worst poetry of any war. One verse of her war poem will set her serious mood.

> Where are you, God,
> In whose hands this great world
> Is like a tiny ball,
> That can be turned and twirled?
> I can't believe that you have seen
> The things that they have done.
> With poison gas and crucifixions
> Battles have been won,
> And yet upon this earth of yours
> There still exists the Hun.
> Where are you, God?

Traveling with her mother on her way to the front to entertain American troops, she wrote:

Paris was full of Americans. We had a lovely apartment at the Crillon, where we kept open house every afternoon, and decided it was a good War. . . .

Paris had not been raided for quite some time. People had almost forgotten to show the new arrivals the spot in the Place de la Concorde where an aviator fell in the last raid. It was old stuff.

Pense tu! They were only waiting for us. In the old Zeppelin days in England we never had the luck to see one. They used to come over and we would read about them next day and hope for better luck next time.

We went to dinner with some Anglo-French friends at their house. We were about twelve, a very gay party, mixing our French and English and American into a cocktail of good-fellowship.

I think it was in the midst of the *salade* that the butler came and stood between the hostess and the gentleman on her left, and addressing them both, said, "The Gothas have arrived, my lady . . . Will you have port, sir?"

The word Gotha at that time meant nothing in my life, but suddenly to my wide-open ears came the most diabolical wail, sounding like a Hippodrome Chorus of lost souls. Our hostess smiled sweetly and said, *"Ah oui! voilà la sirène!"* and that was all . . .

Remarks about other raids and how many were killed floated on cigarette smoke, and were swallowed with a bit of peach Melba. Suddenly Mother came to. She realized that Mousme, our ten-year-old "Peke," Josephine and a very dear girl friend were at the hotel . . . Mother thought she must telephone, but she was wrong, because telephoning is not being done in the best families during an air raid; but we were assured that the guests in hotels were requested gently but firmly to descend to the *cave*—so that was that! By this time, I had

thoroughly bayonetted my peach in its most vital spots, and I could resist no longer, so assuming my most blasé tone of voice, I said: "Do you suppose they are over us now?"

"*Mais non!*" they all cried. "It's always at least twenty minutes before they arrive after the first *'alerte.'* One must wait for the *tir du barrage.*"

"Ah! Now I understand the calmness of everyone. I thought—Boom! boom! boom! went the guns in the suburbs of Paris."

"*Voilà!*" cried one tiny French miss, "they are coming!"

Boom! boom! boom! This time much nearer . . .

Coffee was served.

Boom! This time under my chair, it seemed. I found myself wanting to be near Mother, so we might share the same bomb as we have always shared our joys and sorrows.

Someone went to the window and opened it. The noise was deafening. "They are here," said the window-opener. "Listen, you can hear the planes."

I swallowed my salted coffee and ran to the window. Sure enough—*Brrr, brrr, brrr,* sang the engines. I forgot everything in my anxiety to see.

"Pit pat, pit pat," something was falling like rain.

"Shrapnel," said the hostess.

Boom! brrr—gush!

"*Une bombe,*" said a lady with no back in her dress.

Une bombe! and perhaps twenty souls hurled into eternity without a warning. I came back to earth with a thud. Mother's hand was in mine and the guests had gone into the drawing-room, already bored by the monotony of the guns. I squeezed Mother's hand and said, "Well, dear, if our numbers are up, we will exit together."

We went back into the drawing-room, where to the tune of the *Livery Stable Blues* we danced through the rest of the raid, which lasted an hour and a quarter.

The Huns came the next two nights. In the hotels they put all the lights out when the "*alerte*" is given. So the good old-fashioned candle has come into its own again. The second night we were at the theater—in the midst of a scene a man walked on the stage and said, "*Messieurs et Mesdames, les Gothas sont arrivés—la represèntation continuera*"—and walked off.

There was a buzz all over the theater. I translated it to our American friends for whom it was too fast.

All our party thought the raid would be more amusing than the show, so we went out into the inky darkness, tried to lure a taxi into taking us to the Crillon. He wanted forty francs, which we thought a little high even for an air raid, so we wandered home, arm in arm—looking for things in the sky, trying to make ourselves believe that a shooting star was a falling Boche airplane, and when we reached the hotel the "*berloque*" (All clear!) was given. It was a *fausse alerte.* So we missed both shows.

After this show of blasé bravery, Miss Janis should be left in her more serious mood, with a verse:

> Forgive me, God,
>   If I have doubted you,
> For in my heart
>   I know what you will do,
> Quite soon now you will
>   Send us our release,
> Quite soon in your own way
>   You'll tell us—Cease!—
> And with one mighty stroke,
>   You will send Peace,
> For You are there!

We doubt if this was read by General Pershing. In March, 1918, he placed the American forces at the disposal of the Allied High Command after the German breakthrough. He said, "We are here to be killed."

CHAPTER 38

Hem

Every damn thing is your own fault if
you are any good.

ERNEST HEMINGWAY

O F THE MAKING of books about Ernest Hemingway there will be no
end in our time; literary instincts, good and bad, are at work on
him. He has become an industry. E. E. Cummings had said, "World War I
was the experience of my generation." It was certainly the major lifetime
experience of Ernest Hemingway. He never outgrew it, "and never grew
up," some have added. The sublime, the insoluble parts of him will last
some time.

He was in Paris from 1921 to 1927, and the legends that have grown on
his years there, like tundra moss on Arctic stones, are hard to scrape off,
to reveal the solid rock of what he was and how he got that way.

He was a young man who had come to Europe in 1918—a very young
man—to drive an ambulance on the Italian front. Later he was to claim a
night of love with Mata Hari, who, however, was executed in 1917—a
somewhat incomprehensible copulation by seance. At twenty-two, in December of 1921, he arrived in Paris, a newspaperman with a wife and
letters of introduction to Gertrude Stein and James Joyce from his first
master, Sherwood Anderson. "Mr. Hemingway is an American writer
instinctively in touch with everything worth going on here."

He was a remarkably handsome man with an intoxicating essence of
purpose, and he would recite without much begging, how the 98 or 128

bits of shrapnel had gotten into his legs on the Italian front (the count varied with the number of drinks). He was tense with some ephemeral dream; he was driving, and he worked hard under Gertrude Stein to make himself an original writer. He hung out at Sylvia Beach's bookstore; he ordered a few copies of *Ulysses* when published, and did some drinking with its author. But La Stein was his true teacher, not the little, near-blind Irishman. There is no doubt the young man from the Middle West was touched with genius. One has only to reread the early short stories to find an amazing economy of language, a new power behind simple words, a personal closeness to the physical aspects of nature, as he saw them, to realize this was a gifted youth, already aware of an incipient rebellion within him against a world of clichés.

The good fairies at his birth had however been attended by a few bad ones. He was a mean and cruel man, for all his vitality, audacity, and charm. His father had given him a shotgun at seven, and he was to spend a great deal of his life slaughtering thousands of birds, animals, big fish, and, in the end, the biggest game of all—himself. Mixed with the most subtle sense of the proper word was a fear of natural death, an infinitely complex interior maelstrom. When his father killed himself, Hemingway's mother sent him the gun. He lived a life of self-pity, within a tough husk, much bitterness and a proud futility.

Hemingway was a brilliant student of what Gertrude showed him about prose. About a dozen of his early short stories are masterworks that have a permanent place in world literature. He saw life as fried deer meat, squaw bread, blankets crawling with graybacks, the skills of hunting and courage. The true nature of the careful artist was hidden by a facade of the lusty he-man, hairy and booze-swilling, loving death and blood. To the public he was the bull-fighting *aficionado*, the boxer who could knock you on your ass; not with too much skill but by brute strength. He was very strong.

The mean side of him showed itself against all who were to help him: Sherwood Anderson, whom he nearly destroyed in a cruel parody of his style; in the ungrateful gossip he passed on of Gertrude Stein's private life; Ford Madox Ford, who had both taught him and seen him first published; F. Scott Fitzgerald, who got Scribners to take Hemingway seriously as an important writer. He came to love *la gloire militaire* and to fear and mock the intellectuals.

Of course there were reasons for these protective layers. Hemingway had almost no education and was by the standards of the writers of Paris an illiterate. Sexually he was a problem to himself—in the particular behind the absolute—boasting of his success with women, yet in private there were certain fears. He himself tells us he was impotent in Paris for six months at his second marriage, coming around, as it were, only after some prayers in a church.

He was greatly disliked by his mother; perhaps in consequence his portraits of woman are in the main of dream lays. They are the visions of boys coming into puberty, rather than the true pictures of sexual partners seen by mature men. They become the dream, the too willing slave nurse in *Farewell to Arms,* the sex dolly in the sleeping bag, the contessa in the gondola. All seem to exist out of Tom Sawyer making like Portnoy on a typewriter. And the heroes of his books live humorlessly the privileges and graces of a boy's erotic images.

The handsome young man was accepted and helped by Gertrude, by Ezra Pound, who blue-penciled his manuscripts, by Ford Madox Ford, who printed him in his *Transatlantic Review,* even made him assistant editor. Ford's reward was to be remembered by Hemingway only as the possessor of bad breath. Hemingway paid people back meanly, forgetting Anatole France's remark: "Heroism and devotion are like great works of art—they have no object beyond themselves."

Hemingway was to admit, "Ezra was right half the time . . . Gertrude was always right." Her reward was to be clobbered indecently by her disciple after she was in her grave. If one is to write anything about Hemingway, one must accept his insensitive coarseness to human relationships which would, in time, destroy him and turn him into the comic Papa of *Life* Magazine and the profile in *The New Yorker*—the drunken, maudlin braggart and confessor in public.

At the start Hemingway and Gertrude were, as he wrote, "just like brothers," and she said he was "a delightful fellow." She taught him how to cut his first wife's hair, and she and Alice stood godmothers to the Hemingway's Paris baby. In 1924 he could write her of his writing: "It used to be easy before I met you, I certainly was bad, gosh, I'm awfully bad now but it's a different kind of bad." He was to add, much later, about leaving behind the "lyric facility of boyhood that was as perishable and as deceptive as youth itself." He assumed he was a red meat realist, but was unaware he was extremely defensive and sensitive, a poet in prose. He remained all his life wildly romantic, in the adolescent state he brought to Paris. But his first critics mistook him for a new kind of naturalist, a nut-hard realist. If he was a realist, it was one outfitted by Abercrombie and Fitch, who took pride in the names of exotic drinks and consorted when past his prime with motion picture actors and actresses—*if* they were stars.

He began in Paris writing with emotions having the shock and force of a hemorrhage.

He was never to improve upon the genius of those first stories. His novels do not stand up today except for the brilliant fragments imbedded in them here and there. The sex scenes remain embarrassing. The last books are parodies at times of the early Paris style, but witless.

The break with Gertrude Stein came because it was in Hemingway's nature to turn on all those who helped him. It was a life pattern. His attack on Sherwood Anderson in a too easy burlesque, *The Torrents of Spring*, hurt Gertrude, too, and Hemingway planned it that way, he admitted. "I had attacked someone that was part of her apparatus." There was also a stab directly at Gertrude in such words as, "Right around the corner from where Gertrude Stein lived. Ah, there was a woman I . . . What was at the bottom of it? All that in Paris. Ah, Paris . . ."

1926 was the year Hemingway drifted away from Gertrude. Hurt, she called him "yellow," and wrote he belonged "to the museums." She pointed out he was yellow because he lacked the courage to move out of the safety of his style, his narrow view of life, and his formulas. A Hemingway story at its best was splendid, but hardly ever moved from the protecting cover of his limited way of seeing things, his physical vision of life as action and reaction. She suggested he never dared widen his horizon and write of a fuller spectrum of life, of people who did not hunt or kill, go to war or live in exotic places, ordering exotic drinks by fancy names. He never did come out from the shadow of his narrow duck-blind. And the splendid style wore down and it didn't come on good any-more and the thing wasn't fun anymore, not anymore. The things you did weren't done for the doing, only because they had to be done.

There have been those who felt Gertrude's anger at Hemingway's de-sertion of her was a guilt reaction, for she had done to her brother Leo, consciously or unconsciously, what Hemingway had done to her: cut someone very close out of her life completely.

So much has been made of Hemingway's boxing and horse racing excitement in Paris, his family life over the saw mill, that a warped picture is all we have of what the writer was in those early days, and we shall not here repeat what has been done and done and done in so many books about him.

It must be recorded that Hemingway was happiest in Paris, leaving out all those manly emotions he pumped into himself when gut-shooting a wild animal to fragments or seeing a bull slaughtered or a big hooked, uneatable fish die under the attack of sharks. Paris, he came to reflect, was where he had been the young man, had seen his promise shine and had gone part way toward what his genius might have been. The decisive moments were still ahead, still to be savored. Returning to Paris in 1933, he could admit, "Paris was a fine place to be quite young in and it is a necessary part of a man's education." It wasn't the same, of course, couldn't be, and he knew it. "We all loved it once and we lie if we say we didn't."

As for many Americans, Paris had for him a sexual connection, a sen-sual image of passive raffishness; for Paris "is like a mistress who does not grow old and she has other lovers now." He stood for a moment in repentance, almost in some humble silence, then became Papa again.

Even in Africa Paris was on his mind, and a good part, the best part, of *Green Hills* and some of "The Snows of Kilimanjaro" were about the memories of Paris of a writer who has sold out to fancy living and is dying; the fountains in the Place de l'Observatoire, the Flaubert bronze in the Luxembourg Gardens, the cheap and easy life of the Place de la Contrescarpe. We can almost sense as he looks back, like a medieval Christian, Hemingway already praying for "a good death."

As Hemingway deteriorated as an artist and grew as a public entertainer, the contemporary world would grow hazy at times. He often tried for something that would bring back the days when he was such a magnificent young writer. He was old-fashioned enough to continue to stay at the Ritz when in Paris, and in 1957 a trunk of his that had been there since 1927 was found to contain notebooks of his first impressions of the city. Notes, one gathers, like delicate bister wash drawings. Out of this reminder of his lost youth and some of the notes grew his last book, *A Moveable Feast.* It is no more trustworthy as to facts than Gertrude's *Alice,* but contains the flavor of good wine grown a bit corked; memory padded by nostalgia and to hell with facts and history. The mood is good and the stuff is running fine; no matter what is fiction, what is fact, this is how you are as a dying man and how you see your provocative education as a young writer in Paris where everything was fine, even what later you wouldn't find fine.

There are too many literary anecdotes in the book that have been told

before and are hardly worth repeating, and too many meannesses to old friends—but there are also good warm pictures of cosy cafés and bars you liked going to, of food and drink, of being there and existing, of going to the horse races at Enghein. The favorite café was always the Closerie de Lilas, or the reading done by the fireplace in the bookshop Shakespeare & Company, the "photographs on the wall of famous writers both dead and living . . . even the dead writers looked as though they had really been alive."

A Moveable Feast is not a full picture of Americans in Paris; it leaves out most of the American expatriates whom one didn't care for, the lives of the worthless, lazy Americans, enjoying or suffering in the city. He moved in the book in a cloud made up of himself, his life as a young writer in Paris, and a distaste of those who were even then his friends. The Dôme and the Rotonde crowd were never serious enough for him, and he overdoes his poverty a bit, he was never as hard up as he claimed to be in those days. He knew he had to work hard to make it, and he did. His dedication to his work was good to see, even when it didn't turn out right anymore.

As to Hemingway's intelligence and his wide reading, there are no agreements. Elliot Paul in conversation with this writer insisted, "Hemingway was bright but played dumb—maybe illiterate in most departments except for hunting, fancy sports and the history of screwing. He talked a good line about his vast reading of classics, but if you threw him a question about a writer who wasn't on his Big Boy's list, Turgenev or Stendhal, you'd find him suddenly get started on baseball or bike racers. I don't know . . . And notice how he needs a new wife, nearly for every new book. Tolstoi didn't, and Balzac married late."

This is no place to relate the Paris gossip of his sex life or its effect on him. Paris saw the end of his first marriage by betrayal, saw him come out from the Rue du Cardinal Lemoine and the saw mill on the Rue Notre Dame des Champs, come out as the most talked about, written about American writer of modern times. He moved into a life lavish and discontented; it didn't balance beautifully—like a new gun in his hand should.

He was recognized early. In the small Paris edition of *in our time* (all lower case), Edmund Wilson, the foremost American critic, said, "His little book has more artistic dignity than anything else about the period of the war that has yet been written by an American."

Hemingway's most spectacular entry into Paris was in 1944, when, supposed to be a journalist with the Allied advance on Paris after the

Normandy landing, he organized a romantic band of irregulars to take Paris. They got in the way of serious units fighting their way forward. Hemingway, with much publicity and lots of drinking, attracted world-wide attention. He came into the city with his mob of cameramen, reporters, magazine illustrators, and camp followers and pulled up his motorized detachment in front of Sylvia Beach's bookshop. Hemingway, bearded, marked with head wounds and scar tissue from a London street accident, began to yell, "Sylvia! Sylvia!" She came down to be engulfed by Hemingway in his war journalist's uniform and a cloud of booze, to be swung around and powerfully kissed. He proceeded to the roof top to fire handarms at some snipers. Then he was off in the jeeps, according to him "to liberate the cellar at the Ritz."

It is still impossible today fully to evaluate Hemingway, either the man or the writer. He belongs now to the professors, and the books produced so far about him have been miserable and misleading. The official life by the Princeton professor is dull and out of focus, and the last Mrs. Hemingway worked on it with its author. Generous instincts often become tacky absurdities.

It may well be we have overvalued him as a writer, except for those fine early stories, and his marvelous style, cutting away so much ornamentation from American literary writing. As Faulkner's reputation rises, Hemingway's may decline if one honestly compares the size of the fields of their work. The man Hemingway can perhaps remain forever an enigma of braggadocio and violence, hiding rubbed-raw fears. It was to the public image he devoted most of his life, the making of Papa.

He belonged to a more glorious time, for all its postwar scars, when youth, in spite of all the horrors of war and change, was hopelessly romantic. Perhaps F. Scott Fitzgerald wrote Hemingway's obituary, and all his generation's: "Life hasn't much to offer except youth and in older people the love of youth in others."

CHAPTER 39

Harry's New York Bar

We all had a girl and her name is Nostalgia.

ERNEST HEMINGWAY

N OSTALGIA: *a longing for experiences, things, acquaintanceships, belonging to the past.* So states the dictionary. To the social historian it is a curse. One has to hunt in old clippings to find a true kernel among the chaff surrounding a place like Harry's Bar. Survivors are not to be trusted. So from an item here and there, from some unsentimental report, the place begins to reshape itself as the Mecca, the old clubhouse for so many Americans in Paris.

Harry's New York Bar in Paris is the birthplace of the Bloody Mary and sidecar cocktail. Eight hundred odd cocktails were dreamed up by the barmen at Harry's. Drinkers used to ask for *"sank roo doe noo,"* the phonetic translation of the Harry's Bar address at 5 Rue Daunou. Tourists still do.

Andy McElhone, son of the founder of the fifty-eight-year-old bar in Paris, is boss today. McElhone took over the running of Harry's when his father, the original Harry, died in 1958. He has maintained the bar as his father ran it. It opened its swinging doors to the public on Thanksgiving Day in 1911. A popular American jockey, Tod Sloan, and a New Yorker named Clancey dismantled the latter's bar and shipped it across the Atlantic. Harry McElhone, a Scots bartender, was the man chosen to greet the customers. He took over the bar in 1923.

The mahogany bar once warm to the touch of writers like F. Scott

Fitzgerald, Ernest Hemingway, Ford Madox Ford, William Faulkner, and John Steinbeck still exists. The wood paneling that once decorated the walls of a bar in New York provide a backdrop for the meeting of minds in the back bar at Harry's.

Harry's Bar has seldom missed appearing in the pages of memoirs written by American survivors of the Twenties and Thirties in Paris. "W. W. Windstaff" (pen name of a rich American) in his privately printed memoirs speaks of it as it was in the 1920s. "A damn easy place to be mooched on by shabby sentimental drunks, get picked up by an Irish whore who claimed to be a duchess, and there was always a tout with nicotine-stained fingers who had a sure thing horse running that day if you'd put nine hundred francs on it for the both of you. The drinks were good at Harry's, but not up to the standard of the old Waldorf in New York or the Palace in San Francisco. College boys overcrowded the place."

Its walls were ringed with college pennants from all over the United States. "Those were given to us by visiting students and alumni," McElhone said.

Harry's Bar was the place where Primo Carnera prematurely hung up his gloves in 1929 after losing a bout to young Stribling. Carnera later went on to win the heavyweight championship from Jack Sharkey. The gloves still hang there from a wooden monkey. French playwright Marcel Achard was an official time-keeper when ivy leaguer J. H. Cochrane set Harry's beer-drinking record in 1932 by downing 4.4 pints (two liters) in eleven seconds.

"The younger people aren't happy with the bistros that used to satisfy their fathers. They prefer the atmosphere of bars and pubs." The change is seen in the clientele of Harry's. During the 1920s and 1930s it was unusual to find a Frenchman in Harry's.

Today the fame of cofounder jockey Tod Sloan rests on the fact he popularized the style of riding high up on a race horse's neck with the aid of short stirrups of uneven length. *And* the fact that all American jockeys are still barred from riding races in England since that Derby Day when Sloan pulled the king's horse to lose the race in a deal he had made with a group of gamblers.

"W. W. Windstaff" gives us a good impression of a day at Harry's Bar.

You could get there tacky-eyed about noon in limping reluctance with your tongue hanging out, and the king of all hangovers hammering nails into your head. Chips and Bob, the two barmen, were ready for you. You'd get a sizzling fizzing aid or a glass of bicarb with a raw egg in it and some Worcestershire sauce to settle the coals still smoldering in your gut, and the hair of the dog in the shape of a neat shot glass full of brandy. Or three fingers of Dutch gin, unless you had incipient ulcers.

There would be a few other survivors of the night before, standing around with mesmerized eyeballs, looking at the bottles at the back of the bar, shaking their head in a lazy way or just looking into their drinks as if the whole fucked-up answer to life were printed there. Somebody would be giving advice to a husband or a fag, *plus sage que les sages*. Or a crazy character in baggy dirty tweeds would be talking about his publisher or his broad. If you ate any lunch around two o'clock, you'd be leaning on the bar, or your ass screwed in a chair, and the place would fill up around you. Newspaper bums from the Paris *Herald*, the publisher-editor-owner of the English-language magazine, *Boulevardier*, a fellow named Erskine Gwynne, who was rumored to be a Vanderbilt; Elliot Paul, who was one of the editors of the avant-garde crock of crap *transition* (lower case, of course). Elliot was a fat little butterball of a man—a pussy hunter with a goat's beard, and lots of lies about his life in the Wild West, but with a poignant satanic joy, a proper feeder too, cooking up fine messes when in the mood for American girl art students at Parsons that he'd invite up to sip and sample. Erskine and Eliot usually had been on a party the

night before, and mostly they'd compare the women, the conversation and the games played. I remember the morning I stood against the bar, holding on and waiting for the earth to steady itself, and Erskine and Elliot were at it.

"Sure were swacked, Paul."

"Not at all, just the normal load on."

"You cheated on the game."

"Not at all."

"The most revolting whore in Paris for the prize, right?"

"And to bring her back to the party, to be judged."

Paul laughed, his whole jellylike body shaking, "It was easy."

"Bullshit." Erskine turned to me. "Tell this bastard he cheated."

I didn't have much interest that morning in the games Americans played in Paris. "How did he cheat?"

"The sonofabitch. You see all the men had to go out, in half an hour come back with the most revolting whore in Paris, one still on her feet and walking the *pavés*. You follow?"

"I follow."

"I bring back this old biddy who looked like a hag out of Bruegel, that painter chap, you know. All wrinkles, three teeth, all gums, a face Lautrec; why he'd have given his whiskers just to sketch her, broken nose, *only* three teeth, all pure Camembert . . . and Paul, the sonofabitch, his whore was declared the winner."

I said, "Don't tell me."

"She was no leper or anything," said Paul. "Fine relic, I'll admit. And as E.Q.'s courtesan was about to be crowned, I lifted the skirt of my beauty and I had the winning ticket."

"The sonofabitch, you know why? His whore had one withered leg, the other was cork with metal joints, must have stolen it off a soldier of the war."

Paul smiled. "*La belle dame sans merci.*"

"Very unfair, I mean when you bring a whore in parts."

If it was horse race day, Harry's Bar would empty out, but around five, six, it would fill up, winners and losers, noses sunburned, and just plain drinkers. Some tourists would mosey in to look over the crowd. Often it would be second-class stuff; Kiki de Montparnasse, the gash of anybody, telling when she was a model how some artist would find her seated at the bar and kick out the stool from under her to see her fall on her marvelous ass. Or the Yid publisher from New York, who was trying to be one of the boys and was politely referred to as Mr. Shit. Sometimes Hem, playing the big manly stud, would come by; creeps from colleges with copies of Joyce in the blue paper covers from Sylvia's place, hoping Joyce would drop in and sign their copies. I guess it was at Harry's the story started of Jimmy Joyce standing at the bar and some college boy asking him, "Will you have a small whisky on me, Mr. Joyce?" The answer, "There is no such thing as a *small* whisky for an Irishman." I don't know if it happened like that or happened at all.

Around midnight Roy Barton, Bud Sheppard would make music, piano and guitar.

Harry's wasn't a good place for the cunthunters. For that there was the lobby of the Ritz for flappers and pubescent girls, or some of the cafés where the society tarts showed their legs, sitting back in a chair, toying with a rotten drink with lots of color in it. And Cocteau hunting boys, Augustus John *anything*.

The real racing crowd went to the Chatham on the Rue Daunou, but lots of bets on the Grand Prix de Paris touted by "Peter Pickem" in the *Chi Trib* were made at Harry's, and some money changed hands. There would be a rolling of dice to see who paid for the drinks. Some drinkers stayed right through the dinner hour, just held up a finger and pointed to their empty glass. Some just stood or sat like statues of poured cement, and the same color, too. But around nine, ten, women—hipless, titless, emaciated from reading *Vogue*—and their dates would come in, and there would be lots of laughing and making signals, canting altercations and giving each other the office, arms around shoulders. Christ! the copious felicity, the involved malignity, and everybody drinking, laughing, scratching.

The serious drinkers didn't want to go any place, and the studs were comparing notes where the best parties were—alpha people, top drawer—and who would be there, and what girl you could shaft, and what girl might, and what drip to avoid. Sherwood Anderson would tell some big story of how to get a broad trapped and how to talk to her, and how to avoid tears. Sometimes a bull dyke on her way to Natalie's would bring in a flower dyke who wanted to meet Hendrik Van Loon, or a writer on the *Herald*. But mainly the lezs—they liked to call themselves *amazons*—had their own little bars where they picked up clitoris-bumpers and sent each other tight little bunches of violets.

It was never as wild or exciting as people said it was. But Harry's Bar was a place you could be wry and pungent, meet people you knew and people you wanted not to know. It had the smell and flavor of where you had come from. Nobody had any idea of going home if they could avoid it while little checks kept coming from home, or publishers, or a female friend. Checks from America were fine to have because the rate of exchange was very much in your favor, and you didn't have to take some old dame down to Monte or to Deauville as her joy-boy for coffee and cakes, a little champagne, a wrist watch, or a wop roadster.

The truth was Harry's was an excuse lots of times for the writers not to write much when the Underwood was busted, and for the painters not to paint when the light was always bad. The poets said they were meditating and incubating, and "you *can't* hurry a poem."

If you were in the chips and went to dances at the American Embassy, you bought your clothes at Old England on the Boulevard des Capucines, if not you rummaged in the steamer trunk of someone still trusting and exciting who had come over on the *France*. It was never dull. You took a girl to the *Sarah Bernhardt* to see Pierre Fresnay, the two Guitrys in *Mariette*, or the jazz band at the Jockey. Love began with an evening of hors d'oeuvres, ended in casual conviviality.

While waiting for funds if I had been gambling and losing, a date was taken to Clara Bow at the Paramount in *Wings*, and the Grand Guignol on the Rue Chaptel. And avoiding people you owed money to; the damn landlord, the hotel, all that got snotty shoving their *addition* into your face. *Du sublime au ridicule il n'y a qu'un pas.*

One month after some very crazy play at cards and time with a greedy Hungarian whore, I was down to eating at parties given by Otto Kahn, or drinking at the showing off of a new statue in Joe Davidson's studio. Or even to being present at one of those dismal affairs Elsa Maxwell does for some rich old broad trying to make it in Paris society. With too much fastidiousness and sensibility you could starve in Paris. But I never got down to work as some Americans did at steering customers to Zelli's or the Scheherazade for a bit of a payoff. Once I lived off the sale of a Van Dongen drawing of a long-legged flapper for two weeks, eating the American cooking at Elza Lee's; the manager bought the drawing. Margaret Brown's was the other place that served American food; but you couldn't put it on the slate there, they never took a drawing or a small picture in pay. I had some credit in the Pigalle bars. I usually preferred Luigi's for lunch, but they didn't put your account on the slate either, cold cash only.

Another popular hangout for Americans was Jimmy's Falstaff Bar. Jimmy had been a boxer, came from Liverpool, had worked in a few bars, and in the Twenties was at the Dingo. He was a character, a confidante of the Anglo-American barflies. Hemingway liked Jimmy's service, and Jimmy liked best, as he put it, the hangers-on, the disillusioned (mainly as a result of love complications) and habitual drunks.

Hemingway got a lot of atmosphere and people from Jimmy's place for *The Sun Also Rises*. Among them Pat Guthrie and Lady Duff Twysden, two lovers and soaks who became the Lady Brett and Mike of the novel, almost without change. Robert Cohn, the college boxer who fell for Lady Brett (that brought out Hemingway's anti-Semitism, which people who knew him claimed he carried along most of his life), was actually Harold Loeb, publisher of a small literary magazine that didn't flourish.

Hemingway, a feline observer of others' blemishes, wasn't too popular when his book came out. The citizens of Montparnasse felt he had picked for his main characters the drunks, sex maniacs, and disillusioned bums of the district, and overlooked the serious writers and the people who didn't hang out in bars, get maudlin on Pernod, sit over aperitifs at the Dôme or Coupole all day. Hemingway had called his news story for the

Toronto Star, "American Bohemians in Paris a Weird Lot," and said their hangout, a popular café the Rotonde, "gives you the same feeling that hits you as you step into the bird house at the zoo."

The two stars of Jimmy's Bar, Hemingway and F. Scott Fitzgerald, fought and made up in some deep laid animosity. Hemingway treated Fitzgerald with a sort of snide rancor most of the time. Fitzgerald, an alcoholic, with his wife going insane before his eyes in their Paris apartment, was never too sure of himself. "I was always the poorest boy at a rich man's school." But he was very keen. As he watched Hemingway go from wife to wife, he observed, "Hemingway needs a new woman for each big book." One can almost follow Hemingway's trail through literature by the women he married and dropped; hardly a wife survived more than one major writing project.

Hemingway liked the casual indolence of bars and cafés. And boxing, of which so much has been made in the retelling. The fault of the gossip about his boxing may have been his own, for he had been heard saying, glass in hand, "My writing is nothing, my boxing is everything." At least three people heard him say this at various times.

The flavor of the bar's regulars and guests, if nothing else, is given by Jimmy in a book with his name on it, *This Must Be the Place,* listing Americans and their companions who came into the bar. He may not have been aware that the phrase is taken from a rowdy burlesque routine and refers to a whorehouse. Jimmy remembered bar customers like:

Captain Smith, who went from London to Italy in a canoe; the woman, ashamed because she had a decided moustache on her lip, who became a beauty when she had it removed; Bud Fisher, the creator of Mutt and Jeff; Sam Dashiel, an American journalist, and Hilda, his very English, ex-Tiller-girl wife; Captain Bunny Christiansen, who, though his legs were paralyzed, was a great success with the ladies; Bea Mathieu, who represents the fashion column of *The New Yorker* in Paris; Rea Brown and Flo McCardle, friends of Bea's, and also in the fashion game; Countess de Vitali, a great friend of Pat and Duff; Stephanus Eloff, the grandson of General Kruger of Boer War fame; the American Indian who entertained the Dingo by dancing on nails and swallowing fire or sticking pins into his skin; Jack Dempsey, who visited us once but said nothing; May Manning, the English model; Edward Titus, the husband of Helena Rubinstein, who published *This Quarter;* Lena Hutchins, with her strange Swiss accent and a gray streak in her hair; Victor Pattou, "the Greek God," famous for his looks and magnetic powers; George Gibbs, who was the spitting image of Douglas Fairbanks and liked to be taken for him; John Paul Jones, who died of tuberculosis contracted during the war; Bubbles Williams, whose international romances once occupied considerable space in the American newspapers; Mrs. Van Ness and daughter, Betty, who was brought up in the Dingo; Louise Coons, a writer from Kentucky; Mary Seigert, known as Mary Queen of Scots, and very much liked; and Morton Hoyt; and Martin Somers; and Marjorie; and Hildegarde Martin; and Miss Marney; and Charles Grey; and Glen Goetz . . .

Names now mostly forgotten, they drift in and out of memoirs like passenger lists, old letters, forlorn like the ghost in Gogol's famous story, "The Overcoat," haunting life as if it were a pawnshop. They came and sat in the cafés of Saint-Germain-des-Prés; Lipps, The Flora, the Deux Magots; they hummed "Ramona," "Three O'Clock in the Morning," and claimed all their taxi drivers were czarist colonels unless they were generals. They passed from view, this "lost generation," prodigal, extravagant, insensible and alien, shy, sad, or in obstreperous vulgarity, all seeking layers of subtlety in Paris.

It was a time of names, few of lasting value—in Paris, in the south of France, the Americans couldn't write to each other without spilling each other's names. Wrote F. Scott Fitzgerald mockingly in a letter, sometime in 1926: "There was no one at Antibes this summer except me, Zelda, the Valentinos, the Murphys, Mistinguett, Rex Ingram, Dos Passos, Alice Terry, the MacLeishes, Charlie Brackett, Maude Kahn, Esther Murphy, Marguerite Namara, E. Phillips Oppenheim, Mannes, the violinist, Floyd Dell, Max and Crystal Eastman, ex-premier Orlando, Etienne de Beaumont—just a real place to rough it, an escape from all the world."

It was at times a quest for a society, doomed to frustration by its absurdity, and by the coming world depression.

Among the older generation let us not overlook the name of Eddy Morris Campbell, turn-of-the-century U.S. financier, who collected rare wines—a mixed selection of red Bordeaux, including three bottles of 1870 Château Lafitte, three of 1887 Château Latour, and 1904 Château Rausan-Gassies.

And some of the names were not kind to other names:

> I would rather live in Oregon
> and pack salmon
> Than live in Nice and write
> like Robert McAlmon.

Who was Robert McAlmon? Years later, after he was dead, *The New York Times* summed up his memory:

Born in Kansas and raised in South Dakota, McAlmon blew into Paris like a wind from the prairies. That was in 1921, the year when scores of young Americans came storming into the Montparnasse cafés, all bent on having a hell of a good time before they utterly transformed, or so they hoped, the world of art and letters . . . He wore a broad-brimmed hat that wasn't like a cowboy's, but that still made him look as if he had galloped into town on a Saturday afternoon. He sang Western songs and had enough of a cowboy's energy to carry him through nights of drinking and dancing. He founded *Contact Editions*. Though a very small house, by 1929 it had published the work of several famous or soon-to-be-famous authors—Hemingway (his first two booklets), Pound, W. C. Williams, Mary Butts, H.D., Robert M. Coates and Gertrude Stein—as well as seven books of poetry and fiction by Robert McAlmon.

CHAPTER 40

Isadora Duncan— Dancer by the Seine

I dined yesterday at our Embassy and sat beside the wife of the United States minister to Brussels, an American woman . . . These men and women are destined to be the future Conquerors of the World. They will be the Barbarians of Civilization, who will devour the world.

The Goncourt Journals APRIL 23, 1867

I SADORA DUNCAN was a devourer of life and thought of herself as a conqueror of the new world, but of the world of the dance. She certainly was not a barbarian, unless one took the position of so many Parisians that *anything* American was barbarian and looked best in frontier fur hat, feathers, or cowboy outfit. This was how they remembered Benjamin Franklin, George Catlin's Indian Gallery, and Buffalo Bill's Wild West Show—in their feathers, war paint and buckskin.

When Isadora Duncan did get to Paris, those who noticed her wrote of her in romantic prose, in exotic terms that pictured a creature halfway in elf land and wholly unreal. "Isadora, a virgin, meets Rodin, who pants around her like a fawn, feverish and possessed, pressing every square inch of her flesh. Then later the eternal regret of this woman at not having given the colossus that flesh to crush, her flesh which has since known the ardent embraces of so many." So, in a rather silly, overheated journal, wrote a Paris art dealer, who sold millions of dollars' worth of unremarkable paintings to American millionaires. This was his picture of Isadora Duncan, the pioneer of the modern dance, and for whom Paris contained the greatest tragedy in a life made of so many tragedies.

Called reckless, revolutionary, and resolute, Isadora was born in San Francisco in 1878, and as she put it, her ideas "came from the rhythm of the waves. . . . I was born under the star of Aphrodite, who was also born on the sea." Her Scots father left her Irish-Catholic mother for another love, and the mother, a disciple of Robert Ingersoll, became a vocal atheist. The Duncan family was full of apocalyptic visions and messianic urges; made up of two girls, two boys. They lived on the earnings from the mother's piano lessons and the rather bad poetry they recited when hungry. San Francisco has a story that they raided the orchards of a family named Stein. The Stein daughter was called Gertrude, and they would all meet later in Paris.

Isadora, wild and gay, began dancing and teaching dancing when she was a child. The local ballet teacher refused to instruct Isadora after the third lesson because the child refused to stand on her toes, a stance Isadora insisted was "ugly and against nature." She had a lifetime hate for the formal ballet, preferring the intoxicating ecstasies of inspiration.

Aged seven, she and Mama were in Chicago trying to get someone, anyone, to see Isadora dance Mendelssohn's *Spring Song.* There was a short engagement. Also at twelve there was a passionate platonic love affair with a married Polish painter, which she remembered as "the insane passion with which I had inspired Miroski . . . I decided . . . that I would live to fight against marriage and for the emancipation of women and the right of every woman to have a child or children as it pleased her." Already she agreed with Heraclitus, "Character is fate."

She was bold. To Augustin Daly, the theatrical producer, she made a speech: "I have discovered the dance. I have discovered the art which has been lost for two thousand years . . . For the children of America I will create a new dance that will truly express America."

To stop her flow of words he gave her a small part in a New York pantomime, after which she was a fairy to Ada Rehan's Titania in *A Midsummer Night's Dream* (dancing to the Mendelssohn). The family survived; brother Augustin touring with a road company, Raymond trying newspaper work, and sister Elizabeth helping run Isadora's dance classes. Isadora found revolting *all* bourgeois aspirations and the stale erudition of the ballet.

When unable to pay their bills at the Windsor Hotel, Isadora exclaimed, "The only thing that can save us is for the hotel to burn down." No one investigated the fire the *next* day that burned the hotel to a hollow shell.

The Duncans beat a hasty retreat from unpaid bills, going to England on a cattle boat. In England, guileful and artistic, they lived often on thin soup and penny buns. Isadora joined Frank Benson's Shakespeare Company, again as the first fairy in *A Midsummer Night's Dream*. The Duncans decided Paris was the true Mecca of the modern dance. If not, Isadora would make it so.

Isadora had matured; she was twenty-two, not a beauty. She had a pert nose, was a bit fat in the cheeks, signs of a double chin. But she had fine eyes and a generous body. By today's standards for women as seen in *Vogue* she was too much woman, but in a more Rubensesque day she delighted men. Her true moments of beauty were on stage when she began to dance. Then she became sea born, wave motivated.

The Duncans' Paris was a Paris of dry croissants and no coffee, living hand to mouth, outwitting hotels and landlords, visiting the Louvre to study the Greek vases, statues, bas-reliefs. Isadora wanted solitude to think out, with body and mind, why such grace existed only on pottery and in marble. She experimented with setting those long dead Greek poses to music, to "the rhythms of the feet, the Dionysiac set of the head, and the tossing of the thyrsis." In their studio, brother Raymond, a gifted eccentric who was to become a fixture in Paris for over half a century, painted Greek inspired columns on the walls. The entire family tossed off their shoes and took to sandals. Isadora danced barefoot in a transparent tunic; no tutus or posturing manikins on their toes for her.

It was through friendship with the Japanese Sada Yacco, who was posing for Rodin, that she came into the focus of the bearded sculptor. His artistic drive, satanically sensual, pagan, was amazing and shocking. All Isadora wanted was to learn "the divine expression of the human spirit through the medium of the body's movement . . . I discovered the center . . . the crater of motor power was the solar plexus." Later critics said she advocated the basic dance not as an art but as a biological function, a moving grace, a response to every experience and emotion. Spontaneous movement was her goal, reactions to sensory or emotional stimuli. And she was still a virgin, the oyster that had not yet pearled.

The lecherous Rodin, she sensed, was a mighty artist, pushing life into his clay forms with his brutal yet eager and skilled fingers. She guarded her maidenhead for some dream prince and watched the master at work. Rodin had hardly much to do with the marble and bronze versions of his work. He had a crew of Italian stone workers for that. His bronzes are still being cast to the greedy profit of dealers. Of Isadora he wrote: she "has attained sculpture and emotion effortlessly . . . has properly unified Life and the Dance." Like much of the writing of nonverbal artists it is an easy, shallow statement. It misses the diversity, the nihilistic nature of her intrinsic intentions.

At this point in her life Isadora's virginity irked her as a derision, a lack of a rounded existence (there is no other way to express her condition). If she saw herself as Aphrodite Callipygian—a fair-assed Venus—she knew she wasn't marble. Isadora planned a seduction scene. Sending her family to the opera, she invited a suitor named André to the studio, dressed herself in that see-through tunic, put roses in her hair, got out a hidden bottle of champagne. She waited for André, psychologically, physically ready, "feeling just like Thais." Her story is, when it came to the attack, the sexual assault, André went damp with fear at sight of the body, the roses, and wine, and ran for it. A new male was then enticed to a Paris hotel room, but he merely fell to his knees. As one writer puts it, "Overcome by her purity, she frightened more men than she seduced." Certainly no Paris hotel room rented for intimate moments had ever had such a scene. So, while in time she could claim her life story called for "the pen of Cervantes—or Casanova," at twenty-two Isadora Duncan had a hard time disposing of her virginity.

She decided that perhaps going on tour would help remove her burden. It was in Budapest, dancing the *Blue Danube* by Strauss, that she met *him*, the machinery of her deflowering. He was a second-rate stock company actor, "tall, magnificent . . . of godlike features and stature, who was to transform the chaste nymph that I was into a wild bacchante." Her romantic glow, if it was like her prose, soon bored the Hungarian ham; he recited when he should have kissed. So it was back to the dance: Munich, Berlin, then Greece. Raymond pointed out they should turn their backs on a sanctimonious age and follow the voyage of Ulysses (a route still unknown to us). After setting up a school in Greece, Isadora came to Bayreuth to dance the *Tannhäuser* Bacchanal—of course, her version. Also to fall in love with a German hack novelist, Heinrich Thode, who responded, as did so many men she attacked with no decorum of approach, by staying strictly Platonic. She went on to Moscow to dance to Chopin and try to get the great Stanislavsky into bed. Complete failure. She had not studied the Method, had no time for it. As a *femme fatale* she felt she had no need for lessons.

At twenty-seven, still hunting the secret of the dance and the ideal lover, she met Gordon Craig, stage designer, the son of Ellen Terry, the famous English actress, and one of her lovers. It took just a few hours to light the flame between them and bring on her prose style: "His white, lithe, gleaming body emerged from the chrysalis of clothes . . . upon my dazzled eyes." There was no couch in the studio but for two weeks they remained locked in there, entwined, boa constrictors of passion, sleeping and loving on the floor. The ideal love period passed quickly—the ego of

genius soon loses the sense of shared drama—and they were bickering and quarreling, crying out together the agony of the artist betrayed. No idyllic future together was possible. Isadora went to Holland to have their baby. She named it after a sad Irish queen, Deirdre. Then she ran off with a young Hollander to Russia—with eighteen trunks. "Better the pleasure that lasts a moment than the sorrow which endures forever." They traveled, parted. She moved on. In New York the critics disliked her dancing. Wrote one shocked critic: "Her Beethoven was a perverted use of the Seventh Symphony."

At thirty-two, Isadora, broke, with a child, her family to feed (the other Duncans never were providers) was back in Paris. Here she met the American millionaire, Paris Singer, heir to the sewing machine fortune. She called him Lohengrin. He was a dandy, blond, bearded, tall and stylish, always well dressed, always charming, always with all that money could buy—grand dinners, yachts, fêtes and parties that startled Paris. He gave a festival at Versailles for Isadora where the whole Colonne Orchestra fiddled and tooted in time to her bare feet. Caviar went around by the pound. Off stage Isadora liked frivolous elegance. She learned to enjoy fine wine, developed, in fact, a taste for alcohol, furs, rare scents, gowns from Paul Poiret. By 1911 the romance—her sexual proclivities were international gossip—became Sunday newspaper filler. Leaving for America in the biggest suite afloat, Isadora and Lohengrin had to return when her new pregnancy began to show. Her son Patrick was born in France. She enjoyed motherhood, saw in it the fecundity and resourcefulness of life.

Paris Singer now begged for marriage. But Isadora wanted no bonds, no unconditional surrender to social morality. Again between lovers angry words were thrown, battles and screams took over, so in time Singer felt escape from Isadora's bedlam of talk and rage was his only hope for sanity.

It was not a full break. Apart they longed for each other; together they fought and scratched; a banal novel. There were love meetings between Isadora and Lohengrin, but no marriage, just meetings and partings. When she was thirty-five she and Singer had one of their brief reunions in Paris, like birds mating on the wing. Her two children were sent one day with their nurse for a ride in the automobile. On a steep slope leading down to the river the brakes failed and the car hurled itself into the Seine. Singer came staggering in to Isadora with the news: "The children, the children are dead."

The terrible tragedy changed Isadora. She was never again as she once had been. A blight had set in. Louis Untermeyer, writing of her, said, "Life went on for her but it was another woman who lived it, a coarser woman, suffering less from sorrow than from a self-destructive reckless-ness."

There is no reward for us here to record her decline, her heavy drink-ing, her love affairs. Or of her marriage at forty-two with a twenty-seven-year-old, insane Russian poet, a maniac, cruel and dissolute, who took to wrecking rooms, breaking furniture, holding a pistol to her head. He was locked up in an insane asylum. She freed him. He cut his wrists, wrote a poem with his own blood, and hanged himself. It seemed there could be no going on for Isadora.

Yet in Paris, in July of 1927, Isadora, now near fifty, had recovered her spirit enough to give what many admirers called her greatest dance con-cert. She remained a genius, untrained but eloquent in her movements, and rather silly when she talked about her art and her emotions. Her life was a mixture of artistic cant, banal at times, but her dance was a great cleansing force that purged modern dancing. She undressed the dance, liberated it from its formal duties to the opera house and the theater. It was a revolution created by an aging alcoholic, bloated, and, off stage, no longer attractive. She was a failure as a *femme fatale*. In 1929 William Bolitho could write of her, "She attained a greater fame and influence than any other American woman ever achieved." Perhaps.

Two months after her great success in Paris, while she was riding in a car the end of a flowing scarf she wore around her neck caught in one of the spinning wheels. The scarf tightened, broke her neck, killed her.

It might have been the dramatic world-shocking exit she desired. She had been tired, was fat, addicted to drink, disillusioned with physical love.

She was buried in Paris's famed Père Lachaise. Five thousand people attended her funeral.

Her brother Raymond lived on—a friend of the Steins—one of the sights of Paris in his shoulder-length hair long before the fashion came in, dressed in robes he wove himself, wearing his sandals, preaching sim-plicity and love to an indifferent world, settling for a vegetable diet. A kindly man, a bit impractical but managing to enjoy his way of life. He was there to remind the world there had been an Isadora Duncan in the flesh.

CHAPTER 41

At Natalie Barney's

*I was dealing less with a declining social order than
with a dissolving moment in time, with one of those
perpetually returning epochs which fall between an
age that is slipping out and an age that is hastening in.*

ELLEN GLASGOW

WHY were the young Americans going to Paris? Why were they attempting what Henry Steel Commager called the "Cult of the Irrational" in his book, *The American Mind?* This cult rejected the very concept of principle. It was the rejection—on pseudoscientific grounds— of reason, meaning, normality, morality, continuity, coherence, the rejection of civilization as eccentric and decadent; a passionate interest in the subconscious, unconscious, an enthusiasm for emotion rather than thought, instinct rather than reason, anarchy rather than discipline. It was obsessed with sex, especially in its abnormal manifestations, as the most powerful and pervasive of all the instincts and the interpretation of all conduct in terms of sex. It had a weakness for the primitive: primitive people, Africans, Indians, peasants, and children; primitive emotions and activities, eating, drinking, sleeping, fighting, making love; closely connected with a predilection for violence, the unqualified repudiation of orthodox moral standards, conformities, conventions, acquiescence in a perverse amorality, submission of the highest virtue to instincts. And the formulation of a new language, a new grammar to express impulses emanating from the subconscious.

Certainly the new language and grammar of the arts they saw born in Paris attracted many. But not all were primarily creative artists, not even talkers who claimed to be creative and weren't.

Some came to be frankly hedonists, to live *outré* lives, to escape into sexual patterns frowned upon or outlawed at home.

Henry James was aware of the quicksands glossed over with a social surface that when tested failed. "I have the imagination of disaster, and see life as ferocious and sinister."

It is just before World War I in Paris. Miss Natalie Clifford Barney, rich, beautiful, is a young patron of the arts. She is having a party, giving a reading of Pierre Louys's *Dialogue*, a presentation by two pretty actresses. Everyone applauds the reading, and then down a path through well-trimmed trees, up to the lawn of the reading comes a nude woman riding a white horse, its mane braided with twinkling jewels. The rider is borrowed from the Folies Bergères, a Dutch woman passing as a dancer from Java, whose stage name is Mata Hari. Not that she is completely nude. Since Mata Hari has hardly any breasts, she wears a brassiere. At the time Mata Hari is only a mild sensation in Paris. The writer Colette is present for the strip on horseback; she describes the dancer as having a blotchy skin, heavy nose, but admits "the back and thighs are of the first order."

The dancer dismounts, takes up a wrap and makes a short speech which has not survived. Miss Barney's party is a sensational success.

Mata Hari was invited back to perform a "Javanese dance," naked, at another party of Miss Barney's, "for women only, a Lesbian orgy." Colette was not permitted to attend this delight—her husband Willy objected. Willy was an expert on sensualists himself. Mata Hari was never a spy of any importance, bungling her assignments. The Germans betrayed her to the French in order to get rid of her and she was accordingly shot.

All that was long ago, but Miss Barney herself lived on into a very old age, over ninety, but was known in the early 1970s intimately only to her own fervid circle of followers. In her extreme old age she was living in a 300-year-old house, a house in the narrow and quiet atmosphere of the Rue Jacob. It is a Left Bank spot, "very French," certainly very much a Paris of the past, and an address famous or notorious to the underground American expatriate world. Almost any tourist can prattle of Gertrude Stein, or with a bit of education identify Mary Cassatt. Almost none of the thousands of tourists have heard of Natalie Clifford Barney. She lived on as if hidden in a dream—refusing to open her eyes to the present. Once in her garden, in her salon, the most famous, the most sinful, the artists, composers and their pets had talked and reveled.

There are legends of the street before Natalie's time, when Racine,

Cardinal Richelieu, Balzac met mistresses there, to drink or eat some gourmet's delight. The specter of the past of Paris lingers, even the smell of expensive, obsolete motorcars.

Frankly, as journalists will tell you, Miss Barney has been avoided as subject matter by those writing for American publications about Americans long lodged in Paris. Natalie's life has been strange, wild, and by the Puritan United States' moral standard, sinful. *The New Yorker's* bold, brisk Janet Flanner ("Genêt") stated, Natalie Clifford Barney is "a perfect example of an enchanted person not to write about." Why has she been shunted into a grotesque limbo of forgotten parties?

Natalie's salon was famous; the brilliant, the great, the sensual, and the unbalanced mixed with casual ease. Gossip gave her and her house a reputation for privileged, leisurely vice that research almost validates. She has written books rarely known to Americans, for she became so French that for her the old saying "more royalist than the king" would fit. Her world was beyond the brutishness of professional patriotism, or the public morality of Main Street, U.S.A. *Le dessous de la carte*, the secret of Natalie is available for those who seek it in certain books. She has appeared in fiction, in that once shocking lesbian novel—now so dull and decent—*The Well of Loneliness* by Radclyffe Hall. She is the character called Valerie Seymour. She is described as rich, beautiful, bilingual, *libre penseuse* . . . limbs very perfectly proportioned . . . eyes very kind, very blue, very lustrous . . . slender and shapely shoulders." There is a tribute to her in *Lettres à l'Amazone*, by Remy de Gourmont, and she is also the model for the seductive Laurette in *L'Ange et les Pervers* by Lucie Delarue-Mardrus. She inspired *so* many, becoming the Flossie of a Colette novel, the Moonbeam in a Liane de Pougy story, the sensual Lorelei in some hardly sane passion-love poems of Renée Vivien.

We are dealing with an Amazon monument. Old wrinkled, feeble, Natalie still retained at a very advanced age the aristocratic look, the good clear voice, the stance and control of her body and mind that make one a unique personality, still able to hurl the lance of resentment, remember the dissenters and heroes of her time.

Certainly she was eccentric, self-mocking, firm in her way of life, outlawed, outside the pale of her society. She came naturally to her wandering way. Her family had money in those days when in good families it meant travel for those seeking culture, tone, grace, social nuances, art, and good living for all; people who exist now only in Henry James's novels, the works of Edith Wharton.

Natalie's mother, of Dutch-Jewish stock, had studied painting with

James McNeill Whistler. She signed herself Alice Pike Barney when doing portraits of Bernard Shaw, Gilbert Chesterton, pictures of the social queens of the Eastern Shore, paintings of her daughters, Laura and Natalie. Alice Barney also wrote plays, created a theater in Washington, D. C. The Barney side of the family has some misty connection with the American Revolution, was involved with the deeds of John Paul Jones, Benjamin Franklin, James Monroe. It's very vague and has not been

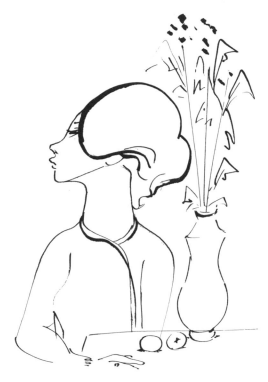

proved to the satisfaction of historians. Natalie in time preferred being her own ancestor.

Natalie Barney, for all her tearing herself out of the American landscape, was born in 1877 in Dayton, Ohio, traveled to Bar Harbor, to Washington, when her mother painted portraits. Her own portrait by Alice Barney shows Natalie was blue-eyed, had shiny waves of mink-colored hair, clear finely defined features. She is boldly staring back at the world. Natalie matured into a fine, shapely, alert teen-ager. She went to Europe to study, settled in on her own in Neuilly, already aware of her sexual and intellectual direction. In 1909 she moved into the house on the Rue Jacob where she was to stay over half a century, near the Boulevard

Saint-Germain, the Seine, the Café Flore, the Café Deux Magots. She was at times the close neighbor of Picasso, Apollinaire, Gertrude Stein, Sylvia Beach. She suggests some lines of George Santayana:

> The crown of olive let another wear;
> It is my crown to mock the runner's heat
> With gentle wonder and with laughter sweet.

She did not feel the need to explain herself as an exile, as did Logan Pearsall Smith: "An Englishman or other who settles in America incurs no kind of moral blame, either in the land he has deserted, or in his new-adopted home . . . But to desert America is somehow regarded as a kind of treachery, as if America were more than a country, were a sort of cause, and its Stars and Stripes the banner of a crusading army which it is dishonorable to desert."

She was one of many American women who felt their personal lives were freer in Paris, and if she had explained, she might have agreed with Willa Cather: "The United States has gotten ahead wonderfully, but somehow ahead on the wrong road." Willa Cather also wanted to settle in Paris but gave it up. "I tried to live in France . . . But when I strike the open plains . . . I'm home. I breathe differently." Actually Willa Cather retreated to a dream America of a pleasant, unreal past, of shadows on the rocks, of Catholic dreams (she was never converted, however) in which a nest of nostalgia of her own making was furnished by fine interior decorating.

Natalie Barney, once settled in Paris, never wanted change, never felt lost or in need of open plains.

Not all the Americans who came to grasp at the arts in Paris were invited to Natalie's salon. But many claimed to have been there, basing their information of the details of her house and garden and guests on the literary and social gossip, the intimate journalism of the city. The name-dropping was like a hailstorm. (As Elizabeth of the *German Garden* fame put it: "Some kiss and tell. Writers often don't kiss—and tell anyway.")

Who hadn't been there to the house on the Rue Jacob? Present at one time or another were George Antheil, Virgil Thomson, Sherwood Anderson, Carl Van Vechten, Ezra Pound, T. S. Eliot, Bernard Berenson, just to name a few of the hundreds of Americans who over the years were greeted by her. And the giants or clowns of Europe: James Joyce, Marcel Proust, to name the high priests first, also the fool and self-proclaimed genius, Gabriele D'Annunzio, and Apollinaire, who always claimed he was sired by a cardinal of the Vatican. André Gide called Natalie "among the few people you have to see." The list of guests is almost endless. Many of the names have become important and many have faded of those who trooped to her garden's stone Temple of Friendship, who ate the famous chocolate cake and other goodies and drank the wines. The guests sipped vintage champagne. Natalie didn't. Of all her vices alcohol was not one. Friday was *the* night one went to Natalie's—Friday if one was part of the group in favor. There was vaudeville, avant-garde show business, events like Colette doing a scene from her *La Vagabonde*, readings of Paul Valéry's verse, a premiere of George Antheil's First String Quartet. When Apollinaire couldn't make an appearance, he wrote a poem of regret. He could compose stuff like *Tant d'explosifs sur le point. VIF!*

Natalie's fame as a hostess to the arts in Paris was hidden in America for decades because of her love of women. Yet some hints were dropped: "Among her passionate friendships one may cite the most beautiful and talented women of Paris." Or "She was most attractive . . . many of her sex found her fatally so. At Miss Barney's one met ladies with high collars and monocles, though Miss Barney herself was so feminine . . ." Another snapshot: "My last glimpse was of a small salon where some young women, transported by literature and champagne, danced madly about in each others' arms." William Carlos Williams remembered "women of all descriptions . . . sneaking off together into a side room while casting surreptitious glances about them, hoping their exit had not been noticed." Dr. Williams somehow retained a hostile Puritanical American streak on his visits to Paris; one did *not* have to sneak or hide one's desires at Natalie's parties.

Natalie had her own answer for her behavior, the open admission of her way of life. "To be one's own master is to be the slave of self." Lesbianism in those days had to be whispered. A play, *The Captive*, could be removed from the stage because one woman gave another woman a bunch of violets.

Writing in *Pensées d'une Amazone,* Natalie said, "That catastrophe; being a woman." She hated sham and pretension, moral hypocrisy. She mocked D'Annunzio as a fellow roué: "You are interested in women only from the waist down, while my interest in men is only from the neck up." Her attitude toward men she once expressed as, "It isn't because I don't think of men that I don't love them, but because I *do* think of them."

She had begun her frank, exuberant life long before coming to Paris. She had frankly arrived at her attitude toward sex in childhood, having seduced a lady visitor in her mother's studio, moving on to conquer a servant girl and a governess to kissing and mutual, intimate, consoling delights. Her girlish days in boarding school, Les Roches at Fountainebleau, completed her emotional education. Sent to Paris with money to have her portrait painted by Whistler, Natalie never showed up, but spent the money entertaining available women partners.

While studying music in Paris, she was introduced to the young Renée Vivien. Some Americans used the polite words "Amazon love," but even whispers of it in those days of buttoned-up Edwardian doings did shock. That is why so many American women of Sappho-like nature settled mostly in Paris and set up lifelong ménages with other women, or sported as flirts and seducers away from Main Street, from San Francisco, Boston, Baltimore, escaping the morals of a nation dedicated to Manifest Destiny, the domination of the Father Image, a materialism based upon that old time religion and the prosperity of the Republican Party. Natalie's father, a clubman of wealth, once intercepted a passionate love letter intended for Natalie. It was a shock to the sophisticated gentleman, a burden to wear on well-tailored shoulders. Her mother illustrated Natalie's first book of poetry. One wonders, did she really not know the meaning of certain loaded lines? A scandal sheet, *Town Topics*, made some innuendoes when Natalie appeared as a character in Liane de Pougy's novel. Natalie kept the book away from her parents' prying eyes. She seduced Lucie, the wife of Dr. Mardrus to whom her parents had sent her. As Lucie could not have children, she suggested Natalie have a child by the doctor. The idea did not appeal to Natalie.

Her first serious love affair started when Natalie was out riding and sighted the celebrated and notorious courtesan, Liane de Pougy, promenading in the Bois de Boulogne. Natalie at once wrote a passionate note, sent fabulous flowers (she still had some of that Whistler portrait money left). She called on Liane, was so profuse that she overwhelmed the high-class whore. They became the closest of lovers. Liane insisted she rationed herself to men so she could save so much more of herself for Natalie, her Flossie, her Moonbeam.

It was in the middle of the Liane de Pougy affair that Natalie, herself a student of music, was introduced to Renée Vivien, as a lover of the muse. Renée had no great physical charm compared to the sensational courtesan. Brown-eyed, still retaining a bit of rounded childishness, she was clumsy, had over-fleshed lips, and her chin was somewhat lacking in length. Rodin sculpted Renée's head, so she must have had charisma not all physical. She had been presented at the Court of St. James. Renée had skated at a rink with Natalie and she then invited her to her flat for full intimacy and perfervid lovemaking.

Natalie, neglecting the old love, Liane, shrugged and said about the discarded one, "Like the season, we must let love pass."

On the surface Renée appeared jolly and pleasure seeking, but the poems she wrote reek with death; the ghastly finality had a burning attraction for her as she wrote of it in her flat among her collection of gold coins, bibelots, enamels, rare jewels, lacquers. Her poetry turned out best, she felt, if she could scale some height of unhappiness. That wasn't easy at first in such comfortable surroundings. Natalie made Renée publish her poems, and in time there was enough unhappiness in the long-lasting ménage of the two lovers to produce a great deal of verse.

Natalie had money and Renée liked to enjoy the wealth of others. For a time Renée had an affair with a rich woman of ostentatious income and habits, who spent without reason and served as the sexual stimulant to more morbid verse. But she was jealous, this rich prey. Renée's servant girl, in the pay of Miss Rich Bitch, intercepted love letters Natalie sent to Renée. It had all the contorted drama of a normal French bedroom farce gone wrong.

Renée remained loyal to the rich friend. Natalie with one of the sisterhood, the opera star Emma Calvé, the Met's Carmen at the time, dressed in the male attire of street singers and went to serenade under Renée's window, hoping to lure her back with song. In time a reconciliation took place, and the two lovers went off to find Lesbos in Greece, where in a golden age Sappho herself had made inexhaustible love—hardly in the style, the calm solemnity of Hellenic sculpture.

As she matured, Natalie became emotionally hardened. She accepted the sexual game and let the romantic naiveté of the impulses fall away. She could say of someone's name mentioned in passing: "Do I like *who?* Heavens no, she and I made love, that's all." She made it clear she never had any regrets for things done with a variegated feeling for youth and ardor. *Ah, merde alors.*

A neighbor of Natalie's, the poet Remy de Gourmont, who knew her well and admired her, published *Lettres à l'Amazone*—letters to Natalie Barney. Gourmont called Natalie the *lis* as in lily. She said "his eyes were like two children living in a ruin."

In rebuttal to his book about her Natalie in her own *Pensées d'une Amazone* set down her ideas on bizarre sexual pleasures. "He who confuses reproduction and love spoils both of them; the result of this mess is marriage." A pretty fair sample of her style and philosophy.

She treated men like hurt dogs, providing Gourmont with money and patrons when he was in dire need. When Picasso's friend, Max Jacob (a

Jew who became a Catholic and who in a vision once claimed to have had an affair with Christ) was hurt in one of those murderous Paris auto accidents, Natalie helped him press his claim for damages in a French court. He lost the case; judges and courts of *le gouvernement français* often favor big corporations. She got Jacob, a wretchedly bad painter, some patrons for his gouaches to keep him from sinking to the life of the dives of the Rue Château Landon.

Marcel Proust kept up a friendship with Natalie, and she inscribed to him a copy of her book, stating that his understanding "merits this expurgated copy." She wondered at Proust's boldness in so fully exposing the sordid side of homosexual life in Paris in his *Cities of the Plain*. She said she worried over what he would do with his tainted women characters.

He answered her, "My Sodomites are all horrible, but my Gomorrheans will be charming."

Proust, who acted as if absurdity might be the essential human condition, doctored himself with patent medicines, even though his brother was a well-known doctor. He lived in that famous cork-lined apartment, went out only at night in his later years. When he visited Natalie late at night, she would have a huge fire burning even if he never took off his black fur coat. She is said to have quoted Satie to him: "Why attack God? He may be as unhappy as we are."

Natalie found James Joyce in his visits to her catty and snide about other writers. While she liked Gertrude Stein and her companion Alice B. Toklas, she felt Gertrude's writing could "never really come to the point at all." However at a party she gave for Gertrude at the end of the Twenties, Ford Madox Ford, gasping for air, stood on the steps of the Temple of Friendship and read out *Homage to Gertrude Stein*. Virgil Thomson, who was to do the music for the Stein opera, *Three Saints in Four Acts*, played some of his music and also sang it.

The years slowed Natalie down, and as she reached past eighty, looking back on a long and sensational life in Paris on the Rue Jacob, she could ask with that ironic stare, "Do I have a salon?" The Friday nights no longer took place every Friday, and the old crowd was dead or senile or locked away; so many reputations forgotten, so many would-be geniuses in fragile inanity turning into mere footnotes. One of her last parties was for the molting old bigot Ezra Pound. Ezra pottering around, was nearly as old as his hostess, still working on his *Cantos*. He was an addled ghost, lamenting a world that would not adjust to his ideas of it. The guests found him as self-contained as a rotten egg in an unbroken shell.

It was a more permissive age as Natalie grew very old. She could be outspoken as an unrepentant hedonist, one who took her pleasures where she found them and smiled at the morality of a society set up as the norm, with a morality secretly broken. One would have liked a recording of her meeting with Edna St. Vincent Millay at one of the Natalie Barney parties; two women of audacious aspirations who burned the candle at both ends and gloried in the light it gave.

Natalie summed up her world of alienated status and corrupt tenderness: "I have gotten from life all I could. I have gotten even more than it contains. Everything I set out to do I did." Neither Napoleon nor de Gaulle could make so positive a statement.

Her love life was notorious, her lovers beautiful, famous, often full of violence. She had produced a bit of literature herself, created a literary salon where the new geniuses were exposed like boiled shrimp on golden toothpicks before being dipped in the best society sauce of her gatherings. She helped with funds, with patrons, the needy writers of merit.

She even suggested her own epitaph: "She was the friend of men and the lover of women, which for people full of ardor and drive is better than the other way around."

CHAPTER 42

Shakespeare & Company—
And Miss Beach

A book? They already have a book.
RADIO JOKE, C. 1929

I N 1919, in a Paris shabby and sad in victory—some claimed a million and a half Frenchmen were dead in the fearful war, a war that was merely the second act of a tragedy that pointed ahead to 1939—a hawk-nosed young woman named Sylvia Beach, with a mop of dark hair crudely cut and brushed carelessly back, opened a Paris bookstore called Shakespeare & Company to handle English-language texts and dedicated to the avant-garde writings; books of authors not yet accepted by the grand literary poobahs who made or broke popular reputations. Among the authors she helped to fame were James Joyce and Ernest Hemingway. Without her, Joyce's *Ulysses* might not have seen print for more long years.

France was fatigued, smirched with compromise, rotted with profiteers, soiled with political expediency; yet Paris began to revive and art was merely dormant.

Sylvia Beach was one of the strange waifs thrown up on the shores of postwar Paris, who, torn from their native land, thought of Paris as the center of the artistic earth. Like the Cone sisters, Dr. Claribel and Etta, she, too, came from Baltimore, Maryland, being born there in 1887. She was descended from nine generations of Presbyterian ministers, all of whom had been steeped in spiritual pieties and rituals. Her mother was born in India, in her parents' missionary setting.

The Beaches, except in death and bereavement, were wanderers moving about a great deal, and always preachers. Sylvia's father, the Reverend Sylvester Woodbridge Beach, D.D., held the pulpit for seventeen years at the Princeton First Presbyterian Church. While at Princeton at various times he preached at three American presidents: Woodrow Wilson, James Garfield, Grover Cleveland. Before the 1914 war broke, the Beach family had been in Paris for two years, and Sylvia was shipped off to a Lausanne school, an ossified institution which she hated for its disciplines, its dated, tepid ideas of the world.

In 1916 during the Great War, as the romantics called it, Sylvia was in Spain, but, itchy-footed, she traveled on to wartime Paris with her most beautiful sister, Cyprian, and they went to live in a Palais Royal apartment. Cyprian had failed in her plans to become a great singer. Patrician yet exuberant, she had become a motion picture actress of some fame, a siren of the silent film's great pioneer days. But time and decay has obliterated her; this writer has been unable to discover anyone who remembers her as a star of the silent films.

However, here were two young American girls in wartime Paris with Cyprian's parrot Guappo. It was a Paris of curfews, darkness, little cellar dives, soldiers on leave in despair before going out to die on the Somme, at Verdun. Confidence in victory was fading, fading fast. The girls moved to the Hôtel Quai Voltaire; it was hard to heat an apartment with fuel shortages, food was mean and coarse when available. From the hotel the girls could look across the street to the Seine and its embankment. Guappo the parrot managed to escape his cage and get out through the window. Misjudging his flying ability, he landed plump in the river. (As one of the Wright brothers was to say, when asked to make a speech at a banquet, "The parrot is the only bird that talks, and is the worst flier.")

Sylvia, seeing the disaster, ran from the hotel in slacks and dived into the river from the bank and swam toward the squawking bird. She managed to capture it before it drowned and returned to the bank with it, swimming with one hand, holding the parrot over her head with the other. There was a nice round of applause from the gathering crowd as she came ashore with a handful of wet animated feathers. But Guappo—his reactions essentially stupid—broke out again a couple of weeks later and was never seen again by the sisters.

With the war ended, the Beach girls went out to Serbia to do Red Cross work, feeling themselves part of a historic moment. It was tough going, riding shaggy ponies in war-ravaged landscapes, flea-carried plagues all around them. A French poet who knew them at the time has recorded that Sylvia looked like the daughter of a Wild West sheriff, hitching her horse outside the Last Chance Saloon. From now on Cyprian fades from our records. Nothing seems on record of her later life.

Sylvia's mind was on literature and a strange, wonderful little book she had read, *A Portrait of the Artist as a Young Man,* by an unknown writer, an exile someplace in Switzerland, an Irishman named James Joyce.

Back in Paris, deloused of Serbian insect life, she found some modern books that bore the rubber stamp of *La Maison des Amis des Livres,* a bookstore of the Left Bank, on the Rue de L'Odéon. She went there and was greeted by a mountain of a woman in a skirt that touched the ground, who was standing in the doorway. A gust of wind at that moment blew Sylvia's hat down the street and the bulky woman sprinted after it, captured it, and returned it to its owner. It all seems a scene from a Mack Sennett comedy of the period. The woman, Mademoiselle Adrienne Monnier, was the owner of the bookshop, established in 1915. The two women took to each other and a lifetime friendship of love and confidence began. The Amazon duet was not odd to Paris, a city that casually accepted many things, as Natalie Barney had discovered. Monnier and her costumes were described by the novelist Byrher as looking "like a French officer in military cape attempting to lead his soldiers back from Moscow." It was true Monnier affected a cloak tight-buttoned around her neck, and never seemed to be out of a ground-touching skirt, at least in public. Sylvia she saw as "a passenger from the Mayflower, with the wind still blowing through her hair." The poet Stephen Spender called the group around Adrienne Monnier "The Vestal Virgins."

Monnier's bookshop had begun as a palm-reading salon, then was taken early into the Dada movement. In the salon behind the bookcases Monnier presented Erik Satie's music, a performance of his *Socrate,* he at the piano and Jean Cocteau reciting the words. Among others present Sylvia noted André Gide and the Catholic bigot and poet Paul Claudel. Art, metaphysics, and personalities filled the place. Incomprehension, overstimulated egos were made into art movements.

Sylvia talked with Monnier of her idea of having her own bookstore, where American and English books and newspapers and magazines would be sold to the growing English-speaking colony of Paris. It was the time of Gertrude's Lost Generation, of escape from Main Street and the Bull Market of Prosperity, the time of Harding and Coolidge. The Americans were favored by a marvelous rate of exchange and were coming to Paris in droves; here the last Puritanical pang could be dissolved.

Sylvia also established a lending library, so the frugal French could read what was being done in English to bring on another revolution—at least in prose. Sylvia spoke a brisk, slang-sprinkled French (the accent faint), flavored by the unique gutter language of Céline, essential in a daughter of nine generations of preachers.

After the shop was found, a failed laundry on the Rue Dupuytren, Sylvia wrote home for help. Her mother bravely entrusted her life savings to her daughter. It came to three thousand dollars. But it was not enough, and over the years cousins and aunts of the Beach family kept bailing out Sylvia's bookstore in Paris, which they could look upon as missionary work of a kind.

James Joyce was now in Paris, led around, half blind, by Ezra Pound, who proclaimed the Irish exile's genius at the salon of Natalie Barney, where artistic dilemmas were mixed with parties.

On Sunday, July 11, 1920, an important date in the history of Joyce, Sylvia Beach met her hero at a poets' party. She looked at the slight figure of the pale little man leaning on a cane, his sick eyes hidden behind dark glasses, a wisp of blond mustache and curl of chin beard. Jesuit trained, an unemployed language teacher, a one-time movie theater manager in Dublin—a hardly published genius.

"Is this," she asked, perhaps in tones of Stanley meeting Livingston, "the great James Joyce?"

He admitted it, "James Joyce," offering to shake hands. When he heard Sylvia ran an English-language bookshop, he was delighted, asking for her address with patrician elegance. Next morning Joyce was at her door in a blue serge suit, dirty tennis shoes, stick in hand and hat on back of his head. He needed a cheap apartment; did Miss Beach know of anyone who needed language lessons? Joyce was a Celtic charmer when he wanted to be; he was to live off of female patrons for some time.

Sylvia became his champion, and was skillfully moved into having her bookstore involved with presenting his novel, *Ulysses*. She was a willing victim. If used by Joyce, and abused, she realized it. She knew Cézanne's remark: "The artist is only the dog of his work, and when the master whistles, he must come—even on Sunday." And Joyce was such a blind dog.

"Would you, Mr. Joyce, let Shakespeare & Company have the honor of bringing out your *Ulysses?*"

Of course Joyce was overjoyed. The book had been finished for three years. It was April, by October the masterwork should be given to the world. He was not a grateful man—his innate sensibility he saved for his work. He treated Sylvia, most historians of the period think, in a brusque and shabby manner. Besides, he had an amazing contract to get 60 percent of the net profits, if any ever would come into being. Geniuses often have senses that are blurred and crusted to those cursed to be intimate with them. He was the master of prose to make articulate the dark processes that create a new art. Meanwhile, waiting for publication, he got patrons to support him with a hundred and fifty dollars a month while *Ulysses* was turned into print ("reek of plug, spilt beer, men's beery piss . . .").

Robert McAlmon, who put up some of the money, got a brisk letter from Joyce telling him he was late with his payment. "I shall be greatly obliged if your monthly cheque arrives punctually on the 1 Nov." Joyce believed in an austere morality with patrons. Joyce's patrons, mostly women, as one writer put it, made it "possible for him to be poor only through determined extravagance."

Sylvia, no Philistine with a genius—always called him "Mr. Joyce," and he answered her as "Miss Beach." In private she and Monnier got into the habit of calling him "Melancholy Jesus" and "Crooked Jesus," terms he

had used himself. The ridge runners of new art are often problems. Sylvia never faltered in her devotion to Joyce.

She found a trusting printer in Dijon, Maurice Darantière, who not only had typesetters, the only ones in France perhaps who could set English prose, but also was dreamer enough to wait for his money until the subscription payments for the novel came in.

At the same time Sylvia moved her shop from the Rue Dupuytren to the Rue de L'Odéon. The shop had high narrow windows, a ladder to climb to find something in the higher stacks, a fireplace Hemingway enjoyed, lots of pictures of authors (often with pipes and tweed jackets), and tables and shelves, usually in disorder. Americans and others came in to warm themselves, often to read and not to buy.

Sylvia's eyes grew dim reading proof for Joyce ("Stately, plump Buck Mulligan came from the stairhead bearing a bowl of lather"). She donned silver-rimmed glasses as she worked on galley sheets late into the night while others sported on the Boul' Mich, ate chocolate, fruits *glacés*, *cacahouètes*. Joyce plagued her, rewriting and rewriting on the proof sheets, so that entirely new typesettings had to be made over and over again. About a good third of the book was actually written by Joyce on proof sheets, and *pneumatiques*, special delivery letters, came in droves.

When the *Circe* section of the book was lost in MS, Sylvia tried to get the New York lawyer and collector, John Quinn, who owned the original manuscript, to lend her the section. He refused. Quinn was an odd, feisty man—a successful rich man—who came to see Sylvia in the bookstore and still refused to lend. It was *his* novel now, the "Quinn Joyce." In the end, pressured by Ezra Pound, Quinn permitted the section to be photographed. Joyce was little help; he was involved in color schemes and insisted the covers of the book be "the blue of the Greek flag," and no color sample seemed to please him. Hunt for the color was made even as far as Germany before he finally accepted a color as "Greek" enough. Joyce's personality was like a Rembrandt painting; the shadows have the most meaning.

Sylvia began to develop bad eyestrain and blinding migraine headaches after a year of battle with the author, the text, and the printer. Darantière had insisted the book could *not* appear on Joyce's fortieth birthday, February 3, 1922. As the project proceeded, disillusionment touched the printer, never Sylvia. She had brought off the greatest literary coup since the publishing of *Du Côté de chez Swann* in 1913.

Joyce, hero of *le monologue intérieur* in Paris art circles, ate in the most expensive restaurants, gave five pound tips to waiters and taximen. Ernest Hemingway, himself still struggling, pointed out that Joyce's admirers thought he was starving while he was actually feasting in gourmet places that he, Hemingway, couldn't afford. Sylvia contended with printers' bills, bookkeeping, sales, subscriptions, as well as taking care of her bookstore. Joyce borrowed books and hardly ever returned them. She was low in funds but she went on, moved Joyce's furniture to a better hotel, sent money orders to Joyce's sister, dug up his favorite yellow medicine, and bottles of his special lotion. Joyce would help himself at the bookshop till and write IOUs. He refused Sylvia any share of the American rights. He got an advance of $45,000 from Random House when they published the book in 1933, at a time when Sylvia almost lost her bookstore. Bennett Cerf made, it was said, nearly a million dollars on Joyce, yet Sylvia never received a share as the original discoverer, editor, and publisher. In the end Sylvia was just a bookseller, and having a hard time of it.

With the Depression Sylvia's bookstore began to lose money. Joyce's royalties were running to hundreds of dollars a month, but it was André Gide who went to Sylvia's aid when she was in trouble, enlisting a group to support the store. No American or English sophisticated pleas for help aided the fun. But Sylvia continued to help artists as if they had no willful eccentricities; George Antheil lived rent free in a room over her own.

There was another world out there in Paris, away from the bookstore, but Sylvia knew very little of it. Were people still doing the Toddle in Paris night clubs to the music of "Stumbling"? Having dinner at the Trianon? Was Flossie Martin, the fat Follies girl, still cursing the tourists? And the street criers selling papers, *Ami du Peuple, Intransigeant, Paris Soir?* Sylvia stayed away from the gay colored Paris of the Fitzgeralds, the *Vanity Fair*, Peter Arno, Clifton Webb set, the neo-Thomism of Jacques Maritain hoping for American converts, nights at the Cole Porter's Paris house. Did she shop at the Galeries Lafayette? Meet some rich American patron getting off the boat train at the St.-Lazare station, or cashing his check at the Guaranty Trust Company? Or carry food to some young, hungry writer stuck at the Paris-New York Hotel on the Rue Vauguirard? We don't know. No one seems to have recorded the details about her life outside the shop, facts that we would have liked to know.

What did Sylvia think of all the talk of the manly writers about the little bulls of Pamplona, or safaris in fancy gear to Africa? We do know how she felt about great literary artists; to her they were like ants that carry burdens several times their own weight and size. How could she avoid helping them. George Antheil, her boarder for a time, the "Enfant Terrible of music" was good for her. The most intimate they ever got was her acting as his banker, often at a loss. Sylvia aided Frank Harris, who wanted her to publish his erotic *Life and Loves*. D. H. Lawrence offered her *Lady Chatterley's Lover*. But she was out of publishing, even when pornographers and geniuses were combined.

War came in 1939. Sylvia was isolated, holed up in her failing bookstore. When the Germans marched into Paris, they planned to seize her stock of books, but she got the volumes off to hiding. She sheltered at great risk many refugees and was part of an underground that clothed, wigged, disguised fugitives from the murderous Germans. Her response and efforts were not just sympathy in her second war against Germans; *they* burned books.

The Germans arrested Sylvia Beach. She was held prisoner in harsh, revolting conditions for seven months. The Gestapo threatened ghastly torture and the firing squad. Pressure by friends, perhaps followers of Pétain, got her released. She retreated to her boarded-up apartment over the store. When liberation came, Ernest Hemingway, delighted at playing at war, led his noisy, jeep-carried band to the Rue de L'Odéon and shouted up to Sylvia that aid had come. *Mourir pour la patrie!*

The rest of Sylvia's life was a continual brave fight of a rearguard action. Her sign, a SHAKESPEARE painted by Monnier's sister, Marie, was stolen by some lover of literature. Others were making fortunes out of Joyce. Personal happiness also had fled from her life. Adrienne Monnier committed suicide in 1955. The rest of her life was marked by mere honorary awards: an honorary degree, her papers sent to Princeton for posterity, appearance as a special guest at the Martello Tower in Dublin (which opens the great book) in memory of James Joyce. With archaic honesty she wrote her book on the history of Shakespeare & Company. It was too bland and kind a book, had few sales. Joyce's books sold in the millions, *Finnegans Wake* half a million alone, and *Ulysses* outdid it fourfold.

There was nothing to do but keep the bookshop neat and wait. Sylvia Beach remained proud, kind, and self-contained to the end. That end came in 1962. When the neighbors got to her, they said, "She was found kneed but not floored." Did she remember, just before the final dark, James Joyce reciting Dante?

> *Io non mori, e non rimasi vivo—*
> I did not die, yet nothing of life remained.

Michel Mohrt wrote in his obituary of her in *Le Figaro Littéraire,* "Was there ever a woman more devoted to literature?"

CHAPTER 43

John Dos Passos Goes to War

Du coton dans les oreilles.

APOLLINAIRE

M OST of the young American college men from ivy league schools
who visited Paris during the first years of the Great War were
shown what the world could become by H. G. Wells and George Bernard
Shaw. These writers pointed out the flaws of their society and predicted
the shape of things to come. The young men were unhappy with the way
their democracy was being used, but as romantics they were ready to
fight a war "To Make the World Safe for Democracy."

Shaw in a Delphic utterance could lambast their hopes, but they
moved to the war fronts in spite of his words: "I have never spoken or
listened to an election meeting without being ashamed of the whole sham
democratic routine. The older I grow, the more I feel such exhibitions to
be, as part of the serious business of the government of a nation, entirely
intolerable and disgraceful to human nature and civic decency."

So many young idealists, yearning for excitement, grads of Roxbury
Latin, Dartmouth, and Yale Law School, were going to war, driven to the
depots (pronounced *de-poes*) at St. Louis, Santa Barbara, New Orleans,
often in the family Pierce-Arrow, Franklin, Stearns-Knight, Packard.

Paris in the years 1914 to 1918 had its quota of war-lured Americans.
Since the start of the Great War Americans had come over to drive
ambulances, join the *Lafayette Escadrille*, serve in the Foreign Legion,

learn names like Sopwith Camel, Fokker, Nieuport. In 1917, a Harvard man just past his twenty-first birthday, John Dos Passos, arrived with a few other Americans in Paris to join the Norton-Harjes Volunteer Ambulance Service, driving Model T Ford ambulances on the Western Front. It was in part a country-club war service; very fashionable with lots of Harvard and Yale and Princeton men, left-wing intellectuals or poets, John Howard Lawson, Robert Hillyer, Frederik van den Arend. As the young Dos Passos, trying to make concrete a transcendental experience, wrote home, "The fellows in the section are frightfully decent—all young men are frightfully decent."

The frightfully decent fellows read Henri Barbusse's *Le Feu*, dreamed of running a better world than the "swagbellied old fogies." They rode the drafty, war-battered trains into Paris—*je n'oublierai jamais*—stopping at stations to buy wine and rolls in the station *buvettes*, and were cheered by widows in drab black and old men bent over canes as "*Les Américains!*"

John came to Paris through the Quai D'Orsay station with other volunteers, all carrying their baggage in the dark, moving toward waiting cabs in a Paris dank and tired of three years of war. John had known Paris as a child, for his mother was not then married to his father, a bristling corporation lawyer with another (legal) family. So John and his mother had often lived abroad during his school years. He had been educated as a boy in England. Now the Paris of his lovely, sad mother, the memory of childhood in green French gardens, horse-cab filled streets, had become this unpainted, war-damaged town; the Germans, lovers of *Kultur*, were still firing their Big Bertha shells into the city. John's hotel had black-out curtains, and there was little of the room service Americans used to get in Paris. However, he had read his emotions, taken his pulse—*this* was a crusade to progress in the human condition.

Next day he went to the Norton-Harjes offices on the Rue François Premier. Here in a happy huddle were others of his Harvard classmates; the *cercle littéraire*, they had been called, and some had appeared in a volume John had edited, *Eight Harvard Poets*. It was a jolly reunion of the decent chaps. E. E. Cummings was coming over to join them. Some wrote to a favorite professor, beginning "*Cher Maître. . . .*" They still lacked uniforms, and the French, slaughtering their hundreds of thousands of citizens, were arresting all young men out of uniform. The French had over a million casualties now, and there was talk of mutiny of entire divisions of weary French soldiers. Why couldn't the French die with the grace of a Rupert Brooke?

As a man who already knew Paris, Dos Passos led his friends down along the Seine to the towers of Notre Dame. It was all a sort of dress rehearsal for the Americans who would come to Paris in the Twenties and made ritual the emancipated, rowdy life that the waiting Red Cross drivers were living in wartime Paris. To find rapture during a cruel war was most likely a sin (Puritanism kept seeping back).

Section I of the American Red Cross was billeted in a very fancy palace at Fontainebleau, its courtyard full of shiny new Model T Ford ambulances. The drivers lived magnificently at the Hôtel François Premier. John welcomed the autumn; Paris looked romantic and weathered as the leaves fell, the woods all around turned red and gold . . . Was there really a war on some place? And did they really do all that drinking? They would expose the sores of war in their poems, their novels; reveal the malformed head of an embryo.

Yes, they'd write how it was. It seemed to be a special American pride, then and later, in the intellectual circles to drink and drink and talk and talk. "Our boast was that we never drank enough." Take a look at Gouverneur Morris, a war reporter, a descendant of that Morris who had been in Paris during the French Revolution, and whose story is an early part of this history. The reporter Morris was noted for saying at table or bar, "Have anuzzer one." Language had lost its grace since the original Morris was in Paris.

They left Paris in their ambulances, driving south to Marseilles, and then were shipped to Italy. It was an Italy still in shock from the great beating taken at Caporetto.

John Dos Passos, after other adventures in other places, was back in Paris in the climactic summer of 1918. But he felt it was no longer the same. "Memories grin at me from street corners . . . the past with its eternal infernal mirror . . . I hate it." Ernest Hemingway turned up and he and John talked writing. Hem was working for the *Toronto Star* in Paris; he had a wife named Hadley and soon a baby called Bumby. Sometimes they all ate lunch together at Lippe's. John had known Hemingway on the Italian front in 1918, when both drove ambulances.

In the Twenties, drinking vermouth cassis at the Closerie des Lilas, corner of Saint-Michel and Montparnasse, they read to each other and were soon to be "the lost generation."

> Arms and the man I sing, who forced by fate
> and haughty Juno's unrelenting hate.
>   [JOHN DRYDEN's translation]

CHAPTER 44

Escadrille Lafayette

"Lafayette, we are here."
Said by CHARLES E. STANTON, *not*
GENERAL PERSHING

T HE MOOD of those who were in France to fight was often as fuzzy as that of the warmakers. Today, in our meaner times, their visions of Paris, of its art, of its women, are not easy to recapture, nor their reactions and emotions.

Of the eager young Americans of those days John P. Marquand said:

The nice thing about a war is that when one comes, you can drop everything and go to it, and everyone will say that you were exactly right . . . We were all caught in an inescapable wave of mass hysteria, which suddenly swamped the country. Definitely . . . it was something over which one had no control. If all your friends were going, it was only common sense to go along. The wave broke over us almost over night, sending us in all directions, and when it receded we were never quite the same again; but it was common sense to go along, although it was difficult to know exactly why we were going, and oddly enough this seemed unimportant. Even at the time, however, the reasons for going to France seemed peculiar. Most of them were based on a generally accepted fact that if we did not go over there, the Germans would certainly come over here. The eagerness to see Paris, to go to the war became contagious. We waited in the rain for three hours outside a Boston office to get our names down, so as to be sure to be among the first. It was unthinkable that we might be left behind when everyone was going. Even so, we lived in hourly fear that we might have applied too late.

As the young Americans saw Paris and died, the desperate romantic atmosphere of their early eagerness evaporated. Of the dead the too neutral philosopher, Santayana, could write in 1917 to a friend this callow letter: "As for deaths . . . I don't much care. The young men killed would grow older if they lived, and then they would be good for nothing; and after being good for nothing for a number of years, they would die of catarrh or a bad kidney, or the halter, or old age—and would that be less horrible? I am willing, almost glad, that the world should be poorer; I wish the population too, could become sparse. . . . People are not intelligent. It is unreasonable to expect them to be so, and that is a fate my philosophy reconciled me to long ago. How else could I have lived for forty years in America."

Having disposed of the young dead, and America, Santayana let others fight his wars and died at a very ripe old age, housed, comforted and fed by strangers of a still not too sparse world.

One of the willing was William Faulkner, very young and eager to fly in the war. "I had seen an aeroplane and my mind was filled with names: Ball and Immelman and Boelcke and Guynemer and Bishop, and I was waiting, biding, until I could get to France and become glorious and beribboned too."

He never got to fly in France, or in any war.

Americans on leave in Paris were to learn to call casually for calvados, marc, brandy on the Faubourg Saint-Martin, as easily as they once had asked for a chocolate soda on Main Street, USA. They even smoked Gauloises when they had to instead of their own Camels or Piedmonts. And to the officers the wearing of a wristwatch was no longer the sign of a sissy.

These Americans had helped reelect Woodrow Wilson, whose posters read, WHO KEEPS US OUT OF WAR? WHO EXTENDED THE PARCEL POST? They learned the enemy were Krauts, Huns, Boches, Fritz, and Heinies. Body louse was the cootie. Short Arm Inspections were army regulations for exhibition of one's genitals to see if romance had turned to clap. And the wood and canvas planes of the *Escadrille Lafayette* seemed so flimsy and small for becoming a hero up there in that big baby-blue sky.

By 1916 there were enough hearty or foolish volunteer American fliers in Paris for the French, in April, to form the *Escadrille Américaine*. At least it was more American than Grog *Américain* or Lobster *Américain*. The officers and ground crew were French. It was in business at Luxeuil-les-Bains, near leaves in Paris. The German Embassy in Washington protested at neutrals fighting for France. *Escadrille des Volontaires* was suggested as a substitute title. It finally became the *Escadrille Lafayette*. The first unit contained thirty-eight Americans. Those who couldn't get in joined the French as members of the Lafayette Flying Corps. In both units over two hundred Americans went to war. Later, in February of 1918, the *Escadrille Lafayette* was absorbed by the U.S. Air Force and became the 103rd Pursuit Squadron.

Norman Prince, an American expatriate in Paris, got the plan rolling. Prince was backed by Dr. Edmund L. Gros, the Paris organizer of the American Ambulance Service. The problem was Washington, and the solution was "Don't tell them we're organized." The Americans did not swear allegiance to France. They were actually privateers. Some Americans in the Legion were transferred to the *Escadrille*.

It was a strange and in some ways a romantically amazing crew. The cynical and depressing talk of the Paris cafés and studios came later. It was in the Twenties before it appeared in print, written by Hemingway, Cummings, and others.

One of the founding group was William Thaw, who had a wacky knee, poor vision, feeble hearing. Others were Elliot Cowdin, James McConnell, Kiffin Rockwell, Victor Chapman, Bert Hall. None had ever fought in the air, but most could somehow—more or less—fly a plane. They were given Nieuports.

They settled in at the Grand Hotel of Luxeuil and began to make life hell for their French officers, Captain Thenault and Lieutenant de Laage de Meux. The flight instructor was Captain Haape. He showed them first where there were emergency landing spots in case the planes proved too balky for them. From French flying groups, Dr. Gros lured over such Americans as Paul Pavelka, Didier Masson, Chouteau Johnson, Raoul Lufbery (these names hardly sounding like old stock Yankees), and Dudley Hill and Clyde Balsley. They were war-blooded stock and able.

Overall, in command, was Captain Thenault. He watched silently as the boys wrecked planes by bad landings and running into hangars. The French public cried out that the damn Americans were living it up in the lap of luxury. The Americans were moved into battle areas around Verdun, where the Germans commanded the air. They took as their insignia a feathered screaming Indian Chief copied from a powder company's trademark, fine painted on their fuselage. This was for real. Thaw nearly bled to death from a bullet wound to a main artery, but spurting blood, he managed to get back to Bar-le-Duc before passing out. Rockwell had his windshield smashed in air battle, which tore his face to bits. Nearly blind, and in agony, he too got back home. Next day, his head was a cocoon of bandages, but he forced himself back into the air.

The boys were unlucky, or perhaps as yet unskilled. Victor Chapman was waylaid by four Germans in the clouds, and got his scalp split. It dug a canyon in his skull. He could not stop the flow of blood. The stabilizing controls of the plane had also been shot away. He just made it to Bar-le-Duc. He was a gory frightening sight, but refused to go to hospital. He only permitted emergency bandaging of his serious wound. The French shrugged their shoulders. Perhaps all this spirit to fight was *"un bon augure."*

Going up as a group under Captain Thenault, Balsley, Rockwell, Clyde, and Prince ran smack into fourteen enemy planes. The Germans circled them like an Indian raiding party, firing all the time. The captain led them in a dash for home. Balsley failed to make his escape and he took on the fourteen Germans. He dove and he banked, trying to give them the slip. They continued to rack him, and one of his legs was torn open. The enemy was using exploding dum dum bullets, in theory out-

lawed for war. Balsley got in the clear, and came down at the airdrome. He could not lift himself from the cockpit. Put in a hospital nearby, he was soon on the road to recovery. His comrades, Chapman, Lufbery, and Prince, getting hold of some fruit, decided to fly to visit Balsley in hospital. In the air, an entire flight of Fokkers jumped them. Chapman's plane went into a burning dive, and hit the earth with fearful impact. Victor Chapman was the first American flier killed in battle. The earnest, worried French decided the Americans were "inexperienced and brash." They were withdrawn from the front and returned to Luxeuil. Here they found fifty Royal Air Force pilots in residence. The Yanks and the Limeys hit it off and bottles passed around, and there was much group singing. Except for taking wounds, the Americans had not been impressive.

On leave in Paris, Lufbery, Hall, and Thaw acquired a snarling lion cub who was promoted to be the squad's mascot and named Whisky. It became a ritual for the Americans to go to Paris on leave, to meet French fliers and to get rid of any remaining Puritan obsessions with the fleshy pleasures available there. A few were said to have visited Gertrude Stein. The madam and her lifelong friend, Alice Toklas, were driving a Model T ambulance.

But the real business of war went on. Rockwell went out of formation in the air to try and get himself a Fokker. The German, diving at over 100 miles an hour, riddled him with the illegal exploding bullets, tearing open Rockwell's throat, mutilating the body in a fearful manner. Photographs of the grim cadaver were sent in protest to Geneva, who did nothing about it. They didn't even appoint a committee, the usual brush-off.

The French decided to put the reckless Americans to escorting bombers. Prince, returning from a flight on a dark night, ran into a high tension wire. His machine spun head-over-teakettle, broke up with tearing sounds. Prince was thrown hard onto the ground. He tried to stand, failed, and discovered both legs were broken. Also his entrails had something wrong with them. He died from internal injuries (and French Army surgery, some claimed) three days later.

The Americans needed replacements; the call was sent from Dr. Gros for volunteers. Fifty showed up. There were those who had been close enough to a plane to touch it. And many who had never seen the inside of a cockpit. The Americans never settled down, but they flew.

The ace of the group turned out to be Raoul Lufbery, who on a cold December day got a German two-seater. Nearby, the great French flier Guynemer shot down his twenty-fifth kill.

The planes they flew were now Spads, with Hispano-Suiza engines that vibrated badly and went weak in power in extreme cold. Landings on icy fields were a problem too. Yet, in January, 1917, Lufbery got his seventh German victory in wind and snow.

There were personalities who were problems. Bert Hall was soon to be sent away to one of the Stork Squadrons. He didn't wear well; his mean and boorish habits, his snide grudges, his ego always trying to outbrag the rest of the group. Put in Coventry, he was to ask for transfer, noting in his diary, "Moved with as little excitement as possible. I hate goodbyes . . . glad to get rid of me. I don't blame them."

Most likely, Hall was too worldly wise, world weary, with a sense of being a rogue in a world of dupes.

It was the tradition—and still is to some historians—to present the air heroes as sterling characters, dedicated to duty and to liberty and country, almost without fault, and modest in behavior. Oh, there was local color added at times, of a little carousing on leave, a lifting of a skirt, or a bottle to release tensions. In the main the individual was outstanding, and many were. But not all.

Bert Hall was a drifter, what used to be called "a soldier of fortune," which could mean an international tramp, a confidence man seeking a free bed, picking his way through life with his eye on the easy dollar, the excitement of trying to get by in charm, storytelling, and never settling down for long. Of Hall it can be said, almost anything could be made of his life; according to what version of his past one wanted to believe. He bragged, he slurred his speech, suggesting a dozen settings for birth, for background.

Basing our information of his past on what he said, he could claim to be born in Kentucky, vaguely about 1880. Or he could say the place of his birth was Higgenville, Missouri. He might have flown and fought in the Turkish-Bulgarian war in 1912; on either side, as his stories changed as to just whom he was flying for in the Balkans. Next night, he could relate he had been at the bloody Battle of Mons with Kitchener's army, which, with his help, saved England. Yet at the same time, if one compared dates, he also claimed to be in the French Foreign Legion, having been in from the start of the war, from August to December of 1914.

He wrote of his adventures as a soldier and flier, but no account is trustworthy. If one began to like him, and wonder perhaps if some of all this yarning was true, he would come up with information that he had guided Dr. Cook, the notorious imposter, to the North Pole. As Cook was proved never to have reached the Pole, Hall must have done it alone.

His collection of medals was amazing. Many were of Orders rare and hardly known. He did shoot down three Germans while with the Americans, to get the *Médaille militaire* and Croix de Guerre. Yet before that, when this war-tested flier transferred from the Legion to the French Air Force, it was discovered he hardly knew one end of a plane from the other. He did become a flier after training, and in time was taken in by the *Escadrille Américaine* in April of 1916. However, his past, either the fiction or the true facts, was catching up with him. The French Secret Service kept close surveillance on him, being sure he was a German spy. Two French Army Intelligence men, posing as student fliers slept in beds on either side of Bert Hall, in case he went out at night to signal the enemy, or perhaps give away secrets in his sleep. Intelligence Services, as we know, are not too intelligent at times, and there was never any evidence that Hall was anything but a blow-hard sponger and a liar on the grand scale.

The Americans with whom Hall flew found him a bit too lucky shooting crap or handling a deck of poker cards, and it was almost impossible to get him to sign for bar or mess chits. The usual explanation given of his departure is that he was "invited" to leave the squadron, with hints it was better than being booted out on his well-traveled arse.

A new recruit was Edmund Genet, descended from that citizen Genet sent to America by the French revolutionary government and who never went home again. Young Genet went AWOL from the U.S. Navy, joined the Foreign Legion, and then got into the air force. He wrote his mother, "If anything does happen to me, you all surely can feel better satisfied with the end than if I was sent to pieces by a shell or put out by a bullet in the infantry, where there are seventy-five out of a hundred possibilities of your never hearing of it. The glory is well worth the loss. I'd rather die as an aviator over the enemy's lines than find a nameless, shallow grave in the infantry."

Enemy anti-aircraft guns killed him, the first American killed after America entered the war. U.S. Army red tape listed Genet as a deserter. After the war, his name was cleared.

CHAPTER 45

Between Leaves in Paris

I N his privately printed book, *A Flier's War*, "W. W. Windstaff," an
American who flew with the RAF, tried to get to Paris on leave as
often as he could. What his life was like while dreaming of Paris in a declining ardor, many Americans also felt.

The lie was the Germans in the air or on the ground weren't as good as we
were, weren't fighting up to snuff any more. Of course, the generals, sitting
snug on their prostates in their big Rolls Royces with an aide carefully putting
the woolen rug over their legs and paunches, insisted that Sacrifice was Glory.
It was for Civilization, for Mankind. We fliers were pretty sick of abstractions:
Vaterland, Freedom, Democracy, the King, the Prince of Wales (poor, creepy
young bastard in his tight little uniform, his sleepy eyes half open, moving
down a safe trench and shaking hands with little undernourished Cockneys). It
was all a bloody sell-out, and we fliers now were aware of it.

And as I flew I wasn't buying Father O'Bein, or Church of England's Cecil,
or Rabbi Haukfliesh and all their fine moral promises and splendid dogmas.
Because there were O'Beins and Cecils and Haukflieshs on the other side, too.
God in that war was divided from his crotch to his eyebrows. He promised
victory through O'Bein, etc., to those who had the faith. I didn't have faith,
only a hatred of official cant. I was becoming an alcoholic, I had crabs, two
cavities in my back teeth. At times I couldn't control the twitch on my face.
My hands had a tremor. I had murdered half a dozen Germans or Austrians or
Roumanians who were out to murder me. And almost everything John and

Chunky and I had believed in as boys was *merde*—plain shit. Fortunately for me I went raving, flaming mad when it got too much. But that came later. I always thought I faked it beautifully—the grimaces, the twitching, the filthy language. But several doctors told me, "No, old boy, you had really gone off your rocker."

After Chunky (another American) went down in flames with nothing left to bury, flying became a horror to us old crocks. We were soon, we were told, going to be withdrawn from the advance airdrome. As we drank our *café-marc* and waited, the war increased in rumors, fury, deadlines. I was leading young English fliers, who barely seemed to understand the theory of it, while the Germans were in a bad way, too, desperately sending staffels of twelve machines out against every patrol, using the Hakberstadt fighter to good advantage, a machine that pulled up in a loop so fast we seemed to be walking.

I'd come in from patrol, goggled eyes still full of pirouetting, burning planes, and the dirty, dusty fields of summer where we were stationed still within sound of the front where the Americans were moving up under their tin hats, faces like the ones I once knew at home in high school. I felt like yelling, "What are you stupid bastards doing here?" But I was developing British phlegm and secret grievances.

Tony, an American who had grown melancholy at missing women, and played all day on a shrill gramophone a recording of Schubert, taught me a bit of Yiddish, and took up the violin, which he played well, but in a gloomy manner.

John (a schoolmate) was flying in a unit fifty miles up the line with the dog Fritz he had inherited when Chunky went, as his only companion in the cockpit. John had threatened his C.O. with a Very pistol cartridge up his arse when the C.O. tried to force on the squadron a plane with elevator controls the factories had put in wrong.

John wrote me, "It's a very starchy war for our Limeys, but you get up there among the cumulous clouds in an F.E.II with the 250 h.p. Rolls Royce engine and they can keep the old crazy worn-down earth. There's a whole universe unused. Say, you long-haired bastard, you ever read *Faust? We fear the blows we never get. And those things we never lose, is what we lament.* Damn good for a Heinie. Faust differs from all other intellectuals in that he hunted experience, besides knowledge. To hold life in total vision is damn hard. If we can get poor Chunky's auto working, we'll come down maybe to your field soon with some native fellows we've been bunking with, of the 12ième Groupe d'Escadrilles de la Chasse, the French elite squadron. Only we call them the Storks. I'm in a bad way, as the poet Hafiz said, Who can't drink, can't love. I've got an ulcer the Doc thinks. No letter from Sue, who is now some place in the Near East with the Red." John wrote, "I don't know, Bill, I'm scared."

That set me back on my heels a bit, solid John cracking.

Tony and I were taking up a wing of twelve. The trouble was that usually there was a strong wind from the west, so that if we took our sucklings, just out of solo school, too far over the German lines and a dog fight broke us up, they'd drift so far east in their excitement, they'd never have the petrol to make it back. They were all as eager as bridegrooms who had read it all in a book. But green, green, *green*.

The Germans had their Aviatik two-seaters out, and we had no back up at all in the air except from the *Escadrille Lafayette* at Bar-le-Duc. We didn't get on too well with them. They had been the *Escadrille Américaine*. N.124, flying the Vosges sector. They felt it was not playing the old ball game for Tony and me to be flying with the lousy Limeys when we could fly with them, real solid American he-men, who were going into the Hat-In-The-Ring group, USA. But they could fly, and could die.

Tony in his flying pants, unshaved, eyes bloodshot, was to fly wing for me and the sucklings. The planes snorted and stank on the flying field, hustling at their wheel blocks, the castor oil a fearful odor, blue smoke tossing pebbles among the dying weeds. I got in my crate, raised my hand to get in the saddle, and we took off into the rising day, bluish shadows in the plane trees we just got over, the air warm as English beer, the day still dark to the east.

The sun was slanting on our left as we wheeled up and up in case the *Staffel* of the late Herr Immelmann were in a paranoiac mood and were hunting our ass. I let the air stream clear my head. I hoped to endure, with care. I was living on coffee, raw eggs and brandy again, and any day I hoped to hear the major say I'd been elevated out of combat and could go to a nice rest in London. Bathe, see a doctor about my nerves, get my teeth fixed, read a book.

Tony was wagging his wing. To the far left I saw were a herd of *Drachen*, German kite balloons up to observe and direct artillery fire. I signaled no. We had to ride a contact patrol with some land action. And the *Drachen* were protected by nasty A.A. fire, and Woleff's and Schafter's pilots lurked some place in the clouds nearby to take care of the foolish fighter who was sucked in by balloons.

I gave my Lewis guns a burst to clear them for action. They often jammed. I was thinking that this horse's nuts air fighting we were doing had no real military value, merely anonymous butchery that the press wrote up, when zam! we walked right into it. The clouds having drifted away, we were blinded by the sun. In two layers, red painted triplane Fokkers were down on us; black crosses and mean. They had been stacked just above the cloud bank. My sucklings ganged up like nervous hens. I dumped my retrospective thoughts, kicked the rudder, went into a roll, saw the babies under my wing try and follow. Tony pulled up in a loop, always a crazy fine flier, and he came around and to the left, firing in bursts. A red-nosed Boche went down and around, wind screaming like a fury through his wires.

A dog fight is a rocketing chaos; I had enough to do chasing tails. Some of the Huns' new planes were firing one pound pom poms. I saw one of my babies go crazy in a tailspin and pour black smoke and come apart. I suppose he

forgot his belt for he fell out screaming, but I was in trouble myself. I put on rudder without banking. I had two enemies, one above me and one below in the blind spot, where it was pumping slugs into me. I could feel canvas and wood splinter and tear, and I prayed ohshitandpiss, if I get it now, give it to me a fast one right through my brain or heart, as I gave a few. No burning, no falling, falling to mash into a field. ("He fell at dawn on a clear quiet day") I kept the trigger finger ready, and kicked up and let the top Hun feel my guns. I let go half a drum, twenty-four rounds, but he ate it all and I knew it wasn't my day. I jabbed at the rudder bar, pushed the stick over and went into a steep dive. But they followed me down. The unshaved bastard behind his goggled eyes was staring at me. I panicked, but my deep inner nerves—who didn't give a damn about my surface ones—they told me what to do and how to do it.

I took a quick look in the blue quadrangle of sky. My flight had blown apart. Some of my babies were scattered, or falling burning or breaking up. Tony—I hunted his ship—he had a thumb-on-nose insignia painted on his fuselage. He was flying far below, near the treetops, dodging three Heinies on his tail, trying to lure them low enough to crash them into the ground. I didn't see more. I was off to the north and they east, the horizon spinning like a fever dream, trying to get clear. One bastard clung just below in the blind zone, and I knew if I kept on going east, I'd run into *Jagdstaffel* interceptors.

I remembered an old bike racing trick John and I had once worked out when we rode for Sunday prizes. I poured on coal to get a black exhaust, suddenly stalled and went down tail first, hoping I could get out of it in time. The Hun shot out in front of me. I came out of the dive, roared up and around and over him. I fired the rest of the drum, put in another drum (try it sometimes if you ever find an old Camel in a museum) working stick, rudder, your elevator controls, feeling the oil gage drop—one hand loading, wind tearing at you, the Hun circling to get behind and below.

And he had me. My motor sounded like a grease-spitting iron skillet frying flounders.

It's marvelous for your nerves, dying in a sodden sun. Makes you think, repent, shrinks your scrotum. I could feel the plane shudder as he fired short bursts but lots of them. Then there was the sound of a Klaxon (we carried them to signal ground patrols) and a big blue fighter with English oval insignia was to the left of us. It had two fixed Vickers guns firing through the air screw, and the Hun just went up into an exploding rose. Breaking at once into fragments. The blue Nieuport wagged its wings. I made a feeble superfluous gesture of thanks—held my hands in prayer position. Then it was that I felt my right leg and hip burn, and I put down a glove furtively to investigate. It came up smeared with black blood. Funny, I hadn't felt it during my funk. I gave a curdled smile. Was I dead or out of the war?

I didn't think I could make it back to the field, so I began to look for a place to bring down my ruptured duck, oil spitting in my face. I couldn't work the rudder, so I used the tail surface for some kind of wearing around and the engine was pissing hot rusty liquid in three places. I couldn't see and the goggles were smeared. I pulled them off It was a fun day and I didn't want to bleed to death at two thousand feet. Tony kept above me on guard, and I came down hard—too hard in the front line trenches of a Canadian outfit, The Princess Pats. A colonel with the A.D.C. said it was a damn improper landing when they brought me through the wire. I smiled and said, "That's right." I passed out there and woke up in hospital with a little New York City doctor shouting: "Beautiful, beautiful. It's a hip wonderful to work on. Give the *povero diavolo* another whiff of ether, Miss Bedpan." I fell way down into happiness and quoted Buddha to myself: "The sword follows space without exertion to the wound." I felt good. The war was over for me. I was a human being again. I hoped the wonderful wop didn't take off the leg; my last thought was, how embarrassing to get into bed with a woman with my leg off—sorry baby, this is all of me. The ether sang in my head. Survival is all. . . .

Book Six
EN FIN DE COMPTE

CHAPTER 46

Scott

A fool is a protector of the wise.

ST. AUGUSTINE

WHAT made post-World War I Paris such an added joy to Americans who wanted to stay on was the low cost of living there in the Twenties and part of the Thirties. It helped the sheer *allégresse* of creating or padded the afflicting blight of inertia.

Morley Callaghan figured out that in 1921 he got to Paris with a scholarship worth $1,000 (about 12,000 francs), and he and his wife lived on that for a year with about $500 in added earnings. "We sat in cafés and rode in taxis, though we could not give American tips; and at the end of the second year, after paying our debts and buying our passage, we arrived in New York with exactly five dollars. By that time it seemed that everyone in Greenwich Village had heard the good news and was planning to live abroad."

Then the *littérateur*, the *bon viveur*, the drifter got a shock. In 1933 the United States went off the gold standard, and the bubble of easy living on less burst in Paris. The Epicure and the Spartan both felt it. The rate of exchange was bad news, living cost more, and old settlers and newcomers to art or frivolity found they had to go back home. The money game of paper and metal as played by the international banking men, and turned into rooms and food and fun, just didn't work as it once had for the Americans. The trek home began, to a nation in trouble, with heads of families handling WPA shovels and Okies fleeing the dust storms, millions unemployed.

The ex-Parisians began hording nostalgia as if it were old Brownie snapshots. A recent letter to this writer from one of those Americans who did nothing much in Paris, though there for years, contains some information of what happened afterward. "It was speak-easies and backseat screwing in the Twenties; Marxist cells and group theater in the Thirties; London and Paris hangovers in the Forties; alcohol and rest homes and second wives in the Fifties; black is sassy and beautiful, and Social Security in the Sixties . . . *en fin de compte.*"

Breaking through the hard shell of symbolism that has become the lives and times of the F. Scott Fitzgeralds in the Twenties, one discovers the fact that if Paris helped many Americans write or paint or compose with more ease, it helped ruin both Fitzgeralds. The fine life did much to limit the output of a writer who many think was the most gifted of his generation, and one who did less with his talents.

One catches a close-up of the two Americans living it up in Paris in a quick portrait of them as Morley Callaghan comes to call on them for the first time. "In that light he looked like the handsome, slender, fine-featured man whose picture I had so often seen, whose profile, in fact, appeared to be copied again and again by magazine illustrators. The vestibule light touched Zelda's blond hair. A handsome woman, her features were as regular as Scott's."

For all his gifts, Scott was to produce very little that came from the deep, solid core of his endowment: *The Great Gatsby*, parts of *Tender is the Night*, and a half dozen splendid stories among the 200 or so he wrote, mostly for *The Saturday Evening Post*. "May Day," "The Rich Boy," and the bittersweet short narrative of "Babylon Revisited"—a return to Paris of one of the Lost Generation when it was all over in the dank Thirties and the Depression had changed everything. It is the saddest and most beautiful of all his memories of Paris when the glow was gone. The hero at last finds a well-remembered bar, now "strange and portentous. It was not an American bar any more . . . It had gone back into France."

Edward Dahlberg had written, "A painter hangs his paintings but a writer can only hang himself." Scott's rope was alcohol—even back in 1925, when it had seemed impossible the time of crepuscular decay, madness, and writer's block would ever come to the golden pair. The Fitzgeralds lived then in a grand apartment, a disordered place but expensive, on the Rue de Tilsitt. They gave parties, took people to drink at the Ritz, to lunch on the Champs Elysées, did all those crazy things, too often retold, while drunk with the *flâneurs* and millionaire whores and fairies; when sobering up, told while posing with their daughter Scottie and saying crisp bright things to quote in the Sunday papers back home as the "historian of the Jazz age" (Scott knew almost nothing of the real jazz).

In a fragment, not intended for publication, Scott caught the easy depravity and wonder of their lives, the wounds made without nails: "Then six of us, oh, the best the noblest relics of the evening . . . were riding on top of thousands of carrots in a market wagon, the carrots smelling fragrant and sweet with earth in their beards—riding through the darkness to the Ritz Hotel and in and through the lobby—no, that couldn't have happened but we were in the lobby and the bought concierge had gone for a waiter for breakfast and champagne."

Like most Americans the Fitzgeralds' Paris of Citroen horns, gendarmes, waiters, concierges, was mostly the Sixth Arrondissement of the city's twenty. Their world ran from the Seine to the Boulevard Montparnasse, with some spillage (*faire le diable à quatre*) over into the Fourteenth Arrondissement. Americans crowded the cafés and *estaminets*, the little galleries on the Rue Bonaparte, the hotels good and bad, grand or sleazy (*sleazy*, a popular word of the period along with such terms as *nifty*, *ritzy*, *snazzy*). If not the Ritz or an apartment on Rue Royale, then attics called studios would do. If there were children, behind the Louvre were the Luxembourg Gardens where one could walk

and wee-wee them; where—does one really believe Hemingway—when hungry for bloody meat, one could kill pigeons with a slingshot? *Il n'est cher que d'appétit.*

Scott early saw Hemingway's genius, and in return for that interest Hemingway took Scott to meet Gertrude. Scott brought out his great charm, which he had when sober; he could be a mean and nasty, destructive drunk. Gertrude liked what Scott said of her work. In time she wrote he was "the only one of the young writers who wrote naturally in sentences."

Hemingway was always meeting people and dropping people; in time he could drop whole groups by pointing out: "Many people went to the cafés at the corner of the Boulevard Montparnasse and the Boulevard Raspail to be seen publicly and in a way such places anticipated the columnists as a daily substitute for immortality."

Certainly Sinclair Lewis at times was at his worst in Paris, even later with his second wife, the burly Brunhilda, Miss Dorothy Thompson, who called him Hal, and castrated him in public. Lewis, often already drunk before arriving, loved the cafés, sitting as if on a duck egg, or leaning on a cane, talking, talking away; a kind of overkeyed elf with a scar-tissue face, eyes as blue as a Siamese cat's, he the creator of American images that the loafers and *flâneurs* at the Dôme and the Rotonde agreed with as being "the real stuff." The intellectual bourgeoisie of Europe also saw his people as the real stuff; Babbitt, Gantry, and Dodsworth. The critics might belittle Lewis, but a man who could etch such copious figures into literature as permanent types was a better artist than his detractors. As with the Fitzgeralds, Paris did Lewis little good and some harm. Basically at times they were Mid-western yokels.

E. E. Cummings caught the innocent, the fun, the pleasant alcoholic side of the American's reaction to Paris.

> make me a child, stout hurdysturdy-
>   gurdyman
> waiter, make me a child. So this is
>   Paris.
> i will sit in the corner and drink
>   thinks and think drinks.

CHAPTER 47

Last Days of Gertrude and Alice

Why is life so tragic; so like a little strip of pavement
over an abyss? I look down; I feel giddy; I wonder
how I am ever to walk to the end.

VIRGINIA WOOLF

AND FAME in all its fireworks and laurels came at last to Gertrude, came as noted with a popular simple book of some small literary merit, the *Alice* book. Fame that came nearly too late. In her younger days Gertrude had often written all night and published almost nothing. She never did publish during her lifetime *Things As They Are*, written in 1903, a Radcliffe girl's Lesbian love story, and the rest of her manuscripts had to wait.

Gertrude's sensual life became calmer when Alice moved in, to provide what Virgil Thomson called "a fertile soil of sentimental security in which other friendships great and small could come to flower."

When young, Gertrude had smoked cigars like General Grant, eaten with relish and no attention to her weight *poularde normande, ris de veau, terrine de canard,* and enjoyed wine. But with fame, from the age of fifty until her death, she ate little, did not smoke or drink.

Alice guarded her: "I'm sorry, Lovey, it wasn't like that at all." "All right, Pussy," Gertrude would say, "you tell it."

Gertrude was five feet two and at first, some felt, nearly as wide. In time she grew thin, showed bone structure; her head lost its padding and the skull began to push out. By the Twenties she had cropped her hair short—Alice had cut it for her—and she wore it often brushed forward, a lock of it in the middle of her forehead.

People feared Alice, who was an inch or two taller than Gertrude, but Thorton Wilder, one of Gertrude's young men, insisted "Alice was merely the dragon protecting the treasure."

Gertrude died in 1946. Alice, alone, began to write. Her cookbook contained the recipes already referred to for *Hashish Fudge*—"two pieces are enough." In her written memory of Gertrude's death she reports: "I sat next to her, and she said to me early in the afternoon, "What is the answer?" I was silent. "In that case," she said, "what is the question?"

And so Gertrude died at seventy-two. The dialogue seems too pat, and no other witness present reports the last words, so proper and fitting for a home-grown enigma.

Life was lonely for Alice with Gertrude gone. Money short, she had to sell Picasso drawings Gertrude willed her. She became embroiled with Gertrude's relatives in court over the twenty-eight Picasso paintings in the collection left her in trust. The collection of cubist works, consigned to a bank vault, went to Gertrude's relatives. Alice Toklas became a Roman Catholic, anxiously asking her priest, "Will this allow me to *see* Gertrude when I die?" She lived alone her remaining years, bedridden, arthritic, having contact only with her maid Yacinta. In 1966 she died, eighty-nine and alone, in Paris.

Gertrude and Alice were luckier than most of the "lost generation." They reached old age. Paris was good to them.

But not to the poet Hart Crane, who wrote of his stay there: "Dinners, soirées, poets, erratic millionaires, painters, translations, lobsters, absinthe, music, promenades, oysters, sherry, aspirin, pictures, Sapphic heiresses, editors, books, sailors. And How!" And then he beat a waiter, knocked over a Paris gendarme, for which he got a week in jail.

Harry Crosby promised to kill himself by "October 31, 1942," by stepping from a plane into a French forest, but long before that date Harry instead put a bullet into his head. Crane had written for both of them, as "one of those emotional derelicts who are nothing but tremulous jellyfish might-have-beens."

Overdocumented, in fact overexposed and overwritten by second-rate authors was the decline and fall of Scott and Zelda Fitzgerald, of what Hemingway called their "festive conception of life." Their Paris visits were no longer cheerful, and when Zelda had a love affair with a French flier named Jozan, Fitzgerald felt something once valid had gone forever from his life. He did not agree with those who blamed their much published crack-ups to her alone. "We ruined ourselves," he wrote to Zelda.

"I have never honestly thought that we ruined each other." As for her, she confessed, "All I want is to be very young always and very irresponsible."

But as she sank into madness, she was no longer the girl of whom it was said, "She lived on the cream at the top of the bottle." Fitzgerald, himself an Irish Puritan under all his posing, felt "sometimes I don't know whether Zelda isn't a character I created myself."

As their visits to Paris grew shorter or were curtailed, Scott's heaviest drinking and Zelda's mounting schizophrenia in her final breakdown in 1930 coincided with the Great Depression. With dreadful fascination Fitzgerald followed her down, like a ghoul with a notebook, charting her sad journey, material for his novel *Tender is the Night*.

The sporting girl seemed to accept her disintegration. As she herself wrote: "We grew up founding our dreams on the infinite promise of American advertising . . . that one can learn to play the piano by mail and that mud will give you a perfect complexion . . . and then never again to know the good gone times when we still believed in summer hotels and the philosophies of popular songs."

When Fitzgerald died, much out of place in that addled Valhalla,

Hollywood, she could only say, "Life seemed so promissory always when he was around." In 1948 she died in a sanitarium fire in Asheville, North Carolina. In some valid moment before the fire she had uttered her last message to the world, "Don't worry . . . I'm not afraid to die."

The Fitzgeralds were never able to accept the text for survival of Edith Wharton, who had stayed on in Paris.

"There are lots of ways of being miserable, but there's only one way of being comfortable, and that is to stop running round after happiness. If you make up your mind not to be happy, there's no reason why you shouldn't have a fairly good time."

CHAPTER 48

Americans with Music—
Harris, Thomson, etc.

In art there are no generations, only
individuals; all times have been modern.

NADIA BOULANGER

You are an expatriate, see?
You hang around cafés.

ERNEST HEMINGWAY

JUST HOW MANY Americans were living in Paris, how many hung out in the cafés, no one will ever know for sure. The American Chamber of Commerce in Herbert Hoover's time, in 1927, figured in some way not fully explained that there were 15,000 Americans living in Paris. Perhaps, it was pointed out, they were only counting people doing business in Paris, not artists. The police said there were 35,000 Americans residing in Paris in 1927. They must have been counting the kind of people the U.S. Chamber of Commerce didn't think worth adding up: painters, writers, composers, plain loafers, who could say to be betrayed at least proves we still exist. All those who sat on the *terrasses* of the Café Du Dôme, Le Select, La Rotonde drinking *marc-cassis*. These cafés and the American Express, where one could pick up checks from home, were best liked by the Montparnasse Americans. Some were poets like Stephen Vincent Benét, who remembered his roots and the American genocide of the Indians.

> I shall not rest in Montparnasse . . .
> I shall not be there, I shall rise and pass
> Bury my heart in Wounded Knee . . .

While a great deal has been printed and gossiped about the writers who found their style or their souls in Paris, the musicians have been only vaguely known, or made into minor figures by the writers of memoirs. American musicians hungered for news of Satie, Nadia Boulanger, the Ballet Russe of Sergei Diaghilev, the new sounds of Debussy and Ravel. The amenities of musical controversy drew young Americans to Paris. From the first notes of *Petrouchka* in 1911, *Le Sacre du Printemps* in 1913 (the latter caused a riot on its first playing) to the final cheers and bravos for *Daphnis et Chloé, L'Après-Midi d'un Faune*. It seemed Paris was making all the right new sounds. The artist could cry, "We are the taste-manipulators, open your ears!"

Virgil Thomson came out of Harvard to run away to Paris from his German music teachers. George Antheil came, Aaron Copland ("For me abroad inevitably meant Paris"). All found the air freer and living costing just a little less. Only the most pessimistic American gave up and went home if he could stay.

In 1918 there was talk of an American Conservatory of Music at Fontainebleau, for American students to spend summers with French teachers to acquire experience and the consciousness of new ideas. By 1921 the school was open in an old palace and first in line as a student was Aaron Copland. Later he and Virgil Thomson and Melville Smith were the first Americans to study with the great Nadia Boulanger, sultana of musical sensitiveness. Studying with Nadia—to the musical world—was the Good Housekeeping Seal of Approval in Modern Music. Copland admitted: "I arrived fresh out of Brooklyn, twenty, and all agog. . . . Her intellectual interest . . . [was] an important stimulus to her American students." She had an irreducible uniqueness, multiple qualities for searching out true talent.

In 1926 she gave a concert of chamber music by American composers, work of her pupils. Roy Harris gave a performance of his Concerto for Piano, Clarinet, and String Quartet. Harris was frontier-Oklahoma by birth, small-town California by growth, before he got to France and Nadia. "Going to Paris was the best thing I ever did. I was just a truck driver then, and had written my first works out of the fullness of my ignorance . . . She said there were three kinds of music students: the kind who had money and no talent, and those she took; the kind who had talent and no money, and those she took; and the third kind had money and talent and those she never got."

Hardly true. Nadia had diverse, conflicting levels of consciousness. She was half Russian and half Gallic, and she could brew up a storm when some pupil didn't seem to follow her tyrannical sway. For the presentation of Harris' Concerto the "best clarinet player in the world" turned up drunk. But he played his part perfectly. He wouldn't have dared do otherwise under Nadia's eye.

George Gershwin could hardly be called a Parisian of long habit, yet his popular *American in Paris* has given him a false position as a musical historian of a mood. Actually when he wrote an *American in Paris* in 1928, he had come over as a tourist to hear his *Rhapsody in Blue* and Concerto in F being played at the Paris Opéra. He wrote *American in Paris*, first draft, in New York before coming over, and finished it after going back and hearing the taxi horns. His program note states the music opens "in typical French style, in the manner of Debussy and The Six . . . to portray the impression of an American visitor to Paris as he strolls about the city . . . listens to various street noises." Some critics have called the music of "great vivacity, but superficial." Gershwin aspired to sonorous eulogies and wrote fine popular songs.

Because the writers created most of the impressions of Americans in Paris in those days, they seem more interesting than the musicians. But the *enfant terrible*, George Antheil, was the equal of Hemingway or Gertrude Stein in attracting attention with an absurdity of nihilism. George was twenty-two when he came to Paris, short, thin, brash, and loud. He carried a pistol in a holster under his evening clothes and would often take it out and place it on the piano when performing in public, the way a poker player in a big game of the old West would place his Colt .45 in plain view to show that he'd stand for no monkey business. George had played piano over most of Europe after coming from Trenton, New Jersey. He was admired by many experts as having great promise. Stravinsky set up a concert for George in Paris, but the young man delayed because a Hungarian girl named Boske with whom he was involved couldn't get a visa to join him and he needed her for her flattering unction to his art. He got to Paris in June, 1923, and cried out, "This is the city of Stravinsky's music!" Hardly news by then, even to the ordinary citizen aware of the city's obsessive cults of art.

George went to work on his *Ballet Mécanique*; his fame rests on that with the public, those who remember him at all. It was scored for eight pianos, a player piano, drums, xylophones, airplane propellers, and other mechanical noisemakers. It was art to some, ubiquitous vulgarity to others. The concert "got catcalls and booing, shrieking and whistling, shouts of 'thief' mixed with 'bravos.' People began to call each other names and forgot there was any music going on." Like so much avant-garde work it was the true stuff only to a small group of social status seekers and to the deep thinkers of the day.

It looked as if George Antheil were going to become the greatest thing in music since the invention of the violin. But George's fame and glory did not last. Platitudes burst like soap bubbles, fame dribbled away. In New York City the *Ballet Mécanique* failed to impress. The all-Antheil concert at Carnegie Hall, in 1927, was looked upon as more of a circus act than the arrival of a musical god. Soon George was a has-been, as Elliot Paul said, "wearing his halo around his balls." George admitted he was corrupted by his first successes. "I had become a mere imitator of the latest and most elegant Parisian (and most decadent), the most recent neoclassicism."

Paris, although more sympathetic to new art than any other city, was a difficult one in which to hold one's artistic integrity. One senses in George's yelps of pain and bowed head the rejected artist, the bitter hemlock of one who had so much within his grasp, yet somehow it got away, an Abraham howling at Sodom, fingers in his ears. George used his own failure to damn *all* that Paris could do for the artist, and he pointed out how bad was that flavor of Paris that some took away with them. "How effete my taste had become in Paris! How effete still were the tastes of my colleagues who had dragged too much of their Paris studies and taste home with them!"

George Antheil ended up in Hollywood writing scores for films, his talent twitching like a damaged muscle; hack work that echoes little of the promise that had excited Paris and its musical critics. George had read William Blake on how one sells out to the *Vegetation*: "This World of Imagination is the World of Eternity; it is the divine bosom into which we shall go after the death of the Vegetated body. This World of Imagination is Infinite & Eternal, whereas the World of Generation, or Vegetation, is Finite & Temporal."

Some stayed on in Paris and husbanded their talent. "On my arrival in 1921 I had become a Parisian instantaneously. Paris was where I felt most at home." So wrote Virgil Thomson, small, round, neat, a composer and critic, who in gratuitous grace wrote the music for Gertrude Stein's opera *Four Saints in Three Acts*. Thomson came over with the Harvard Glee Club. The Glee Club went home after two weeks in Paris, but he stayed on and began the serious study of music. Paris was like some strange foray into the bloodstream. He took lessons from Nadia Boulanger in counterpoint and harmony, and organ lessons from her at the *Ecole Normale de Musique*. He lived on the Rue de Bernie, back of the Gare Saint-Lazare, in a hotel some Americans called a whorehouse. He got a piano up to his small room; he strolled to the hangout of the music students, *Le Boeuf sur le Toit*. Thomson expanded, studied, composed. "I felt at home with France, its music, food, its people, its reading and writing." After the first love, he knew in time, there is no other. No place ever touched him like Paris.

Virgil Thomson was to be a Parisian, with time off for work in America, until 1940, when the Germans were ready to pounce on the city. To help himself live in France he wrote on the music scene for the *Boston Transcript* and the magazine *Vanity Fair*. He gave piano lessons when he had to. His first $500 lasted him seven months, then he lived around "more or less on nothing." He studied and composed, his work being performed around Paris.

In 1926 came Thomson's meeting with Gertrude Stein. George Antheil brought him into the Stein circle. Alice sensed a rival for the affection of Gertrude. "Virgil Thomson she found very interesting although I did not like him," wrote Alice. However it never came to a duel, or a quivering palsy of passion. Gertrude liked being courted. She didn't have much musical sense or appreciation. She still thought "The Trail of the Lonesome Pine" "as pleasing as the heart of a melon and pretty good music." Thomson played Satie's *Socrate* for her. He began to put some of Gertrude's work to music. He had to walk with care. Gertrude could repudiate you, read you out of her circle at any hint you hadn't a keen perception of her genius, no lathering of praise was too soapy for her. She once broke with Thomson by sending him her calling card with the note, "Miss Stein declines further acquaintance with Mr. Thomson."

They didn't speak for some years, but Thomson went on working on *Four Saints in Three Acts*. In private Gertrude could feel with Baudelaire: "I cultivate my hysteria with joy and terror."

Thomson and his music were becoming known; he had some fame in the world outside the narrow inner circle. There were concerts. He now could live in a flat—not a brothel room—on the Quai Voltaire on the Left Bank in a fine eighteenth-century building, just across the way from the Louvre. There were yellow draperies at the windows and paintings on the walls by some of his friends, none of great importance except for a Hans Arp. It was here Thomson began to work seriously on *Four Saints*. Gertrude's favorite saints (she a Jewish atheist) were Saint Francis of Assisi, Saint Teresa of Avila, and Saint Ignatius Loyola; and a few more she dusted off. None of this mattered, as the text of the opera is merely an excuse—something to put music to and to provide a reason for stage decor. For singers it was decided to use an all Negro cast and they could have recited the New York telephone book for text; the inherent empti-

ness of the words never tripped the music. Gertrude wanted each saint "surrounded by younger saints learning the trade" as if they were plumbers' apprentices. Thomson called it "an oratorio about an opera," which seems fair. The value of the words can be judged from the following:

> How many acts are there in it.
> How many saints in all.
> How many acts are there in it.
> Ring around a rosey . . .

Gertrude did not claim the last line was original with her. By July of 1929 the opera was finished, but it didn't get onto a stage until 1934. A museum director at Harvard, A. Everett Austin, president of The Friends and Enemies of Modern Music, "felt *Four Saints* was just the right project to open a new wing of the museum at Hartford, Connecticut." The decor and setting were done with intoxicated ardor by a society painter, Florine Stettheimer, a sort of primitive in mink, who liked fluffy, shiny, slinky material. The sets and costumes were mostly made of cellophane, lace, feathers, glass beads. Thomson picked Negro singers because "they move so beautifully. And they understand Gertrude Stein." The opera was a success. Carl Van Vechten wrote: "I haven't seen a crowd more excited since *Sacre du Printemps*." Which was stretching it a bit as the Hartford opening lacked the Paris riot. The opera was a success later on Broadway and in Chicago.

Thomson got back to Paris as soon as he could. "In terms of just plain good feeling France was in those days, even for the poor, the richest life an artist ever knew."

He had a complete commitment to the city. He confessed he had counted 60,000 painters in Paris and the fact gave him comfort. He wrote the *State of Music*, a very original book on the subject, an impulsiveness and intimacy with music by a musician who wrote brilliantly.

Six days before the Germans took Paris, on June 8, 1940, he was still in the city. He left, made his way to the Spanish border, ran out of money, and got on a ship for America with Man Ray the Jewish Dadaist fleeing Europe. During the war Thomson became music critic for the New York *Herald Tribune*—a very fine one, caustic, firm, volatile, witty. Hardly the usual sloppy, battered prose writer that does most of the musical writing.

Thomson stayed on for fourteen years as critic, and then felt he had enough of it. He wrote his memoirs, *Virgil Thomson by Virgil Thomson*. He wore his rosette of the Legion of Honor. He composed *The Seine at*

Night. In the program notes he confessed: *"The Seine at Night* is a landscape piece, a memory of Paris, and its river . . . faraway Montmartre, fireworks, casual rockets flare and expire . . . between a furry sky and the Seine's watery surface, fine rain hangs in the air. . . ."

It is all like someone finding a love letter one shouldn't read, but does.

CHAPTER 49

Les Maisons de Tolérance—
English Spoken

The French say there are three sexes—
men, women and clergymen.

SIDNEY SMITH

W^HILE THERE is a great deal of information about the more famous love affairs and sexual doings of Americans in Paris, little is said of the average American who wanted the simple sex life of a bachelor or husband, who took his sex in the Parisian dives and brothels, or from streetwalkers, in the traditional and nearly respectable establishments of the Twenties. The best picture of them and of the Americans who were entertained there is in the privately printed memoirs of "W. W. Windstaff."

Skipping the impotent and the pederasts [he begins] all the nookie hunters among the Americans had their heads filled with pictures of sleeky Parisian tarts and hustlers, images already out of date, and mixed up with sepia-colored photos sold to them as "French postal cards." After a while most, if they didn't have a steady lay among the USA art students, or weren't too hot for the fancy parties given by the Porters or the visitors at the Ritz, they would drift down to the Boulevard Edgar Quinet or the Rue de Fourcy, sip a bock and enjoy the life, sleazy and busy in the *brasseries,* kid a couple of whores and buy some drinks, swallow *cacahouètes* (peanuts) but not hurry into anything. There might be some of the big pink Normandy hookers at the Chope du Nègre. Mostly it was the Rue du Faubourg Montmartre when our friends were looking for something in the skin trade and weren't flush enough to afford something, no better but fancier, in silk or furs.

The college boys with their letters of introduction, or frat brothers I'd take

down the line would all go bug-eyed and kind of grin and tell me they felt, oh
hell, "No puritan guilt here." No need to act up at all I'd say, even if there were
maquereaux and *souteneurs*, the streetwalkers' pimps, smoking their foul cigarette butts and paring their fingernails with a sharp frog-sticker. I'd walk the
boys over to the Halles and get them the expected onion soup and let them look
over the parading cunt. Filling them full of oysters and clams at the Chien qui
Fume, telling them it would put lead in their pencils, I found a lot of them
were still cherry. Some would act shy, if they were just in town a week or so,
their Hart, Shaffner and Marx still well pressed, and so I'd have some of the
tarts come on over and jolly the boys a bit and rub their hips against a Yale
man or a blushing kid from Princeton, and say, "*O, le pauvre bébé!*"

Paris whores have a nice sense of camaraderie, but also they are all business,
no heart-of-gold types, the kind American writers from the Middle West like to
put in their novels. Hell, these hustlers were mostly wily small-town girls who
had come to Paris to peddle their ass and get enough of a bank account
together for a dowry so they could marry some clod-kicker back home, or
make a down payment on a bar and eating place, and be so gaddamn respectable the rest of their lives you couldn't even pinch a tit while paying your bill.
Or they died in one of those big dirty hospitals, asking the sister for a priest.

The college boys would buy the whores white wine, a Pernod, café crème,
crème de menthe au cassis, or a shot of apple brandy on a rainy night. The tarts
were hungry, but I don't know why it was that sandwiches, a brioche, an
omelette would take the romance out of it for the boys. They bought drinks,
but it seemed to spoil a whore with sore feet and tired eyes for them that she
could be hungry.

I explained to the college boys a good whore was *sérieuse* about her work
and game for anything. A whore who wasn't earnest was a tramp, a boozer, a
drug sniffer, or daffy from chewing hashish which the Arab rug peddlers sold
them. A good whore, Sherwood Anderson had said, "knows she is sitting on
three square meals a day."

After a while the boys would wander off with one of the tarts to a cheap
hotel, the girl hanging on tight, dark silk shiny on big rumps, pretty breasts
sometimes bobbing up out of the top of her blouse, the tart talking salty street
French to some kid from Cornell or Stanford whose two-year college course of
the language failed him, and he perhaps wondering how he'd perform in the
hot-sheet hotel. And would he get the clap and did the *maquereau* really not
mind selling his girl?

It was very American, thinking of this kind, worrying if a pimp minded
selling his girl's body. Also if some *souteneur* began to slap his woman around
in a bar, hard blows back and forth across her cheeks with the palm and back
of his hand, I had to explain that the girl expected it, was sure her pimp was
showing his love by giving her punishment: "He cared." It's hard for Americans to understand that some lower-middle-class women expect to be beaten by
a lover.

"That's low," a college boy said.

Sure, still I knew some high-class American flappers who didn't mind a chop to the chin before getting into bed.

It was pretty shocking to lots of Americans. In their culture hitting a woman is not a traditional sign of full possession. If they were shy Americans, not at ease in cafés or under the street lights picking up a whore, settling the business of price and place, I'd suggest to them to go to the whorehouses, or "closed houses"—the French term. Running a cat-house in Paris is almost a family heritage, and respectable—as respectable as auto repairing or politics anyway. A good house, polite, established with old customers and a family trade, say, fathers and sons and son-in-laws, was as respectable and ordinary as a green-grocer's. A good closed house had no drunks rolling on the dusty rugs, and your wallet was safe along with your inherited grandfather's gold watch and chain. The girls would not reach for your wang right away or tell you dirty stories, or get boozed up and scream and carry on. It was a serious parlor; oil lamps or gas fixtures converted to electric light, wax flowers under glass, girls and clients sitting around like on a pleasant minor holiday or saint's day. Sometimes a man would even bring his wife to show her what life was like in a cosy *maison de tolérance;* of course saying *he* had heard much of such places, though he didn't himself go there, but his friends, his boss liked to *faire l'amant.* The Madame would grin, he most likely being a cocksman and known to every girl in the place as a stud stallion.

Hem and Scotty [Hemingway and F. Scott Fitzgerald] liked to get their fun by bringing people to the more lively places, but neither of them was what could be called a real gash-hound. They hung sex all over with romantic trimmings. American writers—mostly lousy lays—didn't like the respectable family places. They went to the *tableaux vivants*, joints that had circus acts, sex fantasy acted out for real, where the women and men performing were dressed as admiral's buggering sailors, sailors muff-diving nuns, and a nun being had by Shetland ponies or sheep dogs. The Rue des Victoires was the place for these shows. At some joints I remember seeing Wall Street bankers, Meadowbrook polo players, a Pulitzer Prize winner. Most popular were the *Sphinx* and the *Chabannais,* almost continual circuses. One of the regular boys taking on an "admiral" in such a line-up later became a very famous and very fine French film actor. As he explained it to me a long time later, with a shrug, "It was a trade, and I was hungry and very poor. The *quartier* was poor, we all were poor. It was eating and drinking. The night I stopped all that was when in my sailor suit I looked around and there was an uncle of mine, done up as an admiral—the sod—climbing on my back."

Unlike most sporting houses in the USA catering to the passing scene, the steady clientele of a closed house was very loyal to it, and you didn't even have to open your fly. You'd drink a brandy, read the *Paris Soir,* listen to some music, greet other customers resting their pratt on the leather sofas or cosy around a table, smoking and making small Frenchy jokes, mostly about priests and water closets, or General Joffre's cock.

What gave it away as a snatch shop was the girls were mostly naked, or just wearing stockings and high-heeled slippers, a bit of lace, and they were singing *"J'aime à jamais."* In winter the stove would be overcooking the air, and in summer there would be little buzzing brass electric fans with tricolored ribbons tied to the frames, and the ice in the drinks—if there was ice—would taste like Typhoid Mary.

Closed houses were mostly too bourgeois for those from the USA escaping American morality, and they would go find alcoholic, foul-mouthed whores who were not at all *sérieuse.* Sometimes we'd have to go to Harry's or Jimmy's bar, to see if we could get some American out of jail if he had run into trouble with the law. The French *flics* would usually have worked them over just a bit—not hard as they did the French. The Paris cop is a big mean shit at all times, comes mostly from Corsica, and smells of rum and garlic.

It was Eliot Paul who put it all in its proper place one night, while the *gérante* of a respectable family whorehouse was serving us coffee. "What most Americans object to in a family business like this, Madame and Monsieur Whoremaster, six plump girls, all going to mass and confession, and cousins of Madame, is that there is no sauce of sin, no guilty voluptuousness goes with it. Too open and casual; so easy, just saying *'Je suis prêt.'* But make it a place where your American Babbitt or adolescent has to sneak into, and where it's against the law, and you strip in the dark and the broad is shy about getting your joint copped, and an abandonment of principles is like a sure one-way ticket to hell-fire and the devil's pitchfork, whoopee! Your American will be having the time of his life."

I ordered *les alcools* all round.

The closed house has the smell of spilled drink and dreadful French tobacco, and body powder and sweat, and a hint of cooking with herbs, and often there's an old aunt as housekeeper, once a courtesan or cancan dancer or retired from a *maison de couture*. The decor is lovely—all the crap of six generations: some dead relative in oil paint on the wall, draped in black; sea shells from holidays in August by Madame and Monsieur in the south of France; Monsieur in tropical soldier's gear in Indochina, fat and pink like a roasting pig.

There were also dives where American women could find Amazons to their taste, or Natalie Barney would invite them over for some Lesbian revels. The sissies could find trade in tight pants with a golden head of curls in the Cocteau set, or the fairy writers who adored Gertrude Stein. It was surprising the fancy or important-named Americans in business and politics who went faggot in Paris. The arts, the music schools were just loaded with USA talent, if not genius, composing and admiring the behinds of the waiters and the greedy schoolboys offering themselves. That was the way Paris had been and was, and the way it was always to be for the fun loving Americans.

But of course "Windstaff" was wrong. His picture of the commercial arrangement of sex available in Paris is now long out of date. His genre picture of the legal sex business, healthy, inspected, well medicated, inherited, traditional, hardly survived the Second World War.

The sex trade is underground in Paris today, and the easy, legal, casual pickup over wine, croissants, and espresso is a thing of the past. Once one could take one's time and inspect the flesh parade while reading St. Price in *Le Journal*, or Vaillant Couturier in the Marxist *L'Humanité*. No more. The houses of the Rue de Fourcy are gone, the bistros are called Le Snack, Le Drugstore, and feature Cokes and hot dogs. The Quartier Saint-Paul behind the Hôtel de Ville smells as bad as ever, but men no longer queue up and wait their turn for their favorite Mademoiselle Fifi to be free.

CHAPTER 50

Cole Porter, Parisian

Tobacco, coffee, alcohol, hashish . . .
strychnine are weak dilutions; the surest
poison is TIME.

   EMERSON

A CASUAL READER of memoirs of the Twenties and Thirties would imagine that Americans in Paris who really mattered were writers
and painters, poets and serious composers; that beneath the floss and flutter of the city there were these earnestly engaged people, exploiting the
avant-garde, experimenting with new ways of doing the same old thing.
Even those who sat at the Dôme, the Select, and other cafés, who did little,
still talked of the work in progress, of the book or poem or bit of musical
dynamite they were planning, all fighting the willed commitment, the
need to affirm.

   But there were other Americans in Paris who had nothing to do with
the Steins or the editors of *transition* or Sylvia Beach's bookshop. They
touched fingertips, if at all, only through the F. Scott Fitzgeralds, a sort
of exchange of signals there at the Ritz bar between those who wanted to
be seen with the world-shakers and those who wanted to be the gentry,
the society column faces, the rich or would-be rich "in the social swim."
Those with titles or who knew people with titles were called the international set; later they became part of café society. In the just-gone past
they, or rather their children and grandchildren, were marked down as
the Jet Set. It was a grouping of people into which Greeks with yachts,
motion picture Jews and gentiles had infiltrated; bidders at auctions of a

million dollars for old masters (usually tax avoiding gimmicks), fattish prima donnas, Egyptian television actors, all found access, rife with new pretensions, deceits, pomposities.

One of the true stars of the international set of the Twenties was Cole Porter, one of the most charming, self-admitted hedonists who ever set brilliant lyrics to delightful music since Gilbert and Sullivan. Although a long-time resident in Paris, Cole never met or wanted to meet Hemingway or Joyce, Gertrude Stein, John Dos Passos, or Virgil Thomson. The names one can list of those that surrounded him in his world were almost all human grasshoppers and drones; some had money or titles, some took cocaine, at times smoked opium, were often blandly homosexual. Some got their pictures into those sections of the Sunday papers called Rotogravure; a brownish gravy-colored offset process of printing reproductions on smooth paper, no longer in use. The distortions and involutions of this parasite set made up Porter's world.

In 1916 Porter had come down from Yale *and* Harvard with a fellow college student to put on a musical show in New York City, *See America First.* Clifton Webb, who was a dancer in the show, remembered it with despair. (When Webb, who was devoted to his mother, Mabel, and always traveled with her, wrote his autobiography, some claim it was Cole Porter who suggested as a title *Up in Mabel's Womb*, a pun on a once popular stage play called *Up in Mabel's Room.*)

The play was reviewed as "the newest and worst musical in town." Cole, after trying to study music, decided instead to join the war going on in Europe. It was fashionable for the young college men, Yale and Harvard poets, Princeton football players, to taste the Great War. Most of them went to drive ambulances, some got into the air in French *escadrilles.* And some, like William Faulkner, only got as far as the Canadian Air Force, got drunk, fell out of a plane (while it was on the ground), and gave up trying to fly in the war but wrote some fine short stories of air battles. Faulkner for some time kept giving off the impression he had actually flown with the Royal Flying Corps in the war. This Faustian striving to see war close up was almost a romantic cult among American college boys.

Cole sailed on the *España* and entertained on board ship at the piano and with his zither, an instrument he carried with him at that time. Cole's war record is hard to unravel. His press agents always claimed later he was a bold warrior in the Foreign Legion. We do know he was transferred to the *Ecole d'Artillerie* at Fontainebleau, and perhaps was at the

front with the French 32d Regiment. But mostly he was parading himself
in Paris in various uniforms, none of which Monty Woolley (who had
been at Yale with him) insisted Cole had any right to wear. The Yale
Class of 1913 reported, falsely, "Classmate Cole A. Porter has joined the
American Aviation Forces in France, although nobody seems to know in
what capacity."

What records do exist show that Cole served the American society
matron, Nina Larree Duryea, in Paris, in the relief service she had which
gave aid to battered French villages. Then Cole was at the American
Aviation Headquarters on the Avenue de Montaigne. By April of 1918 we
find Cole in the French Army, the Foreign Legion branch, which was the
only branch an American could join. But he never fought in any battle
except in those at parties he gave in Paris at a marvelous house "lent him
by a French lady." The parties were remembered by the poet Archibald
MacLeish, who was at one of the first of the famous Cole Porter shindigs.
"I was the most naive country bumpkin, but I thought it was pretty big
high life," said the poet. Porter, as the only American in his outfit, was
cherished by his officers and protected from such harm as going to the

front and getting caught under fire. He served in none of the French battalions, no matter what his film biography *Night and Day* claimed. Nor did he ever get the Croix de Guerre (an award which "even street cleaners were getting," as some publications claimed.)

On April 18, 1919, in the French term, he was "stricken from controls," and out of the army. Paris became his playground. He wore pin stripe trousers, carried a Briggs umbrella. Fun and music were foremost on his mind. He never stressed too hard the qualities in which he excelled. He found a society made for fun, and for the music he enrolled in the Scuola Cantorum, where knowledge of counterpoint, harmony, composition, and orchestration was available for the willing student. Porter was no shallow or earnest product of Tin Pan Alley. George Gershwin, as we've noted, who came to Paris later, did surface readings, like the taxi horns, and wrote *An American in Paris* without really knowing the city. Cole Porter, however, became a true Parisian; in time he owned a house there and made it his setting-out point on his many travels, always returning to it. He liked the easy privacies, the social glow of the city. Paris was his home until the Second World War began to loom over Europe.

Cole Porter, the worldly cosmopolitan, was born in Peru, Indiana, in 1891. His mother named the boy Cole, and was told by a gypsy fortune-teller that for a child to make his mark in the world he should have initials that spelled out a word. So he was rushed by his mother Kate at the age of six to the courthouse and there legally listed as Cole Albert Porter; somehow CAP seemed a lucky combination. Kate was a character, as was her hard-shell father, J.O. Cole, usually called just J.O. He had dug gold, grown rich in real estate, and become a millionaire in lumber and West Virginia soft coal. Cole's father, Samuel Fewick Porter ("PORTER THE DRUGGIST. DIRT CHEAP. HE DOES NOT STEAL FROM YOU!") was pushed aside as soon as he had sired Cole, and J.O. took over. A loud, mean, tough, old bastard, he ran everybody's life in sight of his dominating gaze. Cole's father had very little to do with raising the boy; wife and father-in-law and his own innate rectitude make him a minor character in our story.

Kate wanted Cole to be talented, and at an early age he played violin solos in public. In 1901, aged ten, he wrote an operetta of one song, "Song of the Birds." As for Cole's father's reaction to it: "he seemed not to notice." A year later Cole wrote a fake Strauss dance called "The Bobolink Waltz." (His mother with inspired audacity paid a hundred dollars to have a hundred copies printed.) Cole was a lonely child, cradled in a sensuous plenitude. His charm was always part provincialism and part an easy sophistication.

In 1905, at thirteen, Cole Porter was sent east to Worcester Academy, where they processed young Christian gentlemen. Kate insisted on a school in the east, and J.O. stopped speaking to his daughter for several years.

Porter was a charmer at school and everyone liked him. He played the piano for himself, noodling along, and played for group singing. He said his voice was "unpleasant but adequate."

In 1908 Porter took examinations to get into Yale, still a lonesome kid in many ways, never talking of the incongruity of his strange family. A Francophile even before he saw Paris, Cole managed a trip to the city before entering college, living with a French family on the Rue Boissonade, perfecting his French. He differed from almost all Americans who went to Paris by entering French family life and by his remarkable skill with the language.

New Haven, in 1909, took Cole in and made him welcome. During the holidays he visited the homes of his classmates, those he called "the rich *rich*." Being poor seemed such a persistent error. Old J.O. insisted Cole study law, but Cole was more interested in making friends and music. In college he wrote one hundred compositions, and even had the firm of Remick, in Tin Pan Alley, New York City, publish his song, "Bridget." The 1919 tour of the Glee and Mandolin Club had a Porter tune, "Perfectly Terrible," which got special praise. From the start he had an individual identity in college, was someone special.

Besides Monty Woolley, he met at Yale Gerald Murphy, who was rich through his family's Mark Cross, the fancy leather-shop people. (Gerald was voted the "best dresser . . . most thorough . . . greatest social light" and was to become (with his wife Sara) the grand host, a lifetime dilettante, king of the easy livers among the Americans in France and in Paris. Today what fame the Murphys have is based on their toleration of an eccentric and slightly mad Scott and Zelda Fitzgerald, and a few other assorted pithy, scabrous folk.) At Yale Murphy got Porter into Delta Kappa Epsilon, and his song "Bull Dog," composed about that time, is still sung today at Yale.

Porter continued to be a popular piano player. At this time his life pattern could be from the pages of *This Side of Paradise*; he loved society, danced all night on trips to New York. He was an honored Whiffenpoof, made Scroll and Key, sang his song "The Motor Car" on a glee club tour, got good reviews: "A good singing voice and . . . clever imitator, Mr.

Porter is a comedian . . . out of the ordinary in college glee club concerts . . . brought down the house" (Washington *Star*).

When Porter left Yale to study law at Harvard by J.O.'s demand, the class book gives us some information. Cole is listed as a drinker of champagne, gin, Scotch, smoked Fatimas, was fifth as one who had Done Most For Yale; as Most Entertaining, he was first. Most Original, second by five votes, Most Eccentric, the winner. As for his future, J.O. had taken care of that. Cole listed it as "Mining, lumbering or farming." He was Phi Beta Kappa, and tied for the Greek Prize. He was more than just a bunch of narcissistic attitudes. His qualities were sensual, emotional, and intellectual, with a cherubic acceptance of his gifts.

Cole got two songs into two not very successful shows. Sigmund Romberg and Ray Goetz had songs in these shows too, so he was traveling on the fringe of the big league. An agent, Bessie Marbury, sold *See America First* for a New York production, but, as we have already recorded, its failure sent Cole Porter, late of Yale and Harvard, to Paris to join the Foreign Legion. A sort of ritual without an atonement, a romantic role, toward the flames. After the war his army discharge left Porter free to study music, but he found the Scuola Cantorum stuffy in its rejection of any modern experimentation. The classics, he felt, needed an airing, a moratorium from old rules.

Porter didn't give a damn about money, but he liked high living and J.O. was giving him enough to live well in Paris. As Sara Murphy was to put it, their friend Cole "was a natural-born hedonist, which is fine. People like hedonists . . . he wanted to live like a king which was all right too." But Porter wanted more than the Murphy's kind of superficial involvement; he wanted to have his music used.

One of the friendships Cole cemented in Paris was with a large, ugly social parasite, Elsa Maxwell. She had come out of San Francisco from a background somewhat of a mystery, had toured with a Shakespeare company when young. Elsa had played honky tonk piano, sung in a frog's voice, and arranged parties for the shy and shaky socially rich, setting up charity drives for New York Blue Book folk. Cole had first met Elsa in New York after his musical failed, at a party where he had played the piano and sung "They Call Me Ivy But I Cling."

In 1919 Elsa was in Paris trying to get by selling the flavor of *la vie Parisienne* to Americans, exerting herself for the pleasures and pastimes of international society people, moving about in her unprepossessing person. Yet she was always welcome, somehow, always helpful, always getting some cash out of her contacts.

In Porter's life women helped him meet the right people. Besides Elsa there was also Elsie de Wolfe, who became Lady Mendl and did interior decorating, mostly in white. And Mimi Scott, who liked to sing his songs. So he got around; either Elsa, Elsie, or Mimi were always talking up Cole Porter: "Yale, Harvard, marvelous music, charming." Porter got invited to perform all over Paris. No one took him too seriously—his motivations were human but not offensive—just the nice Midwestern farm boy, plays the piano, sings. He felt his work at that time was "too special for the audiences that went to musicals." Good enough for smart parties—*chic* was the word often used.

It was while on a round of parties that Porter met Mrs. Linda Lee Thomas. She was eight years older than Porter, had been an experienced social success, was rich, divorced, courted. Her great admirers called Linda "the most beautiful woman in the world." People who merely liked her called her "*one* of the most beautiful women in the world."

Porter with meticulous seriousness fell madly in love and demanded she marry him. His friends with ludicrous solemnity or mocking disapproval tried to talk him out of it. Sara Murphy put it plainly: "She [Linda] was dull as anything . . . Gerald and I found her stuffy . . . If she came along, it made it sort of heavy going."

How catty or honest Sara Murphy was we don't know. Or how profound and perceptive. Sara, who was for living at one's fullest potential, socially, was no great beauty herself. So what she said of Linda's failure to sparkle is suspect. "Partly it was her great beauty. She was *so* aware of it. She never moved her mouth or made any false gesture that might cause her to develop a line in her face." Other friends merely felt that in her intensely subtle sensibility she was bored by most people and could "freeze up like an icicle." Her relationship to Porter shows loyalty, magnanimity and compassion.

Linda was not photogenic, so we do not know if she was "the most beautiful woman in the world." While she liked Porter and his wonderful suggestive songs, his rhythms and rhymes, she had no desire to marry him. As one studies Linda's life, one wonders if she is not the original of the rich girl, Daisy Buchanan, in F. Scott Fitzgerald's *The Great Gatsby*. Linda was born of a "good family" with monetary problems in Louisville, Kentucky. A daughter of Mr. and Mrs. William Pace Lee, "descended from a signer of the Declaration of Independence," a product of the best folk, the best horses, the best balls and parties. "Everybody knew the Lee girls." At the Kentucky Derby Linda met James Borden Harrison, the spitting image of the character Tom Buchanan, the husband of Daisy in

Gatsby. Harrison had a private railroad car and Linda was seventeen and impressed. Harrison was supposed to be a banker but was more a millionaire sportsman, playboy, and publisher, part of, but a rebel against, the gentlemanly oligarchical society of his class.

They were married in 1901. They lived in jocose, rich nihilism—jewels, yachts, town houses. Linda's father-in-law gave her a $60,000 string of diamonds.

Linda's husband's life often revolved around horses. She had an allergy attack when she came near a horse. It seemed unsporting of her and it helped keep the couple apart. She began to live abroad. "There is no greater pain," wrote Dante, "than in misery to remember happy times." Linda's husband was in a couple of bad auto accidents (an auto accident involving the millionaire playboy Tom is the climax of *Gatsby*). Harrison got mixed up with some international whores, also with Evelyn Nesbit, for whom Harry Thaw shot Stanford White on a celebrated night on a roof garden. Then came Theodore "Teddy" Gerrard, who did a "wild Vampire Dance" on stage.

In 1912 Linda got a divorce and a million-dollar settlement. She took a house in Paris on the Rue de la Baum, a little gem of a place, and became a popular hostess with men (to quote Elliot Paul) "sniffing after her as hounds after a red fox bitch on a Virginia hunting field." Her rite of purification after marriage seemed to be to flirt with the field.

Cole Porter decided marriage was what he wanted now, with Linda, Mrs. Lee Thomas, as she was known in Paris. He tried hard to belong to her group. He wore diamond-studded gold garter clips, bathed in iced champagne, and was the instantaneously accepted entertainer of "the best people," at least those he liked the best. A world of piano keys, Grand Marnier, jazz at Bricktop's Club, steam baths, Harry's Bar, taxi horns after midnight.

He turned on the Porter charm and Linda began to melt. What they had in common was the discovered nostalgia for "the old home grounds"; they would talk and talk of how it had been living in Louisville, Kentucky, and Peru, Indiana. They discovered how much they had to share, and how fine it was to be in Paris together. Not the Paris of Robert McAlmon, Donald Ogden Stewart, Djuna Barnes, or the crowd at Madame Leconte's Rendezvous des Mariniers.

At last Linda threw caution, other suitors, common sense to the winds and told Porter she would marry him. Now came the problem; if he married a rich woman whose money was well invested, how could he with any self-respect live on her income? No, he would go back to America and get his feisty grandfather, J.O. Cole, to increase his allowance to that proper amount by which a man could keep a beautiful society wife in Paris.

In the spring of 1919, Porter was on a ship headed for New York, and by those games chance plays to redirect a man's destiny, on board was a famous comedian and Broadway producer, Raymond Hitchcock. Few remember him, but he was then as popular as Bob Hope is today, with more reason. Hitchcock had a yearly show in New York called *Hitchy-Koo*, and he was searching for material for the version of 1919. In life the banal plot is often the true reality.

Hearing that Hitchcock was interested in material, Cole played for him a half hour of music and songs on one of the ship's pianos. Hitchcock listened expressionlessly, showing no sign that he liked or disliked the material. At the end of the session he simply said, "I'll take them."

"Which one, Mr. Hitchcock?"

"Take the lot."

Dillingham and Erlanger, the producers of the Hitchcock show, who put up the money for *Hitchy-Koo*, weren't too sure it was such a bargain. They asked Porter to do a number to fit some discarded costumes made

up as flowers that Ziegfeld had rejected and that had never been used. Cole wrote "An Old Fashioned Garden," one of his first hits.

But Indiana, not Broadway, was the main reason he had come home, come to get J.O. to jack up his allowance so he could marry Linda. J.O. scowled; he had raised the boy to be a lawyer, not a vulgar songwriter. Also why the hell had Cole served with the damn French Army when the United States at war was available? Allowance? Marriage? The old man —the report is—beat the arm of his chair in rage and said not until this foolishness of being a songwriter was discarded. However, Porter's mother promised him in secret that she would give him the extra money, if he didn't let on to J.O. Porter promised and trained back to New York.

At the Liberty Theatre on 42nd Street, Porter faced his second opening of a musical, himself done up in topper, hammertailed evening coat, and splendid stiff shirt. Cole made a few jests to some of the audience that he had wanted the show presented "in schools and Second Presbyterian churches and such instead of a theater." It was a good show. *The New York Times*'s critic (name not given) called it "the best review in town . . . music and lyrics are the work of Cole Porter, who has made a particularly clever job of the lyrics and a good tinkling one of the music." Cole's song, "An Old Fashioned Garden," sold 100,000 copies, which is like a million today. Magazine writers claimed he had written the song during World War I near the Front. Some musical pedant claimed the tune was a direct copy of a colonial ditty, "The Quilting Party." However come by, success was toasted in bootleg armagnac and vermouth.

Back in Paris, on December 18, 1919, Cole Porter and Linda Lee Thomas were married in the mayor's office of the Eighteenth Arrondissement. It was for him total, incomprehensible happiness. He had his bride, his hit show, a smash song, and his mother was raising his allowance. To bring into being what we have imagined is the hardest miracle. That Linda was older and wiser did confuse some of Porter's friends. Reports of their objections stressed that some felt it was, in one way, a mother-and-son relationship; that Linda was a replacement in Porter's mind for Kate back in Peru, Indiana. We do not know enough of that relationship to be that sure. Certainly Linda, besides physical pleasure, filled some deep psychic urge, alleviated some grievances created by the vagaries of the odd family in Indiana.

Back from the honeymoon around Europe, Mr. and Mrs. Cole Porter chose Paris as their home base, complete with the friendships of Michael Arlen, at times the Scott Fitzgeralds, Diaghilev, Lifar, the Murphys, Dolly Sisters, and the rest of the international set. All came to their apartment at the Ritz to carry on the task of the hedonists of the Twenties. Porter's mother and J.O.'s second wife, Bessie, visited the young married folk and were bug-eyed at their fancy way of life. Back home in Indiana, Bessie told old J.O., "Linda has a maid."

"Well, dammit, you, too, have a maid, haven't you?"

"I don't mean kitchen maid. A personal maid. She even pulls on Linda's stockings."

J.O. exploded. "What the hell is wrong with her? She sickly or something?"

It might be pointed out that there were some basic deficiencies in Linda and Cole in their seeking transitory pleasures. Perhaps—but it could also be that they had rich tastes and just gave way to them. No artistic attic in Paris for them, no sacrificing comfort to attain some genius's goal. If there were sublimated frustrations, Linda soothed them by collecting antiques, French and Chinese art objects. They indulged their flagrant vanity; they bought an open Rolls-Royce; most stuffy people bought closed black Rolls. Dogs, too, came into their life; more than a dozen dachshunds, and also a hairy-faced sheep dog named Major, who rode in wind-whipped glory up front with the chauffeur. When Linda at a party wore one of her diamond and sapphire bracelets, a young woman guest asked her, "Are they real?"

Linda just shrugged. "Real *what*?"

It was a line of dialogue that could have come from the popular novel and play, *The Green Hat*, or from the lines a young man named Noel Coward was beginning to write about the glossy mediocrities of the international set.

Living at the Ritz was fine for a while, then the Porters bought a beautiful house at 13 Rue de Monsieur. Linda furnished it with style and taste, moved in her collections. It was the Cole Porters' home until the shadow of World War II forced them from Paris, and the international set became passé. The floors and some walls were done in zebra hide, red chairs in white kid, one room that became the talk of Paris, *mon cher*, had platinum wallpaper. When the Porters traveled, and they traveled a lot, they often hired a private railroad car and carried along a number of free-loading, titled or notorious friends, as well as Cole's valet, Eugene, and Linda's maid Weston (who pulled on Linda's stockings to shock J.O.).

Cole exploited his hedonism with good taste; he was hardly ever vulgar, even with the imbecile, gullible press. He still wore gold buckles on his garters at a time men were advised by advertising, "If you wore your garters around your neck, would you change them more often?" The stories about him spread; the press expanded them. Writers used their imagination, picturing the Porters as scatterbrained rich. When Porter tried to explain their way of life, he only made it worse. "But don't you understand, everyone lived like that in those days." Everyone being the international loafers, moochers, titled bums of both sexes—those he thought of as his friends. He could be at ease with close friends with titles, Duke Fulco di Verdura, Baron Nicolas de Gunzberg, and a few, too, not in the high born record books.

Some of their friends had drinking problems. One was Howard Sturges, out of Yale, in Paris to study music, but really boozing himself into a stupor. Linda would find him lying in a gutter, load him into her car, and drive him to a drying-out sanitarium, a place popular with American alcoholics in Paris. Linda got Sturges to go on the wagon, and it is said he never drank again after one really violent bout she dried him out of—for which good deed Sturges sent Linda a yearly gift of some fine jewel.

Names appear as the Porters' Paris friends, people from Yale or from Linda's social set. They remain mostly names for us. Len Hanna, Arnold Whiteridge, and others still remembered as the Murphys (Gerald and Sara), Monty Woolley—without a beard in those days.

In 1923 J.O. died at eighty-five. Porter got $250,000 from the estate, which he proceeded to spend at great speed in high and fancy living, before the stock market crash in 1929 wiped out nearly a million dollars left to the other and more frugal heirs. Porter put a lot of his money into a Venice palazzo for holiday fun-making, a place for wild and fancy doings on land and water. Its histories, scandals, hysterics kept the international press busy for years. Venice, a city sinking into the muck, with its ancient, never removed, sacred *merde* over everything, attracted wealthy Americans, elegantly or vulgarly epicurean, from Princess Jane di San Faustino ("a rich American broad who married a title and as a widow in black was a knockout"), to Peggy Guggenheim, who was to bring a modern collection of art to Venice, after exploding like a bombshell in Paris where, she claims in her book, *Out of This Century*, she had a problem. "About this time I was worried about my virginity . . . I found it burdensome . . . [Florenz] said we would go to a hotel room sometime . . . That's how I lost my virginity . . . Florenz had a pretty tough time because I demanded everything I had seen depicted in the Pompeian frescos."

The Cole Porter crowd in their deliciously ironic sinfulness did not care to mingle with Ezra Pound, Glenway Wescott, E. E. Cummings, the ragtag and bob of the Gertrude Stein crowd. Even Elsa Maxwell, laughing it up like an articulate oboe, had a hard time staying with the Cole Porter gang. Linda insisted Elsa cheated at bridge, and took Cole as a pigeon by teaching him Mah-Jongg. In the end Elsa was exiled from the gay Porter group because she was breaking the rules of the game.

CHAPTER 51

More Porter—and Bricktop

Pray madam, who were the company?
Why, there was all the world and his wife.

JONATHAN SWIFT

I T was a time of names, a time of precocious, lunatic banging about in search of other names. In Paris or Venice one might find such American guests at the Porters as Tallulah Bankhead, Grace Moore, Irving Berlin, George Gershwin, George Jean Nathan. The John Barrymores came too, and John offered his daughter, Diana (of tragic destiny in middle age), to Cole and Linda "to raise for me." They declined Diana, claiming they had a progeny of eight dogs on their hands. Among the titled there was Princess Oduskuki, and the English fascist leader and his wife, Sir Oswald and Lady Cynthia Mosley. Cole and Linda had no political sense of any sort; it was enough that the banks of the republic should pay a good percentage and stock dividends keep rising. The rest of the world was a menagerie to them, a disgruntled truculence one handed tips to.

Although deep in his thirties, Porter was still not sure he was a professional song writer. Bored, with self-deprecating humor, he invented a rich Oklahoma oil millionaire couple, "Mr. and Mrs. S. R. Fitch." Porter sent items to the Paris edition of the New York *Herald* about the Fitches; one was that Elsa Maxwell had given a huge dinner party in their honor, the guest list bearing names of international figures, English, French, Russian (White), and Hindu. Elsa guessed it was Cole's work and went

along with the gag. A rich man's humor, she knew, is *always* funny. The
Fitches began to appear every place, according to press items about
them. Tired of the joke, Cole finished it off by posing Elsa in a Mack
Sennett bathing suit and sporting a Kaiser Bill mustache. Cole sent the
pictures around to the papers as "S. R. Fitch of Muskogee, Oklahoma."
The jest was over.

There was no color line in Porter's make-up, and he saw Negro performers, often the rage of Paris, as human beings and friends whom he
would invite to his home on the Rue de Monsieur. Among them was the
amusing red-haired Negro who was called Bricktop, who ran a very
fashionable club called Bricktop's. She came to the Porters' house and
taught the Aga Khan, Elsa Maxwell, the Prince of Wales, and other
Porter friends the latest hip-jolting, leg-jerking version of the Charleston.

When Bricktop felt left out at the Paris Opera Ball, Porter had Captain
Molyneux, the designer, do her a gown copied from one he had designed
for Princess Marina of Greece. Bricktop wore it, loved it, enjoyed the
ball. Most of the opera patrons were outraged, and there was talk of
"what was the Opera Ball coming to?" When Porter was questioned, he
just said Bricktop was "as much a lady as anyone at the ball."

Fanny Brice, the comic singer, was also a Porter guest. Vulgar, loud,
she was married at one time to the confidence man and convicted bond
thief Nicky Arnstein, by whom she had two children. They changed their
names to Brice (the son became a so-so painter). Fanny was loud, funny;
Porter insisted she was "one of those rare personalities who adapted to
any level. Royalty and gangsters were *all* the same to her." But Bricktop
remained a favorite.

The Negro in Paris in the twentieth century played a crucial part in
American life there, and while his umbilical cord pulled him back toward
Harlem, the freedom of Paris seemed a better system. Getting off the
ship, he or she could repeat Cocteau's line: "Life is dead, long life life!"

Gaby Deslys, the chanteuse with American millionaire lovers, in 1917,
returning from New York, brought a jazz band to the Casino de Paris.
Writers like Blaise Cendrars took up the Negro cult, wrote *Anthologie
Nègre*; the composer Francis Poulenc made music of *Rhapsodie Nègre*.
And when entertainers like Josephine Baker and Bricktop began to
shake and sing, the news was *"Elle a chaud au cul."*

The Great War had made the bisexual Senegalese soldiers popular in
the Madeleine quarter of Paris, the section known as "Sodom and
Gomorrah," with its notorious brothel, the *Chambannais*. The Negro's
popularity could be expressed by the poet, Louis Aragon, speaking of the

popular beginning of the war, by the line, "We loved the war like a Negress."

Bricktop, Negro singer and club owner, was known on her passport as Ada Smith du Conge. She was a long entrenched American celebrity in Paris. Her greatest glory came in the Twenties. She was always ready to talk about her life—even to give the date of her birth, "1876, in Alderson, West Virginia, red-haired and freckle-faced but 100 percent American Negro." She was reared in Chicago. By the time she was seventeen she was singing in night clubs, among them Murray's on Central Avenue in Los Angeles. She went to New York. In 1924 the management of the Grand Duke, a Paris bistro, sent for "that fresh little red-haired girl from Chicago."

Bricktop's first impression of Pigalle was disappointing:

"The place was no bigger than a room." I said, "The bar is nice but *where* is the cabaret?" I found out that was all. I sat down and cried. I wasn't crying later when I had the kings of Europe sitting at those fourteen tables.

Regulars at the *Grand Duke,* which came to be called *Bricktop's,* included Scott Fitzgerald and his wife, Zelda—she was nice. Hemingway, already famous, Louis Bromfield, and John Steinbeck. Steinbeck, he's my darling of all my darlings, except, of course, Cole Porter. He was my favorite in all the world. Cole Porter heard me. He came again bringing Elsa Maxwell and a large party of guests. He said, "I know you can sing, but can you dance? I want you to teach me the Charleston."

So Bricktop was teaching all of Paris to Charleston. One night at a party she was presented to the Prince of Wales. "He knows how to Charleston; he wants you to teach him the Black Bottom." So it went, even if all recalled scenes are composed of inexactitudes. The prince reciprocated by having a party opening night at a club of her own that Bricktop had acquired.

"I stayed in Paris almost until Hitler was coming down the Champs Elysées. The Duchess of Windsor and Lady Mendl paid my fare home in 1939. I never have a dime. The money I didn't give away I spent on living, my only vice."

Bricktop spent the war years in the United States, for a time ran a night club in Mexico City. She returned to Paris in 1949 and was bitterly disappointed. "I opened up a club again, but it wasn't the same. It was not that Paris didn't try to be chic and elegant. The French just don't like us. They gave me a lot of trouble about my licenses and taxes, although I had paid more taxes in that city than any five night clubs. My waitresses stood around, talking about 'those vulgar bastards, the Americans.' "

The *cote fleurette* of postwar France toward Americans shocked those who had been there in the Twenties. There were no more unqualified enthusiasms. Bricktop gave in. "I just tossed the keys of the club into the middle of the street and went to Rome."

Bricktop's in Rome was on the Via Veneto, right between the Flora Hotel and the Excelsior. "It was on the mad, mad mile, as we called it. Bricktop's is where I am; it's always been that way." But she failed to recapture—as the world failed—the old *succès de snobisme* of that other Paris, of the Prince of Wales doing the Charleston to the cheers of American tourists. As for those nonexistent kings at those fourteen tables— Bricktop was never good at history.

Jean Cocteau had found a broken-down Negro boxer dancing at the Caprice Viennois. Panama Al Brown had been bantam-weight champion of the world, but lost it, and now after two years of dissipation in Paris he was a wreck, aged thirty-four, a has-been. By some personal magic Cocteau got Brown to train—like "Christ raising Lazarus"—and on March 4, 1938, at the Palais des Sports Brown won back the title. But then he was back on drugs, went on tour as a dancer with the Amar Circus, in the end was in the United States as a dishwasher in Harlem. On Saturday nights he would show up at Small's Paradise on 123rd Street, in his only remaining Paris item, a smoking jacket. He made the journey to Bellevue Hospital, lungs failing, and died at the Seabright Clinic. His body was displayed on a truck in the streets of Harlem to collect coins for his burial.

The life of Mr. and Mrs. Porter, "run for fun," ran on. When his brother-in-law died, Porter left his Venice palazzo, the Rezzonica, in charge of Elsa, who needed a place to live, on the promise she would not do any razzle-dazzle stunt while he was off mourning his dead. A rapacious press always exploited any mention of the Porters' lives. On the day of the burial Elsa Maxwell gave one of her wild, eye-popping parties, and the world press carried the news with exuberant additions of its own. Linda rushed back, and with a gesture worthy of Tallulah Bankhead threw Elsa out. "Get out of my house!" It ended forever any close friendship between Elsa Maxwell and the Cole Porters.

If Porter had not been writing music and gaining a reputation as a songwriter, his life would hardly be worth writing about today. It was the same, gay, empty round of fun and games, banal jests and practical jokes by people who made news of sorts, but nothing much else. In 1923

Porter had a show opening in Paris at the Champs Elysées Theater, called *Within the Quota.* Although it was a success in Paris, it failed when moved to New York. Porter continued to work on his music without requests by any producer. It was 1927 before anyone asked for music. The manager of the Paris night club, Des Ambassadeurs, Edmund Sayag, got the idea of a review based on the theme of the United States, which he knew mostly from gangster films and Hollywood musicals. He boldly announced he had signed Fred Waring, Gershwin's sister Frances, Morton Downey, Georgia Hale, and others. Georgia—a party-goer— loudly suggested Porter do the score for Des Ambassadeurs.

The show opened in May of 1928, and Cole had two dozen songs ready. Opening night prices for dinner and show (wine extra) were seventy dollars a head. Young William Randolph Hearst, Jr., on his honeymoon, gave a huge party to help things along. When Clifton Webb joined the show a little later, Porter wrote "Wake Up And Dream" for him.

It was the beginning of his prime as a songwriter. From then on Cole was almost always busy, always involved in writing or rehearsing a show. His next show was called *Paris,* starring Irene Bordoni. This text is not a history of his music, so we can just record he went on to do *Fifty Million Frenchmen, The New Yorkers, Gay Divorce, Kiss Me Kate, Dubarry Was a Lady,* and others. In passing it might be mentioned that he wrote "Night and Day" for Fred Astaire in *Gay Divorce,* while staying with the Vincent Astors in Newport. The film became *The Gay Divorcée. Time* Magazine said he liked cats, parties, scandal, swimming, crime news, Peru, Indiana. Disliked baseball, golf, poetry, Belgium, pressed duck. Some of this was true.

The years passed, the home in Paris remained filled with guests, parties rocked the roof.

In 1937 Porter was a guest at the Countess Edith de Zoppola's house at Oyster Bay, Long Island. Wanting to ride, Porter and some others went to the Piping Rock Club in Locust Valley to get horses. Porter, against advice, picked a skittish, jumpy animal. While he was riding the horse took fright and reared. Porter, legs still in the stirrups, fell with the horse, which rolled on him, crushing first one leg and then the other. The bones of Porter's legs were pulverized.

The gods no longer smiled. The end of the good, gay times had come. His motto became, "For Christ's sake, don't sympathize." Doctors considered amputation. Porter pleaded to save the legs, and went through agonizing years of operations, months in casts, always in grinding pain, long periods of depression. Operations followed each other in series. Years later one leg had to be removed, and Cole became a semirecluse. The absurdities of ill health, the unpredictable declines took over.

After the accident Cole was under strong sedation. To Clifton Webb, who came to visit him with Elsa Maxwell, he whispered, "Just goes to show, doesn't it, fifty million Frenchmen can't be wrong. They eat horses, don't ride them."

In 1938, he was forty-seven, and that day, celebrating, he slipped on a marble staircase, rebreaking his left leg. He still thought both legs could be saved and that his disability was temporary. But the bone marrow infection, osteomyelitis, had set in. Life itself was a temporary ailment, as a guest at one of his parties had once said.

Paris, where therapy and uplift might have been possible, was lost to him. Linda had closed the house on the Rue de Monsieur, gotten rid of the grand wine cellar's contents; she wasn't going to leave that for Hitler's generals. Cole would have to accept the grim possibilities of change.

Both the Porters were now ill, but they refused a friend's suggestion to try sessions with a psychiatrist. Cole repeated the remark created by Sam Goldwyn's press agent: "Anyone who goes to a psychiatrist should have his head examined." As a friend put it, "From their point of view psychiatrists might have been witch doctors." A great many people held the same view. And Cole lacked metaphysical sensibilities.

The years were filled with pain. The Germans were in Paris, then the Germans were out of Paris. But it wasn't the same. Linda was suffering from emphysema; the walls of her lungs were losing their elasticity. She said sadly to Porter, "I hate being forgotten . . . a flower or something could be named for me." Porter got a patent on the *Linda Porter Rose*. Linda died in May of 1954.

Returning to Paris alone, Porter found it a strange "combination of joy and sadness . . . lunched with Sir Charles Mendl . . . he was helped into lunch . . . He didn't know anyone was there except at rare intervals . . . I dread old age."

However there was a bit of cheer. His song, "*C'est Magnifique*," was the number one hit in France. "Nice to find that when I tried to write a typical French popular song . . . dismissed by American critics . . . it has at last become a typical French song."

He died in 1964, and only his valet accompanied his body back to Peru, Indiana, for burial. There were few survivors of the Cole Porter set still active at parties—even in Paris.

Book Seven

REMEMBER AND REMEMBER

CHAPTER 52

Tropic of Henry Miller

I do not say a better world order.
I say merely a necessary one.

HENRY MILLER

T HE PARIS of Henry Miller is as alien to that of the Stein-Hemingway circle as it is to the gay Lost Generation sports and spenders of the Cole Porters'. He came later, with no sophisticated modes, after the stock market collapse, when the Depression had bitten hard. His Paris was glum and worried about falling prices and unemployment. This was a Europe of harsh, doctrinaire gothic grotesques. Many Americans had gone broke, suicidal, or alcoholic. Worse, many had gone back to Kansas or Ohio, to the family hardware store, to teaching in some whistle-stop, jerkwater college. He did not belong to that generation with its sense of life almost too poignant to face.

Miller, a German-American from Brooklyn, scarcely educated, a great reader and fornicator, once employed in his father's tailor shop, later by Western Union, had drifted through life thinking of writing, but formless and stumbling, seemingly trapped in the wearisome existence of mortality.

Certainly it was Paris and the two masterly novels by Céline—*Journey to the End of the Night, Death on the Installment Plan*—that started him toward *Tropic of Cancer*. In style, in manner, in use of language, he owes much to the French genius, a fecund, heterogeneous nature seeming to lack sanity and form.

Miller had first come to Paris in 1928, but only for a visit. He settled in

Paris in 1930. The first time he had brought over his second wife, whom he had picked up in a New York dance hall. He loved her but their life **was** a bickering hell; the battling "Jiggs and Maggie" of the comic strips with erotic overtones. Miller's true contribution to frank writing about sex was the simple, animal pleasure of it, free of the burden of guilt or seriousness. No regard for romance can be seen, or tender feelings, no spiritual emotion or reaction, beyond banging away at the physical fun of the act. He seemed susceptible to no exquisite response with a woman.

There is hardly any sad fornication in his various books, nor any revealed intuition or love of the female beyond the moment of pronged attachment. He acted, on his pages, with a naive credulity, a ludicrous incongruity.

In 1930 Miller was in Paris alone, drinking at a Montparnasse café, saucers piled up before him. He was nearly forty, green-blue eyes, bald, a Chinese seer's opium mask look to his face. He presented a serenity of detachment, the philosopher of the casual lay. Miller was basically a talker, to anyone, about anything, at any time. To Americans in Paris, Germans, Russian exiles, if they would listen, he'd talk.

Broke, often homeless—Miller's natural states—he stayed on in Paris. He'd cop an overcoat, or in cosy *Gesellschaft* get into bed with someone's wife or girl friend. He had no sexual loyalty. He felt he needed release; his scheme was to try Paris as a base for writing. He had to come through as a writer of a book or be a failure.

America, he felt, was a place where the artist was a bum, a pariah. In Paris the artist could have pride, retain his dignity. This was the nonsense Americans in Paris had been talking for years. But Miller was always a bit dated, even at his best. He took over the slogans of the Twenties in post-depression Paris. Miller would often pay for his drinks with his watch and hope for ten dollars at American Express next day.

Alfred Perkes took Miller in when the American was at low ebb. Perkes had come from Vienna, worked as a journalist in the Twenties and Thirties on the Paris edition of the Chicago *Tribune*. (By his own confession he had been a dishwasher, a fortuneteller, barman, ghost writer, card shark, sandwichman, and the guinea pig for some monkey gland experiments.) He followed the law of inevitability: something would always turn up. Miller agreed with him.

Miller's philosophy was, "I have no money, no resources, no hopes. I am the happiest man alive." He lived like one, even if it was not always true. He was a great eater when he could get it. He ate with animal gusto—*Gemütlichkeit*—and yet was not a gourmet. *La bonne chair* was his trademark. In his books his Paris was the low life, the drinkers of *vin ordinaire*, the parade of shabby whores selling themselves to the market folk on the Boulevard Edgar Quinet. Their price two francs, or as Miller figured it, the cost of two packs of American cigarettes in Brooklyn. Twenty-five cents.

Mostly Miller talked; drunk or sober he was a voice, going on about any subject, all undigested fragments of his hurried, disordered reading, his devouring of exotic books, masterworks, ideas of his own often hardly half resolved. He saw his ideas as a vision of categorical truth, a self-commanding, sacred animality.

The Americans of long standing in time avoided the tourist crowded cafés, the Dôme, the Coupole. But not Miller. He held court there, mooched, took solace in amiable debate with eccentrics. To the cafés came the failed Americans of the Thirties, mostly the bad artists, unpublished writers, the kooks, the addled, often in odd costumes: pajamas, sandals, Greek robes. The haggard livers on the wind were there, hunting food, drink, a patron, available women. Few had money. The quality of Americans had run down since the Depression. Rug peddlers hopelessly solicited their trade, pearls and peanuts were offered. The entertainers were sidewalk singers, floozies, plain beggars.

The Greenwich Village tourists, the last of the Babbitts, were Miller's prey. He would take a drink, a meal, a pair of pants, a shirt in exchange for his talk. He would happily pick the pockets of friends; loose coins he looked upon as his own heaven-sent gifts.

Among the friends he made was Michael Fraenkel, a naturalized American of Russian beginnings, who had made money in the stock market and retired to Paris to write of his favorite subject; death. He was fascinated with the utter futility of living, of breathing. The idea of death attracted him in all its forms, its sidelights. Miller played up to Fraenkel. There were also Richard Osburn, Walter Freeman, Samuel Putnam, Edward Titus (Helena Rubinstein's husband who ran a bookstore). So many Americans and near Americans, most of them only names now, but all moving about Paris in the Thirties, making art, talking of little magazines, of publishing, most of them skirting the irrational. So Miller amused them, and they fed him, often sheltered him when he lacked a room. He articulated their vague or messianic hopes.

It was not the gay life of Whistler or the Fitzgeralds anymore, the bohemian world of the early decades of the century; not the gay Lost Generation of the Twenties, so sure they could unknot the modern dilemma. These Miller years were made up of often desperate people; more and more Spanish, German artists, writers, journalists, and plain refugees were crowding into Paris. And among refugees honesty is an extravagance, unjustifiable by the logic of survival.

Sometimes Miller wrote for the Sunday magazine section of the *Tribune* under Perkes' name. His piece "Rue Lourmel in Fog" attracted the attention of the English critic and editor, Cyril Connolly, who was running the magazine *Horizon* in London. He found it was actually Miller who had written the piece, and he became the first of the important critics to recognize Miller. Later he lost his excitement for the American; too much improvization, a narrow horizon, damp fireworks.

Perkes got Miller a job as a proofreader on the Paris *Tribune* for a short time; Miller was not really interested in work. He had decided to be the fully unentangled man, free-loading if he had to, to create his fifteen, twenty pages of prose a day, his own personal writing. Miller was an expert speed typist, and often to many readers what he wrote was just speed typing. The germ of *Tropic of Cancer* was forming in his mind. Céline had shown him the power of low-life jargon, the argot of the streets, the way to shock by direct, unornamented statement, a denigration of love and loyalties to a quick, lucid copulation.

Wambly Bald had started a magazine, *The New Review,* aided by the

American Samuel Putnam, a scholar and gifted translator, long resident in Paris. The magazine published Miller's short story, "Mlle Claude," his first in France. Putnam had to take a business trip to America, and, in an absent-minded way, turned the editorship of the magazine over to Miller and Perkes. They threw out most of the material carefully prepared for the issue, and in Laurel and Hardy haste filled it with something else, including a manifesto, *The New Instinctivism,* a sort of parody of the Dada and Surreal manifestoes that had gone before. It was to be taken as "a gob of spit upon the face of humanity . . . from odd axioms to a study of *les maladies des voies urinaires.*" The printer sent the galleys of this text to Putnam, who ordered the manifesto killed. No copy of the unique manifesto exists today.

Anaïs Nin entered Miller's life. Anaïs Nin had some vague Spanish-French background, was the daughter of Joaquim Nin, the concert pianist. Miller found her with forty-two volumes of her detailed diary and at once proclaimed her "a genius!" He stated: "There are lines in it that are Immortal—not lines only, but whole passages . . . some so cruel and revolting as to seem unhuman." Anaïs Nin was to spend a lifetime at her literary mirror, searching out her every thought and idea, setting them down for an unaware posterity. Perhaps she needed Miller as a father image; others in her past had let her down. Now Miller treasured her, she was magnificent. As he, too, needed praise, they lathered each other's genius delightfully. (His evocation of her work insisted, "The whole thing is a bloody emission, the orgasm of a monster.") What could be nicer. No way-out egotist could resist such praise to her pathological greatness.

There were other women in Miller's life. He was a hasty Don Juan of the cafés and the walk-up studios; often the zipper-down-Casanova rather than the full stripper. Some women he took to bed, some fed him and helped clothe him. All he enjoyed with that unthinking, evangelical pleasure in human intimate friction—four legs in a bed—that was his charm and his virility. He never said *Merci*; he took, and smiled, and left. *L'homme n'est ni ange ni bête.* He liked to suffer perhaps, liked to be tormented by a woman. An affair could end if the woman wasn't bitch enough to satisfy his needs for a bit of roughhouse. Refined women, even if abandoned to passion, were not enough for Miller's provocative, hilarious sex play.

Miller often hit rock bottom in Paris; no warm room, no food, no bed, or body, for the night. Hope, he insisted, was a bad thing. "It means you are not what you want to be." As a philosophy it saw him through hard times. He still loved eating, and getting enough food was the big problem. Scientifically he made a card index of all of his friends, a card for each. The system was simple. Two cards a day, lunch and dinner mooched from two friends, would see him through the day. Fourteen friends free-loaded would take care of a week of being fed. As he was popular with some people, he had more than a dozen or so friends able to feed him, so he could pick his meals with the clear, studied eyes of a gourmet. He was aware now of the best in the *cuisine bourgeoise*. In this food game he was all system, letting the donors of the meals know just *when* he'd show up to feed, the day and hour.

Sleeping was no real problem. Michael Fraenkel, the death-lover, owned a house in Paris, the Villa Seurat. For a time Miller lived in the corner of the living room. There was a kitchen and a bathroom with American plumbing—Miller was a learned authority on the human turd. Fraenkel was a hard man to get to part with a franc, but Miller dazzled him with his knowledge of his favorite subject in exchange for a mangy sofa and the flush plumbing. Fraenkel was a bore and pedant about all perishable things on earth, the final dissolution of all living matter. He was full of grimy, necrophilic themes which Miller could embroider in all-night sessions. Talk was of rot, bodies burned alive in wet, toady graves; the charnel house never spoiled Miller's appetite for food. When all else failed, Miller, as said, would pick any pockets in the house he could lay hands on, whatever could be turned into a bottle of wine, a meal. Fraenkel never seemed to notice the petty larceny going on under his nose while Miller warmly regaled him on the subject of some gruesome burial custom.

Miller never failed to do his stint of so many pages of prose a day, now forming into what was to be the *Tropic of Cancer*, around him the air thick from the Gauloise cigarettes he smoked, *trente sous le paquet de vingt*, rumor being they were made from the droppings of the horses of the French police. Miller was a daytime nap man; when his writing task was done, he would take off all his clothes, get into wrinkled pajamas and cork off. "Sleep puts velvet in my vertebrae."

Walking about Paris was his form of exercise. "A man need not feel rich. A man does not need to be rich, nor even a citizen, to feel his way about in Paris." Although in some ways naive to the extreme, he had an ear, eye, nose for the streets, the idiosyncrasies of individuals.

Miller made himself the disturbing poet of the beggars, the refugees, the forgotten, the diseased of Paris. The underworld of the poor, the filthy, the broken, the dispossessed, the exiled delighted him. He had no feeling for politics or plans to improve mankind. Modern politics was a progressive paralytic disease. The sordid, the revolting excited him. His landscape was the gutter, the fleabag hotels, the bars of pederasts and lesbians; all held a fascination that he was able to turn—as his master Céline did—into a kind of instant literature, but without Céline's bitter curses on life. Miller would talk to anyone; any strange acquaintance might have a story for him. He adored mad people; the insane were a tonic to him; the black contrasts of human behavior his cocktails. If criminals were depraved and interesting enough, he saw them as part of the whole. As far as the true systems that make up the social order, the power game, he was to remain naive, finding that in the gutter the puddles reflect stars.

Dope addicts, *femmes honnêtes*, all were to be recognized and spoken to in his walks around Paris. *Les bas-fonds* claiming to be poet or painter, no matter how glazed with filth, the tramps were human interest for him. And always there was an affluent middle class to search out for food and shelter.

By 1932 Miller shared a flat in Clichy with Perkes—a *domicile fixe*, a home. No more borrowed sofas, hasty banging of one-night hostesses.

For a while, no more flophouses were the bedbugs drove him scratching into the cold night air. Miller never did sink to the Salvation Army boat moored at the Pont du Carousel to exchange a kip and a plate of gruel in return for a half dozen hymns. Nor has anyone yet claimed Miller slept under bridges with *tireurs de pieds de biches* and *clochards*. He was fed and cared for by Russians, Balkans, Jews; even, one Nanantattee, a Hindu who sold pearls.

Owning half of a flat, Miller could enjoy from time to time a good solid meal. Their grocer permitted credit; he respected Americans. Were not Rockefeller, Henry Ford, J. P. Morgan, Rudy Vallee Americans? *Vive l'amitié franco-américaine!*

Miller, with no disposition to a melancholy view, got by on his humor, his true good nature. People shrugged, smiled at some small, dishonest deed, often at an improper advance to a wife, or a mistress not his own. "*C'est un admirable paillasse.*"

He finished *Tropic of Cancer*, his first real book. He had written a book in New York, *Crazy Cock*, but now he saw it was no good, too loose, no discipline; it dangled. He felt he had come through with *Cancer* as a writer. But who would publish him? Bennett Cerf, if the hot stuff was by Joyce, Harper and Brothers? No, of course not. There was Jack Kahane, an Englishman, half-Irish, half-Jewish, to hear him tell it, who had founded and ran the Obelisk Press of Paris, specializing in obscene English-language novels. It was not, he would claim, actually pornography, but he begged booksellers to *not* display his wares in their windows. Tourists who could read English flocked to the bookshops to ask for the gamy products of the Obelisk Press. When short of the right kind of author, Jack Kahane, the publisher, often became the author himself, writing many of his early grimy books under the pen names of Basil Carr and Cecil Barr.

As Kahane prospered, he published Frank Harris's *My Life and Loves* (actually a reprint, for Harris had privately published it earlier), Lawrence Durrell's overripe *Black Book*, and Cyril Connolly's delightful *Rock Pool*.

Miller had let William Aspenwall Bradley, a literary agent, read a first version of *Tropic of Cancer*, and in despair of getting a proper publisher Bradley had recommended it to Kahane. It was a daring book to publish, even in Paris, for it used all the crude four-letter words of folk talk, all the direct sexual terms, and the fornications were fully spelled out. Unlike most erotic writing, there was no fancy romancing, no imaginary, unreal orgies. It was plain as a grocery list. Kahane decided to publish. He tried to sneak it out to his various outlets without publicity, and at the smut hounds' special price of fifty francs a copy. Again the warning from the publisher was *Ce volume ne doit pas être exposé en vitrine.* A second edition sold out. Stray copies appeared in the United States and England, where it was at once barred—after all the officials had read it over a few times. Miller was suddenly a sensational, a notorious literary figure.

CHAPTER 53

"Saint Erotica" Miller Canonized

"We're as happy as can be,
Doing the what-comes-Naturally."
    IRVING BERLIN, *Annie Get Your Gun*

T ROPIC OF CANCER and James Joyce in its blue cover were the two items the intellectual or horny American tried to smuggle past the yahoos at customs. Jack Kahane, the publisher, modestly announced, "The *Tropic of Cancer* is the first full-length work of an American writer of genius, comparable to Céline's *Journey to the End of the Night*." Anaïs Nin had written a preface: "The violence and obscenity are left unadulterated, a manifestation of the mystery and pain which ever accompanies the act of creation." The Obelisk Press added a blurb: "In no work here hitherto has there been such an entire laying bare of body and spirit, such a remorseless description of thwarted appetites and unappeased desires." The customer who didn't think he was getting a "dirty book" couldn't read. *Tropic* was a pulsating, miraculous, underground best seller.

The book was also a work of fine, original literary merit, to be recognized as the work of one who could, at times, be a skilled writer, bringing to modern writing hidden-away subject matter, distasteful to many, but vital. It had fewer of the faults Miller was to develop *ad nauseam* later on. It was tighter and more coherent than the sprawling, indifferent work he was to produce over the years as he wrote mechanically on and on. Miller earned the praise of some of the best critics (T. S. Eliot!) and was the point of the driving wedge that was to open up the free and direct expository writing of today, where anything goes from *Naked Lunch* to Portnoy's dismal finger exercises.

As the published author of an obscene book, a kind of fame came to Miller, and most of those who approved of him pointed out the vital, natural vulgarity of his effective humor, his happy, direct approach to sex that made his writing almost wholesome compared to what had been done in that field before. He made a picture of loosely affiliated greeds, sexual and visceral, as everyday as spitting. It must be remembered that the Thirties were not the present time with its permissive language about gut and genitalia in the novel. The publishers and the public were still extremely cautious about certain four-letter Anglo-Saxon words. Even the realists like Dreiser or the manly seeming authors like Hemingway either left a dash or used another word.

No great flood of cash came in. Miller and his group could not afford *canard à la presse*, or a quartet of cooked ortolans. Nor could they ride too often in taxis; some of them took to riding bikes. Miller enjoyed peddling to the Seine, to Suresnes and Saint-Cloud, even to Versailles; routes by transportation the American traveler seldom thought of taking. Miller studied Paris as even a Parisian would not study it, visiting the shacks of the disinherited, the hovels where chickens ran with naked children. He found blacksmiths that still shoed horses; the bloody horse butchers, themselves fat as Percherons, prepared their version of *Steak Dumas*. He knew the alleys and the stairways where ivy and moss ran wild like carpeting, streets with old broken trees, still alive in spots and putting forth courageous buds of green. He tested the last of the Art Nouveau urinals. And where there was a folksy neighborhood whorehouse, Miller sniffed it out. Not for Miller the ennui of just any new school of the avant-garde.

He found unfashionable streets as Utrillo and Van Gogh had painted them, watched processions of nuns steering lines of orphans with runny noses, peeked into curio shops, greengrocers, read the obscure newspapers and publications of odd societies, special groups. He saw the Paris of imprisoned currents of age-old habits.

Eating was still his great pleasure—next to bed, the hiss of long hair on a warm pillow. With some money from his publisher the flat in Clichy in time served up *hors d'oeuvres*. Perkes remembers eggs mayonnaise, shrimp, olives, green, black, and stuffed, Bayonne ham, celery *rémoulade*, tomato, cucumber, and potato salads, selected *cochonnaille d'Auvergne*. This to start with; then, first appetite appeased, came a *poulet de Bresse*,

a huge *Châteaubriande* accompanied by *pommes alumettes*, vegetables in season, of course. There was a Miller delight of a salad—*n'oubliez pas la gousse d'ail*. It hardly seems possible to go on, but there was a *soufflé à l'Armagnac*, cheese, nuts, fruit. All this washed down with some *pichet d'arbois*, Mouton Rothschild with the red meat, Vittel with salad, Gevrey-Chambertin with the *fromage de chèvre*. Is this report of a Miller party's intake serious? Those who knew Miller at table insist the account is not too far from the truth of the pleasures of eating at Clichy *when* there was money to pay for it.

Mona, Miller's second wife, came back to Paris; and while the two fought and loved with swollen expectancy and heavy voices, it was clearly only a matter of time before they would again part. Mona's pale face was made up in a dance-hall hostess facade, her black hair swept long over her shoulders; in dress she was addicted to a long theatrical cape. She was sloppy; her cosmetic jars and scent bottles, her intimate womanly drugs were all over the place.

They were said not to emerge from Miller's bedroom for days at a time. They were biological conspirators rather than lovers. Their meals in bed added to the mess. Angry voices would be heard, then the sounds of passion rushing along in its old habitual way, to an abating, diminishing gasp for oxygen.

Miller, with Mona in residence, no longer wrote; sensation took its place. Other women came to visit Miller while the rituals of the Mona and Henry version of Venusberg were going on. A great slanging match between Mona and Miller took place over these "outsiders." Violence and tongue lashings, cruel hurts were hurled in proprietary jealousy. It was soon clear Mona would be returning to the United States. Miller was in no mood for a permanent domestic setup, and Mona could not rationalize her dissatisfactions—so witnesses tell us.

Times could be hard for Miller, even as a published author, and the municipal pawnshop saw one or more of the typewriters of the flat in Clichy from time to time. (Three hundred francs was average on a typewriter.)

Much of Miller's Paris is closely connected with the Villa Seurat, the neighborhood that is so much the setting for *Tropic of Cancer*. Miller is the valid historian of tramp life, the true genre painter of this shabby world. The Café Zeyer, where a *fine à l'eau* was one franc seventy-five (price was important), was all red plush, spotted mirrors, and shiny brass. When funds were flowing, there was the bistro Bouquet d'Alesia for a *vin blanc cassis*, a *café arrosé rhum*. It was a good dive to gossip and listen to Miller talk on any subject, while the *patronne* sat at her place counting and recounting the francs the customers offered for pay. The Fourteenth Arrondissement was a sinister, depressing section; the drunkards lying around, the lowest kind of whores on patrol, rough kids smoking short butts, mean-eyed and unwashed. The houses looked as if they were from Doré illustrations of the past. Miller delighted in the stucco or brick with diseased surfaces of faded pinks, sick greens, red turned *merde*-brown. But there were also big studios, central heating for those who could pay, bathrooms and electric lights. Dali and Soutine had once worked there, also Grommaire, Lurcat, and hosts of forgotten artists.

The romantic district of Montparnasse was going through change. The Americans were almost gone. The quarter was filling up with German refugees from Hitler and his Master Race, from the land of Bach and Goethe and Dürer. What had happened, Miller wondered, to the most cultured people in Europe, people who wept at Mendelssohn and sighed over Heine?

The terraces of the Dôme and the Coupole were full of proud, once rich-living German writers, artists, businessmen, professors, who suddenly, like Cinderella at midnight, were transformed into sad, worried Jews, friendless in the French Republic, people making one more step in massive misery. Soon Montparnasse would seem like a German settlement. Miller was apolitical. If he visited his publisher, Kahane, to ask for money, his only other interest would be the location of "the john, the toilet, the *lavabo, le cabinet, quoi!* Where is it quick . . ." His friends explained he was *homo naturalis*, that's all.

For Miller there was still the reward of debating at the Café Zeyer with Fraenkel, who always had funds when Miller had not, death still his *idée fixe*, and all the varieties of dissolution. All the time Miller would be shouting his order: "Waiter, *double fines à l'eau.*"

The two men decided to make a book of their exchange of letters on the subject and related ideas. Hamlet was the key that set them off in a long exchange, from the sublime to the prosaic. The first volume was published in a very fancy edition by Fraenkel himself, in 1939. Miller's sections are verbal raids on reason, as with guerrilla cunning he bangs away.

Not all of Miller's friends talked merely of death. Among Americans there was Betty Ryan, who had a studio nearby. Then Lawrence Durrell appeared. He was an Anglo-Indian from Corfu, Greece, not yet the author of the *Alexandria Quartet*. Durrell saw in Miller a master to shout greetings to. Miller was always exciting to those disciples who were quick to talk up his greatness; he had little critical background to give praise its true value. It was not Durrell but another admirer, Moriband, who insisted: "You are a living explosive shell forever in search of a detonator." Blaise Cendrars, a one-armed adventurer, best known in America for his novel, *Sutter's Gold*, shouted to Miller, *"C'était pas malin d'être né en Amérique."*

In 1937, for three issues, Miller and Perkes got control of a magazine called *The Booster*. It was originally the publicity organ for an American promoter in Paris named Elmer Prather, who had built a golf course twenty miles east of the city at Ozoir-la-Ferrière. There were few golf clubs around Paris, and those very exclusive; so Mr. Prather in his innocence thought a popular golf course would do fabulously. Few American businesses ever did well investing in a French project. There was the traditional red tape, small officials in power, and finally, as one American put it, "the outstretched palm that made graft and pay-off part of the national Gallic culture." There were harassing inspections, permits, favors demanded, free-loading *and* loss in translation, so the American seeking to set up a French business had his problems. "The rubbed thumb and forefinger should be the ubiquitous symbol of France, not the rooster."

Elmer Prather was sixty-nine years of age, and as president of the American Country Club of France, he looked about him and waited for the Americans and the English in Paris to drive their golf balls off on his rugged greens, so he could earn back the one million francs he had put into the project. To publicize the club he had created the monthly magazine, *The Booster*. At first he edited it himself, hoping to support it with golfing supply advertising, selling space to drink and food purveyors calling attention to their products on the magazine's pages. It was when the magazine became too bothersome to handle that Prather turned it over to Perkes as its new editor-owner, who was to support it by seeking advertising. Perkes and Miller at once began to scheme to make *their* magazine a shocker. They didn't expect to run it for long, for the advertisers would drop out after a few issues once they saw its contents. But until then the new editors felt they could go hog-wild. As Perkes put it later, "The idea was to run the *Booster* into the ground and make a spot of literary history while doing it."

Lawrence Durrell was visiting Miller and he, too, joined the fun. Over the *roquefort au beurre* that followed a huge steak filet, Miller announced the new version of the old golfing magazine. The reborn publication came out in September of 1937 (Munich was just a year away). The masthead listed as Literary Editors: Lawrence Durrell, Henry

Miller, William Saroyan. (How Saroyan got into the picture was never made clear. The second issue published a story of his.) Oddly listed was Anaïs Nin as Society Editor, and Henry Miller as Fashion Editor. Under "And Metaphysics" was the name of Michael Fraenkel. Mr. Prather, who still paid the bills, was confused by what was happening to his creation and never could understand how the full-page advertisement for the North British Rubber Company (golf balls) was lost to be replaced by some avant-garde filler.

The magazine ran an Eskimo legend ("The girl was sitting at one end of the igloo. So lovely he turned hot and almost died of want . . .") and Mr. Prather called the story and the publication filthy and pornographic. The editors were warned they must not again use the title of *Booster* for their new issues. The third and final issue of *The Booster*, January 1938, featured *The Air Conditioned Womb Number*. After that the magazine was called *Delta*. It staggered on until just before the war, making no great impression in literature, publishing work by Durrell, Miller, Kay Boyle, Fraenkel, Anaïs Nin, Karel Capek, a poem by Dylan Thomas. The Christmas issue after Munich was called *Special Peace and Dismemberment Number With Jitterbug-Shag Requiem*. A bit of heavy-handed wit that has lost its humor with time.

The war was nearly upon them when Miller's *Tropic of Capricorn* was published by Obelisk Press, and Kahane had to put out a good fat royalty (for him) to Miller, who was the best seller on his strange list.

With its publication Miller's major adventure in Paris ended. He was on his way to Greece, to live, or to imagine the background, for his book, *The Colossus of Maroussi*. The war would cut short that trip, and Miller would return to America and enter legend. He settled for some years at Big Sur on the rugged California coast. He kept on writing, almost automatically; the critics felt the first lyric drive was gone, and while one could still find here and there the early Miller vitality, one had to turn over a hundred pages or so to find one that lived up to the early promise. Miller surged on in a living immediacy; writing, painting, etching, marrying a few times more, settling near Hollywood. He became one of the sacred objects of a cult and ended up with the Westwood Art Center, a sort of guru to its swinging social pendulum.

With war actually begun, the Americans in Paris in the main went home, even Man Ray, the Dadaist. The picture Miller gives us can be taken as the true image of his Americans in Paris during the Thirties. The people of the Gertrude Stein and the Edith Wharton backgrounds and their admirers were aging, living in another world. They would vanish

into some fairly safe region of France, where they could remain unknown, or move to England.

The Miller people, his cult and followers, were all that could be called
an American-Paris movement of the Thirties. They had had little contact
with the earlier generation, the stars of the Murphy, Sherwood Anderson,
Hemingway worlds. They came and went.

CHAPTER 54

Richard Wright—Black Exile

*Dear Richard: It is obvious that you and I
are the only two geniuses of this era.*

GERTRUDE STEIN

GERTRUDE STEIN could hardly ever forget a compliment; she would lather praise on the giver, often beyond reason. So when Richard Wright wrote her that he liked her short story about a Negress, "Melanchtha," Gertrude could do no more than include him in her company as the genius. Gertrude seeking praise was once compared to a man who takes a hot bath on a sinking ship.

Richard Wright was a good and serious writer, the first Negro really to touch middle-class America with a popular novel, a sensational yet true book. Wright grew up in a world where bigotry was a thick miasma. Born in 1908 in Natchez, Mississippi, he had muscled his way upward and made a position for himself as a writer. By 1945, married, with a child, he was living on Charles Street in New York City.

As he sat writing one December morning, about seven, the phone rang. It was a long distance call from Paris. A member of the French government wanted to speak to "Monsieur Wright." The message was: would he come to France as a guest of the government? Wright cried out, "It's not possible!" meaning, of course, he'd come, but it was such an unexpected honor.

Wright told his wife Ellen the news, and made plans to take their daughter Julie out of school. As the war was just over, they reserved passage on a troop carrier, the *S. S. Brazil*. He waited, but no official confirmation of the invitation came from the French Embassy in Washington. Had he imagined it? He had read Baudelaire: "The deed is not sister to the dream."

The American passport office then notified him he couldn't go anyway: "Application rejected." The excuse: conditions in postwar Europe made it impossible. Besides, Wright might be stranded there without money. Wright wrote back he was making $30,000 a year from his books. The State Department sneered (a knack they had perfected via plain typing) and again said no. Wright's lawyers admitted no American had a *right* to a passport; it was by State Department juggling only a privilege, not a right to have a passport. These weren't the days of Jefferson; the State Department was a private government in itself.

Wright's protests grew louder. Gertrude Stein was alerted in Paris, friends in America began to insist on a passport for Richard Wright. It appeared that the man had no sense of protocol, no respect for the etiquette of the State Department. The French, too, were puzzled. How could Mr. Wright think he was still going to Paris when they remembered he had shouted on the phone at the man inviting him, "It's not possible!" However, if he still wanted to come, of course the French would welcome him. A formal invitation was sent, not only offering to take care of Wright, but paying the passage of the family, the hotel, *all* costs for three months.

With the French invitation in hand, Wright had proof he was wanted in Paris. He mailed off the formal invitation, registered, to the State Department. The Department in abysmal self-depreciation immediately announced it had lost the document; *lost* usually being the easy way of getting rid of Americans who insisted in fighting the power of the department, resisting its autocratic rule from which one never got any full explanation. Wright asked the French for another invitation, and this one was sent direct to the State Department. A phone call from Wright to the State Department brought out the answer, "No such invitation has been received." Wright said he would fly to Washington and face them with the facts. He was told *not* to waste his time; he wasn't going to Paris.

Wright flew to Washington and, desperate, used names and pressure of right-wing reactionary groups. (After all, he had once been a member of the Communist Party; what *better* weight could he swing?) Through friends he met "a certain man" of the right. Wright had his passport in an hour. No questions asked, no documents "lost." He discovered there were those who controlled the State Department.

Wright crossed the Atlantic with wife and child. As he landed in France, he felt, "For the first time in my life I stepped on free soil." A foolish remark, as colonial blacks and Algerians in France were in no paradise. An American remark, as well.

Leaving the boat train at the Gare Saint Lazare, Wright faced Gertrude Stein, unstylish in a baggy brown tweed coat and mannish derby hat. The American Embassy man was there, too, to give élan to a now accepted American author, with two, not one, *two* long Lincoln limousines. Also in the welcome group was the editor of *Les Lettres Nouvelles*.

Gertrude had made reservations for the Wrights at the Hotel Trianon, but first she proudly took them in the Embassy car through the Tuileries Gardens, up the Champs Elysées and the quais.

The cold spring of 1946 did not chill the heart of the Wrights. After all, Wright felt, this was Paris, this was the American ambassador's car. And sitting there beside them was Gertrude Stein, she who had by now become The Mother of Us All.

Gertrude said to the Embassy man, "Don't you feel the privilege we have in revealing all this to a tender heart?" The answer is not of public record. It may be in the department's archives.

Gertrude and Alice were then living on the Rue Christine, and there lunch was ready for the guests. Wright, looking about him at the picture-

filled walls, tried to sit down but was stiffened by a chilling war whoop, as Alice Toklas pulled out from under his rump a small Louis XV chair on which in *gros point* she had worked out an original design by Picasso. Wright's near squat put him in Alice's bad graces.

The press and cameras waited outside the hotel, and Wright found himself answering the usual questions to an American Negro celebrity in Paris. As for Alice Toklas, either because of the affair of the chair, or just because Gertrude liked Wright, she didn't thaw toward the Negro writer. Alice was the matriarch protecting Gertrude, not the other way around, in the ménage of "Lovey" (Gertrude) and "Pussy" (Alice). All friendships are composed of inexactitudes, but Wright and Gertrude got along very well.

It was to be for the Wrights a week of interviews, cocktails, more talks with Gertrude, meetings with those *monstres sacrés*, the French publishers and translators. Wright got up early mornings to walk the Paris streets. "I'm at last in Paris, city of my dreams! . . . will I ever be myself again?"

The Wrights in their first weeks in Paris were isolated from reality by their fame, their official standing, and the kind of friends they made, mostly friends who existed in luxurious superfluities. At last they moved into an apartment on the Boulevard Saint Michel, near the Sorbonne. Mrs. Wright developed appendicitis, and Wright, forgetting how superior the French were in everything compared to dismal America, insisted his wife be operated on by two Army doctors at the American Hospital. A wise move. Wright was more chauvinistic than he suspected. Then daughter Julie developed hives of an amazing size, and she, too, went under American care at the hospital.

In July Wright met André Gide, "an honest man and a superb craftsman." Gide, of esoteric repute, asked the expected question about the "white assassins of the dignity of black men in America." Wright missed a chance to ask Gide about the mass murder of yellow men committed by the French in what was to be North and South Vietnam, or the dreadful torture the French were putting to Algerian terrorists in North Africa. Gide, of course, didn't mention the French colonial massacres. He struck a puerile pose and recited: "The more uncivilized the white man, the more he fears and hates all those who differ from him." He may have been talking of the reaction to homosexuals, whose grand master he was in France. Wright was often the victim of some French *joli garçon* using him as a decoy.

Wright's conversations with Gertrude Stein were simply her own words, as she did most of the talking, much of it incomprehensible. However she delighted him by her loquacity. "How she can talk! What absolute genius this pioneer-looking American has." Again Wright, an honest man, was overemotional. Gertrude Stein could be mordantly funny in conversation; she knew her worth as a character; but she was hardly American in look or spirit. She had been away too long, much too long. When Wright could get a few words in concerning the doom of Negroes "who are yet unborn," Gertrude inevitably added, "Rose is a rose—a Richard is a poet is a poet." Not one of her better efforts. Wright's own efforts at epigrams are not good either.

Wright had accepted an invitation to a reception of the *Société des Gens de Lettres.* Gertrude said it would be boring and highbrow, and "they wouldn't know your work anyway." Gertrude herself had never been invited.

Wright decided to settle his family in Paris permanently. He went back to America to clear out his assets, and came back to Paris in August of 1947. The house on Charles Street was sold, the furniture put in storage. He was coming back with trunks, boxes of food (carrying food to France! the home of the best!), a cargo of seventeen crates in all. And there was a big black Oldsmobile in the hold of the S.S. *United States.* Also making the crossing was Knobby, the Wright's Siamese cat, in a cage. Wright gave a last snarl at his homeland as represented by the ship's crew. "Americans do not know how to render service; the ship is democratically shoddy, and . . . Americans . . . internationally wet behind the ears."

French road signs often have wit, but are not too clear as to direction. Wright lost his way three times as he drove his new car between Boulogne and Paris, the Oldsmobile outfacing the Peugeots and Renaults on the narrow cart roads. Wright got to Paris at seven o'clock and all seemed well. He had a brandy with his wife and cried out exultantly, "Paris!" in the manner of a Balzac hero promising himself fame and fortune.

Wright was an excellent novelist. He had hoped Paris would bring out the best in him in some wider literary spectrum. But somehow he could not work on the new novel as he planned. His work habits in new surroundings seemed to disintegrate. He wrote of despair, of domestic accidents in his journal. When he turned on the faucet to shave, no hot water. He went out to register with the police—something no one did in reactionary America. His car began to sputter. The French mechanics at the General Motors garage said it was a ruin, the car, we are *désolé—*

there are so many things wrong. What? And the gas tank, to begin with, must come out. As Wright realized he was about to be cheated by the French on a grand scale, an American walking by looked in and examined the motor. He said it was merely a short circuit of two wires. There was more hanky panky at the garage where he parked his auto; he found the car was being used by others after he left it. The animal kingdom was also a problem. Knobby, the cat, ate chicken bones and had to be rushed to a vet to have them removed.

Carson McCullers was living in Paris and called Wright to come to visit her. She was ill. Wright knew it was "all from too much drinking." She was drinking hard, and when he got to her flat, they began with four bottles of cold beer followed by a bottle of brandy. Carson drank down a full glass. "It's because I'm so glad to see you," she explained. A Southern writer of the Faulkner school, she had made a reputation when very young with two strange well-written novels. Illness and drink had kept her production small. Taut, neurotic, in ill health, a drinker, her life span would be short. Paris had proved no help to her problems. Her husband Reeves (they had made up, she told Wright as they drank) was in the American hospital with a leg infection. Carson shook her head about him. Reeves was a mental case, maybe taking drugs. He insisted people were always watching him, staring at him. Wright stayed to calm her worries. They had dinner, drank wine, had a cognac with coffee. He thought to himself, "Nobody can worry like a Southern woman." It was clear Wright carried the folk myths of his childhood with him, even to Paris.

Here in Paris he had hoped to have the perfect place to write, and had found what? Medical problems, sick cats, dishonest garage men, writer's block. And now, primed by drink, he was facing this sick, boozy woman, and he felt, "Why does she repel me . . . the one person whom I want to like?" He seems to have been infected with Carson McCullers' prose style.

Next morning, Carson, wild with panic, was on the phone to Wright. Reeves had come home after all, after spending a day and night drinking in bistros and cafés.

The Wrights went out the following night with the McCullers—Reeves a small, blond Irishman, tried to seduce Wright's wife. Still friendship was friendship when Carson was taken to the hospital with a stroke, her third or fourth, her kidneys ruined from drink. Certainly for Richard Wright this was not the Paris of E. E. Cummings and Cole Porter.

Seeking solitude, Wright rented a dirty little place to write in. It cost a hundred old francs a day. He had carried his old Underwood there, his collection of pills—the C.B.D. vitamins, the three favorite brands of anti-acid pills. His three books had come out in French translations. Tomorrow he would begin writing seriously. He did two thousand words the next day. He also discovered the landlady of their flat, Odette, was taking dope, a little "doctor" coming every day to give her a shot. The Wrights would have to move. It wasn't vice *à la* Caligula, still there *was* the child.

So now began apartment hunting in a Paris where livable apartments hardly existed. At last, somehow, they found a place on the Avenue de Neuilly at Neuilly-sur-Seine for 194,000 old francs, 50,000 of which was security. There was furniture to buy, ice to bring home. "Another day lost," he wrote in his journal. He was thirty-nine, he discovered one day. Time for ripeness. He must participate more in French intellectual activities.

He became close to Sartre and Simone de Beauvoir. When first meeting the mistress of the existentialist philosopher, Wright generalized about *all* French women: "They like men and know what to do with them."

In May of 1948 the Wrights moved again to be near the American Community School for Julie, now six. The French school she had attended insisted Julie color cherries red or yellow, *not* blue. So that ended French schooling. The new place was a five-room flat; it seemed fine. In January of 1949 Julie had a sister born at the American Hospital at Neuilly—seven and a quarter pounds. They named her Rachel.

Still Montparnasse bistros, Algerian rug sellers, vermouth and calvados aperitifs didn't make an American Negro a Frenchman.

A company was formed to film *Native Son*. Wright was talked into playing the main role, the character of Bigger Thomas. It was a halting, lame production. Wright was a poor actor, the company and production were second rate. It took three years to work out the film, a cut and mutilated version. And Wright made only three thousand dollars for all his time and work and the use of his best-selling book.

He was not writing. He'd work a bit on two novels, but nothing really vital and sustained was in progress. He was too often a speaker at lunches; he was honored, interviewed, but his work did not go well. At last he managed to get together over six hundred pages of a novel called *The Outsider*. How would it do? Was he still important?

Wright began drinking heavily. Asked why he drank, he said his soul needed it. Did it make him feel better? "No," he said, "it makes me feel less." Apprehension giving way to apple brandy.

It was Wright's first book in eight years. It was not accepted by readers. The critics panned it. White and black disliked it. One critic wrote, "Come back to us, Richard." But he wanted no Harlem, no Village, no America.

Wright began work on a new novel in which only white characters appeared—an international writer could leave out the black folk he knew. He called it *Savage Holiday*. He finished it in March of 1953. No hard-cover publisher would print it. It appeared after long delay in paperback, unreviewed. Was it too argumentative, showing an instability of temperament—or did Wright just not know whites?

From now on his books were not to have the success of his early ones. Although Wright may have guessed that he missed most in his work his American roots, yet he stayed on in Paris, or he traveled to conferences of colored people. A time came when he feared his passport would be taken away. Joe McCarthy was on the loose, peddling his evil judgments and analogies. The old General read Zane Grey in the White House. The Senate sat on its hands. Passports became a way to punish.

Wright had fallen on Paris as some people fling themselves on rocks from a height. He had hoped to find there the core of the mythologies of the Greek, Christian, and Marxist protagonists, to make literature of it all. He was hopeful, but very vulnerable. Peace had not come to him in Paris, not even in a good clean place to work at ease. The dialogues he had with the intellectuals, the writers, the opinion makers, the French thinkers would often sting like scorpions' tails. He saw we become creatures of our deeds; but were all his deeds behind him in a country he could not live in? Or which he thought he could not live in? Forgiveness is a great luxury, and he could not forgive the dreadful childhood, the agony and poverty of the cities, the way the color of his skin marked him out. He wrote off living in America.

Paris was perhaps Richard Wright's biggest disappointment. But he never said so. As he grew older, he lost, too, that pride in his body, his private kingdom of muscle and bone as it grew weaker. Paris, what was it? a city of Picasso shapes, of androgynous floor shows, of drinking in cafés, in salons, at parties, drinking, talking. The museums soon become tombs of the past if one went to too many of them.

In Wright's journals there are so many querulous complaints against small tasks, household duties, the family's domestic life as it touched or hindered his work. As his books lost their popular appeal, Wright could not accept the fact that critics get jaded, new rebels are promoted by the media, the Mafia of publishers and critics that sells personalities, not truth. Wright began to think that his skill, his talent were perhaps irretrievably lost.

In May of 1954 came the news he dreaded; the State Department was going over its list of 30,000 Americans living in Paris. A weeding out process was to take place, "a tightening up of restrictions," the Paris *Herald* called it, with Joe McCarthy howling like a rabid wolf along the corridors of Washington. If one were critical of the government, of one's country, "the State Department will try and get him back home as quickly as possible."

Wright was most fearful of the grim-eyed female who sat in control of the Passport Department at the pinnacle of merciless power. In print some called her the "Spider," others spoke of a State Department "Witch Hunt." It was the moment of lost equilibrium. The newspapers wrote the Spider had fifty henchmen turned loose in Paris, who in plainclothes haunted cafés and eating places, galleries and parties, listening in on Americans and reporting back what they heard to the Passport Department. Americans in Paris became a paranoiac colony.

By 1956 Wright was sure he would lose his passport. He did not know "the day or the hour when my American passport might be taken from me and I shall be faced with being semi-stateless . . . they burn up at the idea of an independent Negro . . . saying what he likes."

The world seemed mad. Henry James had long ago sensed it. "A subject may well reside in some picture of this overwhelming, self-defeating chaos or cataclysm towards which the whole thing is drifting . . . the deluge of people, the insane movement for movement, the ruin of thought, of life, the negation of work . . . the swelling, roaring crowds, the 'where are you going?' . . . the American, the nightmare . . . the mad, ghastly climax or denouement. It's a splendid subject—if worked round a personal action—situation . . . The Americans looming up—dim, vast, portentous—in their millions—like gathering waves—the barbarians of the Roman Empire."

But for Wright there was no leisure to seek out old texts that predicted the dreadful present. People whispered rumors in voices sounding as if they came from a pocket. Someone wrote a letter to *Life*, signed by someone else's name, a friend of Wright. The letters were very pro-Communist and by a party member. The FBI stepped in, perhaps endeavoring to nab Wright as the letter writer. But another Negro writer, whom Wright had suspected of being a State Department agent, was trapped by his handwriting. He confessed to authoring the letters. Black and white agents provocateurs were found in Paris doing their mischievous business.

In 1959 Dr. Martin Luther King came to Paris and met with Richard Wright. They talked of the Negro problem. Wright did not see eye to eye with King, but he trusted the man and felt him to be honest. King urged Wright to go on writing as he had in the past.

Richard Wright was not well. He had been to the Bandung Conference and had brought back a sick stomach and bowel. He had applied in London for a permanent visa to live there if he lost his passport. Weeks passed and it did not come. Then Wright was told his request for a residence visa had been rejected. An English official was persuaded by some of Wright's powerful friends to see him, but he snarled a final "No!" It seems that Wright had refused to sign certain biased statements. The official threw Wright's passport onto the floor, turned on his heels and walked away. Wright had to pick up the passport. He stood there trembling at this official Tartuffism. England would not be a new refuge for the Wrights.

John Strachey brought the matter of the Wright rejection to the floor of Parliament as a question, to produce a reason for the refusal. It was parried and nothing came of it. A member *disjecta* of society was nothing new in international politics.

Wright was taking shots of three million units of penicillin, massive doses of sulfa, emetine, and bismuth. He had been told his amoebic illness, picked up in the tropics, was cured. But he felt weak, jumpy, no *cote fleurette* as his French friends put it. He rested a great deal, swallowed large doses of bismuth. He spent three weeks in the American Hospital, where they proved the fact that he still had amoebic infection. But Wright felt they had not given him the proper medical aid. He had lost eighteen pounds and his night sweats were weakening. He brooded, had bad moments. Life seemed empty—like a deserted house where the daily newspapers clutter the uncut lawn.

It was a Russian, Dr. Vladimir Schwartzmann, who had insisted on the huge doses of medication and had sworn Wright was cured. Yet the weakness, the ennui, the despair continued. Wright could not accept the fact that he was a sick man. The Russian doctor began to inject him with vitamin B-12 and more bismuth. His emaciated appearance was a shock to friends.

One cold November day he entered the *Clinique Chirurgicale Eugène*

Gibez for more amoeba tests. His wife was in London and he placed a phone call to her. He planned to begin a long novel. On November 28, 1960, Wright read an evening paper, joked with his nurse. About eleven o'clock the nurse noticed his réd signal light was on. She went into his room. He seemed, she said later, to smile at her, then the smile fell quickly away. Richard Wright was fifty-two when he died in Paris. The city had been neither a restful haven for the writer nor a place of peace to produce literary inspiration.

His wife Ellen came over from London the next day and saw him in the hospital mortuary, where his body was kept packed in chipped ice. Some flowers were in the hands folded on his chest. On a cold, rainy day Wright was cremated at Père Lachaise with a copy of his book *Blac':* *Boy*. The ashes were placed in an urn and put in a niche.

Richard Wright, a good man, lived in exile in a city where the conditions for a successful writer were by his time no better than they would have been in America. The French police and other native restrictive regulations were even more oppressive than in New York, Chicago, or Los Angeles. Wright had lived with an incandescent rage and a disastrous candor, close to the sounds he often thought of as the maniacal screams of the world in agony. Everything for Wright seemed at times bathed in the cold sweat of international rapacity. All fine words and intentions were tarnished and had turned reprehensible. Of him his Paris friends could, in the words of La Rochefoucauld, say, *Il est plus facile d'être sage pour le autres que pour soi-même.* "It is easier to be wise for others than for oneself."

CHAPTER 55

Paris Revisited

Disillusion is the only safe foundation for happiness.
SANTAYANA

FLYING into Paris on a recent revisit I was reading of the age of the grand tour, when American colonials and Englishmen saw Paris. Wrote one eighteenth-century tourist: "The water . . . from the river Seine is neither well tasted nor very wholesome . . . giving violent gripes and purging."

Nugent's grand tour guide book of the same gamy period is properly British about the native cooking: "As for French cuisine, for wholesomeness they are inferior to ours, most of their dishes being too highly seasoned, and some of them a perfect hodge-podge . . . as medicine for a sick dog . . . The wine the best in Europe and very reasonable."

Like many male travelers, the English came to Paris seeking sexual adventures. *Milord Anglais*, if he were wise, provided himself with the condom he called "the French letter." (And which the French called "the English sheath!")

James Boswell, a notorious flesh hunter by his own confession in his journals, records visiting Mme Hecquet's knocking shop and Mme Dupuis's brothel in the Hôtel Montigny. He found the first "as in a fever . . . elegant!" He did patronize the Grand Horizontals—but accepted whatever took his fancy and was available for cash, from the Palais Royal to any handy alley.

The tourist of that day visited St. Denis' Benedictine Abbey to gape at marble sepulchres of dead French kings, Marshal Turenne's tomb, Charlemagne's crown, spurs, and chess set. More suspect as mere props were Roland's horn, Joan of Arc's sword.

Travel by post chaise, diligence, private coach was back-breaking on the poor French roads, and the streets of Paris were little better.

There was no Ritz, Crillon, Maurice, George V ("and thank God, no Hilton"). The best places for the traveler were in the Faubourg Saint Germain, the Imperial, the Anjou in the Rue Dauphin. There was the choice of the Orléans, the Picardie, the oddly named Doge of Venice on the Rue de Boucherie. James Boswell preferred the Hôtel du Dauphin on the Rue de Teranne for its pretty maids.

The word *restaurant* was yet to be invented and eating places were called *ordinaires*. Prices then, compared to the thirty to one hundred dollars a day now asked, were mouthwateringly cheap. On the fashionable Faubourg Saint Germain the minister, William Cole, paid about twenty dollars a *month* for two rooms—for himself and valet. Edward Gibbon paid about thirty dollars a month for a suite of four rooms.

The rooms were larger, more ornate than today's, the drapes and furniture fine in the best places. There was, of course, no running water

—hot or cold, it was carried up in cans. And the buckets and chamber-pots were carried off to add to the odors of Paris. Outdoors the danger of being hit by chaises, cabriolets, carriages was great, as there were hardly any sidewalks. Walking was a danger, and children and old folk were often run over and killed by hackney carriages, the taxis of their day (four thousand cruised Paris in the eighteenth century), or the lumbering two-wheeled carts that fed Paris or carried off its leavings.

It was a smaller, more packed city. The Russian traveler Karamzin figured it bigger than London or Constantinople, with a population of 1,130,500, and he says 150,000 were foreigners, 200,000 servants. The *ancien régime* lived high, wide, and handsome—and gamy. Bathing was not popular. Scent, hair powder, and pomade gave the well-off or well-connected a facade. People used doorways and staircases as privies—usually a neighbor's.

Paris was not neat and clean in those times. "A dirty town with a dirtier ditch calling itself the Seine" (Horace Walpole). "That durty Theatre of all Nations" (James Howell). "Paris is a beast of a city" (William Hazlitt). But they all came to Paris. Still the English did not consider it with grace. "I see nothing here that we have not finer and better in England" (Lord Chesterfield to the Duchess of Marlborough).

A great deal has changed in Paris. The return there of those who remembered only pleasant times has a certain sadness. The writer, Jack Smith, remembers such a return in March of 1970.

In the morning I bundled up and went out in the streets. My face turned numb. Paris was icy. I walked up the Boulevard des Capucines to a sidewalk café. It was glassed in for the winter.

I ordered coffee and croissants and took my time, like any Frenchman at his amenities, watching the shopgirls trotting off to their situations. They were armored against the cold in suedes and fake furs and shiny vinyl, like play soldiers in the Opéra Comique. Their cheeks were red and their legs flashed blue and pink through the slits in their flapping maxis.

I left the café and stepped into the quick parade. The day was mine. Alone in Paris! My eye caught a gaudy painted sign above a cinema. It showed *Bob & Carol & Ted & Alice*, all in one bed. "*Imaginez*," it said, "*toutes les possibilités!*"

I walked till I came to the Arc de Triomphe and turned into the Avenue des Champs Elysées and walked to the Place de la Concorde, vast and familiar under the towering pink obelisk from Luxor. Alas, the place is disfigured now, like most of the urban world, by parked autos. I walked on into the Tuileries Gardens. Its trees were sticks, its pools icy, its nudes cold. It was bleak and beautiful, quivering with the spring juices inside it, waiting to burst out.

I walked through the courtyards of the Louvre and took the Pont Neuf over the river to the Left Bank and walked in narrow streets to the Boulevard Saint Germain. It began to rain. I ducked into a bar and ordered a café and drank it slowly, looking around at the other patrons. Near the door a stocky man with a stiff gray beard and a face like pink granite was looking down through gold-rimmed spectacles at a paper on his table, working at it with a pencil in his rawboned hand. *Incredible!*

As I left the café I gave him a closer look. It wasn't Hemingway, of course, but some lesser exile. He was working on the crossword puzzle in the Paris *Herald-Tribune*. I took a taxi back to the hotel.

There is often this recall to the Paris of the Twenties, mostly by Americans who were not there then, but have been steeped in all that has been printed and talked of about that period. A period more often myth than fact.

And how does the intelligent American visitor in Paris spend his time today? How do the American and his wife, no longer young, revisit a Paris they once knew? Jack Smith skillfully sets down their routine.

It was a Sunday, a day so cold and so beautiful that you ached from the cold and the beauty. We had a room in a small hotel on the Left Bank, four flights

up and no elevator, around a corner from the Place Saint-Germain-des-Prés, with its old cafés and old church, the oldest church in Paris.

Church bells woke us, the sound deep and measured; old bells, the same bells that had awakened Molière and Berlioz and Alice B. Toklas, and might at this very moment be waking a new Voltaire.

We walked down the Boulevard Saint Germain to the Seine, and then across the bridge to Notre Dame. A priest in red, the archbishop himself perhaps, was singing the mass in French. We walked down the south aisle and stood in the light of the great rose window, beside the statue of Saint Joan of Arc. The maid seemed supple and alive in the light of half a dozen votive candles. The priest's voice was high and reedy against the deep distant voice of the great organ. Then he called the communicants to the altar and they streamed forward to receive the bread and wine.

We had lunch in a glassed-in sidewalk café on the Avenue des Champs Elysées, warming ourselves first with a *lait Gabrielle*, a nectar made of hot milk, honey, rum, and cinnamon. The Sunday promenade was in full tide. Tens of thousands of Parisians were out on their splendid boulevard—the rich and the bohemian and the bourgeois; young lovers and old roués and married couples *en famille*, pushing red-cheeked infants in perambulators. Up one side they came and down the other, walking swiftly in the cold . . .

If this was all that civilization had brought us to, a *lait Gabrielle* in a sidewalk café on a cold Sunday in Paris, watching the people walk on the Champs Elysées, it had all been worth it, all the centuries. We descended into the underground and took the Métro back to the Place Saint-Germain-des-Prés, and when we came up to the street again it was snowing.

We had dinner in an old restaurant from *la belle époque,* looking unabashedly at all the people and being looked at, sharing the communal sense of joy and excitement, and feeling quite lucky to be human.

Monday we flew back to Los Angeles. We drove home in the dusk over the Santa Monica Freeway. It is our Champs Elysées where we see each other's cars, not each other.

Epilogue

*The newspapers have given the rage of going to Paris
a good name; they call it the French disease.*

HORACE WALPOLE

HE had not yet won the Nobel Prize; that was to be a few years in the future. William Faulkner and I that afternoon were supposed to be working on a film play for a young actor named Ronald Reagan; the studio was finding it difficult to procure simple enough roles for him. The final film we wrote—*Stallion Road*—was reviewed in one line by a New York critic: "If you are a horse, you will like this movie." Faulkner and I were drinking bourbon with what he called "branch water," and we were looking at the wall on which hung reproductions of some of my Paris sketchbooks from a show being held at the Los Angeles Art Association. There was always about his stance an ironic eloquence topped by an ambiguous stare.

Faulkner took a sip and nodded toward the wall. "Why, now, do you think all of us half-assed Americans went to Paris?"

"Why did you go, Bill?"

"Well, now, the literary boys were always talking about it, and saying you had to be there, feel it, taste it, go see the mother hen, Gertrude Stein, dust her feathers. So you do—you go, you walk where Ben Franklin and Henry James, and who was the jim-dandy who gave out gold twenty-dollar coins when he had a load on?"

"James Gordon Bennett."

William Faulkner got up and walked toward the drawings on the wall and stared at them. "We all went, come around to that, because the American strain for the writer fellow, the painter, the poet had become thin here, petered out. The sounds, the colors, the taste of Paris to us felt better than the country cooking we grew up on. Paris for us young fry was good as sun on your back, an eager look at things you maybe felt had meanings you didn't get from the folks back at the store . . . Maybe, maybe."

I said, "Was it busting out, Americans getting away? Was it all the reading we had done, all the whispering that came back from travelers, about this and that?"

He shrugged his tweed-covered shoulders and held out the glass. I poured, and Faulkner stood there, small, graying, the ice cubes clicking as he rattled them, the neat clipped mustache over the pursed mouth, ready to speak.

"Maybe it was some goddamn kind of subtile genetic circle in the blood, like a compass pointing us back to our original roots. Maybe our artists felt that here in the native grass there was an utter futility in trying to write deep tragedy that had bite, form, art. Give it any fancy name . . . I don't know why we pull tracks, head for the French—maybe because here at home the real events are hidden, covered over by the obvious ones. Any which way we figured it, it was all a good excuse to go to Paris."

"Could be," I said.

I tried to think it out. Why did Paris still draw us to its fascination, why did it draw those who felt themselves creative—talent or no talent? Why had it been, since Franklin, that all of us felt that we were seeing something freer *there* than elsewhere? Why did art, literature, and sex, and the feeding and drinking seem more genuine there? Generations of Americans had run a whole gamut of desires, hopes in Paris—all so opposite to those they had found at home, on the farm, in the city, with the accustomed smell of old gym shoes in high-school locker rooms, the twist of the Santa Fé rails beyond San Berdoo, the familiar chatter of girls loosely walking along Main Street or down Fifth Avenue on those long American legs.

I still have the notes I made in a journal of our conversation that afternoon. William Faulkner, glass in hand, eyes half-hooded, hawk-nosed, said, "Maybe, Steve, Paris is the grab bag for us because it skirts the irrational, yet seems to find now and then the potential for genius in embryonic shape . . . All right, it also has for us a high falutin' esoteric reputation, and you can escape there getting entangled, sure, entangled in moral alternatives. We're such black Calvinistic bastards at home. In the end you may get a belly-full of it, Paris . . . but you always want to go back. It leaves you spooked with a world of invisible presences. We go there hunting some damn evocative quality, maybe we come back and feel that only the unrealized parts of our lives seem perfect . . . That's what keeps Paris green for us. It's something we are sure is there only we ourselves never fully realized it."

I said we could drink to that.